Cognitive Intelligence refers to the natural intelligence of humans and animals, it is considered that the brain performs intelligent activities. While establishing a hard boundary that distinguishes intelligent activities from others remains controversial, most common behaviors and activities of living organisms that cannot be fully synthesized using artificial means are regarded as intelligent. Thus the acts of sensing and perception, understanding the environment, and voluntary control of muscles, which can be performed by lower-level mammals, are indeed intelligent. Besides the above, advanced mammals can perform more sophisticated cognitive tasks, including logical reasoning, learning, recognition, and complex planning and coordination, none of which can yet be realized artificially to the level of a baby, and thus are regarded as cognitively intelligent.

This book series covers two important aspects of brain science. First, it attempts to uncover the mystery behind the biological basis of cognition, with a special emphasis on the decoding of stimulated brain signals or images. Topics in this area include the neural basis of sensory perception, motor control, sensory-motor coordination, and understanding the biological basis of higher-level cognition, including memory, learning, reasoning, and complex planning. The second objective of the series is to publish consolidated research on brain-inspired models of learning, perception, memory, and coordination, including results that can be realized on robots, enabling them to mimic the cognitive activities performed by living creatures. These brain-inspired models of machine intelligence complement the behavioral counterparts studied in traditional artificial intelligence.

The series publishes textbooks, monographs, and contributed volumes.

More information about this series at http://www.springer.com/series/15488

Lei Chen

Deep Learning and Practice with MindSpore

Lei Chen
Department of Computer Science and Engineering
Hong Kong University of Science and Technology
Kowloon, Hong Kong

Translated by
Yunhui Zeng
Beijing, China

ISSN 2520-1956   ISSN 2520-1964 (electronic)
Cognitive Intelligence and Robotics
ISBN 978-981-16-2235-9   ISBN 978-981-16-2233-5 (eBook)
https://doi.org/10.1007/978-981-16-2233-5

Jointly published with Tsinghua University Press
The print edition is not for sale in China (Mainland). Customers from China (Mainland) please order the print book from: Tsinghua University Press.
ISBN of the Co-Publisher's edition: 978-730-25-4661-0

Translation from the Chinese Simplified language edition: 深度学习与*MindSpore*实践 by Lei Chen, and Yunhui Zeng, © Tsinghua University Press 2020. Published by Tsinghua University Press. All Rights Reserved.

This Springer imprint is published by the registered company Springer Nature Singapore Pte Ltd.
The registered company address is: 152 Beach Road, #21-01/04 Gateway East, Singapore 189721, Singapore

Foreword by Zhijun Xu

MindSpore Empowers All-Round AI

AI has spread much faster and wider than any other general-purpose technology in history. There is little doubt that this new general-purpose technology will have a profound impact on every aspect of the economy and society. However, different industries and organizations have adopted AI at different rates: Traditional industries are still in the initial stages of adoption, whereas the Internet industry embraced it from the beginning. Although most industries are already using AI to some extent, they have not witnessed the expected changes, meaning that there is still huge room for improvement. Some industries have still not found an effective way to realize the value of AI.

In general, there are three main reasons for this. First, the development of AI applications and solutions is challenging, requiring an expert skill set that millions of IT engineers have yet to acquire. Second, unlike the Internet, which has a relatively simple environment, AI applications have complex operating environments and must adapt to meet a diverse range of requirements. For example, the various cloud, edge computing, and terminal device scenarios have different requirements, and AI applications must not only collaborate with existing production systems in various industries and related processes, but also integrate with traditional IT applications. Third, the diversity and complexity of applications in various industries bring new requirements, such as robustness, security, and interpretability, for AI algorithms and theories. AI has therefore undergone rapid, continuous improvement and adaptation, creating a range of challenges for new entrants wanting to master AI technologies.

Central to Huawei's AI strategy is the continuous investment in full-stack, all-scenario AI solutions with the aim of accelerating AI development. To this end, Huawei released its full-stack, all-scenario AI solution in October 2018, and officially unveiled MindSpore—an all-scenario AI computing framework—in August 2019. Many people have asked why Huawei launched MindSpore despite there being many other frameworks available. The main considerations for investing in MindSpore at that time were as follows. First, no existing framework was able to support all scenarios seamlessly. Because Huawei services cover device, edge, and cloud scenarios, and privacy protection is becoming increasingly important, we need a computing framework that supports all scenarios to empower all-round AI. Second, we have learned from Huawei's AI applications and research over the past few years that the development of AI computing frameworks is far from converging. Exploratory research into technologies such as AI acceleration for just-in-time compilation (which is used in automatic differentiation and tensor calculation) and automatic parallelization for ultra-large neural networks, as well as new research areas such as deep probabilistic programming and graph neural networks, require further development of AI computing frameworks.

MindSpore is a connecting link in the full-stack, all-scenario solution, playing a pivotal role in tackling the practical challenges involved in AI development. When developing MindSpore, Huawei's main objectives were to enable both a friendly development environment—to minimize the development time and training costs—and efficient operations. The optimization technology for just-in-time compilation, when used in collaboration with Huawei AI processors that feature the self-developed Da Vinci architecture, can maximize the hardware capabilities and deliver optimal performance. More importantly, MindSpore enables AI to adapt to every scenario (including the device, edge, and cloud) and implement on-demand collaboration among these scenarios, empowering all-round and trusted AI while also ensuring user privacy.

This book takes a systematic approach in providing you with a basic understanding of deep learning and related practical applications of MindSpore. It aims to help you not only achieve greater results more quickly in your basic research and development of AI applications and solutions, but also fully utilize MindSpore and the AI computing power of Ascend series chips. Through this book, we hope to achieve a wider, deeper, and all-round application of AI.

January 2020

Zhijun Xu
Deputy Chairman of the Board and Rotating
Chairman of Huawei
Shenzhen, China

Foreword by Wenfei Fan

Over the last decade, we have witnessed not only surging volumes of data, but also major improvements in computing power and breakthroughs in algorithms, all of which have driven rapid development in the new generation of AI. By giving machines perception, cognition, and even intelligence capabilities, AI touches every aspect of society. It is pleasing to see that Huawei's AI strategy focuses on layout and investment in basic research, full-stack solutions, open ecosystem, and talent development, and contributes to inclusive intelligence.

From the perspective of data scientists, data is undoubtedly a vital element of deep learning. Huge volumes of data are generated due to the explosive growth of information, laying a rich and solid foundation for AI. However, deep learning requires more than just mass data—it also requires the data to be high quality. Some of the key aspects that affect the precision and performance of training models include how the raw data is processed, how the training data is labeled, and how the inferior data is cleaned up. This book enables you to understand the basics and applications of deep learning by describing the related theories and practical applications in a simple, easy-to-understand way, and provides unique insights into data processing. Through its clear explanations of data preparation, data augmentation, and data visualization technologies, this book shows that rational data processing significantly helps reduce model complexity, shorten training times, and improve model performance.

With MindSpore—Huawei's self-developed AI computing framework—data scientists working with AI no longer need to master complex programming skills in order to apply deep learning frameworks; instead, they are able to focus on algorithms and logic. This is extremely attractive to researchers across multiple fields, such as data science, physics, mathematics, chemistry, and life sciences, because it can help them quickly develop AI applications.

It is a pleasure to see Prof. Lei Chen publishing this book in cooperation with Huawei, uncovering the charms of deep learning and helping not only developers to develop ideal AI applications, but also graduates and undergraduates who are majoring in AI. It will also benefit engineers and scientists who are involved in AI development with access to MindSpore's AI ecosystem. The book offers readers the chance to explore the combination of deep learning and logical methods in order to achieve success in the field of AI and advocates us embracing the future era of intelligence to facilitate an inclusive AI.

December 2019   Wenfei Fan
Foreign Member of the Chinese Academy of
Sciences (CAS), Fellow of the Royal Society
(FRS), Fellow of the Royal Society of Edinburgh
(FRSE), Fellow of the Association for Computing
Machinery (ACM), and Member of Academia
Europaea (MAE)
Edinburgh, UK

Preface

From computers to the Internet and then to AI, people from my generation have witnessed and participated in the magnificent feast of science and technology in society that has turned science fiction into reality. Technologies such as machine learning, virtual reality, and cloud computing—technologies that were once used by only leading scientists—have now become a part of our lives and are familiar to ordinary people. Realizing how deep learning will affect all walks of life, Huawei has launched MindSpore, its self-developed all-scenario AI computing framework. By combining hardware and software, and leveraging the superb computing power of Huawei Ascend chips, MindSpore unlocks the full potential of the hardware.

Supporting the models used in all current mainstream deep learning frameworks, MindSpore enables full-stack, all-scenario device–edge–cloud collaborative development. By adapting to all AI application scenarios, MindSpore significantly lowers the development threshold and dramatically shortens the time needed for model development. In addition, MindSpore supports local AI computing, further resolving the problem of privacy security and protection, which is a big concern in the industry.

In the current era where speed and execution are crucial, AI developers need to simplify complicated things, and quickly learn how to use different tools properly and efficiently, in order to resolve the problems they encounter. Helping people achieve this is the ultimate goal of this book. Unlike many deep learning textbooks that focus on theories and the basics, this book aims to make theory simple while focusing on practical application. It offers you a basic understanding of deep learning and describes various related models in a simple way, using multiple examples to explain how you can use MindSpore to implement deep learning theories and algorithms while leveraging the strong computing power of Ascend chips to create many things that other frameworks cannot do.

I sincerely hope that this book enables all developers to benefit from the powerful functions of MindSpore as soon as possible and allows them to realize their full potential while playing their part in this great, rapid, and thrilling technological revolution.

I would like to thank the MindSpore development team for taking time out of their busy schedules to write and proofread all the sample program code in this book. Without their full support, it would have been a difficult task to complete the book. I would also like to thank the MindSpore documentation team for reviewing the book from cover to cover. They went to extraordinary lengths in terms of content arrangement and text layout and made significant contribution to the writing of this book. My thanks also go to Ms. Shen Yanyan, a teacher from Shanghai Jiao Tong University, and Zhang Yongqi and Di Shimin, students from The Hong Kong University of Science and Technology, for their contributions. I must also express my gratitude to my colleagues in the book reviewing team for meticulously checking omissions and adding in the missing parts, and for giving many valuable suggestions. Furthermore, thank you to my colleagues at the Central Software Architecture and Design Management Department for their careful editing and modification of illustrations, ensuring that the content is clear and vivid, and for explaining concepts more specifically and definitively. In addition, I am extremely grateful for my colleagues at the Strategy and Business Development Department, Cloud BU, who frequently communicated with Tsinghua University Press to get this book published quickly. My thanks also go to Mr. Sheng Dongliang and Ms. Zhong Zhifang from Tsinghua University Press for their strong support. Their careful and meticulous work has ensured the quality of this book. Finally, I'd like to thank Huawei for its support during the writing of this book.

I have written this book to the best of my ability but due to limited knowledge, there might be omissions or deficiencies. I therefore welcome and encourage your comments and criticisms.

Kowloon, Hong Kong   Lei Chen
November 2019

About This Book

This book systematically introduces the theory of deep learning and explores practical applications based on the MindSpore AI computing framework. Split across 14 chapters, the book covers deep learning, deep neural networks (DNNs), convolutional neural networks (CNNs), recurrent neural networks (RNNs), unsupervised learning, deep reinforcement learning, automated machine learning, device–cloud collaboration, deep learning visualization, and data preparation for deep learning. To help clarify complex topics, this book includes numerous examples and links to online resources based on MindSpore.

In addition to providing a reference as well as learning material for software development engineers and scientific researchers engaged in deep learning, this book offers a solid foundation for graduates and undergraduates majoring in artificial intelligence (AI), intelligent science and technology, computer science and technology, electronic information engineering, and automation.

Contents

Chapter 1
Introduction

This chapter starts by outlining the historical development trends of AI and then explains what deep learning is and how it performs in practical applications. The chapter concludes by briefly describing the features of MindSpore, Huawei's self-developed deep learning framework.

1.1 The History of AI

AI dates back to the 1950s. Its development was extremely slow in those days because each field had a unique definition, and understanding of AI, the content and methodology of studies were inconsistent, and the sharing of technology and information was limited. At the 1956 Dartmouth Summer Research Project on Artificial Intelligence, John McCarthy et al. unified the descriptions of "human-like computing" and "machine intelligence" in different fields for the first time, and formally proposed the term "AI". This gave birth to the development of artificial intelligent and clarified its primary mission: using algorithms to build a dynamic computing environment to mimic human intelligence. Over the two decades that followed, AI achieved remarkable milestones in speech processing and problem solving. During that period, the "general problem solver" and "LISP AI voice" were two among many successful applications of AI. Nevertheless, AI in those days was severely limited and could only handle simple problems, offering unsatisfactory performance in practical applications. Furthermore, perceptron theory—a cutting-edge achievement in neural networks—was strongly criticized at that time, leading to a rapid cooling in the first wave of AI development. Various investors, including governments, stopped funding projects involving AI, resulting in it entering its first winter.

A resurgence did not occur in the field of artificial intelligent until the end of the 1980s, when expert systems began attracting research. Affected by symbolism, researchers of expert systems—deemed to be of high commercial value—hoped that machines could perform logical inference like a human does and then mimic

© Tsinghua University Press 2021

L. Chen, *Deep Learning and Practice with MindSpore*, Cognitive Intelligence and Robotics, https://doi.org/10.1007/978-981-16-2233-5_1

a human's cognitive process. This led to the emergence of many programming languages, such as Prolog, oriented to logical calculus, but the resurgence did not last long because the expert systems were dependent on expensive computing platforms. As the performance of personal computers improved, expert systems were gradually phased out in favor of low-cost personal computers. In the end, the hardware market built up around AI declined sharply and AI entered its second winter.

Since the mid-1990s, in accordance with Moore's Law, computing power has increased exponentially and various machine learning algorithms have been rapidly verified, trained, and applied, directly triggering a renaissance of AI. During this period, machine learning methods such as support vector machine (SVM), boosting, and kernel method achieved excellent performance in practical applications such as handwritten digit recognition, stock prediction, sentiment classification, and click-through rate prediction. In 1997, Deep Blue—a chess-playing computer developed by IBM—defeated Garry Kasparov, the then world champion, in a chess match. This milestone event attracted a great deal of attention and rekindled people's interest in artificial intelligent. Since then, a new wave of AI has gradually swept the world.

In today's burgeoning field of AI, one of the most valuable and influential areas of research is deep learning, which has already achieved revolutionary advances in many aspects such as data representation, feature extraction, and feature interaction. As a representative method of machine learning, deep learning uses an artificial neural network (ANN) as the basic framework and benefits from the continuous accumulation of big data and rapid development of computers. Massive data resolves the problem of overfitting during neural network training, and high-performance hardware makes model training possible. In recent years, as research into deep learning has grown, we have witnessed Google's AlphaGo beat a human world-champion Go player. With the vigorous development of various intelligent technologies, such as unmanned vehicles, there is again hope that AI will eventually surpass human intelligence.

Due to the remarkable effects brought by AI and the rapid pace at which it is developing, various industries have integrated it into practical applications across fields such as computer vision, natural language understanding, speech recognition, and intelligent games. There is little doubt that AI will have a profound impact on society as a whole, and it is already changing our daily lives, albeit gradually at this time.

As a new AI technology, deep learning absorbs knowledge from massive data, interacts with the external environment, and learns interactive policies through feedback. In both the theoretical methods and practical applications of deep learning, a number of disruptive results have already been achieved. In the next section, we explore what deep learning is and how it can be applied practically.

1.2 What is Deep Learning?

Deep learning is a class of machine learning algorithms that use a multi-layer structure to automatically learn and extract higher-level features from raw data. In most cases, this extraction process is extremely difficult to achieve. Deep learning represents the raw data as a nested hierarchy of features, enabling each layer containing these features to be defined and calculated using simpler features. Of particular importance is deep learning's ability to automatically learn how to place different features optimally at specific layers. Unlike traditional machine learning algorithms that require features to be handcrafted, deep learning automatically learns how to extract features. There is therefore no need for complex and time-consuming manual feature engineering in deep learning, unlike traditional machine learning algorithms.

The word "deep" in deep learning represents the use of multiple layers needed to transform data into the required data. For a given model used with data input, the depth of the model is equal to the length of the longest path in the flowchart that describes how the model obtains output. Conversely, in the deep probabilistic model, the depth of the model is equal to the depth of the graph that describes how the concepts are associated with each other, rather than the depth of the computational graph. It is worth noting that the computational graph represented by the latter for calculation may be much deeper than the conceptual graph. Because these two opposing views exist, there is generally no consensus on how deep a model needs to be before it can be considered a "deep" model. Broadly speaking, however, deep learning generally refers to models that require more calculation steps or concept learning than traditional machine learning.

The ANN is the foundation on which most deep learning models are built. Based on the human brain, the ANN is a set of interconnected, hierarchically organized units called neurons, where different layers perform different transformations on the input to obtain different levels of abstraction and feature extraction. The connections between different neurons are assigned different weights, representing the impact of one neuron on another. The earliest model that is able to learn weights from sample data is perceptron, whose learning algorithm is a parameter learning method for the linear model. Although the linear model is still in widespread use, it has many defects, most notable of which is perceptron's inability to learn the XOR function.

Today, the most common deep learning model framework is the feedforward neural network, also known as multi-layer perceptron (MLP). "Feedforward" means that the information flow passing through the network is transferred in the forward direction. Specifically, data is used as input, and it is then computed at the intermediate layer to obtain the final output. The entire structure has no feedback connection, and the information is propagated in one direction only: forward. The feedforward neural network is the foundation for many practical deep learning models—an example of this is the CNN for computer vision tasks. When a feedforward neural network is extended to allow feedback connections, it is called an RNN. Both CNNs and RNNs have achieved significant success in practical applications, and these networks form the basis for implementing many of deep learning's practical applications, as described in the following section.

1.3   Practical Applications of Deep Learning

In recent years, the deep learning revolution has profoundly changed—and is expected to succeed in—many fields of application, including automatic speech recognition (ASR), image recognition, natural language understanding, and numerous other interdisciplinary fields (such as health care, biology, and finance). The following briefly describes these typical practical applications of deep learning.

1.3.1   ASR

ASR is a technology that converts speech into text. From early template-based methods to strict statistical models, and on to deep models in use today, speech recognition technologies have undergone several generations of change. Prior to deep learning models, the hidden Markov model (HMM) was the most popular speech recognition model, which required a four-step procedure for all ASR systems: feature extraction, acoustic modeling, language modeling, and decoding search. Before a speech signal enters the acoustic model, which is mainly used for feature conversion and representation, noise must be eliminated and the signal amplified and converted from the time domain to the frequency domain. A language model is then used to sort the results during the decoding search, and the text sequence with the highest score is selected. An early approach to implementing acoustic modeling was to use a DNN. However, because the DNN required fixed-size inputs, a method for processing speech signals of different lengths was needed. In addition, effectively modeling the long-term dynamic correlation is important due to the speech signal being a non-stationary timing signal. RNNs excel in performing these tasks, leading to the long short-term memory (LSTM) network—a variant of the RNN—becoming the most widely used deep learning model for ASR. Speech recognition systems based on the RNN significantly lower the recognition error rate and are therefore the go-to choice for mainstream commercial speech recognition devices (such as Amazon's Alexa).

1.3.2   Image Recognition

Image recognition is one of the most successful applications of deep learning. The first breakthrough in the field of computer vision came in 2012, when Professor Hinton's research team used AlexNet, a CNN architecture, to significantly reduce the error rate of image classification at the ImageNet Large Scale Visual Recognition Challenge (ILSVRC), winning the contest. Since then, new architectures based on CNNs have been proposed (including GoogleNet, VGGNet, ResNet, DenseNets, and Inception), offering continuous improvement in the accuracy of image classification while also continuously increasing the depth of the network. In addition, deep learning has been applied to other computer vision tasks, including object detection, image segmentation, image annotation, behavior analysis, facial recognition, and neural style transfer and video generation that are based on the generative adversarial network (GAN). The deep CNN, a deep learning model, plays a key role in these tasks. It involves convolution and pooling—the most important operations in the CNN—and is well suited for processing image data due to its parameter sharing and sparse connectivity. By stacking multiple layers, the CNN can continuously extract higher-level features from lower-level ones and achieve superior processing of downstream tasks. As proposals for new network architectures continue to emerge, it is hoped that deep learning will make significant headway in the field of image recognition.

1.3.3   Natural Language Processing

Neural networks have been applied to language models gradually since 2000 and have achieved promising results in natural language understanding tasks such as constituent parsing, sentiment analysis, information extraction, machine translation, and text classification. One of the most significant among these results has been the learning of word vectors. A word vector is a method for converting a word into a vectorized positional representation in the hidden space by using a DNN. Word vectors, when used as input into an RNN, enable sentences and phrases to be parsed effectively through the synthetic vector grammar, which can be considered a probabilistic context-free grammar implemented by the RNN. In terms of machine translation and language modeling, as well as other aspects, the RNN represented by the LSTM network performs exceptionally well. Over the past few years, proposals have emerged for new DNN structures (such as Transformer), in addition to the RNNs. By learning the long-term dependency and hierarchical structure in text sequences, these structures have achieved remarkable results in natural language processing (NLP) tasks. In addition, unsupervised models based on pre-training, such as the Bidirectional Encoder Representations from Transformers (BERT) model based on Transformer, use transfer learning and fine-tuning to further push the technical frontier of deep learning methods in NLP tasks. As the deep learning architecture for NLP tasks continues to evolve, its use in both reinforcement and unsupervised learning is expected to yield enhanced models.

1.3.4 Other Fields

Deep learning is also prevalent in other fields, such as biology, health care, and finance. For example, in biological research, deep learning algorithms can discover features that are either impossible or unfeasible for humans to capture. Researchers use these algorithms to classify cell images, establish genome connections, and speed up drug development. In the healthcare field, deep CNNs are applied to medical image analysis tasks, such as cancer cell classification, lesion detection, organ segmentation, and image enhancement, achieving good results. Deep learning is also applied in the financial field, where it is used to detect financial fraud and money laundering, and even to complete complex tasks such as stock screening, timing, and risk control by simulating the behavior of traders. Additionally, it can be used for credit scoring and detecting abnormalities.

1.4 Structure of the Book

This book introduces deep learning at three levels, starting with an introduction to various deep learning models and algorithms from a theoretical perspective. It then explores how deep learning methods can be used in various applications, and the performance results these methods achieve, from a practical application perspective. Finally, the book combines theory and practical application in explaining how to implement high-performance deep learning models and achieve effective learning through MindSpore, Huawei's self-developed deep learning computing framework.

1.5 Introduction to MindSpore

MindSpore is Huawei's next-generation deep learning framework. By leveraging the computing power of Huawei Ascend processors, enabling flexible deployment in device, edge, and cloud scenarios, and integrating the industry's best practices, MindSpore lowers the threshold for AI development and defines a new paradigm in AI programming.

At Huawei Connect 2018, Huawei set out the ten key challenges of AI technology, among which were the long training time (taking days or even months), the lack of powerful and cost-effective computing, and the labor-intensive approach used in data annotation. Issues such as huge development costs, long deployment cycles, and reliance on highly skilled experts have impeded the development of the AI developer ecosystem. In order to help developers and the industry tackle these system-level challenges and lower the threshold for AI development, MindSpore delivers a wealth of features such as simple programming, device–cloud collaboration, easy debugging, exceptional performance, and open-source components.

1.5.1   Simple Programming

Many developers involved in deep learning know how complex and error-prone the development process can be. MindSpore is based on a differentiable programming architecture that enables developers to focus on the mathematical primitive expression of the model algorithm, thereby allowing them to automate this complex process and minimize potential errors through automatic differentiation.

The technologies that enable automatic differentiation in deep learning frameworks are categorized into the graph method (represented by Google's TensorFlow), the operator overloading method (represented by Facebook PyTorch), and the source code conversion method (represented by MindSpore Source to Source, S2S), as shown in Fig. 1.1.

The graph method is easy to implement, while the data structure of a graph is easy to optimize and parallel. However, programmability is challenging, as this method requires users to understand the concepts and interfaces of the graph, including data, communication, and computing nodes, and data, dependency, and reference edges. Furthermore, representations of the control flow and higher-order derivation in the graph method are complex.

The operator overloading method suits the programming habits of users and is especially popular in academia. Nevertheless, this method introduces high overheads, as it uses the interpreter of the host language and records the running process to a tape (sometimes called a Wengert list). Additionally, the dynamic nature of this method makes it unsuitable for optimization of the reverse performance.

The S2S automatic differentiation technology balances both programmability and performance. It not only offers a consistent programming experience, but can also utilize the optimization capabilities of modern compilers due to being based on the intermediate representation (IR) granularity. This technology uses a differentiable programming architecture that is highly efficient and easy to debug. Through Python programming interfaces at the interface layer, including control flow representations, users are able to get started quickly. For example, as shown in Code 1.1, we start by defining a computational graph (function) using Python code. Then, we use the reverse interface provided by MindSpore to perform automatic differentiation, and obtain a backward computation graph (function). Following this, we provide some inputs in order to obtain the derivative of the computational graph (function) at a given point. In this example, the results of automatic differentiation are the derivatives of

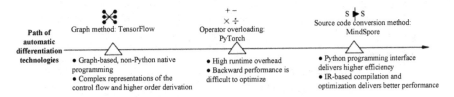

Fig. 1.1 Path of automatic differentiation technologies

all inputs in the graph. The reverse interface of MindSpore also provides an option
to calculate the derivatives of one or a given number of inputs.

Code 1.1 Native Python Programming Experience

```
def cost(x, y): return x * (x + y)

@mindspore
def test_grad (x, y):
    return grad_all(cost)(x, y)

def main():
    test_grad(2, 1)
```

As mentioned earlier, S2S is based on the IR granularity, meaning that it can
convert user-defined network source code into the IR defined by MindSpore (Mind-
Spore IR) and then generate the reverse code by using the IR mutator method. Other
techniques such as operator fusion are also used in this process to further improve
the reverse performance.

As shown in Fig. 1.2, a control flow expressed in MindSpore includes loops
and conditions. The programming style is consistent with native Python, but
unlike Python, MindSpore does not expand the loop when it generates the reverse
control flow. Instead, it performs IR-based reverse computation, thereby improving
performance by avoiding the need to expand the expression.

Compared with other frameworks, MindSpore reduces the amount of core code
by up to 20%, lowering the threshold for development and increasing the efficiency
by over 50% in some cases. Furthermore, because MindSpore inherently supports
compilation optimization, it significantly improves code efficiency and simplifies
research projects. MindSpore's automatic differentiation code is as follows:

Code 1.2 Example of Automatic Differentiation Code at the Graph Level

```
class Net(Cell):
    def __init__(self):
        self.w = Parameter(Tensor(np.ones([10])))
    def forward(x, y)
        return x + y
#Defining net
net = Net()
x = Tensor(np.ones([10]))
y = Tensor(np.ones([10]))
#Automatic differential derivation
gout = grad_all(net)(x, y)
```

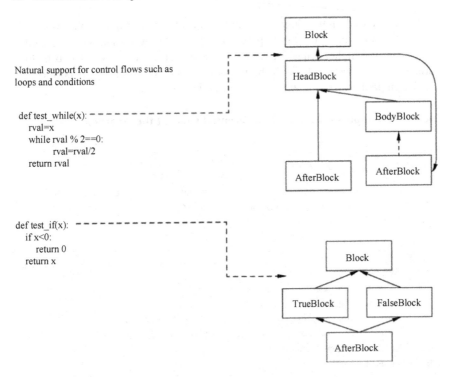

Natural support for control flows such as loops and conditions

```
def test_while(x):
    rval=x
    while rval % 2==0:
        rval=rval/2
    return rval
```

```
def test_if(x):
    if x<0:
        return 0
    return x
```

Fig. 1.2 MindSpore expression of a control flow

In addition to graph-level automatic differentiation, MindSpore also supports operator-level automatic differentiation. As well as providing operators of mainstream deep learning networks, MindSpore provides a tensor engine (and related interfaces) that enables users to customize operators using Python domain specific language (DSL). Through Python DSL, users can customize operators in Python as a mathematical form, similar to defining functions as formulas in mathematics. The operator-level automatic differentiation interfaces provided by the tensor engine can directly differentiate operators that are defined by DSL, again similar to mathematics where we would use a differential sign to express derivation. This approach more closely matches the code writing habits of users, as shown in Code 1.3. In the example code, we use DSL to define the forward operator, which is the objective of operator-level automatic differentiation, and use the tensor engine's reverse interface to derive the backward operator. For a multi-input operator, we can specify one or more forward operator inputs for the backward operator interface, enabling automatic differentiation calculation to be performed concurrently on these inputs. In operator-level automatic differentiation, the result of automatic differentiation on the upper-level operator in the reverse graph (the lower-level operator in the corresponding forward graph) is used as the input, and the result of the backward operator is calculated based on the chain rule—this approach differs from graph-level automatic differentiation. Using MindSpore, we can use the reverse interface repeatedly to calculate the higher-order derivative of the operator. This is similar to mathematics, where we would obtain the higher-order derivative by repeatedly performing calculation on the function by using the differential operator.

Code 1.3 Example of Automatic Differential Code at the Operator Level

```
def sigmoid(x):
#DSL implementation of the forward operator
    From te.lang.cce import vrec, vadds, vexp, vmuls
    res = vrec(vadds(vexp(vmuls(x, -1.0)), 1.0))
    return res

def sigmoid_ad(dout, x):
    import te
    #Forward operator reference
    out = sigmoid(x)
    #Generate a backward operator after automatic
    #differentiation of the forward operator
    [dx] = te.differentiate(out, [x], dout)
    return dx
```

We can apply many optimization techniques to operator-level automatic differentiation at the IR layer because it uses the IR method. For example, MindSpore's tensor engine provides zero-removal optimization at the IR layer according to the operator features of deep learning. The efficiency of operations such as summation may be significantly compromised if there are many zero elements in the unoptimized backward operator, so the tensor engine uses automatic differentiation to eliminate these zero elements through cyclic axis merging and cyclic domain scheduling transformation. This not only improves code efficiency but also simplifies the code to facilitate subsequent deployment. In addition, the tensor engine adopts the polyhedral model to overcome cyclic deformation dependence; to implement automatic operator scheduling, automatic memory optimization, and optimal memory configuration; and to deliver optimal operator performance. This frees users from the details of manual scheduling and tuning, allowing them instead to focus their attention on the algorithms.

Through the operator-level automatic differentiation interface, MindSpore supports not only automatic generation of the backward operator, but also manual optimization of the derivative formula. Specifically, the operator-level automatic differentiation function divides the operator into several complex operations of simple functions. Derivation is then performed sequentially by using the derivatives of the known basic functions and the derivation rule, following which the derivative of the composite function is calculated according to the chain rule. Once this has been completed, the tensor engine's built-in mathematical formula simplifier is used to simplify the derivative. Although this is sufficient for most users, MindSpore also provides an interface that allows users with higher requirements for performance or code deployment to use their own optimized derivative formulas in order to replace one or more of the steps involved in automatically generated differentiation, as shown in Code 1.4. While MindSpore can complete the derivation of the sigmoid function in the preceding example, some users may want to calculate it using the manually derived derivative $dy = y (1 - y)$ of the sigmoid function so that they can use the result obtained through the forward function. In this case, the manual derivative formula is added to the function custom_sigmoid_fdiff, and the derivation of this part is reloaded in the automatic differentiation. The custom_sigmoid_fdiff parameter is used as the output to calculate the derivative of x while automatic generation of other parts is preserved. By taking this approach, MindSpore ensures consistency of the automatically differentiated backward operator and the manually tuned backward operator, making it easier for users to call the operator at the graph layer.

Code 1.4 Example of Automatic Differentiation Code for Manual Tuning

```
def sigmoid_ad_optimized(dout, x):
    import te
    #Forward operator reference
    out = sigmoid(x)
    #Manual tuning
    def custom_sigmoid_fdiff(out, inputs, grad):
        return [out * (1.0 - out)]
    #Generating backward operator
    [dx] = te.differentiate(out, [x], dout, override= {out:([x],
    custom_sigmoid_fdiff)})
    return dx
```

In summary, by saying that MindSpore realizes simple programming, we mean that it simplifies the development process and improves both code readability and efficiency by not only considering user requirements for manual tuning of the backward operator, but also combining automatic differentiation and manual tuning. In addition to supporting operator-level automatic differentiation, MindSpore also optimizes the backward operator at the IR layer, thereby meeting developer requirements for automatic generation of the backward operator.

1.5.2 Device–Cloud Collaboration

By leveraging Huawei's "device–edge–cloud" service scenarios, MindSpore supports all-scenario deployment and enables cloud-to-device processes with a particular focus on ensuring complete privacy protection. It enables developers to quickly develop and deploy cloud-based, edge-based, and mobile-based AI applications—and interconnects all scenarios to improve resource utilization and privacy protection—by providing capabilities such as consistent development and deployment along with on-demand collaboration capabilities for any scenario.

Although the industry and academics have yet to define "device–cloud collaboration", the device–cloud interactive learning pattern is generally considered a device–cloud collaboration system. For example, the application of technologies such as model compression, on-device inference, on-device training, transfer learning, and federated learning can be considered as device–cloud collaboration. This involves building, pre-training, or hosting models on the cloud, executing or training models on the device, and transferring models or weights between the cloud and the device.

In on-device inference, the cloud model is compressed and converted into an on-device inference model, which is then loaded into an on-device inference framework to infer local data. The dataset used for cloud-based model pre-training and the real device data typically differ, so to achieve an accurate and personalized user experience, real device data needs to be used for model training. Because of device limitations in terms of computing power, energy, and data storage, training a model from scratch is impractical and therefore transfer learning technology is used for on-device learning. A number of device–cloud federated learning methods and frameworks have been proposed to combine multiple devices in order to train a global model and implement on-device privacy protection, aiming to make full use of device data and on-device training capabilities. For example, Google pioneered a federated learning approach and framework in 2016, following which Yang Qiang et al. proposed methods such as horizontal federated learning, vertical federated learning, federated transfer learning, federated reinforcement learning, and their corresponding frameworks. On-device inference, transfer learning, and federated learning are different stages of device–cloud collaboration, all of which are combined in MindSpore's device–cloud collaboration framework in order to streamline the entire device–cloud process, as shown in Fig. 1.3.

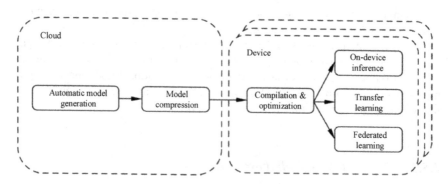

Fig. 1.3 Device–cloud collaboration architecture

This process, covering model generation, model compression, compilation optimization, and on-device learning, is streamlined through MindSpore's device–cloud collaboration framework integrating both the cloud and device frameworks. In terms of establishing model libraries, MindSpore provides neural architecture search (NAS) capabilities for automated model generation and uses its model compression module to prune and quantize models. And to subsequently convert and optimize the models, MindSpore uses its compilation optimization capabilities while also accelerating operator execution through methods such as neural processing units (NPUs), graphics processing units (GPUs), and ARM NEON.[1] MindSpore's device–cloud collaboration framework offers the following features[2]:

(1) Rapid deployment in multiple scenarios. The framework constructs a diversified model library by using NAS technology so that models can be quickly adapted to different types of hardware on multiple devices. In this way, we can search the library for a model that satisfies the performance constraints of a given application, and use the model directly without additional training.

(2) Full stack performance optimization. The framework enables users to optimize the precision, size, and latency of models in order to achieve ultimate performance through methods such as NAS, model compression (pruning, distillation, and quantization), and compilation optimization (operator fusion, constant folding, and hardware acceleration).

(3) High flexibility and ease of use. The framework supports multiple strategies, including model generation, model compression, and compilation optimization, and not only streamlines the entire device–cloud process, but also centrally manages the strategies and configurations throughout the process, delivering tangible benefits in terms of improved ease of use.

(4) Various learning patterns. The framework supports advanced learning patterns that require on-device training capabilities, including transfer learning and federated learning, as well as basic patterns such as on-device inference (support for different learning patterns is being added gradually).

1.5.3 Easy Debugging

Along with visualized AI development, MindSpore makes the debugging process simple and offers both dynamic and flexible development debugging. After developing a single codebase, we can easily switch between the dynamic and static graph debugging modes by changing only one line of code. For example, if we frequently need to perform development debugging, we can select the dynamic graph mode for convenient and flexible debugging using a single operator or subgraph. Or if we need to ensure high running efficiency, we can switch to the static graph mode, compile

---

[1] See: https://developer.arm.com/architectures/instruction-sets/simd-isas/neon.

[2] The framework is continuously evolving in order to remain at the cutting edge of AI development. Get the most up-to-date information at https://mindspore.cn.

and execute the entire graph, and obtain high performance through efficient graph compilation optimization. The simple code needed to change between debugging modes in MindSpore is as follows:

Code 1.5 Example of Code for Switching Debugging Modes

```
def ssd_forward_run():
    net = ssd_resnet34_224(batch_size=8)
    #Switching to the graph execution mode
    context switch_to_graph_mode()
    model.train(epoch=10, train_dataset=dataset)
    #Switching to the debugging execution mode
    context.switch_to_pynative_mode()
    model.train(epoch=10, train_dataset=dataset)
```

1.5.4 Exceptional Performance

MindSpore not only maximizes the heterogeneous computing power of all Huawei "device–edge–cloud" scenarios through AI Native, but also leverages Huawei Ascend chips for on-device execution, highly efficient AI data format processing, and depth map optimization to deliver optimal performance, helping minimize training time and improve inference performance. In addition, MindSpore implements automatic model parallelization, automatically dividing and optimizing models by using flexible policies and cost models. This is especially important due to the difficulty involved in dividing and debugging the models manually, which would lower the development efficiency, and addresses the fact that a single computer is unable to provide sufficient memory and computing power to handle the ever-increasing size of datasets and models. MindSpore's automatic parallelization code is as follows:

Code 1.6 Example of Automatic Parallelization Code

```
def ssd_forward_compile_auto_parallel(loss, opt, dataset):
    net = ssd_resnet34_224(batch_size=8)
    #Defining a distributed optimizer
    distributed_opt = DistributedOptimizer(optimizer=opt,
    degree=1)
    #Automatic parallelization among eight devices
    model = Model(net,loss,distributed_opt,data_parallel_size=8)
    model.train(epoch=10, train_dataset=dataset)
```

1.5.5 Open-Source Components

One of the key objectives of MindSpore is to ensure the continued prosperity of the AI development ecosystem. Through open-source components and an extensible architecture, MindSpore helps developers flexibly expand the capabilities of supporting third-party frameworks and third-party chips in order to meet a multitude of different customization requirements. As MindSpore continues to evolve, more and more learning resources, online support, and additional services will be provided at https://www.mindspore.cn/en and in open-source communities.

Chapter 2
Deep Learning Basics

This chapter describes several commonly used algorithms and basic concepts related to deep learning.

2.1 Regression Algorithms

Regression algorithms typically use a series of properties to predict a value, and the predicted values are continuous. For example, the price of a house is predicted based on the house's features, such as its location and number of bedrooms, or weather forecasts are predicted according to the previous week's temperatures and weather maps. Using the first example, if the actual house price is CNY 5 million, and the value predicted through regression analysis is CNY 4.99 million, the regression analysis is considered accurate. For machine learning problems, regression analysis includes linear regression, polynomial regression, logistic regression, and others. This section focuses on linear regression algorithms due to their simplicity, offering an ideal starting point for those wanting to quickly understand the basics of deep learning. Section 2.3 builds on this basic understanding by elaborating on logistic regression.

Let's start by looking at a linear regression problem with only one variable. Table 2.1 shows the given data, also called a dataset.

Each group of data is denoted as $(x^{(i)}, y^{(i)})$, and there are m groups of data in total. The goal is to obtain a model through which a value of y is predicted based on a newly given value of x. For linear regression, the model is a linear function, and the formula is as follows:

$$h(x^{(i)}) = w_0 + w_1 x^{(i)} \tag{2.1}$$

where w_0 and w_1 represent parameters that need to be obtained through training.

© Tsinghua University Press 2021
L. Chen, *Deep Learning and Practice with MindSpore*, Cognitive Intelligence and Robotics, https://doi.org/10.1007/978-981-16-2233-5_2

Table 2.1 Given data

x	– 12	– 4	1	10	20	29	43	60	…
y	0	2	3	5	8	7	10	15	…

This model is also called hypothesis. Linear regression aims to obtain an optimal group of w_0 and w_1, so that the hypothesis is close to the dataset shown in Table 2.1. In this way, we hope that the w_0 and w_1 obtained through training can fit the given dataset as closely as possible, as shown in Fig. 2.1.

So how do we obtain the optimal w_0 and w_1? We can achieve this by converting the training goal into minimization of the following function:

$$J(w) = \frac{1}{2m} \sum_{i=1}^{m} (h(x^{(i)}) - y^{(i)})^2 \tag{2.2}$$

A function that needs to be minimized is called a loss function, and more than one may exist. The one given above is called the mean square error function, which is typically used to solve regression problems. For classification problems, the cross-entropy loss function is typically used. An example of this is:

$$J(w) = -\frac{1}{m} \sum_{i=1}^{m} y^{(i)} \log h(x^{(i)}) + (1 - y^{(i)}) \log(1 - h(x^{(i)})) \tag{2.3}$$

The final optimization goal is to minimize the error between the predicted value $h(x^{(i)})$ and the actual label $y^{(i)}$ in the training data.

For the sake of simplicity, let's assume that the input data x has only one property, although in practical applications it may include n properties ($n \geq 1$). In this case, $n + 1$ parameters w need to be obtained through training, $w = [w_0, w_1, ..., w_n]$, where w_0 is a bias, and w_i ($i = 1, 2, ..., n$) is a weight of the ith property. In summary, the regression problem can be expressed as follows:

Fig. 2.1 Linear regression model

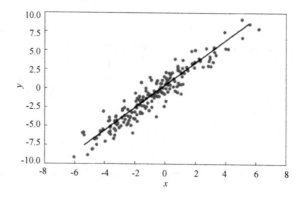

(1) Dataset

$$\{(x^{(i)}, y^{(i)})\}_{i=1}^{m}, x = [x_1, x_2, \cdots, x_n]$$ (2.4)

(2) Parameter

$$w = [w_0, w_1, \cdots, w_n]$$ (2.5)

(3) Hypothesis

$$h(x^{(i)}) = w_0 + \sum_{j=1}^{n} w_j x_j^{(i)}$$ (2.6)

(4) Loss function

$$J(w) = \frac{1}{2m} \sum_{i=1}^{m} (h(x^{(i)}) - y^{(i)})^2$$ (2.7)

For brevity, the dataset is expressed as an $m \times (n + 1)$ matrix X, where the first element of each row is always 1, which is followed by n properties of $x^{(i)}$, that is:

$$X = \begin{bmatrix} 1 & x_1^{(1)} & x_2^{(1)} & \cdots & x_n^{(1)} \\ 1 & x_1^{(2)} & x_2^{(2)} & \cdots & x_n^{(2)} \\ \vdots & \vdots & \vdots & \ddots & \vdots \\ 1 & x_1^{(m)} & x_2^{(m)} & \cdots & x_n^{(m)} \end{bmatrix}$$ (2.8)

In addition, the target value is also denoted as a vector form $y = (y^{(1)}; y^{(2)}; \ldots; y^{(m)})$, meaning that the linear regression problem can be expressed as follows:

$$w^* = \arg\min_{w} \frac{1}{2m}(y - Xw)^{\mathrm{T}}(y - Xw)$$ (2.9)

In order to find an extremum w^*, we can calculate the gradient of w to obtain:

$$\frac{\partial J(w)}{\partial w} = \frac{1}{m} X^{\mathrm{T}}(Xw - y)$$ (2.10)

When $X^{\mathrm{T}}X$ is a full-rank matrix or a positive-definite matrix, let the gradient $\frac{\partial J(w)}{\partial w} = 0$ in order to obtain:

$$w^* = (X^{\mathrm{T}}X)^{-1} X^{\mathrm{T}} y$$ (2.11)

where $(X^{\mathrm{T}}X)^{-1}$ is an inverse matrix of the matrix $X^{\mathrm{T}}X$.

After obtaining w^*, for any sample x, let $\hat{x} = [1, x]$, so that we can predict a regression value of x as follows:

$$h(x) = \hat{x}^{\mathrm{T}}(X^{\mathrm{T}}X)^{-1}X^{\mathrm{T}}y \qquad (2.12)$$

However, in practical applications, $X^{\mathrm{T}}X$ is unlikely to fully meet the conditions of the full-rank matrix or the positive-definite matrix. For example, the quantity of properties in some tasks might be large, potentially even large enough to exceed the quantity m of samples, that is, $n \geq m$. As a result, the quantity of columns in the sample matrix X would be much larger than the quantity of rows. In this case, $X^{\mathrm{T}}X$ is unable to meet the conditions of the full-rank matrix.

In the linear regression problem, let $\frac{\partial J(w)}{\partial w} = 0$, so that we can obtain an analytical solution of the optimal parameter w^*. However, for models or loss functions that are more complex, there is usually no analytical solution. Section 2.2 will describe gradient descent, an algorithm that has found wide use in the field of machine learning. By minimizing the loss function, this algorithm obtains, through training, the parameter w^* that needs to be calculated.

2.2 Gradient Descent

Gradient descent is a first-order optimization algorithm used to find the local minimum of a loss function (or objective function). Using this algorithm, also called steepest descent, we need to move a distance proportional to the negative of the gradient (or approximate gradient) corresponding to the current point of the function in order to implement iterative search. The converse of this is called gradient ascent, whereby if we move a distance proportional to the positive of the gradient, we will approach the local maximum point of the function. This section focuses exclusively on gradient descent.

Gradient descent is based on the following observation: If a real function $J(w)$ is differentiable and defined at w, then $J(w)$ decreases fastest at the point w along the direction $-\nabla J(w)$, which is opposite to the gradient. As shown in Fig. 2.2, if we

Fig. 2.2 Gradient over ridges

follow the middle route, we would travel a much shorter distance than if we traveled along either the left or right route.

Based on this, the concept of gradient descent includes the following parts:

(1) Selecting an initial point w_0.
(2) Gradually updating the parameter in the negative direction of the gradient, $w_t = w_{t-1} - \alpha \, \nabla J(w_{t-1})$ until convergence.

Here, $\alpha > 0$. Also known as learning rate, α is step size whose value can be set before training, or it can be adjusted according to the training situation. Based on the definition of gradient, if the value α is small enough, $J(w_t) \leq J(w_{t-1})$. If an appropriate step size is given, starting from w_0, smaller loss functions $J(w_0) \geq J(w_1) \geq J(w_2) \geq \ldots$ are obtained gradually. In theory, the sequence w_t will gradually converge to the minimum of the loss function, as shown in Fig. 2.3.

Assume that the loss function J is defined on a plane and looks like a bowl. The elliptical curves represent contour lines; that is, the function J is a curve formed by a set of constants, where the value becomes smaller as it approaches the center. If an initial point w_0 is selected arbitrarily, the arrows point to the negative direction of the gradient (the gradient direction is perpendicular to the contour line of the point). In this case, the parameter w is gradually updated along the descending direction of the gradient until it reaches the bottom of the bowl, that is, it reaches the minimum point of the function J.

Because we can convert the problem of solving the linear regression, mentioned in Sect. 2.1, into one of minimizing the loss function $J(w)$, we can use gradient descent here. For a given dataset $\{(x^{(i)}, y^{(i)})\}$, the parameter w is defined according to the number of properties of x. The linear equation $h(x^{(i)})$ and the loss function are as follows:

$$J(w) = \frac{1}{2m} \sum_{i=1}^{m} (h(x^{(i)}) - y^{(i)})^2 \tag{2.13}$$

Fig. 2.3 Illustration of gradient descent

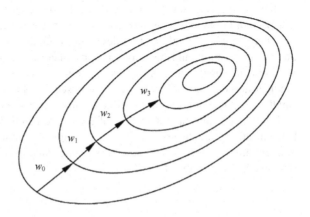

First, we need to randomly select an initial point w_0 and an appropriate step size α. The gradient calculation formula is as follows:

$$\nabla J(w) = \frac{1}{m} \sum_{i=1}^{m} (h(x^{(i)}) - y^{(i)})\hat{x}^{(i)} \tag{2.14}$$

where $\hat{x}^{(i)} = [1, x^{(i)}]$. A dimension of a constant 1 is added to the original property vector to update the bias w_0.

The parameter w_t can be updated step by step based on the gradient $\nabla J(w)$, and the optimal parameter value can be obtained by using $w_t = w_{t-1} - \alpha \nabla J(w_{t-1})$. In addition to being used in linear regression, gradient descent can also be used for minimizing the loss function to solve many problems in machine learning.

This versatile algorithm is also called batch gradient descent, where "batch" means that the total quantity m of training samples is used. In practical problems, the quantity of samples may be large (e.g., the quantity of students in a school, clients in a bank, and files on a hard disk). The quantity of parameters may also large, especially for complex learning models such as the DNN. Using all data samples in each gradient calculation will produce large results or even make the calculations impossible. The batch gradient descent algorithm can be thought of as a random process, in which only one point is randomly selected at a time, which is expected to be roughly similar to the sum of all points. This means that the gradient of a single point, called stochastic gradient, can be used instead of the average gradient, and the overall gradient can be regarded as an expected value of the stochastic gradient. An iterative algorithm for a linear programming problem based on stochastic gradient descent involves the following formula:

$$w_t = w_{t-1} - \alpha(h(x^{(i)}) - y^{(i)})\hat{x}^{(i)} \tag{2.15}$$

where $x^{(i)}$ is the sample randomly selected from m data samples during the tth iteration.

Because only one sample is used for each update without traversing all datasets, the speed of iteration is relatively fast. However, the gradient direction selected each time may be not optimal due to a deviation of random sampling, meaning that the quantity of iterations and the minimum value of convergence may also not be optimal.

In practical applications, mini-batch gradient descent—a trade-off between batch gradient descent and stochastic gradient descent—is a more popular algorithm. A small batch of samples with a sample quantity of b ($b < m$) are randomly selected each time, speeding up calculation of the entire batch. In addition, using a small batch in calculating the gradient direction yields greater accuracy than the stochastic gradient direction, which is based on only one sample. Mini-batch gradient descent is shown in Algorithm 2.1.

Algorithm 2.1 Mini-batch gradient descent

Input: Dataset $\left\{\left(x^{(i)}, y^{(i)}\right)\right\}_{i=1}^{m}$, step size α, mini-batch training sample size b, and iteration quantity T

Output: Converged parameter w_T

(1)   Initialize the parameter w_0

(2)   *for* $t \in \{1, 2, ..., T\}$.

(3)   Select b samples uniformly at random from m samples

(4)   Calculate the gradient and update the parameter

$$w_t \leftarrow w_{t-1} - \frac{\alpha}{b} \sum_{i \in m_b} \partial_w J_i(w) \tag{2.16}$$

Algorithm 2.1 summarizes the main process of mini-batch gradient descent, where m_b is an index set of b samples randomly selected from m samples, and $J_i(w)$ is a loss function on the ith sample. We will describe selection of a step size, conditions for convergence, and other relevant aspects in subsequent sections.

2.3   Classification Algorithms

Unlike a regression problem, the output of a classification problem is a discrete value rather than a continuous value, that is, the category of the sample. Classification problems are widely used in real-world applications, for example, to perform handwritten digit recognition, email spam classification, and facial recognition, and even to distinguish cats and dogs in images. Such problems include binary classification ("yes" or "no") and multi-class classification (where one of multiple categories needs to be determined). All multi-class classification problems can be converted into multiple binary classification problems. For example, when animals are classified, each animal can be systematically determined using "yes" or "no" in order to achieve the goal of multi-class classification. This section focuses on the binary classification problem.

Consider the following question: Can we solve a classification problem by using the same method we use to solve a regression problem? The answer is yes. The main difference between classification and regression problems is that a series of discrete values, rather than a straight line or curve, is to be fit. The logistic regression mentioned in Sect. 2.1 is ideal for the linear binary classification problem.

Logistic regression is based on the logistic function (also known as a log probabilistic function) shown in Fig. 2.4, that is:

Fig. 2.4 Logistic function
$\text{sigmoid}(x) = \frac{1}{1+e^{-x}}$

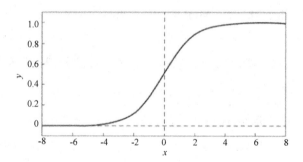

$$\text{sigmoid}(x) = \frac{1}{1 + e^{-x}} \qquad (2.17)$$

where $e^{(\cdot)}$ is an exponential function.

Any given input value x is mapped by the logistic function to a value in the range 0–1. The output value is closer to 1 if $x > 0$, and closer to 0 if $x < 0$. When $x = 0$, it indicates an inflection point with the maximum slope value. The output value of the logistic function is usually regarded as the probability that the output is 1. The logistic function is a monotonically differentiable function, which is an important property that allows gradient descent to be used for model training.

For a given sample property x, assume that the label $y \in \{0, 1\}$, and the predicted value $z(x) = w^T \hat{x}$, where $\hat{x} = [1, x]$. For classification problems, if $z(x) > 0$, the predicted value is 1, whereas if $z(x) < 0$, the predicted value is 0. In this way, the predicted value $z(x)$ can be substituted into the logistic function to obtain:

$$h(x) = \frac{1}{1 + e^{-w^T \hat{x}}} \qquad (2.18)$$

From the perspective of probability, the classification probability can be expressed as $P(y = 1|x, w) = \frac{1}{1+e^{-w^T\hat{x}}}$. Similarly, $P(y = 0|x, w) = \frac{1}{1+e^{w^T\hat{x}}}$.

For a given dataset $\{(x^{(i)}, y^{(i)})\}_{i=1}^{m}$, in the linear regression problem, the optimization goal is to minimize the mean square error. However, in the logistic regression model, the optimization goal is to maximize the likelihood function L. The calculation formula for L is as follows:

$$L(w) = \prod_{i=1}^{n} P(y^{(i)}|x^{(i)}, w) = \prod_{i=1}^{n} (h(x^{(i)}))^{y^{(i)}} (1 - h(x^{(i)}))^{1-y^{(i)}} \qquad (2.19)$$

If the quantity of samples is too large, numeric overflow may easily occur due to the characteristics of computer floating-point numbers. Because the form of consecutive addition is easier than consecutive multiplication, in terms of gradient calculation, we usually take the logarithm of multiple consecutive multiplication terms. Specifically, we can use the log-likelihood function shown in the following formula:

$$l(w) = \log L(w) = \sum_{i=1}^{n} y^{(i)} \log(h(x^{(i)})) + (1 - y^{(i)}) \log(1 - h(x^{(i)})) \qquad (2.20)$$

Now we can use the gradient descent described in Sect. 2.2 to minimize the loss function in order to train the parameter w, that is:

$$J(w) = -\sum_{i=1}^{n} y^{(i)} \log(h(x^{(i)})) + (1 - y^{(i)}) \log(1 - h(x^{(i)})) \qquad (2.21)$$

This loss function is also called cross-entropy. When the value of $y^{(i)}$ is 1 or 0, the loss function $J(x^{(i)}, y^{(i)}, w)$ on a single sample corresponds to the left or right part of formula (2.21) respectively. As shown in Fig. 2.5, when $y^{(i)} = 0$, if $h(x^{(i)})$ approaches 0, the value of the loss function becomes smaller, as too does the slope. The opposite is true if $y^{(i)} = 1$. The logistic function generates larger penalty values and larger gradients for incorrectly classified samples.

The logistic regression model defines linear binary classification problems from the perspective of regression probability. Figure 2.6a shows a graphical representation of the linear classifier. For dark-colored samples, $y = 0$; for light-colored samples, $y = 1$. The boundary in the middle is the linear classification boundary $z(x) = w^{T}x = 0$, which is obtained through training. When $z(x) < 0$, that is, a point is above the boundary, the predicted value is 0; otherwise, the predicted value is 1.

The linear classifier offers good interpretability, but in practice, the boundary of samples is not linear for a nonlinear classifier shown in Fig. 2.6b. This means that different parameter models need to be defined, such as the polynomial model, the SVM, and the neural network model, to learn complex nonlinear classifiers. Nevertheless, it is worth noting that the nonlinear classification problem can also be split into two parts:

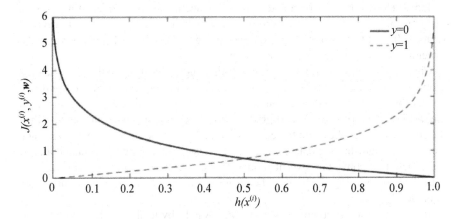

Fig. 2.5 Curve of a relationship between a single sample and a loss function

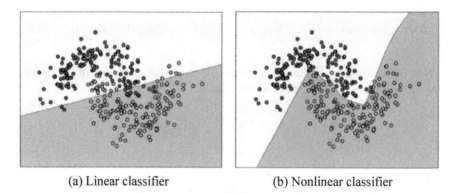

(a) Linear classifier   (b) Nonlinear classifier

Fig. 2.6 Representation of the linear classifier and the nonlinear classifier

(1) Mapping samples to linear space by using the feature function.
(2) Learning the final classification boundary by using the linear classification model.

Chapter 3 will describe how to use the logistic regression model to train neural networks.

2.4 Overfitting and Underfitting

In machine learning, the terms overfitting and underfitting mean that the selected model does not optimally fit the data. In other words, the model is either too complex or too simple. An overfit model typically includes more parameters than the features of the data. In order to fit as much data as possible, some incorrect samples are included. However, these parameters may produce noise due to overfitting of data. The opposite of overfitting is underfitting, in which the selected parameter or model is not sufficiently complex. For example, using a linear model to fit a nonlinear structure can be considered as underfitting.

Figure 2.7 shows the problems of overfitting and underfitting in the classification problems. For a nonlinear model, if the linear model in Fig. 2.7a is used, it will not be possible to fit the nonlinear boundary. This case is called underfitting, in which the model cannot provide a good prediction effect. To fit as much data as possible, the complex model shown in the curve in Fig. 2.7c may be selected. Although such a model distinguishes the data completely, it does not optimally fit the data features. For a new test point, this overfit model may cause an error in distinguishing the data. The curve in Fig. 2.7b offers better generalization and is therefore the model of choice.

If the regression problem shown in Fig. 2.8 is fit by using a light-colored polynomial curve, although all data points can fit perfectly, the features of the data are lost. This means that the model cannot be satisfactorily generalized. For example, for

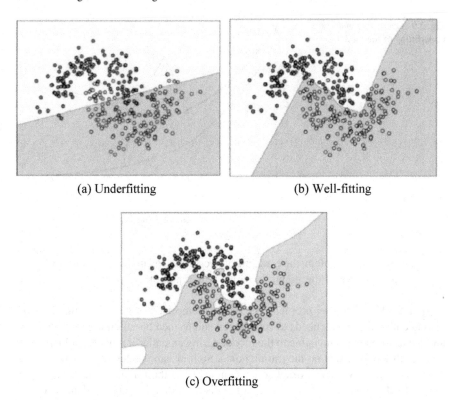

(a) Underfitting   (b) Well-fitting

(c) Overfitting

Fig. 2.7 Underfitting, well-fitting, and overfitting in classification problems

Fig. 2.8 Overfitting in regression problems

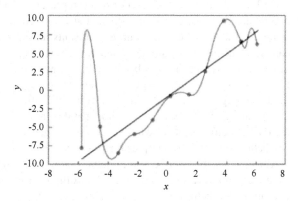

any unknown data point between the first point and the second point on the left, the predicted value is extremely large, resulting in a significant deviation. Conversely, the dark-colored linear model reflects a change trend of the data and can achieve higher accuracy when predicting a new data point.

Fig. 2.9 Overfitting and
underfitting of the model

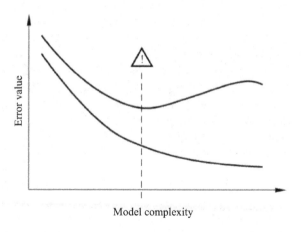

In the preceding problem, the concepts of overfitting and underfitting are explained from the perspective of the graph. Now we will explain them from the perspective of data.

In a machine learning problem, the data is comprised of both training data and testing data—the model needs to be selected and trained based on the training data, and the testing data is invisible to the model. Using an underfit model would achieve a noticeably poor effect on the training data. So how can we determine whether the model is overfit? We can extract some samples from the training data to form one piece of validation data. Assuming that the distribution of validation data is similar to that of the training data and testing data, we can determine whether the model is overfit based on the model's performance on the validation data.

In Fig. 2.9, the horizontal coordinate represents model complexity, the vertical coordinate represents an error value, the lower curve represents an error on the training data, and the upper curve represents an error on the validation data. We can see that, when the model complexity increases, the error on the training data gradually decreases. This is because the complex model fits the data more easily. However, the error on the validation data decreases before it increases, because the model undergoes a gradual transition from underfitting to overfitting. The validation data is intended to help select the model at the dashed line. The model optimally fits the data, meaning that we can expect a better generalization effect—the algorithm can better adapt to new samples (testing data).

Chapter 4 will describe some methods for enhancing the generalization ability of the model to prevent overfitting. Controlling the model complexity can alleviate overfitting and help learn the rules behind the data.

Chapter 3
DNN

This chapter introduces several important concepts related to DNN and presents some examples of using MindSpore to implement simple neural networks.

3.1 Feedforward Network

Deep learning uses neural networks to perform high-level data abstraction—a key difference compared with traditional machine learning. The most basic neural network structure is feedforward neural network (FNN), also known as MLP.

Before describing MLP, we will first look perceptron, which is the basic unit of a neural network. As shown in Fig. 3.1, x_1, x_2, ..., x_n are inputs, w_1, w_2, ..., w_n are corresponding weights, and w_0 is a bias. The perceptron performs weighted summation on these inputs and adds the bias w_0, and then obtains the outputs of neurons by using the activation function f (•). The logic function $\text{sigmoid}(x) = \frac{1}{1+e^{-x}}$, which we mentioned in the classification problem, is a commonly used activation function. It can be used to squeeze a value that changes within a large range to an output value range of (0, 1) or to output a probability value corresponding to 0/1. The double cosine function $\tanh(x) = \frac{e^x - e^{-x}}{e^x + e^{-x}}$ and the rectified linear unit (ReLU) function $\text{ReLU}(x) = \max(x, 0)$ are also common activation functions for neurons. All these activation functions can be used to perform nonlinear operations on neurons, but note that nonlinear functions are more expressive than linear ones. Figure 3.2 shows the shapes of these three activation functions.

Although a single neuron of a nonlinear activation function has a nonlinear feature, this function has only one layer of neurons. It has a very limited learning ability and can handle only linearly separable problems. To solve nonlinearly separable problems, which are more complex, MLP is therefore proposed.

Figure 3.3 is a simple three-layer FNN model that includes an input layer, a hidden layer, and an output layer. Data x is provided to the input layer as inputs, which are processed through linear mapping and nonlinear activation functions at the hidden

© Tsinghua University Press 2021
L. Chen, *Deep Learning and Practice with MindSpore*, Cognitive Intelligence and Robotics, https://doi.org/10.1007/978-981-16-2233-5_3

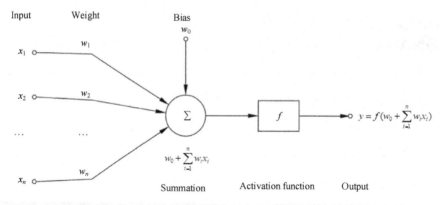

Input   Weight   Bias
                                    w_0

x_1 w_1

x_2 w_2

Σ f $y = f(w_0 + \sum_{i=1}^{n} w_i x_i)$

...   ...

$w_0 + \sum_{i=1}^{n} w_i x_i$

x_n w_n

              Summation   Activation function   Output

Fig. 3.1 Perceptron

layer. The processed data is then transferred to the output layer. At the input layer, the number of nodes depends on the number of properties of the data, whereas at the output layer, the number of nodes is equal to the number of categories, abstract features, or other dimension. The number of hidden layers is specified manually to be one or more, and at each hidden layer, one category of nonlinear activation functions can be set. After linear combination and nonlinear transformation, the function model formed by multiple layers of neurons develops a more powerful learning ability.

3.2   Backpropagation

Chapter 1 explored how we can use the gradient decent algorithm to train the regression model. Although we must use this algorithm in the neural network model to update parameters, a neural network usually includes millions of parameters. This means that it is important to calculate these parameters in an efficient manner. To this end, the backpropagation algorithm is used in neural networks to improve the calculation efficiency.

Before describing backpropagation, we will first explain the chain rule. Assume that there are two functions $y = g(x)$ and $z = h(y)$. The derivative of z with respect to x is obtained as follows:

$$\frac{\partial z}{\partial x} = \frac{\partial z}{\partial y} \frac{\partial y}{\partial x} \tag{3.1}$$

Now assume that there are three functions $x = g(s)$, $y = h(s)$, and $z = k(x, y)$. The derivative of z with respect to s is obtained as follows:

$$\frac{\partial z}{\partial s} = \frac{\partial z}{\partial x} \frac{\partial x}{\partial s} + \frac{\partial z}{\partial y} \frac{\partial y}{\partial s} \tag{3.2}$$

Fig. 3.2 Shapes of the three common activation functions

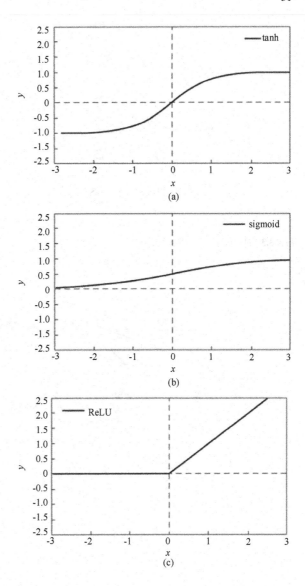

The gradient calculation of neural networks relies on layer-by-layer backpropagation based on the chain rule.

In the FNN shown in Fig. 3.4, the input layer includes n properties $x_1, x_2, \ldots, x_n$, the intermediate hidden layer includes p neurons, and the jth neuron is h_j, where $j \in (0, p-1)$.

The output layer has q dimensions. For each neuron h_j at the hidden layer, we use the following formula first to perform linear transformation:

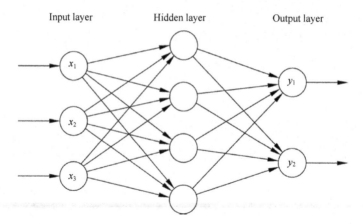

Fig. 3.3 Three-layer FNN model

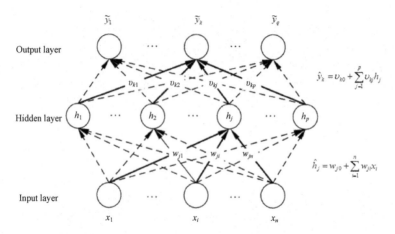

Fig. 3.4 Neural network structure

$$\hat{h}_j = w_{j0} + \sum_{i=1}^{n} w_{ji} x_i \qquad (3.3)$$

where w_{j0} is a bias, and $w_{j1}, w_{j2}, \ldots, w_{jn}$ are weights applied to properties $x_1, x_2, \ldots, x_n$.

After we input $\hat{h}_j$ to the neuron and apply the activation function, we obtain $h_j = \alpha_1(\hat{h}_j)$. Similarly, a neuron is input at the second layer:

$$\hat{y}_k = v_{k0} + \sum_{j=1}^{p} v_{kj} h_j \qquad (3.4)$$

The output is $\tilde{y}_j = \alpha_2(\hat{y}_j)$. This is the forward propagation process of the FNN.

For a single data sample $(\boldsymbol{x}, \boldsymbol{y})$, if we assume that the loss function is a mean square error, then the loss for the kth output is:

$$J_k = \frac{1}{2}(\tilde{y}_k - y_k)^2 \tag{3.5}$$

Through the chain rule, the gradient of the loss function to the weight v_{kj} is:

$$\frac{\partial J_k}{\partial v_{kj}} = \frac{\partial J_k}{\partial \tilde{y}_k} \cdot \frac{\partial \tilde{y}_k}{\partial \hat{y}_k} \cdot \frac{\partial \hat{y}_k}{\partial v_{kj}} \tag{3.6}$$

where the first term is $\frac{\partial J_k}{\partial \tilde{y}_k} = (\tilde{y}_k - y_k)$, and the third term is $\frac{\partial \hat{y}_k}{\partial v_{kj}} = h_j$.

For the second term, if we assume that the activation function is a sigmoid function, we can determine that the gradient has a good property, namely:

$$\frac{\partial \tilde{y}_k}{\partial \hat{y}_k} = \tilde{y}_k(1 - \tilde{y}_k) \tag{3.7}$$

We can then multiply the three terms to obtain:

$$\frac{\partial J_k}{\partial v_{kj}} = \tilde{y}_k(\tilde{y}_k - y_k)(1 - \tilde{y}_k)h_j \tag{3.8}$$

Because the label y_k is given by the data, and both the output values $\tilde{y}_k$ and h_j are calculated by using the forward propagation algorithm, each intermediate layer weight v_{kj} can be easily calculated. In addition, the calculation process can be carried out concurrently.

To obtain the cumulative gradient of the loss value on the hidden unit h_j, we can use the following:

$$
\begin{aligned}
e_{h_j} = \frac{\partial J}{\partial h_j} &= \sum_{k=1}^{q} \frac{\partial J_k}{\partial \tilde{y}_k} \cdot \frac{\partial \tilde{y}_k}{\partial \hat{y}_k} \cdot \frac{\partial \hat{y}_k}{\partial h_j} \\
&= \sum_{k=1}^{q} \tilde{y}_k(\tilde{y}_k - y_k)(1 - \tilde{y}_k)v_{kj}
\end{aligned} \tag{3.9}
$$

Similarly, we can obtain the gradient of the loss function to the first layer weight w_{ji} based on the chain rule (assuming that the activation function of the hidden layer is a ReLU function):

$$\frac{\partial J}{\partial w_{ji}} = \frac{\partial J}{\partial h_j} \cdot \frac{\partial h_j}{\partial \hat{h}_j} \cdot \frac{\partial \hat{h}_j}{\partial w_{ji}}$$

$$= e_{h_j} \cdot \frac{\partial h_j}{\partial \hat{h}_j} \cdot x_i \qquad (3.10)$$

where $\frac{\partial h_j}{\partial \hat{h}_j} = \begin{cases} 0, \hat{h}_j \leq 0 \\ 1, \hat{h}_j > 0 \end{cases}$.

After e_{h_j} is calculated, $\frac{\partial J}{\partial w_{ji}}$ can also be calculated efficiently and concurrently.

In the preceding process, we assume that the loss function is a mean variance error and that the activation functions are sigmoid or ReLU functions. These assumptions are effective for any differentiable loss function and activation function. As we can see from the calculation process, after the values of the hidden and output layers are obtained through forward propagation, the gradient is calculated starting from the loss function and then the top layer, and the gradient is propagated layer-by-layer back to the input layer. The sequence in which this process is performed is the reverse of forward propagation, and therefore the algorithm is called backpropagation. After we have obtained the gradients of all parameters through backpropagation (see Fig. 3.5), we can use the gradient descent algorithm to update and iterate the parameters in order to train the neural network. The neural network training process is described in Algorithm 3.1.

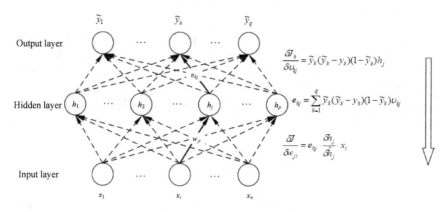

Fig. 3.5 Backpropagation

Algorithm 3.1 Neural Network Training Process

Input: Dataset $\{(x^{(i)}, y^{(i)})\}_{i=1}^{n}$, step size α, mini-batch training sample size b, and the number

T of iterations

Output: Trained neural network

(1)   Initialize the network parameter w_0

(2)   for $t \in \{1, 2, ..., T\}$

(3)   Select b samples m_b uniformly at random from m samples

(4)   Perform forward propagation and calculate parameters of hidden layers layer-by-layer to obtain sample output $\tilde{y}$

(5)   Calculate the error by using the loss function to obtain the gradient of the output layer

(6)   Perform backpropagation and calculate gradients of the hidden layers layer-by-layer

(7)   Calculate the gradients of the connection parameters, and update the parameters

$$w_t \leftarrow w_{t-1} - \frac{\alpha}{b} \sum_{i \in m_b} \partial_w J^{(i)}(w) \tag{3.11}$$

3.3   Generalization Ability

In earlier sections that explained overfitting and underfitting, we introduced the concept of generalization ability, that is, the ability of a machine learning algorithm to adapt to new samples. Overfitting of the training set can easily occur because the neural network includes a large number of parameters and has a strong nonlinear transformation ability. Although the accuracy of the model is very high on the training set and the loss is very low, the accuracy is quite low on the test data. In other words, the model cannot adapt to the new samples due to lack of generalization ability. If the model remembers the labels of some samples, it is possible that the model will have high accuracy on the training set; however, it will not learn the features of the data. This memory-based learning does not work on new test samples.

A lack of generalization ability may result from noise in the dataset, insufficient training data, or high model complexity due to over-training of models. In order to improve the model's generalization ability, a number of solutions have been proposed, some of which are as follows: reducing the depth and width of the model to reduce its complexity; performing data augmentation on datasets such as image rotation, translation, or zooming; adding regular noise such as Gaussian noise; adding the regularization term to control parameter complexity; and using the early stopping method during training.

In Sect. 3.4, we will introduce the specific training methods used to improve the generalization ability of the DNN.

3.4 Implementing Simple Neural Networks Using MindSpore

The interfaces and processes of MindSpore may constantly change due to iterative development. For all runnable code, see the code in corresponding chapters at https://mindspore.cn/resource. You can scan the QR code on the right to access relevant resources.

LeNet is typically used to identify and classify handwritten characters. Proposed in the 1990s, it has been used in a number of banks across America to automatically classify handwritten digits on bank checks. Comprised of several different layers, such as the convolution layer, pooling layer, and ReLU layer, LeNet is a CNN that was unable to handle complex problems due to the limited performance of computing hardware and lack of large-scale training data at that time. However, because of its simple structure, LeNet is ideal for beginners wanting to gain an understanding of neural networks.

3.4.1 Parameters at Each Layer

LeNet-5 is highly representative of early CNNs. Excluding the input layer, it is comprised of seven layers, each of which includes training parameters and multiple feature maps. Each feature map includes multiple neurons and extracts an input feature by using a convolution filer.

1. **Input layer**

   The first layer is a data input layer, where the size of each input image is normalized to 32 × 32.

   Note that this layer is not included in the LeNet-5 structure, as traditionally it is not considered as one of the network hierarchies.

2. **C1 layer—Convolution layer**
   Details about the C1 layer are as follows:

   (1) Input image size: 32×32.
   (2) Convolution kernel size: 5×5.
   (3) Convolution kernel type: 6.
   (4) Output feature map size: 28×28 (28 is obtained by calculating "$32 - 5 + 1$").
   (5) Number of neurons: $28 \times 28 \times 6 = 4704$.
   (6) Training parameters: $(5 \times 5 + 1) \times 6 = 156$.
   (7) Number of connections: $(5 \times 5 + 1) \times 6 \times 28 \times 28 = 122{,}304$.

3. **S2 layer—Pooling layer (downsampling layer)**
   Details about the S2 layer are as follows:

   (1) Input size: 28×28.
   (2) Sampling area: 2×2.
   (3) Sampling mode: Four inputs are added up, the sum is multiplied by the training parameters, and then the training bias is added to the product.
   (4) Sampling type: 6.
   (5) Output feature map size: 14×14 (the size is one-fourth of that in C1; i.e., "28/2").
   (6) Number of neurons: $14 \times 14 \times 6 = 1176$.
   (7) Training parameters: $2 \times 6 = 12$.
   (8) Number of connections: $(2 \times 2 + 1) \times 6 \times 14 \times 14 = 5880$.

4. **C3 layer—Convolution layer**
   Details about the C3 layer are as follows:

   (1) Input: Combination of all or some of the six feature maps in S2.
   (2) Convolution kernel size: 5×5.
   (3) Convolution kernel type: 16.
   (4) Output feature map size: 10×10 (each feature map in C3 includes all six features connected to S2, indicating that the feature map at this layer is different combinations of those extracted from the previous layer).
   (5) Training parameters: $6 \times (3 \times 25 + 1) + 6 \times (4 \times 25 + 1) + 3 \times (4 \times 25 + 1) + (25 \times 6 + 1) = 1516$.
   (6) Number of connections: $10 \times 10 \times 1516 = 151{,}600$.

5. **S4 layer—Pooling layer (downsampling layer)**
   Details about the S4 layer are as follows:

   (1) Input size: 10×10.
   (2) Sampling area: 2×2.
   (3) Sampling mode: Four inputs are added up, the sum is multiplied by the training parameters, and then the training bias is added to the product.
   (4) Sampling type: 16.

(5) Output feature map size: 5 × 5 (the size is one-fourth of that in C3; i.e., "10/2").
(6) Number of neurons: 5 × 5 × 16 = 400.
(7) Training parameters: 2 × 16 = 32.
(8) Number of connections: 16 × (2 × 2 + 1) × 5 × 5 = 2000.

6. **C5 layer—Convolution layer**
    Details about the C5 layer are as follows:

    (1) Input: All 16 feature maps of the S4 layer (fully connected to S4).
    (2) Convolution kernel size: 5 × 5.
    (3) Convolution kernel type: 120.
    (4) Output feature map size: 1 × 1 (1 is obtained by calculating "5 − 5 + 1").
    (5) Training parameters/Connections: 120 × (16 × 5 × 5 + 1) = 48,120.

7. **F6 layer—Fully connected layer**
    Details about the F6 layer are as follows:

    (1) Input: C5 120-dimensional vector.
    (2) Calculation mode: The dot product between the input vector and weight vector is calculated, to which the bias is added.
    (3) Training parameters: 84 × (120 + 1) = 10,164.

8. **Output layer—Fully connected layer**
    The output layer is a fully connected layer that includes ten nodes, which are represented by 0–9.

3.4.2 Implementation Process

The following describes how to implement training and inference using LeNet and includes a number of code examples to help clarify the process.

1. **Loading the MindSpore module**

    Import the MindSpore API and auxiliary module. The core code is as follows:

    Code 3.1 Importing the MindSpore API and Auxiliary Module

    ```
    import mindspore.nn as nn
    from mindspore.train import Model
    from mindspore import context
    ```

2. **Importing a dataset**

Create an MNIST dataset using the MindSpore data format APIs. For details about these APIs and how to implement the train_dataset() function, see Chap. 14.

3.   **Defining LeNet**

Define the LeNet-5 network structure. The core code is as follows:

Code 3.2 Defining the LeNet-5 Network Structure

```
class LeNet5(nn.Cell):
    def __init__(self):
        super(LeNet5, self).__init__()
        self.conv1 = nn.Conv2d(1, 6, 5, pad_mode="valid")
        self.conv2 = nn.Conv2d(6, 16, 5, pad_mode="valid")
        self.fc1 = nn.Dense(16 * 5 * 5, 120)
        self.fc2 = nn.Dense(120, 84)
        self.fc3 = nn.Dense(84, 10)
        self.relu = nn.ReLU()
        self.max_pool2d = nn.MaxPool2d(kernel_size=2)
        self.flatten = nn.Flatten()

    def construct(self, x):
        x = self.conv1(x)
        x = self.relu(x)
        x = self.max_pool2d(x)
        x = self.conv2(x)
        x = self.relu(x)
        x = self.max_pool2d(x)
        x = self.flatten(x)
        x = self.fc1(x)
        x = self.relu(x)
        x = self.fc2(x)
        x = self.relu(x)
        x = self.fc3(x)
        return x
```

The __init__() function initializes the convolution layers and the fully connected layers. Initialization parameters include the number of inputs, number of outputs, parameters of the convolution layers, and size of the convolution kernel. Because the image size of the original dataset is 28 × 28, the input size needs to be converted to 32 × 32 when the dataset is imported.

The construct() function implements forward propagation. Operations such as convolution, activation, and pooling are performed successively on the inputs according to the definition, following which the calculation result is returned. Before the data is propagated to the fully connected layer, we can expand the data using the Flatten() function, which flattens the input tensor while retaining axis 0.

4. **Setting hyperparameters and creating networks**

Define the loss function as SoftmaxCrossEntropyWithLogits, using Softmax to calculate the cross entropy. Select the Momentum optimizer, and set its learning rate to 0.1 and momentum to 0.9. The core code is as follows:

Code 3.3 Setting Hyperparameters and Creating Networks

```
batch_size = 32
epoch_size = 2
lr = 0.1
momentum = 0.9

ds = train_dataset()
network = LeNet5()
network.set_train()
loss = nn.SoftmaxCrossEntropyWithLogits(is_grad=False,
sparse=True)
opt = nn.Momentum(lr, momentum, network.trainable_params())
```

5. **Training a network model**

Load the network, loss function, and optimizer into the model, and call train() to start training. The core code is as follows:

Code 3.4 Training the Network Model

```
model = Model(network, loss, opt)
model.train(epoch_size, ds)
```

Chapter 4
Training of DNNs

This chapter starts by describing the main challenges that face deep learning systems. It then explores the fundamentals involved in the training of DNNs, and concludes with some examples of using MindSpore to implement DNNs.

4.1 Main Challenges to Deep Learning Systems

In this section, we look at the main challenges that face the deep learning systems from six aspects: large dataset requirement, hardware requirement, overfitting, hyperparameter optimization, non-transparency, and low flexibility.

4.1.1 Large Dataset Requirement

To train an effective deep learning model in the deep learning systems, we often need extremely large datasets. In most cases, the larger the dataset is, the more likely we will be in obtaining a more powerful deep learning model. In the field of speech recognition, for example, a large amount of voice data covering different accents and intonations is required to train a model for learning a language. Researchers must therefore have extremely strong data-processing capabilities and spend a great deal of time processing the data. To some extent, the size of a dataset often determines the effects of the deep learning systems.

© Tsinghua University Press 2021

L. Chen, *Deep Learning and Practice with MindSpore*, Cognitive Intelligence and Robotics, https://doi.org/10.1007/978-981-16-2233-5_4

4.1.2 Hardware Requirement

Even if researches can obtain large datasets for the deep learning model, they often face another challenge: How can they process the data quickly and efficiently. To overcome this challenge, the machines involved in the deep learning system need to have sufficient computing power. Data scientists now tend to use multi-core, high-performance GPUs in computing, but GPUs are expensive and power-hungry.

In addition, different application scenarios have different hardware requirements. For example, industrial deep learning systems require powerful data-processing centers, and mobile intelligent devices such as drones and robots often require small but efficient computing devices. Based on the preceding information, we can therefore surmise that it is an expensive and complex task to deploy deep learning systems in the real world.

4.1.3 Overfitting

In deep learning systems, models are often judged by the data collected for them, even though there are significant differences between training datasets and unknown datasets. Typically, researchers train models to deliver maximum performance on training datasets. This means that the models memorize the examples on the training datasets, but are unable to fit new cases and examples; we call this the overfitting phenomenon of the deep learning system. In practical applications, we should judge the ability of a model by unknown and invisible data, not by the training data provided to it.

4.1.4 Hyperparameter Optimization

Unlike the parameters in model training, hyperparameters are defined before model learning begins. In practice, the settings of hyperparameters have a significant impact on a model's performance, with even minor adjustments leading to dramatic effects. If they are not optimized and instead their default settings are used, a model may not deliver the expected performance.

Unfortunately, the settings or adjustments of hyperparameters often depend on the experience of researchers or the final training results of the model. This means that for people without the relevant experience, it can be a long and laborious process to obtain a good set of hyperparameters.

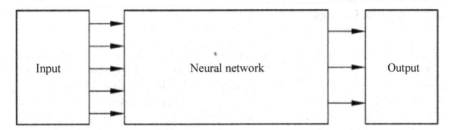

Fig. 4.1 Black-box problem in deep learning

4.1.5 Non-transparency

To train deep learning models, we provide the models with known data. Then, from millions of data points, deep learning algorithms find and select patterns and correlations that may be imperceptible to humans, thereby providing us with solutions. However, the way in which these models make inferences from the given data is often not understood.

As shown in Fig. 4.1, the deep learning model is essentially a black-box algorithm. If the model is given an input, we are only able to observe the output. Because the model's internal learning and operations are largely invisible to us, it is extremely difficult for us to understand the advanced knowledge of deep learning at the abstract level. This is not a problem when the deep learning system is used to perform a trivial task, as it achieves high performance with little chance of making a harmful wrong decision. However, such a system does not apply to areas that focus on critical validation processes. For example, if a deep learning system was used to determine someone's fate in a court case or the treatment of a patient, a wrong decision may have catastrophic consequences.

4.1.6 Low Flexibility

As mentioned earlier, a well-trained deep learning model can provide extremely efficient and accurate solutions to specific problems. However, this also poses a problem to the deep learning system. At present, most deep learning systems are designed specifically for a given subject and can only be used for that subject. Regardless of how good they are at solving the original problem, these systems usually cannot be applied directly to solving a new problem, even if both problems are similar. To overcome this limitation, researchers are currently working on developing deep learning models that can be used for multitasking without retraining and assessment.

4.2 Regularization

In Sect. 2.4, we described the concepts of overfitting and underfitting in deep learning systems and the problems they entail. Overfitting and underfitting can be considered as poor performance of models in testing data. To solve these problems, regularization aims to reduce the generalization error of the model by modifying the learning algorithm; however, this approach often increases the training error of the model. In general, the only way to modify a learning algorithm is to add or reduce some functions. Using weight decay in linear regression, the following describes how to modify the learning function in the model.

In Sect. 2.1, we explained that the loss function $J(w)$ of linear regression is a mean square error. The linear regression of weight decay is designed to minimize both the mean square error and a weight expression that prefers a smaller L2 norm, that is:

$$\tilde{J}(w) = \frac{1}{2m} \sum_{i=1}^{m} \left(h\left(x^{(i)}\right) - y^{(i)} \right)^2 + \lambda w^T w \tag{4.1}$$

where λ is defined in advance to represent the desire to have a small weight.

When λ is set to 0, it indicates that the L2 norm of the weight is not considered. Conversely, when λ is set to a larger value, the model will force the L2 norm of the weight to be smaller. Minimizing $\tilde{J}(w)$ leads to a tradeoff of weight w between fitting the training data and selecting a smaller L2 norm. This determines whether the solution focuses more on having a smaller slope or obvious features.

In Fig. 4.2, the graphs show the model fit with different weight decay parameters λ when data is distributed over the quadratic function. Because a large λ is used in Fig. 4.2(a), the model is forced to learn a constant function with no slope (a constant

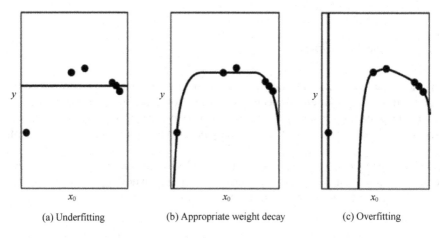

(a) Underfitting   (b) Appropriate weight decay   (c) Overfitting

Fig. 4.2 Weight decay for linear regression

function can only underfit the model). Figure 4.2(c) uses a λ close to 0, so that the model allows a larger slope but leads to overfitting. In Fig. 4.2(b), the model is fitted closely when an appropriate λ is set. Although this model can represent more complex functions than the model shown in Fig. 4.2(a), the small weight decay coefficient forces it to output a simpler function.

In general, the model fitting can be adjusted and controlled by expressing a preference for a function. In weight decay, we expressed our preference for a linear model defined with a smaller weight, but there are many other ways to express preferences for different models and solutions. The methods used for adjusting models are collectively called regularization. Typically, researchers regularize a deep learning model by adding a regularization term to the original loss function. In the preceding weight decay example, the regularization term is $\Omega(w) = w^T w$; yet there are many methods for regularizing deep learning. The following sections describe some of the important methods.

4.2.1 L2 Norm Regularization

The weight decay, also known as ridge regression, is L2 norm regularization. Based on Occam's razor, which states that the simpler or falsifiable hypothesis should be adopted if more than one exists for the same phenomenon (and was applied to the statistical learning theory in the twentieth century), the L2 norm regularization prevents overfitting by reducing the model complexity. The objective of the original linear regression model is to minimize empirical risks. The formula is as follows:

$$\text{min imize} J(w) = \text{minimize (Loss(Data|Model))}$$
$$= \text{minimize MSE} \qquad (4.2)$$

L2 norm regularization aims to minimize loss and complexity, that is, to minimize the structure risk. The formula is as follows:

$$\text{minimize } \tilde{J}(w) = \text{minimize (Loss(Data|Model)} + \text{complexity(Model))} \qquad (4.3)$$

In L2 norm regularization, the quadratic sum of all feature weights is defined as the complexity of the model, that is, $w^T w$. To gain a greater understanding, we will examine the gradient of the objective function for L2 norm regularization. Assume that a model has a regular objective function, as shown in the following formula:

$$\tilde{J}(w) = \frac{\lambda}{2} w^T w + J(w) \qquad (4.4)$$

The corresponding gradient can be calculated as follows:

$$\frac{\partial \tilde{J}(w)}{\partial w} = \lambda w + \frac{\partial J(w)}{\partial w} \tag{4.5}$$

After the stride of ε is used and the weights are updated iteratively, the following result is obtained:

$$w \leftarrow (1 - \varepsilon\lambda)w - \varepsilon\frac{\partial J(w)}{\partial w} \tag{4.6}$$

We can see from Formula (4.6) that the learning rule is modified when the weight decay increases. The weight decay method multiplies the weight vector by a constant factor at each step before performing the usual gradient update. So how does weight decay affect actual machine learning? The following uses the same linear regression problem as an example to answer this question:

$$w^* \underset{w}{\arg\min} \frac{1}{2m}(y - Xw)^{\mathrm{T}}(y - Xw) \tag{4.7}$$

The corresponding solution of the objective function is as follows:

$$w^* = (X^{\mathrm{T}}X)^{-1}X^{\mathrm{T}}y \tag{4.8}$$

After L2 norm regularization is added to the original objective function, the objective function becomes:

$$w^* = \underset{w}{\arg\min} \frac{1}{2m}(y - Xw)^{\mathrm{T}}(y - Xw) + \frac{\lambda}{2}w^{\mathrm{T}}w \tag{4.9}$$

And the solution becomes:

$$w^* = (X^{\mathrm{T}}X + \lambda I)^{-1}X^{\mathrm{T}}y \tag{4.10}$$

The matrix $X^{\mathrm{T}}X$ in the original solution is replaced by the matrix $(X^{\mathrm{T}}X + \lambda I)^{-1}$. As a result, the original matrix is added with a diagonal matrix of λ, which represents the variation of each input feature. L2 norm regularization enables the learning algorithm to perceive the input data with a larger variance, which also reduces the weight of the feature compared with the covariance of the output target.

4.2.2 L1 Norm Regularization

L2 norm regularization, described in Sect. 4.2.1, is one of the most popular weight decay algorithms. Another way to control the complexity of weights is through L1 norm regularization, also known as Lasso regularization. Unlike L2 regularization,

L1 regularization adds the absolute value of the weight coefficient as a regularization term to the loss function. Given the weight coefficient w of the model, the L1 regularization term is defined as follows:

$$\Omega(w) = \|w\|_1 = \sum_i w_i \qquad (4.11)$$

where $\| \cdot \|_1$ indicates the L1 norm.

Compared with L2 norm regularization, L1 norm regularization reduces some insignificant feature coefficients to zero during training so that some features disappear completely. This means that L1 norm regularization allows appropriate selection of features for the model when there are a large number of features. The regularized loss function formula is as follows:

$$\tilde{J}(w) = \lambda\|w\|_1 + J(w) \qquad (4.12)$$

The corresponding gradient is:

$$\frac{\partial \tilde{J}(w)}{\partial w} = \lambda\, \text{sign}(w) + \frac{\partial J(w)}{\partial w} \qquad (4.13)$$

According to the above formula, we can see that L1 norm regularization has a completely different effect on the gradient compared with L2 norm regularization, which makes w affect the gradient of each step linearly. In L1 norm regularization, the effect of w on the gradient becomes a constant factor, and its symbol is consistent with that of w.

4.3 Dropout

In deep learning systems, training a large network is often a slow and time-consuming process. Although the regularization approaches described in Sect. 4.2 can alleviate overfitting to some extent, another method to achieve this is called dropout. Dropout was first proposed by Hinton to solve the overfitting problem. However, subsequent research has proven that it can be used not only to alleviate overfitting of deep learning systems, but also to shorten the time needed for network training.

Unlike the regularization approach, which adds a regularization term to a loss function, dropout changes the learning process in the training process. The functioning of some detectors in the training of deep learning models relies on other detectors—this is called interaction between detectors. To prevent overfitting, dropout proposes to improve the performance of neural networks by blocking the interaction between feature detectors. In each training batch, dropout aims to reduce the interaction between hidden-layer nodes, and thereby alleviate the overfitting problem, by ignoring half of these nodes in the network.

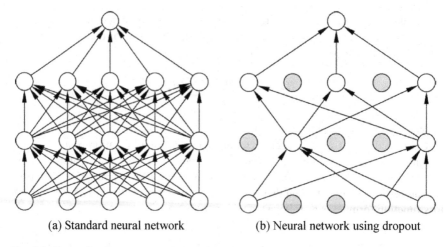

(a) Standard neural network   (b) Neural network using dropout

Fig. 4.3 Comparison between neural networks (1)

As shown in Fig. 4.3, dropout allows certain neuronal activations to stop working at a certain probability when the standard neural network performs forward propagation. By doing so, the dependence of the model on local features can be reduced, and the generalization ability of the model can be improved. This therefore alleviates the overfitting problem. The following describes the general process of implementing dropout in the deep learning system.

In the standard neural network, after the given input x is propagated in the forward direction on the network, the error is propagated in the reverse direction. This is performed to determine how best to update the parameters for optimal learning, resulting in the output y. In the network on which dropout is used, the process is as follows:

(1) Delete half of the hidden-layer neurons in the network at random, but do not change the input and output neurons. In Fig. 4.3b, the gray circles represent the deleted neurons in this training batch.

(2) Propagate the input x in the forward direction through the neural network modified in the previous step and then propagate the loss result in the reverse direction. After a batch of training samples is completed, the corresponding parameters are updated on the remaining neurons by using the stochastic gradient descent method.

(3) Restore the deleted neurons. Note that the deleted neurons remain unchanged, but the neurons that were not deleted are updated in the previous batch.

(4) Execute the next batch of training samples and repeat the preceding steps.

Derivation of a series of formulas after the neural network uses dropout is introduced below. For the sake of simplicity, we will review the standard neural network as shown in Fig. 4.4a. The calculation formulas are as follows:

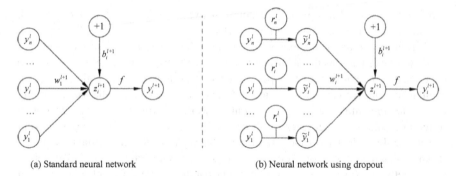

(a) Standard neural network   (b) Neural network using dropout

Fig. 4.4 Comparison between neural networks (2)

$$z_i^{l+1} = w_i^{l+1} y^l + b_i^{l+1} \tag{4.14}$$

$$y_i^{l+1} = f(z_i^{l+1}) \tag{4.15}$$

In a neural network on which dropout is used, some hidden-layer neurons are randomly closed before each training batch. If we assume that the probability of each neuron being closed is p, we can use Bernoulli distribution to express the probability of closing the jth neuron at layer l as follows:

$$r_j^l \sim \text{Bernouli}(p) \tag{4.16}$$

where when r_j^l is 0, the jth neuron at layer l is closed;
when r_j^l is 1, the jth neuron at layer l is opened.
The corresponding forward process is shown in Fig. 4.4b, and the expression formulas are as follows:

$$\tilde{y}^l = r^l * y^l \tag{4.17}$$

$$z_i^{l+1} = w_i^{l+1} \tilde{y}^l + b_i^{l+1} \tag{4.18}$$

$$y_i^{l+1} = f(z_i^{l+1}) \tag{4.19}$$

In practical applications, dropout is more effective than other regularization approaches. The test results of a model using dropout on the validation dataset are often better than those when using other regularization approaches. With large datasets, dropout can significantly improve the generalization ability of the model. Furthermore, dropout has a very low computational overhead, meaning that only the time complexity of $O(n)$ in each training batch is increased. In addition, unlike many regularization approaches that have clear limitations on applicable models, dropout can be used in a variety of neural network models, such as feedforward, convolutional, and recurrent neural networks.

Why can we improve the final performance of the model by randomly closing part of hidden-layer neurons in each training batch? To answer this question, we need to examine how we can improve the performance of a standard model without dropout. Similar to what we can do with ensemble learning, we can use the same training dataset to train multiple different neural networks. Through this, we can obtain different results, and then average these results—this method can usually prevent overfitting. In each step, dropout randomly closes part of the hidden-layer neurons, meaning that the entire dropout process is equivalent to averaging on many different neural networks (averaging offsets different overfitting on different networks). In addition, dropout reduces the complex coadaptation relationship between neurons. Because two neurons may not be opened every time when dropout is used, the update of weights no longer relies on the co-action of hidden-layer nodes with fixed relationships. This forces the network to learn more robust features rather than only a few local ones.

4.4 Adaptive Learning Rate

Following an introduction to the methods for improving the performance of deep learning models, this section focuses on how to optimize the training process of deep learning systems. The learning rate in the training process is problematic for both the basic gradient descent algorithm and other optimization algorithms described in Chap. 2. The invariable learning rate affects a model's convergence speed, while the training time increases and the computational overhead remains high. If, however, we use a variable learning rate, we can significantly improve the convergence speed. In this section, we describe three commonly used adaptive learning rate algorithms: AdaGrad, RMSProp, and Adam.

We start by reviewing the gradient descent formula:

$$w_t = w_{t-1} - \alpha \, \nabla J(w_{t-1}) \tag{4.20}$$

where α, is the learning rate, and

$\nabla J(w_{t-1})$ is the direction.

4.4.1 AdaGrad

Each parameter has a different updating direction and amplitude when the gradient descent algorithm is applied. At any given time, some variables may approximate their minimum values while others remain close to their initial positions, leading to problems occurring when the learning rate remains unchanged. If the learning rate is high, the parameters close to their minimum values may become unstable, whereas if the learning rate is low, the convergence is slow even when a small number of parameters are updated. AdaGrad attempts to solve this problem by setting different learning rates for different parameters. The learning rate is first set to a larger value in order to decrease the gradient quickly, and then the learning rates of the parameters that have fallen considerably are reduced (a higher rate is retained for other parameters).

AdaGrad calculates the gradient and then accumulates its square. The formulas are as follows:

$$g_t = \nabla J(w_{t-1}) \tag{4.21}$$

$$r \leftarrow r + g_t \oplus g_t \tag{4.22}$$

Based on the cumulative square of the gradient, the update calculation formula is as follows:

$$w_t \leftarrow w_{t-1} - \frac{\varepsilon}{\delta + \sqrt{r}} \oplus g_t \tag{4.23}$$

where

δ is a minimum value used to prevent the denominator from being 0, and.

ε is a global learning rate.

As the training process continues, the cumulative gradient becomes larger and larger, thereby lowering the overall learning rate. Although AdaGrad can automatically change learning rates through iterations, it has one significant disadvantage: The cumulative sum of its denominators is always increasing. Due to this disadvantage, the learning rate is reduced and becomes infinitely low, preventing the algorithm from updating the weights. The AdaGrad algorithm is shown in Algorithm 4.1.

Algorithm 4.1 AdaGrad Input: Global learning rate ε, minimum value δ (generally set to 10^{-7}), and cumulative gradient variable $r = 0$.

Output: Converged parameter w_T.

(1) Initialize the parameter w_0
(2) Execute the following when the stopping conditions are not met:
(3) Select m samples uniformly at random from data $\{(x^{(i)}, y^{(i)})\}$
(4) Calculate the gradient:

$$g_t \leftarrow \frac{1}{m} \nabla \sum_i J(w_{t-1}) \tag{4.24}$$

(5)   Calculate the cumulative gradient:

$$r \leftarrow r + g_t \oplus g_t \tag{4.25}$$

(6)   Calculate the update:

$$w_t \leftarrow w_{t-1} - \frac{\varepsilon}{\delta + \sqrt{r}} \oplus g_t \tag{4.26}$$

4.4.2 RMSProp

With AdaGrad, the main problem is that the learning rate will be infinitely low. RMSProp, as an extension to AdaGrad, solves this problem by finding the logarithmic mean value of the square gradient in the current state. The formula for defining the mean square gradient of time t is as follows:

$$r_t = \gamma r_{t-1} + (1 - \gamma)g_t \oplus g_t \tag{4.27}$$

where r_t is the mean square gradient at time $t-1$, and.

γ is the proportionality coefficient of the logarithmic mean.
    The corresponding gradient update is as follows:

$$w_t \leftarrow w_{t-1} - \frac{\varepsilon}{\sqrt{\delta + r_t}} \oplus g_t \tag{4.28}$$

where the settings of δ and ε are the same as those in AdaGrad. RMSProp differs from AdaGrad in that averaging, rather than summing, is performed to effectively avoid an infinitely low learning rate.
    The RMSProp algorithm is summarized in Algorithm 4.2.

Algorithm 4.2 RMSProp Input: Global learning rate ε, minimum value δ (generally set to 10^{-7}), and proportionality coefficient γ (generally set to 0.9).

Output: Converged parameter w_T.

(1)   Initialize the parameter w_0
(2)   Execute the following when the stopping conditions are not met:
(3)   Select m samples uniformly at random from data $\{(x^{(i)}, y^{(i)})\}$
(4)   Calculate the gradient:

$$g_t \leftarrow \frac{1}{m} \nabla \sum_i J(w_{t-1}) \tag{4.29}$$

(5)   Calculate the mean square gradient at time t:

$$r_t = \gamma r_{t-1} + (1 - \gamma) g_t \oplus g_t \tag{4.30}$$

(6)   Calculate the update:

$$w_t \leftarrow w_{t-1} - \frac{\varepsilon}{\sqrt{\delta + r_t}} \oplus g_t \tag{4.31}$$

The RMSProp algorithm outperforms AdaGrad in non-convex settings by accumulating gradients into a weighted mean value, but AdaGrad can quickly converge when being applied to convex functions. Training of a neural network usually involves non-convex functions. As AdaGrad reduces the learning rate, it may become too low before reaching the minimum value. To achieve quick convergence, RMSProp uses a weighted mean value to discard distant information. Through many deep learning experiments, the RMSProp algorithm has been proven an effective and practical neural network optimization algorithm.

4.4.3 Adam

Adaptive moment (Adam) is also a commonly used adaptive learning rate algorithm and can be considered as an optimization of RMSProp. Unlike RMSProp, Adam has less deviation in the early stages of model training. In Adam, selection of hyperparameters is usually quite stable, but the learning rate may need to be changed occasionally. To begin with, Adam calculates the first-order gradient deviation according to the following formula:

$$s_t = \gamma_1 s_{t-1} + (1 - \gamma_1) g_t \tag{4.32}$$

where
g_t is the gradient at time t, and.
γ_1 is the first-order gradient cumulative coefficient.
Similar to RMSProp, Adam then calculates the square gradient cumulative coefficient according to the following formula:

$$r_t = \gamma_2 r_{t-1} + (1 - \gamma_2) g_t \otimes g_t \tag{4.33}$$

where γ_2 is the square gradient cumulative coefficient.
After s_t and r_t are calculated, Adam calculates the first- and second-order corrections:

$$\tilde{s}_t \leftarrow \frac{s_t}{1 - \gamma_1} \tag{4.34}$$

$$\tilde{r}_t \leftarrow \frac{r_t}{1 - \gamma_2} \tag{4.35}$$

Based on the first- and second-order corrections, Adam updates the weight:

$$w_t \leftarrow w_{t-1} - \varepsilon \frac{\tilde{s}_t}{\delta + \sqrt{\tilde{r}_t}} \tag{4.36}$$

The Adam algorithm is summarized in Algorithm 4.3.

Algorithm 4.3 Adam Input: Global learning rate ε (generally set to 0.001), minimum value δ (generally set to 10^{-7}), first-order coefficient γ_1 (generally set to 0.9), and second-order coefficient γ_2 (generally set to 0.999)

Output: Converged parameter w_T

(1) Initialize the parameter w_0
(2) Execute the following when the stopping conditions are not met:
(3) Select m samples uniformly at random from data $\{(x^{(i)}, y^{(i)})\}$
(4) Calculate the gradient:

$$g_t \leftarrow \frac{1}{m} \nabla \sum_i J(w_{t-1}) \tag{4.37}$$

(5) Calculate the first-order gradient deviation:

$$s_t = \gamma_1 s_{t-1} + (1 - \gamma_1)g_t \tag{4.38}$$

(6) Calculate the second-order gradient deviation:

$$r_t = \gamma_2 r_{t-1} + (1 - \gamma_2)g_t \otimes g_t \tag{4.39}$$

(7) Calculate the first-order correction:

$$\tilde{s}_t \leftarrow \frac{s_t}{1 - \gamma_1} \tag{4.40}$$

(8) Calculate the second-order correction

$$\tilde{r}_t \leftarrow \frac{r_t}{1 - \gamma_2} \tag{4.41}$$

(9) Calculate the update:

$$w_t \leftarrow w_{t-1} - \varepsilon \frac{\tilde{s}_t}{\delta + \sqrt{\tilde{r}_t}} \tag{4.42}$$

4.5 Batch Normalization

In the deep learning system, adjusting the training parameters of the DNN is extremely difficult. To help the model achieve faster convergence during training, it is often necessary to try different regularization approaches and learning rates. One of the main difficulties in training the DNN is the strong correlations between layers of the neural network. These correlations lead to internal covariate shift.

Internal covariate shift means that slight changes in the underlying network parameters are magnified with the deepening of network layers, because of the linear transformation and nonlinear mapping at each layer. In addition, when the parameters of a layer change, so does the distribution of inputs to subsequent layers. The network has to continuously re-adapt to these shifts in input distributions, making it extremely difficult to train models. In other words, parameter changes in the network will shift the distribution of internal node data during the deep network training process. Internal covariate shift poses two problems to the deep network training. The first problem is that continuous re-adaptation to shifts in input distributions leads to a lower learning rate. The second is that the training process may easily fall into the gradient saturated region, slowing down the convergence of the network.

To overcome internal covariate shift, batch normalization provides a method that simplifies calculation while also ensuring the original expression ability of data. In addition, because the input of full-batch training data requires a large amount of memory and each round of training is excessively long, mini-batch training is typically used in a deep learning system. Batch normalization is a method based on mini-batches.

Here we will start by reviewing the feedforward formulas of layer $l + 1$ of the neural network:

$$z_i^{l+1} = w_i^{l+1} y^l + b_i^{l+1} \tag{4.43}$$

$$y_i^{l+1} = f(z_i^{l+1}) \tag{4.44}$$

where y^l is the output of layer l.

For all neural nodes at layer $l + 1$, the mean value and variance are calculated during batch normalization according to the following formulas:

$$\mu = \frac{1}{m} \sum_{i=1}^{m} z_i^{l+1} \tag{4.45}$$

$$\sigma^2 = \sum_{i=1}^{m} (z_i^{l+1} - \mu)^2 \tag{4.46}$$

After the mean value and variance are calculated, the output of layer $l + 1$ is normalized:

$$\tilde{z}^{l+1} = \gamma \frac{z^{l+1} - \mu}{\sqrt{\sigma^2 + \varepsilon}} + \beta \qquad (4.47)$$

$$y_i^{l+1} = f(\tilde{z}^{l+1}) \qquad (4.48)$$

In practice, batch normalization has been proven able to facilitate neural network training. This is due to several advantages inherent in batch normalization. First, batch normalization ensures that the mean value and variance of inputs at each layer of the network are within a certain range, meaning that the next layer does not need to continuously re-adapt to changes in the output of the previous layer. The distribution of inputs at each layer is relatively stable, facilitating a faster learning rate of the model. Second, in the DNN, the weight initialization method and appropriate learning rate are used carefully to ensure stable training of the network. Batch normalization can reduce the model's sensitivity to the parameters in the network and simplify the process of parameter adjustment. In addition, batch normalization allows the network to use saturated activation functions such as sigmoid and tand. Any changes in the underlying network can easily accumulate in the upper-layer network, causing the model to enter the gradient saturated region of activation functions and, subsequently, causing the gradient to disappear. These saturated activation functions can alleviate gradient disappearance. Finally, batch normalization can produce some regularization effects in practical applications. As the mean values and variances of different mini-batches are used as an estimate of all training samples, additional random noise is caused in the learning process, which is similar to the random closure of neurons in dropout.

4.6 Implementing DNNs Using MindSpore

The interfaces and processes of MindSpore may constantly change due to iterative development. For all runnable code, see the code in corresponding chapters at https:// mindspore.cn/resource. You can scan the QR code on the right to access relevant resources.

AlexNet is a CNN designed by ImageNet championship winner Hinton and his student Alex Krizhevsky in 2012. AlexNet has carried forward the ideas of LeNet and applied basic principles of the CNN to deeper and wider networks.

4.6.1 Parameters at Each Layer

Excluding the input layer, AlexNet is comprised of eight layers: The first five are convolution layers, and the last three are fully connected layers, resulting in a distribution covering 1000 class tags.

1. Input layer
    The first layer is a data input layer, the size of which is 224 × 224 × 3.
2. C1 layer—Convolution layer
    Details about the C1 layer are as follows:
(1) Input: 224 × 224 × 3.
(2) Convolution kernel size: 11 × 11.
(3) Convolution kernel type: 96.
3. C2 layer - Convolution layer
    Details about the C2 layer are as follows:
(1) Input: 27 × 27 × 96.
(2) Convolution kernel size: 5 × 5.
(3) Convolution kernel type: 256.
4. C3 layer—Convolution layer
    Details about the C3 layer are as follows:
(1) Input: 13 × 13 × 256.
(2) Convolution kernel size: 3 × 3.
(3) Convolution kernel type: 384.
5. C4 layer—Convolution layer
    Details about the C4 layer are as follows:
(1) Input: 13 × 13 × 384.
(2) Convolution kernel size: 3 × 3.

   Convolution kernel type: 384.

6. C5 layer—Convolution layer
    Details about the C5 layer are as follows:
(1) Input: 13 × 13 × 384.
(2) Convolution kernel size: 3 × 3.
(3) Convolution kernel type: 256.
7. F1 layer—Fully connected layer
    Details about the F1 layer are as follows:
(1) Input: 6 × 6 × 256.
(2) Output: 4096.
8. F2 layer—Fully connected layer
    Details about the F2 layer are as follows:
(1) Input: 4096.
(2) Output: 4096.
9. F3 layer—Fully connected layer
    Details about the F3 layer are as follows:
(1) Input: 4096.

(2)   Output: 1000.

4.6.2   Implementation Process

The following describes how to implement training and inference using AlexNet and includes a number of code examples to help clarify the process.

1.   Loading the MindSpore module

Import the MindSpore API and auxiliary module. The core code is as follows:

Code 4.1 Importing the MindSpore API and Auxiliary Module

```
import mindspore.nn as nn
from mindspore.train import Model
from mindspore import context
```

2.   Importing a dataset

Create an ImageNet dataset using the MindSpore data format APIs. For details about these APIs and how to implement the de_train_dataset() function, see Chap. 14. According to the AlexNet model, the de_train_dataset() function uses the following input:

resize_height = 227.
resize_width = 227.

3.   Defining AlexNet

Define the AlexNet network structure. The core code is as follows:

Code 4.2 Defining AlexNet

```
class AlexNet(nn.Cell):
    def __init__(self, num_classes=10):
        super(AlexNet, self).__init__()
        self.conv1 = nn.Conv2d(3, 96, 11, stride=4,
        pad_mode="valid")
        self.conv2 = nn.Conv2d(96, 256, 5, stride=1,
        pad_mode="same")
        self.conv3 = nn.Conv2d(256, 384, 3, stride=1,
        pad_mode="same")
        self.conv4 = nn.Conv2d(384, 384, 3, stride=1,
        pad_mode="same")
        self.conv5 = nn.Conv2d(384, 256, 3, stride=1,
        pad_mode="same")
        self.relu = nn.ReLU()
        self.max_pool2d = nn.MaxPool2d(kernel_size=3, stride=2)
        self.flatten = nn.Flatten()
        self.fc1 = nn.Dense(6*6*256, 4096)
        self.fc2 = nn.Dense(4096, 4096)
        self.fc3 = nn.Dense(4096, num_classes)


    def construct(x):
        x = self.conv1(x)
        x = self.relu(x)
        x = self.max_pool2d(x)
        x = self.conv2(x)
        x = self.relu(x)
        x = self.max_pool2d(x)
        x = self.conv3(x)
        x = self.relu(x)
        x = self.conv4(x)
        x = self.relu(x)
        x = self.conv5(x)
        x = self.relu(x)
        x = self.max_pool2d(x)
        x = self.flatten(x)
        x = self.fc1(x)
        x = self.relu(x)
        x = self.fc2(x)
        x = self.relu(x)
        x = self.fc3(x)
        return x
```

4.   Setting hyperparameters and creating networks

Set hyperparameters such as batch, epoch, and classes import a dataset and create a network. Define the loss function as SoftmaxCrossEntropyWithLogits, using Softmax to calculate the cross-entropy. Select the Momentum optimizer, and set its learning rate to 0.1 and momentum to 0.9. The core code is as follows:

Code 4.3 Setting Hyperparameters and Creating Networks

```
context.switch_to_graph_mode()
batch_size = 32
epoch_size = 2
lr = 0.1
momentum = 0.9
num_classes = 1000


dataset = de_train_dataset()
network = AlexNet(num_classes)
network.set_train()
loss = nn.SoftmaxCrossEntropyWithLogits(is_grad=False,
sparse=True)
opt = nn.Momentum(lr, momentum, network.trainable_params())
```

5.   Training a network model

Load the network, loss function, and optimizer into the model, and call train() to start training. The core code is as follows:

Code 4.4 Training the Network Model

```
model = Model(net, loss, opt)
model.train(epoch_size, dataset)
```

Chapter 5
Convolutional Neural Network

In this chapter, we describe the CNN. This network is a special neural network that uses convolution instead of general matrix multiplication at one or more layers. In essence, it is a feedforward neural network that uses convolutional mathematical operations.

5.1 Convolution

The convolution operation is fundamental in the CNN. Unlike the dot product accumulation operation in the MLP, the convolution operation is like a sliding window that slides from left to right and from top to bottom. (In this section, we focus exclusively on two-dimensional convolution operations.) Each time the window slides from one point to another, a weighted mean value focused on a small piece of data or local data is obtained. The convolution operation consists of two important components: input matrix and convolution kernel (also known as the filter), which correspond to the input and the weight in the perceptron, respectively. As shown in Fig. 5.1, we can obtain the desired output matrix (also known as a feature map) given the input matrix by sliding the kernel matrix on the input matrix.

The calculation is performed as follows during the convolution operation: First, the kernel matrix is applied to the 3×3 blocks in the upper left corner, as shown in Fig. 5.2a. The first output value 5 is obtained from the dot product. Then the kernel matrix is moved to the right twice. For each move, the output in one block is obtained, as shown in Fig. 5.2b, c. The output values 5, 8, and 5 in the first row are obtained. Similarly, the convolution of the second row is calculated to obtain the final output result, as shown in Fig. 5.2f.

We can see that the convolution kernel repeatedly calculates convolution for the input matrix and traverses the entire matrix. Furthermore, each output corresponds to a local feature of a small part of the input matrix. One advantage of the convolution operation is that the output 2×3 matrix shares the same kernel matrix; that is, it

© Tsinghua University Press 2021
L. Chen, *Deep Learning and Practice with MindSpore*, Cognitive Intelligence and Robotics, https://doi.org/10.1007/978-981-16-2233-5_5

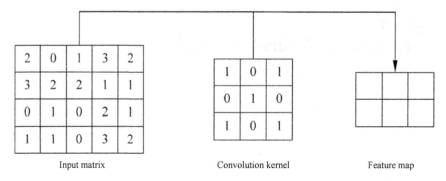

Input matrix   Convolution kernel   Feature map

Fig. 5.1 Components of the convolution operation

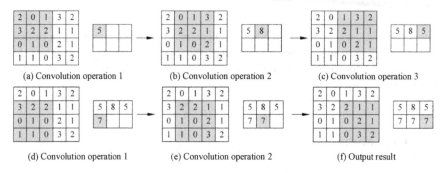

(a) Convolution operation 1   (b) Convolution operation 2   (c) Convolution operation 3

(d) Convolution operation 1   (e) Convolution operation 2   (f) Output result

Fig. 5.2 Steps of the convolution operation

shares the same parameter setting. If the full-connection operation is used, a 25×6 $\gg 3 \times 3$ matrix is required, and each convolution operation in Fig. 5.2 is independent. This means that we do not need to slide the window from one point to another in order to perform convolution calculation. Instead, the convolutional values of all the blocks can be calculated concurrently for efficient operation.

Sometimes the output matrix needs to be resized, and this can be accomplished by using two important parameters: stride and padding. As shown in Fig. 5.3, the stride for lateral movement is 2 instead of 1, (this means that the 3×3 blocks in the middle are skipped), whereas the stride for longitudinal movement is 1. By setting a stride greater than 1, we can reduce the size of the output matrix. The other important parameter is padding. As shown in Fig. 5.4, padding allows the calculation of the kernel matrix to be extended beyond the confines of the matrix. This is achieved by padding one row of 0 s (false pixels), one column of 0 s, and two columns of 0 s on the lower, left, and right sides of the original matrix. The padding increases the size of the output matrix and allows the kernel function to be calculated around the edge pixels. In convolution calculation, the size of the output matrix can be controlled based on the stride and padding parameters. This can be useful if we want to obtain

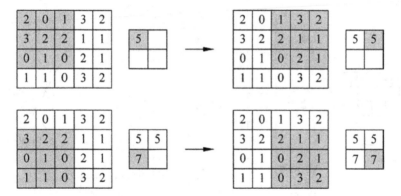

Fig. 5.3 Stride

Fig. 5.4 Padding

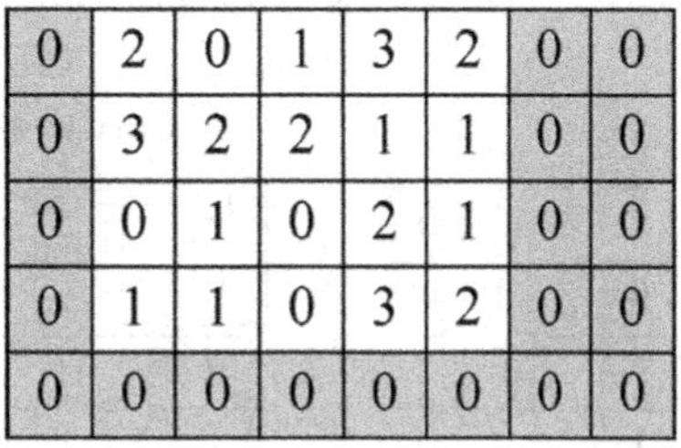

a feature map with the same length and width, or half-length and half-width, for example.

The convolution operation above involves only one input matrix and one kernel matrix. However, we can superimpose multiple identical matrices together. As an example, take an image, which typically includes three channels that represent the three primary colors: red, green, and blue. In a multi-channel convolution operation of an image (as shown in Fig. 5.5), the red, green, and blue channels are tiled first. These channels are convoluted by using their respective kernel matrices, and then three output matrices are added to obtain a final feature map. Note that each channel has its own kernel matrix. If the number of input channels is c_1 and the number of output channels is c_2, a total of $c_1 \times c_2$ kernel matrices are needed.

5.2 Pooling

As described in Sect. 5.1, we can reduce the size of the output matrix by increasing the stride parameter. Another common method for such reduction is pooling. For example, a 4×4 feature map can be reduced to 2×2 regions, which are then pooled as a 2×2 feature map, as shown in Fig. 5.6. There are two common types of

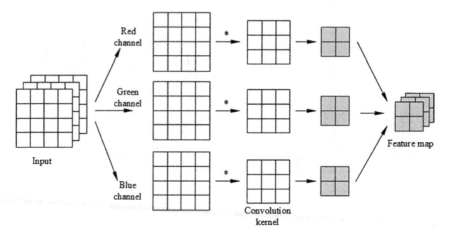

Fig. 5.5 Multi-channel convolution operation

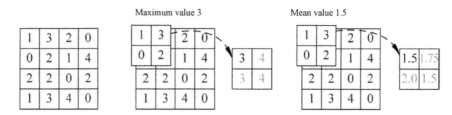

Fig. 5.6 Pooling

pooling: max-pooling and mean-pooling. As the names imply, max-pooling selects the maximum value of a local region, whereas mean-pooling calculates the mean value of a local region.

Max-pooling can obtain local information and preserve texture features more accurately. It is ideal if we want only to determine whether an object appears in an image, not for observing the specific location of the object in the image. Mean-pooling, on the other hand, can usually preserve the features of the overall data and more suitable for highlighting background information. Through pooling, some unimportant information is discarded, while information that is more important and more favorable to a particular task is reserved, to reduce dimensionality and computational complexity.

Similar to the convolution operation, the pooling operation can be adapted to different application scenarios by overlapping and defining parameters such as stride. Unlike the convolution operation, however, the pooling operation is performed on a single matrix, and convolution is a kernel matrix operation on an input matrix. We can understand pooling as a special kernel matrix.

With a basic understanding of the convolution and pooling operations, we can take LeNet in Fig. 5.7 as an example to examine what comprises a CNN. Given a 1×32

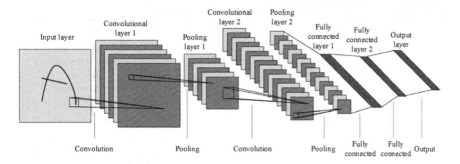

Fig. 5.7 LeNet

× 32 single-channel grayscale image, we can first use six 5 × 5 convolution kernels
to obtain a feature map of 6 × 28 × 28, which is the first layer of the network. The
second layer is the pooling operation, which reduces the dimension of the feature
map to obtain one that is 6 × 14 × 14. At the last two layers, the convolution kernel
performs further pooling operations, giving us a 16 × 5 × 5 feature map. After the
convolution operation is performed at the last layer, each output is a 1 × 1 point. In
addition to this, we obtain an eigenvector with a length of 120. Finally, we obtain
an output vector, that is, a category expression, through two fully connected layers.
This is the classical LeNet model, in which the CNN is used to extract the feature
map, and the fully connected layer is used to convert the feature map into the vector
expression and output form.

5.3 Residual Network

By increasing the number of layers in the CNN, we are able to extract deeper and more
general features. In other words, we can deepen the network level in order to enrich
the feature level. However, when the number of network layers increases, gradient
disappearance or explosion may occur, making it difficult to train the network. This
section introduces residual network (ResNet), a solution that effectively solves the
problem caused by increasing the depth of the neural network.

The basic element of the residual network is called a residual block and is shown
in Fig. 5.8. Unlike the common connection network, the residual block includes a
special edge, which is called a shortcut. The shortcut enables the input x_l of the upper
layer to be directly connected to the output x_{l+1}, that is, $x_{l+1} = x_l + \mathcal{F}(x_l)$, where $\mathcal{F}(x_l)$
$= W_2 \text{ReLU}(W_1 x_l)$ indicates a nonlinear transformation and is also called residual.
Let us assume that we want to learn a mapping function $\mathcal{H}(x) = x$. In this case,
learning $\mathcal{F}(x) = 0$ is much easier than learning $\mathcal{F}(x) = x$, because it is easier to fit
the residuals. This is why such a structure is called a residual block.

As mentioned earlier, the residual network can solve the problem of gradient
disappearance or explosion. We are able to observe this by deducing backpropagation

Fig. 5.8 Residual block

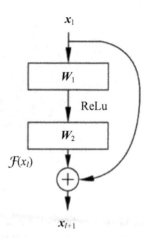

in the residual network. If we assume that the network includes L layers, we can obtain the output from any layer l through recursion:

$$x_L = x_l + \sum_{i=l}^{L-1} \mathcal{F}(x_i) \tag{5.1}$$

Assuming that the loss function is E, then we can obtain the gradient of the input x_l according to the chain rule:

$$\frac{\partial E}{\partial x_l} = \frac{\partial E}{\partial x_L} \cdot \frac{\partial x_L}{\partial x_l} = \frac{\partial E}{\partial x_L} \left(1 + \frac{\partial}{\partial x_l} \sum_{i=l}^{L-1} \mathcal{F}(x_i) \right) \tag{5.2}$$

The independent "1" allows the gradient of the output layer to be propagated directly back to x_l, thereby avoiding gradient disappearance. Although the gradient expression does not explicitly give the reason for preventing the gradient explosion problem, the use of the residual network helps solve this problem in practical applications.

In Fig. 5.9,[1] we can see that the residual network includes layers of residual blocks. Each intermediate residual block adjusts the padded value to ensure that the number of input dimensions is equal to the number of output dimensions, and the shortcut allows us to add or reduce the number of network layers in order to ensure the feasibility of model training. The residual network, therefore, has significant influence in the development of the CNN.

---

[1] Source: https://arxiv.org/pdf/1512.03385.pdf.

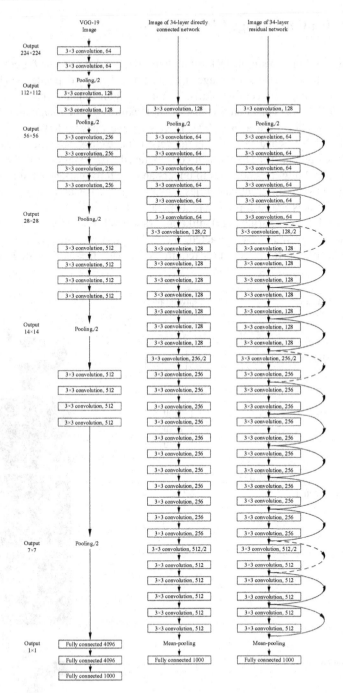

Fig. 5.9   Residual network

5.4   Application: Image Classification

Image classification is a simple task for humans, but is a difficult one for computers. The traditional method used for image classification is heavily dependent on humans having strong image processing skills. In this method, humans manually design features, extract local appearances, shapes, and textures on the image and then use a standard classifier, such as an SVM, to classify the image. However, the emergence of the CNN has had a significant impact on image classification, promoting its ongoing development. The DNN can directly extract deep semantics from the original image level, enabling the computer to understand the information in the image and distinguish between different categories. Taking Fig. 5.10 as an example, different convolution kernels can perform different operations on images, such as edge contour extraction and image sharpening. Unlike the traditional method mentioned earlier, where features are manually extracted, the CNN can automatically learn feature extraction according to specific task requirements. This means that the CNNs are

Operation	Convolution kernel	Result
Self-mapping	$\begin{bmatrix} 0 & 0 & 0 \\ 0 & 1 & 0 \\ 0 & 0 & 0 \end{bmatrix}$	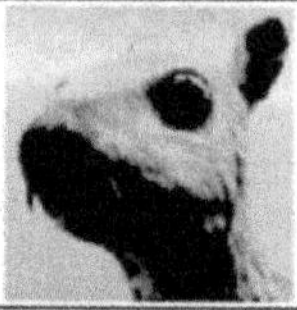
Edge detection	$\begin{bmatrix} 1 & 0 & -1 \\ 0 & 0 & 0 \\ -1 & 0 & 1 \end{bmatrix}$	
	$\begin{bmatrix} 0 & 1 & 0 \\ 1 & -4 & 1 \\ 0 & 1 & 0 \end{bmatrix}$	
	$\begin{bmatrix} -1 & -1 & -1 \\ -1 & 8 & -1 \\ -1 & -1 & -1 \end{bmatrix}$	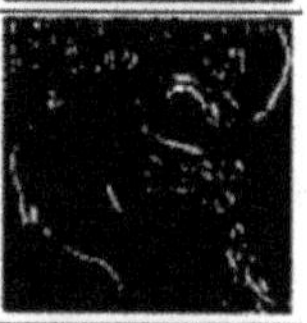
Sharpening	$\begin{bmatrix} 0 & -1 & 0 \\ -1 & 5 & -1 \\ 0 & -1 & 0 \end{bmatrix}$	

Fig. 5.10 Functions of different convolution kernels on images

Fig. 5.11 MNIST handwritten image recognition

able to deliver better image classification effects as well as being suitable for more task data scenarios.

The earliest application of image classification is MNIST handwritten image recognition—one that has subsequently become a classic. As shown in Fig. 5.11, data samples are 10 handwritten numbers ranging from 0 to 9, and each image is a grayscale image of 28×28 pixels. If a fully connected network is used for classification, each image needs to be expanded into a vector with a length of 784. This approach will result in the loss of the image's spatial information, and requires too many training parameters, potentially leading to overfitting. We can solve these two problems by using CNNs. First, the operations of the convolution kernels will not change the spatial pixel distribution of the images, meaning that no spatial information is lost. Second, because the convolution kernels are shared on images, the overfitting problem can be solved more effectively.

The CNN first extracts the contour information of the numeral image by using the lower convolution kernel. It then reduces the dimension of the image, abstracts the information into features that the computer can understand, and finally classifies the number through the fully connected layer. As shown in Fig. 5.12, many of the images that are misclassified by the neural network are also difficult for humans to identify. However, this indicates that the CNNs have actually learned the semantics of the numbers in the images.

Now we will look at the application of color image classification—Canadian Institute for Advanced Research-10 (CIFAR-10) data classification. The dataset includes 60,000 32×32 color images that represent 10 categories of natural objects, such as aircrafts, automobiles, and birds. Figure 5.13 shows the 10 categories and some examples of each category. The semantic information in CIFAR-10 is more complex

Fig. 5.12 Misclassified MNIST images

than that in numbers, and the input color data includes three channels rather than only one in the grayscale image.

Figure 5.14 shows convolution kernels at different layers of CNNs. The layers progressively get deeper from left to right. We can see that the convolution kernels at shallow layers are used to learn the features of edges. With the deepening of the layer, the local contour and even the overall semantics are gradually learned, and the initial states of these convolution kernels are all random noises. We can also see that the CNNs have a strong ability for learning image features, resulting in the rapid development of computer vision in 2012.

As the CNN has developed, the application of image classification has grown to cover the classification of complex objects in photographs (as shown in Fig. 5.15), facial recognition (as shown in Fig. 5.16), and other fields such as plant identification. We can therefore conclude that the application of image classification is inseparable from the CNN.

Aircraft

Car

Bird

Cat

Deer

Dog

Frog

Horse

Ship

Truck

Fig. 5.13 CIFAR-10 dataset

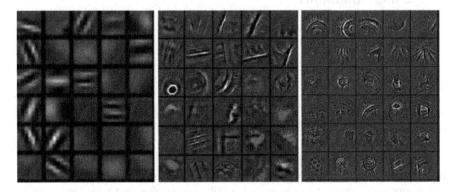

Fig. 5.14 Convolution kernels at different layers of the CNN

Fig. 5.15 Complex objects in photographs

Fig. 5.16 Application of image classification

5.5 Implementing Image Classification Based on the DNN Using MindSpore

The interfaces and processes of MindSpore may constantly change due to iterative development. For all runnable code, see the code in corresponding chapters at https://mindspore.cn/resource. You can scan the QR code on the right to access relevant resources.

In Sect. 5.4, we described the functions of the CNN in image classification. Building on that, we use MindSpore in this section to systematically implement an image classification application based on the ResNet50 network.

5.5.1 Loading the MindSpore Module

Before network training, it is necessary to import the MindSpore module and third-party auxiliary library. The core code is as follows:

Code 5.1 Importing the MindSpore Module and Third-party Library

```
import numpy as np
from mindspore.nn import Conv2d, BatchNorm2d, ReLU, Dense,
MaxPool2d, Cell, Flatten
from mindspore.ops.operations import TensorAdd, SimpleMean
from mindspore.common.tensor import Tensor
from mindspore.train.model import Model
from mindspore.nn import SoftmaxCrossEntropyWithLogits
from mindspore.nn import Momentum
from mindspore import context
```

5.5.2 Defining the ResNet Network Structure

The steps for defining ResNet50 are as follows:

(1) Perform operations such as conv, batchnorm, relu, and maxpool for the bottom input connection layer.
(2) Connect four sets of residual modules, each with a different input, output channel, and stride.
(3) Perform max-pooling and fully connected layer operations on the network.

The details of each step are as follows.

1. Define basic operations

(1) Define a variable initialization operation.

Because each operation for constructing the network requires initialization of variables, a variable initialization operation needs to be defined. Here, we use **shape** to construct a tensor that is initialized to 0.01. The core code is as follows:

Code 5.2 Defining the Variable Initialization Operation.

```
def weight_variable(shape):
    ones = np.ones(shape).astype(np.float32)
    return Tensor(ones*0.01)
```

(2) Define a conv operation.

Before constructing a network, define a set of convolutional networks, that is, conv.

Set the convolution kernel sizes to 1×1, 3×3, and 7×7, and set the stride to 1. The core code is as follows:

Code 5.3 Defining conv

```
def conv1x1(in_channels, out_channels, stride=1, padding=0):
    """1x1 convolution"""
    weight_shape = (out_channels, in_channels, 1, 1)
    weight = weight_variable(weight_shape)
    return Conv2d(in_channels,
                  out_channels,
                  kernel_size=1,
                  stride=stride,
                  padding=padding,
                  weight_init=weight,
                  has_bias=False,
                  pad_mode="same")
def conv3x3(in_channels, out_channels, stride=1, padding=1):
    """3x3 convolution"""
    weight_shape = (out_channels, in_channels, 3, 3)
    weight = weight_variable(weight_shape)
    return Conv2d(in_channels,
                  out_channels,
                  kernel_size=3,
                  stride=stride,
                  padding=padding,
                  weight_init=weight,
                  has_bias=False,
                  pad_mode="same")

def conv7x7(in_channels, out_channels, stride=1, padding=0):
    """1x1 convolution"""
    weight_shape = (out_channels, in_channels, 7, 7)
    weight = weight_variable(weight_shape)
    return Conv2d(in_channels, out_channels,
                  kernel_size=7,
                  stride=stride,
                  padding=padding,
                  weight_init=weight,
                  has_bias=False,
                  pad_mode="same")
```

(3) Define a BatchNorm operation.

Define the BatchNorm operation to perform the normalization operation. The core code is as follows:

Code 5.4 Defining the BatchNorm Operation

```
def bn_with_initialize(out_channels):
    shape = (out_channels)
    mean = weight_variable(shape)
    var = weight_variable(shape)
    beta = weight_variable(shape)
    gamma = weight_variable(shape)
    bn = BatchNorm2d(out_channels,
                     momentum=0.1
                     eps=1e-5,
                     gamma_init=gamma,
                     beta_init=beta,
                     moving_mean_init=mean,
                     moving_var_init=var)
    return bn
```

(4) Define a dense operation.

Define the dense operation to integrate the features of the previous layers. The core code is as follows:

Code 5.5 Defining the Dense Operation

```
def fc_with_initialize(input_channels, out_channels):
    weight_shape = (out_channels, input_channels)
    bias_shape = (out_channels)
    weight = weight_variable(weight_shape)
    bias = weight_variable(bias_shape)
    return Dense(input_channels, out_channels, weight, bias)
```

2. Define the ResidualBlock module

Each ResidualBlock operation includes Conv > BatchNorm > ReLU, which are delivered to the MakeLayer module. The core code is as follows:

Code 5.6 Defining the ResidualBlock Module

```
class ResidualBlock(Cell):
    expansion = 4
    def init(self,
             in_channels,
             out_channels,
             stride=1,
             down_sample=False):
        super(ResidualBlock, self).__init__()

        out_chls = out_channels // self.expansion
        self.conv1 = conv1x1(in_channels, out_chls,
        stride=stride, padding=0)
        self.bn1 = bn_with_initialize(out_chls)

        self.conv2 = conv3x3(out_chls, out_chls, stride=1,
        padding=0)
        self.bn2 = bn_with_initialize(out_chls)

        self.conv3 = conv1x1(out_chls, out_channels, stride=1,
        padding=0)
        self.bn3 = bn_with_initialize(out_channels)

        self.relu = ReLU()
        self.add = TensorAdd()

    def construct(self, x):
        identity = x
        out = self.conv1(x)
        out = self.bn1(out)
        out = self.relu(out)
        out = self.conv2(out)
        out = self.bn2(out)
        out = self.relu(out)
        out = self.conv3(out)
        out = self.bn3(out)
        out = self.add(out, identity)
        out = self.relu(out)
        return out
```

Code 5.7 Defining the ResidualBlock Module

```
class ResidualBlockWithDown(Cell):
    expansion = 4
    def __init__(self,
                 in_channels,
                 out_channels,
                 stride=1,
                 down_sample=False):
        super(ResidualBlockWithDown, self).__init__()

        out_chls = out_channels // self.expansion
        self.conv1 = conv1x1(in_channels, out_chls,
        stride=stride, padding=0)
        self.bn1 = bn_with_initialize(out_chls)

        self.conv2 = conv3x3(out_chls, out_chls, stride=1,
        padding=0)
        self.bn2 = bn_with_initialize(out_chls)

        self.conv3 = conv1x1(out_chls, out_channels, stride=1,
        padding=0)
        self.bn3 = bn_with_initialize(out_channels)

        self.relu = ReLU()
        self.downSample = down_sample

        self.conv_down_sample = conv1x1(in_channels,
        out_channels, stride=stride, padding=0)
        self.bn_down_sample = bn_with_initialize(out_channels)
        self.add = TensorAdd()

    def construct(self, x):
        identity = x
        out = self.conv1(x)
        out = self.bn1(out)
        out = self.relu(out)
        out = self.conv2(out)
        out = self.bn2(out)
        out = self.relu(out)
        out = self.conv3(out)
        out = self.bn3(out)
```

```
identity = self.conv_down_sample(identity)
identity = self.bn_down_sample(identity)
out = self.add(out, identity)
out = self.relu(out)
return out
```

3. Define the MakeLayer module

Define a set of MakeLayer modules with different blocks. Set the input, output channel, and stride. The core code is as follows:

Code 5.8 Defining the MakeLayer Module

```
class MakeLayer0(Cell):
    def __init__(self, block, layer_num, in_channels,
                    out_channels, stride):
        super(MakeLayer0, self).__init__()
        self.a = ResidualBlockWithDown(in_channels, out_channels,
        stride=stride, down_sample=True)
        self.b = block(out_channels, out_channels, stride=1)
        self.c = block(out_channels, out_channels, stride=1)

    def construct(self, x):
        x = self.a(x)
        x = self.b(x)
        x = self.c(x)
        return x


class MakeLayer1(Cell):
    def __init__(self, block, layer_num, in_channels,
                    out_channels, stride):
        super(MakeLayer1, self).__init__()
        self.a = ResidualBlockWithDown(in_channels, out_channels,
        stride=stride, down_sample=True)
        self.b = block(out_channels, out_channels, stride=1)
        self.c = block(out_channels, out_channels, stride=1)
        self.d = block(out_channels, out_channels, stride=1)
```

```
    def construct(self, x)
        x = self.a(x)
        x = self.b(x)
        x = self.c(x)
        x = self d(x)
        return x


class MakeLayer2(Cell):
    def __init__(self, block, layer_num, in_channels,
                    out_channels, stride):
        super(MakeLayer2, self).__init__()
        self.a = ResidualBlockWithDown(in_channels, out_channels,
        stride=stride, down_sample=True)
        self.b = block(out_channels, out_channels, stride=1)
        self.c = block(out_channels, out_channels, stride=1)
        self.d = block(out_channels, out_channels, stride=1)
        self.e = block(out_channels, out_channels, stride=1)
        self.f = block(out_channels, out_channels, stride=1)

    def construct(self, x):
        x = self.a(x)
        x = self.b(x)
        x = self.c(x)
        x = self.d(x)
        x = self.e(x)
        x = self.f(x)
        return x


class MakeLayer3(Cell):
    def __init__(self, block, layer_num, in_channels,
                    out_channels, stride):
        super(MakeLayer3, self).__init__()
        self.a = ResidualBlockWithDown(in_channels, out_channels,
        stride=stride, down_sample=True)
        self.b = block(out_channels, out_channels, stride=1)
        self.c = block(out_channels, out_channels, stride=1)

    def construct(self, x):
        x = self.a(x)
        x = self.b(x)
        x = self.c(x)
        return x
```

4. Define the overall network

Once the MakeLayer modules have been created, define the overall ResNet50 network structure. The core code is as follows:

Code 5.9 Defining the Overall ResNet50 Network Structure

```
class ResNet(Cell):
    def __init__(self, block, layer_num, num_classes=10):
        super(ResNet, self).__init__()

        self.conv1 = conv7x7(3, 64, stride=2 padding=3)

        self.bn1 = bn_with_initialize(64)
        self.relu = ReLU()
        self.maxpool = MaxPool2d(kernel_size=3, stride=2,
        pad_mode="same")

        self.layer1 = MakeLayer0(
        block, layer_num[0] in_channels=64, out_channels=256,
        stride=1)
        self.layer2 = MakeLayer1(
            block, layer_num[1] in_channels=256, out_channels=512,
            stride=2)
        self.layer3 = MakeLayer2(
            block, layer_num[2] in_channels=512, out_channels=1024,
            stride=2)
        self.layer4 = MakeLayer3(
            block, layer_num[3] in_channels=1024,
            out_channels=2048, stride=2)

        self.pool = SimpleMean()
        self.fc = fc_with_initialize(512 * block.Expansion,
        num_classes)
        self.flatten = Flatten()

    def construct(self, x):
        x = self.conv1(x)
        x = self.bn1(x)
        x = self.relu(x)
        x = self.maxpool(x)
        x = self.layer1(x)
        x = self.layer2(x)
        x = self.layer3(x)
        x = self.layer4(x)
        x = self.pool(x)
        x = self.flatten(x)
        x = self.fc(x)
        return x

    def resnet50(num_classes):
        return ResNet(ResidualBlock, resnet_shape, num_classes)
```

5.5.3 Setting Hyperparameters

Set hyperparameters related to the loss function and optimizer, such as batches, epochs, and classes. Define the loss function as SoftmaxCrossEntropyWithLogits, using Softmax to calculate the cross-entropy. Select the momentum optimizer, and set its learning rate to 0.1 and momentum to 0.9. The core code is as follows:

Code 5.10 Defining Hyperparameters

```
context.switch_to_graph_mode()

epoch_size = 1
batch_size = 32
step_size = 1
num_classes = 10
lr = 0.1
momentum = 0.9
resnet_shape = [3, 4, 6, 3]
```

5.5.4 Importing a Dataset

Create an ImageNet dataset using the MindSpore data format APIs. For details about these APIs and how to implement the train_dataset() function, see Chap. 14.

5.5.5 Training a Model

1. Use train_dataset() to read data

```
ds = train_dataset()
```

2. Use resnet() to create the ResNet50 network structure

```
net = resnet50(num_classes)
net.set_train()
```

3. Set the loss function and optimizer

```
loss = SoftmaxCrossEntropyWithLogits(is_grad=False, sparse=True,
sens = (1.0/batch_size))
opt = Momentum(lr, momentum, net.trainable_params())
```

4. Create a model and call the model.train() method to start training

```
model = Model(net, loss, opt)
model.train(epoch_size, ds)
```

Chapter 6
RNN

6.1 Overview

Calculations performed in the CNN are independent, meaning that there is no relationship between the previous and current inputs. However, we need to deal with sequence relationships in many tasks. Take a sentence as an example. If we try to understand a sentence, we must deal with the entire sequence formed by all the words—it is not sufficient to understand only each separate word. We need the ability to predict what word will follow previous ones in a sentence. Another example is video processing, where analyzing each frame separately would produce inadequate results, meaning that we must analyze the entire sequence formed by all the frames. The RNN has emerged to solve such problems.

Figure 6.1 shows the structure of a simple RNN. The structure includes an input layer, a hidden layer, and an output layer. We can understand an RNN as multiple replications of the same network—during each replication, a state is transferred to the next layer.

In Fig. 6.1, X_t is the mini-batch input of the t-th time step in the sequence, and H_t is the hidden variable of the time step. The RNN stores the hidden variable H_{t-1} for the previous time step and introduces a new weight parameter W_{hh} to describe how the hidden variable of the previous time step is used for the current time step. We can therefore ascertain that the calculation for the RNN is recurrent. The hidden variable H_t of the time step t is determined by both the input of the current time step and the hidden variable of the previous time step. The formula is as follows:

$$H_t = \text{sigmoid}\,(W_{xh}X_t + W_{hh}H_{t-1} + b_r) \tag{6.1}$$

The hidden variables can be used to capture the historical information of the sequence up to the current time step. This means that the neural network is able to memorize information. Because the formula is recurrent, the neural network is called an RNN. The calculation formula for the output layer is as follows:

© Tsinghua University Press 2021

L. Chen, *Deep Learning and Practice with MindSpore*, Cognitive Intelligence and Robotics, https://doi.org/10.1007/978-981-16-2233-5_6

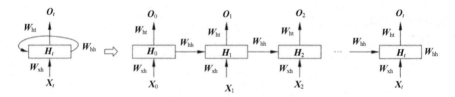

Fig. 6.1 Structure of a simple RNN

$$O_t = \text{sigmoid}\,(W_{ht}H_t + b_o) \tag{6.2}$$

The parameters of the RNN include the hidden-layer weights W_{xh} and W_{hh}, the hidden-layer bias b_r, and the output-layer weight W_{ht} and bias b_o. The RNN always uses these parameters, even at different time steps. An expanded RNN calculation formula is shown in Formula (6.3), demonstrating that the RNN can memorize and use information about the previous time step.

$$
\begin{aligned}
O_t &= \text{sigmoid}\,(W_{ht}H_t + b_o) \\
&= \text{sigmoid}\,(W_{ht}\text{sigmoid}\,(W_{xh}X_t + W_{hh}H_{t-1} + b_r) + b_o) \\
&= \text{sigmoid}\,(W_{ht}\text{sigmoid}\,(W_{xh}X_t + W_{hh}(\text{sigmoid}\,(W_{ht}\text{sigmoid}\,(W_{xh}X_t \\
&\quad + W_{hh}H_{t-2} + b_r) + b_o)) + b_r) + b_o)
\end{aligned} \tag{6.3}
$$

6.2   Deep RNN

In deep learning applications, RNNs with multiple hidden layers (also called deep RNNs) are often used. Figure 6.2 shows the hidden state of hidden layer i.

The calculation formula is as follows:

$$H_t = \text{sigmoid}(W_r X_t + W_{hr}H_{t-1} + b_r) \tag{6.4}$$

Like an MLP, the number L of hidden layers in Fig. 6.2 is a hyperparameter. If we replace the calculation of the hidden state with that of the gated recurrence unit (GRU) or short-term memory, we can obtain a GRU.

6.3   Challenges of Long-term Dependency

When the time step is relatively large or small, gradient decay or explosion may easily occur in the RNN, and capturing the dependency of a large time step in a

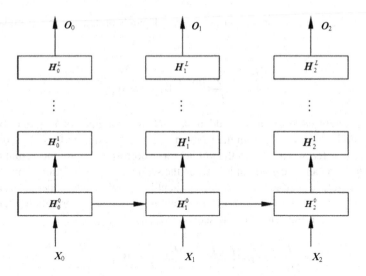

Fig. 6.2 Hidden state of hidden layer i

time sequence is difficult in practice. Here, we will examine the gradient decay or explosion by using the calculation for the backpropagation in the RNN as an example.

With an understanding of the forward propagation algorithm in the RNN, we can deduce the process of the backpropagation algorithm. The idea of the backpropagation algorithm in the RNN is the same as that in the CNN. Specifically, appropriate RNN model parameters W_{xh}, W_{hh}, W_{ht}, and b_o are obtained iteratively using the gradient descent method. Because this algorithm is time-based, it is sometimes referred to as backpropagation through time (BPTT). However, the BPTT and the backpropagation in the DNN differ significantly. That is, all model parameters are shared at each location in the sequence, and the same parameters are updated during backpropagation.

To simplify the description, we can assume that the loss function is a cross-entropy loss function, the output activation function is the Softmax function (represented by l), and y_t represents the real result value. The activation function of the hidden layer is the tanh function. For the RNN, because there is a loss function at the t-th time step of the sequence, the loss function of T (the total number of time steps) time steps is as follows:

$$L = 1/T \sum_{t=1}^{T} l(O_t, y_t) \tag{6.5}$$

We can determine the gradient calculation for output O_t by using the following formula:

$$\frac{\partial L}{\partial O_t} = \frac{\partial l(O_t, y_t)}{T \times \partial O_t} \tag{6.6}$$

The gradient calculation for parameter W_{ht} depends on O_t, and the formula is as follows:

$$\frac{\partial L}{\partial W_{ht}} = \sum_{t=1}^{T} \text{prod}(\frac{\partial L}{\partial O_t} \times \frac{\partial O_t}{\partial W_{ht}}) \tag{6.7}$$

The gradient calculation for hidden state H_t and parameters W_{xh} and W_{hh} is more complex. We can see from the RNN model that the gradient loss at a sequence location t is determined by both the gradient loss corresponding to the output of the current location and the gradient loss when the sequence index location is time step t + 1. We therefore need to calculate the gradient loss of W at the sequence location t step by step from high to low in backpropagation. The gradient formula for defining the hidden state at time step t of the sequence is as follows:

$$\frac{\partial L}{\partial H_t} = \text{prod}\left(\frac{\partial L}{\partial O_t} \times \frac{\partial O_t}{\partial H_t} \right) = W_{ht} \times \frac{\partial L}{\partial O_t} \tag{6.8}$$

Because L is also dependent on H_t through H_{t+1}, the gradient calculation formula based on the dependency is as follows:

$$\frac{\partial L}{\partial H_t} = \text{prod}\left(\frac{\partial L}{\partial O_t} \times \frac{\partial O_t}{\partial H_t} \right) + \text{prod}\left(\frac{\partial L}{\partial H_{t+1}} \times \frac{\partial H_{t+1}}{\partial H_t} \right) \tag{6.9}$$

After being expanded, the formula becomes:

$$\frac{\partial L}{\partial H_t} = W_{ht} \times \frac{\partial L}{\partial O_t} + W_{hh} \times \frac{\partial L}{\partial H_{t+1}} \tag{6.10}$$

$$\frac{\partial L}{\partial H_t} = \sum_{i=t}^{T} (W_{hh})^{T-i} \times W_{ht} \times \frac{\partial L}{\partial O_{T-i}} \tag{6.11}$$

As described earlier, the RNN algorithm can deal with the time sequence problem effectively. However, a number of problems remain—specifically, gradient disappearance or explosion (which is caused by the backpropagation algorithm and the long-term dependency). Note that the gradient disappearance here is different from the backpropagation, and mainly refers to a phenomenon where the memory value is small due to the excessively long time. Accordingly, a series of improved algorithms have emerged, including LSTM and GRU. The LSTM and GRU algorithms employ the following strategies for dealing with gradient disappearance or explosion:

(1) For gradient disappearance, because the two algorithms store memories using a special approach, memories with a larger gradient in the past will not be erased immediately (unlike a simple RNN). In this way, the algorithms are able to overcome gradient disappearance to some extent.

(2)   For gradient explosion, the solution to overcoming this issue is gradient clip-
      ping. Specifically, the gradient is set to c or $-c$ when the calculated gradient
      exceeds the threshold c or is less than the threshold $-c$.

6.4   LSTM Network and GRU

The ability of the RNN to address current problems by applying previous information
has contributed significantly to its emergence. For example, a previous image can
help us understand the content of the current image, and when we deal with the current
task, it is important for us to see some previous image information. We can take a
language model as another example, in which we would need to know the previous
text in order to predict what the next word might be. Given the words "the clouds are
in the", we could easily assume that the next word would be "sky", without needing
any more information. In this case, the gap between the content to be predicted and
the relevant information is very small, and the RNN can easily implement content
prediction by using the previous information.

6.4.1   LSTM

An LSTM network is a special RNN that was first proposed by Hochreiter and
Schmidhuber in 1997 [1]. It has since been improved by many researchers and widely
used to solve various problems, achieving remarkable results and gaining popularity.

The LSTM network is designed primarily to avoid the long-term dependency
mentioned earlier, and its key characteristic is to easily remember information for a
long time.

Figure 6.3 shows the LSTM network structure, which includes three gates: input
gate, forget gate, and output gate. It also includes memory cells with the same shape
as the hidden state to record additional information.

The forget gate controls whether to store or discard the previous cell information
C_{t-1}. The strategy is to calculate the sigmoid function based on the information of the
previous hidden state H_{t-1} and the current input X_t. The output range is [0, 1], where
0 means "completely forgotten", and 1 means "completely stored". The calculation
formula is as follows:

$$f_t = \text{sigmoid}(W_f X_t + W_{hf} H_{t-1} + b_f) \tag{6.12}$$

The input gate controls new information that needs to be added to the cell state.
There are two steps: The input gate determines which values need to be updated,
and then the tanh layer creates a new C_t value (a candidate cell). The calculation
formulas are as follows:

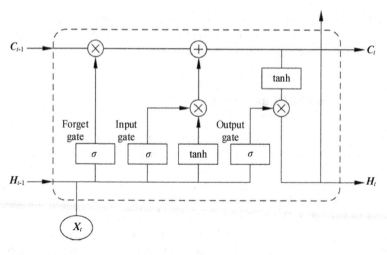

Fig. 6.3 LSTM network structure

$$i_t = \text{sigmoid} \ (W_i \mathbf{X}_t + W_{\text{hi}} H_{t-1} + b_i) \qquad (6.13)$$

$$\mathbb{C}_t = \tanh \ (W_C \mathbf{X}_t + W_{hC} \mathbf{H}_{t-1} + b_C) \qquad (6.14)$$

The cell state is then updated. The formula is as follows:

$$C_t = f_t \mathbf{C}_{t-1} + i_t \mathbb{C}_t \qquad (6.15)$$

Finally, the output needs to be determined, and is a filtered version based on the current cell state. The output gate is calculated by using the sigmoid function to determine which cell state needs to be output, and then the cell state is calculated by tanh and multiplied by the output gate. The calculation formulas are as follows:

$$\boldsymbol{O}_t = \text{sigmoid} \ (\boldsymbol{W}_o \boldsymbol{X}_t + \boldsymbol{W}_{ho} \boldsymbol{H}_{t-1} + \boldsymbol{b}_o) \qquad (6.16)$$

$$\boldsymbol{h}_t = \boldsymbol{O}_t \times \tanh \ (\boldsymbol{C}_t) \qquad (6.17)$$

6.4.2 GRU

The GRU is proposed to capture the dependency more effectively if there is a relatively large time step in a time sequence. The GRU controls the flow of information by a learning gate, and introduces the concepts of reset gate and update gate. In this way, it changes the calculation of the hidden state in the RNN, as shown in Fig. 6.4.

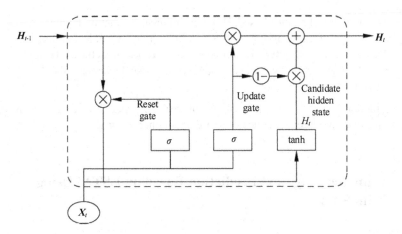

Fig. 6.4 GRU

The calculation process of the GRU is as follows:

(1) The reset gate is calculated, determining which of the previous hidden states can be maintained. The calculation formula is as follows:

$$R_t = \text{sigmoid}\,(W_r X_t + W_{hr} H_{t-1} + b_r) \tag{6.18}$$

(2) The calculation formula for the update gate is as follows:

$$Z_t = \text{sigmoid}\,(W_z X_t + W_{hz} H_{t-1} + b_z) \tag{6.19}$$

(3) The calculation formula for the candidate hidden state is as follows:

$$H_t = \text{sigmoid}\,(W_h X_t + W_{hh} H_{t-1} + b_h) \tag{6.20}$$

(4) The calculation formula for the output state is as follows:

$$H = Z \times H + (1 - Z) \times H \tag{6.21}$$

6.5 Application: Text Prediction

For text prediction, most sentences are meaningless without context, even if they conform to grammatical rules. In Sect. 6.6, we will look at the model for implementing text prediction by using MindSpore in the LSTM network. Although this model cannot learn the meaning of words, we need to consider the following points.

(1)   The model is character-based. When training starts, the model does not know how to spell English words, nor does it know that a word is a unit of text.
(2)   The output text structure is similar to the scenario structure: The text block usually begins with the name of a speaker, and like the name in the dataset, the name is in capital letters.

The model is trained on small batches of text (100 characters each) and is still able to generate a longer sequence of text with a coherent structure.

6.6   Implementing Text Prediction Based on LSTM Using MindSpore

The interfaces and processes of MindSpore may constantly change due to iterative development. For all runnable code, see the code in corresponding chapters at https:// mindspore.cn/resource. You can scan the QR code on the right to access relevant resources.

6.6.1   Loading the MindSpore Module

Code 6.1 is an example operation for importing a dependency package.

Code 6.1 Example Operation for Importing a Dependency Package

```
import mindspore.nn as nn
from mindspore.ops import operations as P
from mindspore.train.model import Model
from mindspore import context
```

6.6.2   Preparing Data

Create an NLP dataset using the MindSpore data format APIs. For details about these APIs and how to implement the train_dataset() function, see Chap. 14.

6.6.3 Defining the Network

Use the LSTM function in MindSpore to implement the LSTM layer. Multiple network cells (nn.Cell) can be combined into the LSTM, which implements forward propagation. The code for defining the LSTM layer is as follows:

Code 6.2 Defining the Network

```
class SentimentNet(nn.Cell):
    def __init__(self,
                 vocab_size,
                 embed_size,
                 num_hiddens,
                 num_layers,
                 bidirectional,
                 labels,
                 weight= 'normal'):
        super(LSTM, self).__init__()
        self.embedding = nn.Embedding(vocab_size,
                                      embed_size,
                                      embedding_table=weight)
        self.embedding.embedding_table.requires_grad = False
        self.trans = P.Transpose()
        self.perm =(1, 0, 2)
        self.encoder = nn.LSTM(input_size=embed_size,
                               vocab_size=vocab_size,
                               hidden_size=num_hiddens,
                               num_layers=num_layers,
                               bidirectional=bidirectional,
                               dropout=0)
        self.concat = P.ConcatV2(1)
        if bidirectional:
            self.decoder = nn.Dense(num_hiddens * 4, labels)
        else:
            self.decoder = nn.Dense(num_hiddens * 2, labels)

    def construct(self inputs):
        #(64, 500, 300)
        embeddings = self.embedding(inputs)
        embeddings = self.trans(embeddings, self.perm)
        output, hidden = self.encoder(embeddings)
        #states[i] size(64, 200) - > encoding.size(64, 400)
        encoding = self.concat((output[0], output[-1]))
        outputs = self.decoder(encoding)
        return outputs
```

6.6.4   Parameter Description

Define the network parameters, loss function, and optimizer. The core code is as follows.

Code 6.3 Defining the Network Parameters, Loss Function, and Optimizer

```
num_epochs = 5
vocab_size = 20000
embed_size = 300
num_hiddens = 100
num_layers = 2
bidirectional = True
batch_size = 64
labels = 2
lr = 0.8
loss = nn.SoftmaxCrossEntropyWithLogits (is_grad=False,
sparse=True)
opt = nn.Momentum(lr, 0.9, net.trainable_params())
```

The parameters at each layer have the following meanings:

(1)   num_epochs: The number of epochs
(2)   vocab_size: The number of words
(3)   embed_size: The dimension of the word vector
(4)   num_hiddens: The number of dimensions of the hidden-layer state
(5)   num_layers: The number of RNN layers
(6)   bidirectional: It indicates whether the RNN is bidirectional. It is set to False by default, indicating num_directions = 1. When set to True, num_directions = 2.
(7)   batch_size: The size of each batch
(8)   labels: The number of categories.

The output of the LSTM network is: out. 0 indicates negative, whereas 1 indicates positive.

After defining the parameters, define the loss function as SoftmaxCrossEntropy-WithLogits, using Softmax to calculate the cross entropy. Then, select the momentum optimizer, and set its learning rate to 0.8 and momentum to 0.9.

6.6.5 Training a Model

Create the network, model, and training dataset. Then, load the network, loss function, and optimizer into the model, following which call model.train() to start training. The core code is as follows:

Code 6.4 Training the LSTM

```
context.switch_to_graph_mode()
ds = train_dataset()
net = SentimentNet(vocab_size=(vocab_size + 1),
            embed_size=embed_size,
            num_hiddens=num_hiddens,
            num_layers=num_layers,
            bidirectional=bidirectional,
            labels=labels)
net.set_train()
model = Model(net, loss, opt)
model.train(epoch_size, ds)
```

Reference

1. S. Hochreiter, J. Schmidhuber, Long short-term memory, in *Neural Computation* (2017)

Chapter 7
Unsupervised Learning: Word Vector

In the field of NLP, as well as for the processing of text data, the first thing we need to consider is how we can express the text mathematically. Through this, we are then able to derive the concept of word vector or word embedding. Word vector, as its name implies, maps a word to a vector space, maximally retaining the original semantics of the word. In this important tool for understanding natural language, we can use a word vector as the smallest unit for mining corpus data or as an input to complex models.

Table 7.1 describes the mainstream methods for generating common word vectors.

7.1 Word2Vec

Word2Vec, created by a team of researchers at Google, is a group of related models used to produce word vectors. The Word2Vec algorithm uses a shallow neural network to perform efficient training on hundreds of millions of datasets. After training, each word can be mapped to a corresponding vector to represent the relationship between the word and the word vector.

7.1.1 Background

Words are the smallest granularity in an NLP task. They form sentences, and sentences form paragraphs. Each word, in a language such as English, Latin, or Chinese, is usually represented as a token and needs to be converted into a numerical value. The process of embedding a word into a mathematical space is called word embedding—a typical example of this is Word2Vec [2]. In Word2Vec, the main body of the model is a three-layer fully connected neural network. Word2Vec includes the continuous bag-of-word (CBOW) model, which predicts the current word according

© Tsinghua University Press 2021
L. Chen, *Deep Learning and Practice with MindSpore*, Cognitive Intelligence and Robotics, https://doi.org/10.1007/978-981-16-2233-5_7

Table 7.1 Summary of mainstream word vector generation methods

Category	Meaning	Representative algorithm
Bag-of-words (BOW) model	BOW involves two steps: (1) Creating a unique tag for each word in the entire document (or a document set) and forming an out-of-order set of words disregarding grammar and even word order (2) Creating an eigenvector for each document (or each document in the document set) that primarily includes the number of times each word appears in the document. Some words may rarely appear in a document, potentially leading to a sparse matrix	One-hot representation Term frequency-inverse document frequency (TF-IDF) Text rank
Topic model	Being a relatively simple vector space model, it introduces the concept of "topic" to facilitate understanding of text semantics	Latent semantic analysis (LSA) Singular value decomposition (SVD) Probabilistic latent semantic analysis (PLSA) Latent Dirichlet allocation (LDA)
Fixed representation based on word vectors	Fixed representation uses a static word vector and cannot solve problems such as polysemy	Word vector computing tool (Word2Vec) Word vector and text classification tool (fast text) Word representation tool based on global word frequency statistics (Global Vectors for Word Representation, GloVe[1])
Dynamic representation based on word vectors	Dynamic representation uses a word vector based on a language model. Typically, it uses the LSTM network or Google's Transformer to extract features and then uses a unidirectional/bidirectional language model	Embedded language model (ELMo[1]) Language model pre-training method: Generative pre-training (GPT)[2] Bidirectional pre-training language model (BERT)[3]

---

[1] See: Peters ME, Neumann M, Iyyer M, et al. Deep Contextualized Word Representations [EB/OL]. 2018 [2019-11-10] https://arxiv.org/pdf/1802.05365.pdf.

[2] See: Radford A, Narasimhan K, Salimans T, et al. Improving Language Understanding by Generative Pre-Training [EB/OL]. 2018 [2019-10-28] https://s3-us-west-2.amazonaws.com/openai-assets/researchcovers/languageunsupervised/language understanding paper.pdf.

[3] See: Devlin J, Chang M W, Lee K, et al. Bert: Pre-training of Deep Bidirectional Transformers for Language Understanding [EB/OL]. 2018 [2019-11-10] https://arxiv.org/pdf/1810.04805.pdf.

Fig. 7.1 Network architecture of the CBOW model

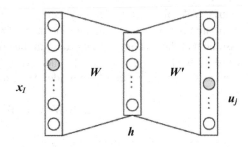

to the context, and the Skip-Gram model, which predicts the context according to the current word.

In general, Word2Vec is a fast shallow neural network training method based on word vectors. It aims to obtain word vectors, the by-product of training, and overcomes the difficulties involved in handling discrete data in classifiers. To some extent, Word2Vec provides smart feature representation, but it suffers from a number of disadvantages. First, it is unable to obtain complete semantic information of the word vector. For example, Word2Vec can obtain only one word vector for a polysemous word that has two or more different meanings. Second, Word2Vec uses a BOW model and therefore ignores the word order. Instead, it assumes that words are independent of each other, even though words typically interact with each other.

7.1.2 Development Status

The research team at Google published a set of open-source TensorFlow-based Word2Vec code. As of August 2, 2019, there were 2952 Watches,[4] 56,068 Stars, 35,055 Forks, 1402 Open issues, and 3093 Closed issues on corresponding GitHub pages.

7.1.3 Technical Principles

1. **CBOW model**

The CBOW model is primarily used to predict the current word according to a number of surrounding context words. Figure 7.1 shows the model's network architecture. Between the input layer and the hidden layer in the network, the weight

---

[4] Watch, Star, etc., are code states on GitHub. "Watch" represents the number of people who pay close attention to dynamics of the project; "Star" represents the number of people who like the project; "Fork" represents the number of people who copy the project; "Issue" is similar to a to-do list containing the tasks that need to be done (where "Open" represents the number of pending tasks, and "Closed" represents the number of completed tasks).

matrix is W, $W \in \mathbb{R}^{V \times N}$. Here, V is the total number of words in the dictionary, N is the number of units at the intermediate layer of the network, and $V \gg N$. If we assume that there is only one word w_I in the context, the input one-hot vector of the word w_I is $x_I = [x_1, x_2, \ldots, x_V]$, where $x_I = 1$, $x_{I'} = 0$, and $I' \neq I$, then we can express the output vector of the hidden layer as:

$$h = W^T x_I = W_I^T = v_{w_I}^T \tag{7.1}$$

where

h is the output vector of the hidden layer, and
v_{w_I} is the row vector of W, which is also the word embedding vector of the word w_I.

The weight matrix from the hidden layer to the output layer is W', $W' \in \mathbb{R}^{N \times V}$. Basing our calculation on the matrix, we can obtain the following prediction value of the output value:

$$u_j = v_{w_j}^{'T} h \tag{7.2}$$

where

v_{w_j}' is the jth column vector of W', and
u_j is the output value of the jth neuron at the output layer.

By combining the Softmax function, we are able to obtain the following posterior probability distribution function of the prediction word:

$$p(w_j|w_I) = y_j \frac{\exp(u_j)}{\sum_{j'=1}^{V} \exp(u_{j'})} \tag{7.3}$$

where

y_j is the output of the jth unit normalized by using the Softmax function, $j \in \{1, 2, \ldots, V\}$, and
$p(w_j | w_I)$ is the probability that the prediction result obtained based on the context w_I is word w_j.

After we transpose formulas (7.1) and (7.2) into formula (7.3), we obtain the following formula:

$$p(w_j|w_I) = \frac{\exp(v_{w_j}^{'T} v_{w_I}^T)}{\sum_{j=1}^{V} \exp(v_{w_j}^{'T} v_T w_I)} \tag{7.4}$$

where

$\boldsymbol{v}_{w_j}$ is the jth row vector of the matrix $\boldsymbol{W}$ from the input layer to the hidden layer; $\boldsymbol{v}'_{w_j}$ is the jth column vector of the weight matrix $\boldsymbol{W}'$ from the hidden layer to the output layer; and

$\boldsymbol{v}'_{w_j}$ and $\boldsymbol{v}_{w_j}$ are word embedding vectors of the word w, which are called word vectors.

The parameters at each layer in the network are sequentially and reversely updated based on the backpropagation process.

The backpropagation process is as follows:

(1) Updating the weight from the hidden layer to the output layer based on backpropagation

The goal of the CBOW model is to derive the maximum likelihood function, which we can express as follows:

$$
\begin{aligned}
L &= \max \log p(w_O | w_I) \\
&= \max \log y_{j*} \\
&= \max u_{j*} - \log \sum_{j'=1}^{V} \exp(u_{j'})
\end{aligned}
\tag{7.5}
$$

where j^* is the ID number (or position or index) corresponding to the ground truth prediction word in the dictionary, and $j^* = 1$.

The partial derivative e_j of L relative to u_j is as follows:

$$
e_j = \frac{\partial L}{\partial u_j} = t_j - y_j
\tag{7.6}
$$

where

u_j is the output of the jth unit of the output layer, and
y_j is the output of the jth unit normalized by using the Softmax function.

y_j is expressed as:

$$
y_j = \frac{\exp(u_j)}{\sum_{j'=1}^{V} \exp(u_{j'})}
\tag{7.7}
$$

$t = [t_1, t_2, \ldots, t_V]$, where t is the one-hot vector of the ground truth prediction word, and $t_{j*} = 1$. The partial derivative of L relative to u_j is the deviation between the prediction value obtained based on the model and the real value. The partial derivative of L relative to the output-layer weight W'_{ij} is expressed as follows:

$$\frac{\partial L}{\partial W'_{ij}} = \frac{\partial L}{\partial u_j} \frac{\partial u_j}{\partial W'_{ij}} = e_j h_i \tag{7.8}$$

where

W'_{ij} is the element in the ith row and the jth column of the weight W' from the hidden layer to the output layer, and
u_j is the output of the jth unit normalized by using the Softmax function.

According to the stochastic gradient ascent algorithm, we can therefore determine that the column vector in the matrix W' is v'_{w_j}, where $v'_{w_j} = \left[W'_{1_j}, W'_{2_j}, \ldots, W'_{N_j} \right]$. The update rule of the column vector is as follows:

$$v'_{w_j} = v'_{w_j} + \eta e_j h, \quad j \in \{1, 2, \ldots, V\} \tag{7.9}$$

where

e_j is the partial derivative of L relative to u_j;
h is the output vector of the hidden layer; and
η is the learning rate, which is greater than 0.

Given this, we can therefore conclude that the change of the word vector v'_{w_j} is mainly related to the difference e_j between the prediction value and the real value.

(2) Updating the weight from the input layer to the hidden layer based on backpropagation

After the previous step is performed, the update rule of the weight W' from the hidden layer to the output layer is obtained. According to the chain rule of backpropagation, the partial derivative of the loss function L relative to the ith unit h_i of the hidden layer is:

$$r_i = \frac{\partial L}{\partial h_i} = \sum_{j=1}^{V} \frac{\partial L}{\partial u_j} \frac{\partial u_j}{\partial h_i} = \sum_{j=1}^{V} e_j W'_{ij} \tag{7.10}$$

where

e_j is the partial derivative of L relative to u_j, and
$W_{ij}{}'$ is the element in the ith row and the jth column of the weight W' from the hidden layer to the output layer.

We can then obtain the weighted partial derivative from the input layer to the hidden layer based on $h_i = \sum_{k=1}^{V} x_k \bullet w_{ki}$ by using the following formula:

$$\frac{\partial L}{\partial W_{ki}} = \frac{\partial L}{\partial h_i} \frac{\partial h_i}{\partial W_{ki}} = r_i x_k \tag{7.11}$$

where

r_i is the partial derivative of L relative to h_i, and
x_k indicates the partial derivative of h_i relative to W_{ki}.

The matrix form of formula (7.11) is as follows:

$$\frac{\partial L}{\partial W} = x r^{\mathrm{T}}, r^{\mathrm{T}} = [r_1, r_2, \ldots, r_i, \ldots, r_N] \tag{7.12}$$

where $\frac{\partial L}{\partial W}$ is the partial derivative vector of L relative to W, and $\frac{\partial L}{\partial W} \in \mathbb{R}^{V \times N}$.

Because x is a one-hot vector and there is only one nonzero element, only the row vector corresponding to $\frac{\partial L}{\partial W}$ is nonzero.

Furthermore, given our assumption that there is only one word w_I in the context, only the word vector corresponding to w_I is updated in the matrix W, as shown in formula (7.13):

$$v_{W_I} = v_{W_I} + \eta r^{\mathrm{T}} \tag{7.13}$$

where

v_{W_I} is the representation vector of the word w_I;
r^{T} is the partial derivative vector of L relative to h; and
η is the learning rate, which is greater than 0.

The partial derivatives of other row vectors are zero, so they remain unchanged. $v_{W_{I,1}}, v_{W_{I,2}}, \ldots$, and $v_{W_{I,C}}$ are input word vectors that correspond to the row vectors of the matrix W. By averaging the word vectors of multiple words in the context, we can obtain the output vector h of the hidden layer:

$$h = \frac{1}{C} W^{\mathrm{T}} (x_1 + x_2 + \cdots + x_C) = \frac{1}{C} (v_{w_{I,1}} + v_{w_{I,2}} + \ldots + v_{w_{I,C}})^{\mathrm{T}} \tag{7.14}$$

where

$x_1, x_2, \ldots, x_C$ are input one-hot vectors of C words in the context, and
$v_{W_{I,1}}, v_{W_{I,2}}, \ldots, v_{W_{I,C}}$ are the representation vectors of C words in the context.

Figure 7.2 shows the network architecture of the CBOW model, assuming that $(w_{I,1}, w_{I,2}, \ldots, w_{I,C})$ is the set of multiple words in the context.

The input one-hot vectors are $(x_1, x_2, \ldots, x_C)$, and multiple words in the context are used to predict output words. The maximum likelihood function is as follows:

$$L = \max \log p(w_O | w_{I,1}, w_{I,2}, \ldots, w_{I,C})$$

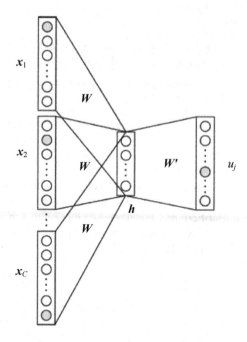

Fig. 7.2 Network architecture of the CBOW model (in the multi-word context)

$$= v'_{w_O} \bullet h - \log \sum_{j=1}^{V} \exp(v'_{w_j} \bullet h) \tag{7.15}$$

where

v'_{w_O} is the representation vector of the prediction word w_O, and
$p(w_O \mid w_{I,1}, w_{I,2}, \ldots, w_{I,C})$ means predicting the probability of the word w_O based on the context $(w_{I,1}, w_{I,2}, \ldots, w_{I,C})$.

The update rule of the weight matrix W' from the hidden layer to the output layer is the same as that of the word context, meaning that all word vectors are updated as follows:

$$v'_{w_j} = v'_{w_j} + \eta e_j h, \quad j \in \{1, 2, \ldots, V\} \tag{7.16}$$

where

v'_{w_j} is the jth column vector of the weight matrix W' from the hidden layer to the output layer, and
e_j is the partial derivative of L relative to u_j.

For the weight matrix W from the input layer to the hidden layer, the row vectors of the words $(w_{I,1}, w_{I,2}, \ldots, w_{I,C})$ in the context need to be updated as follows:

$$\boldsymbol{v}_{w_{I,c}} = \boldsymbol{v}_{w_{I,c}} + \frac{1}{C}\eta \boldsymbol{r}^{\mathrm{T}}, \quad c \in \{1, 2, \ldots, C\} \tag{7.17}$$

where

the uppercase C is the number of words in the context;
the lowercase c is an integer in $\{1, 2, \ldots, C\}$ and generally indicates a word in the context set;
$\boldsymbol{v}_{w_{I,c}}$ is the representation vector of the cth word in the context; and
$\boldsymbol{r}^{\mathrm{T}}$ is the partial derivative vector of L relative to $\boldsymbol{h}$.

2. **Skip-Gram model**

Figure 7.3 shows the network architecture of the Skip-Gram model.

Different from the CBOW model, Skip-Gram uses the word w_I to predict its context. If we assume that its context includes multiple words $\{w_1, w_2, \ldots, w_C\}$, we will obtain C prediction words as output, with the following output probability:

$$p_c(w_j|w_I) = y_{c,j} = \frac{\exp(u_{c,j})}{\sum_{j'=1}^{V} \exp(u_{j'})},$$

$$c \in \{1, 2, \ldots, C\} \tag{7.18}$$

Fig. 7.3 Network architecture of the Skip-Gram model

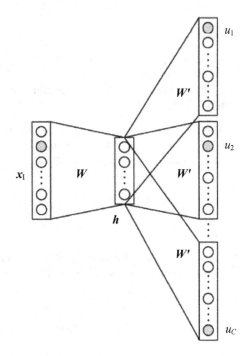

where

$u_{c,j}$ is the prediction value of the jth unit at the output layer when the cth word is predicted;

$y_{c,j}$ is the output of the jth unit normalized by using the Softmax function when the cth word is predicted; and

$p_c(w_j| w_I)$ is the probability that the cth word in the context is the jth word w_j in the vocabulary.

The loss function of the Skip-Gram model differs slightly from that of the CBOW model. Given the word w_I, the likelihood function of the joint probability distribution being the real context set $\{w_{O,1}, w_{O,2}, ..., w_{O,C}\}$ is as follows:

$$L = \log p(w_{O,1}, w_{O,2}, \ldots, w_{O,C}|w_I) = \log \prod_{c=1}^{C} \frac{\exp(u_{j_c^*})}{\sum_{j'=1}^{V} \exp(u_{j'})} \tag{7.19}$$

where j_c^* is the real location of the word $w_{O,c}$, which is in the real context set, in the dictionary.

The partial derivative of the loss function L relative to $u_{c,j}$ is as follows:

$$e_{c,j} = \frac{\partial L}{\partial u_{c,j}} = t_{c,j} - y_{c,j} \tag{7.20}$$

where

$y_{c,j}$ is the output of the jth unit normalized by using the Softmax function when the cth word is predicted, and

$t_{c,j}$ is the value (0 or 1) corresponding to the jth element in the one-hot vector form of $w_{O,c}$.

The vector $o = [o_1, o_2, ..., o_V]$ is defined, where the sum of errors between the prediction value of each element being the word j and the true values of all the words in the context set is expressed as follows:

$$o_j = \sum_{c=1}^{C} e_{c,j} \tag{7.21}$$

where $e_{c,j}$ is the partial derivative of the loss function L relative to $u_{c,j}$.

This means that the partial derivative of L relative to W' is as follows:

$$\frac{\partial L}{\partial W'_{i,j}} = \sum_{c=1}^{C} \frac{\partial L}{\partial u_{c,j}} \bullet \frac{\partial u_{c,j}}{\partial W'_{ij}} = \sum_{c=1}^{C} e_{c,j} h_{c,i} \tag{7.22}$$

where $h_{c,i}$ is the output value of the ith unit at the hidden layer when the cth word is predicted.

The element $W'_{ij} \in W$ is updated based on $W'_{ij} = W'_{ij} + \sum_{c=1}^{C} e_{c,j} h_{c,i}$, and therefore, the column vector v'_{w_j} is updated based on the following:

$$v'_{w_j} = v'_{w_j} + \eta \sum_{c=1}^{C} e_{c,j} h_c, \quad j \in \{1, 2, \dots, V\} \tag{7.23}$$

where h_c is the output vector at the hidden layer when the cth word is predicted.

This formula is similar to formulas (7.15) and (7.16), except that the prediction error is based on all the words in the context set. The method for updating the weight matrix W from the input layer to the hidden layer is as follows:

$$v_{W_I} = v_{W_I} + \eta r^{\mathrm{T}} \tag{7.24}$$

where r is an N-dimensional vector. The N-dimensional vector of the ith element is shown in formula (7.25).

$$r_i = \sum_{c=1}^{C} \frac{\partial L}{\partial h_{c,i}} = \sum_{c=1}^{C} \sum_{j=1}^{V} \frac{\partial L}{\partial u_{c,j}} \frac{\partial u_{c,j}}{\partial h_{c,i}}$$

$$= \sum_{c=1}^{C} \sum_{j=1}^{V} e_{c,j} W'_{ij} \tag{7.25}$$

where W'_{ij} is the element in the ith row and the jth column of the weight matrix W' from the hidden layer to the output layer.

7.1.4 Technical Difficulties

In the three-layer network model of Word2Vec, when a training sample is received, all outputs of the Softmax layer are calculated, and the weight matrix from the hidden layer to the output Softmax layer is updated. In other words, the word vectors v'_w of all the words in the dictionary are updated, and all the weight coefficients are adjusted with billions of training samples. This requires a huge amount of computation. The computational complexity of the CBOW model is $O(V)$, whereas that of the Skip-Gram model is $O(CV)$ due to its predicting C words. To address the significant computational requirements and accelerate training, Mikolov [2] introduces two optimization algorithms: hierarchical Softmax and negative sampling.

1.   Hierarchical Softmax

Hierarchical Softmax is an efficient method for calculating Softmax functions. This method offers high-speed training and is suitable for use with large data and deep models. It uses a binary tree, as shown in Fig. 7.4, to represent all words in a dictionary.

The leaf nodes of the binary tree are words, and the total amount of words is V, meaning that the binary tree includes $V - 1$ inner nodes. Before we can use hierarchical Softmax, we must first calculate the Softmax probability for all output elements and update V word vectors. Hierarchical Softmax starts with the root node and traverses the tree structure to the leaf node where the prediction word is located. Consequently, only $\log V$ inner nodes, approximately, need to be evaluated.

If we assume that a random walk process is performed from the root node to the leaf node w_O, the jth inner node corresponds to the output vector $v'_{n(w_O,j)}$ along the path from the root node to the leaf node w_O. In this case, we can calculate the probability of w_O being the output word as follows:

$$p(w = w_O) = \prod_{j=1}^{T(w)-1} p(n(w_O, j), \text{left})^{d_j} \, p(n(w_O, j), \text{right})^{1-d_j} \qquad (7.26)$$

where

$T(w)$ is the height of the binary tree, and
$n(w_O, j)$ is the jth inner node on the path from the root node to the leaf node w_O in the binary tree.

Binary classification needs to be performed once on each non-leaf node $n(w_O, j)$. The probability of walking either left ($d_j = 1$) or right ($d_j = 0$) can be expressed by using the logistic regression formula $\sigma(x) = \frac{1}{1+e^{-x}}$:

$$p(n(w_O, j), \text{left}) = \sigma(v'^{T}_{n(w_O,j)}h) \qquad (7.27)$$

Fig. 7.4 Implementing hierarchical Softmax using a binary tree

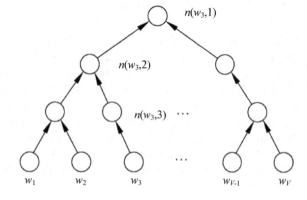

$$p(n(w_O, j), \text{right}) = 1 - \sigma(v_{n(w_O,j)}^{\prime\mathrm{T}}h) = \sigma(-v_{n(w_O,j)}^{\prime\mathrm{T}}h) \qquad (7.28)$$

where $\sigma(\bullet)$ is the sigmoid function.

In the Skip-Gram model, $h = v_{w_I}$, whereas in the CBOW model, $h = \frac{1}{C}\sum_{c=1}^{C} v_{w_{I,c}}$. When the current node is $n(w_O, j)$, the probability of a walking direction is determined by two factors: the inner product of the current node's representation vector $v_{n(w_O,j)}^{\prime}$ and the output vector h of the hidden layer.

For a given training instance $\{w_I, w_O\}$, the goal is to maximize the likelihood function. We can achieve this as follows:

$$L = \max \log p(w = w_O | w_I) = \sum_{j=1}^{T(w)-1} \log \sigma([\bullet]v_{w_j}^{\prime\mathrm{T}}h) \qquad (7.29)$$

where $[\bullet]$ can be either 1 or -1, which indicate "walking left" or "walking right," respectively, and $v_{w_j}^{\prime}$ is a simplified form of $v_{n(w_O,j)}^{\prime}$. The partial derivative of L relative to $v_j^{\prime}h$ is as follows:

$$\frac{\partial L}{\partial v_j^{\prime}h} = \left(\sigma([\bullet]v_{w_j}^{\prime\mathrm{T}}h) - 1\right)[\bullet] = \sigma\left(v_{w_j}^{\prime\mathrm{T}}h\right) - t_j \qquad (7.30)$$

where $j = 1, 2, \ldots, T(w) - 1$; when $[\bullet] = 1, t_j = 1$; or when $[\bullet] = -1, t_j = 0$.

The partial derivative of the representation vector $v_{w_j}^{\prime}$ of L relative to the intermediate node $n(w_i, j)$ is as follows:

$$\frac{\partial L}{\partial v_{w_j}^{\prime}} = (\sigma(v_{w_j}^{\prime\mathrm{T}}h) - t_j) \bullet h \qquad (7.31)$$

The update formula of $v_{w_j}^{\prime}$ is as follows:

$$v_{w_j}^{\prime} = v_{w_j}^{\prime} + \eta(\sigma(v_{w_j}^{\prime\mathrm{T}}h) - t_j) \bullet h \qquad (7.32)$$

Here, t_j is equivalent to the true value. At inner node $n(w_i, j)$, $t_j = 1$ if the next step is walking left; otherwise $t_j = 0$. $v_{w_j}^{\prime\mathrm{T}}h$ is the prediction result. If the prediction value $v_{w_j}^{\prime\mathrm{T}}h$ is almost equal to the true value t_j, it indicates that the vector $v_{w_j}^{\prime}$ has changed slightly. Otherwise, $v_{w_j}^{\prime}$ will be updated to decrease the prediction error.

In order to backpropagate the error to the weight of the input layer, a partial derivative of the output vector relative to the hidden layer needs to be obtained as follows:

$$r = \frac{\partial L}{\partial h} = \sum_{j=1}^{T(w)-1} \frac{\partial L}{\partial v_{w_j}^{\prime}} \bullet \frac{\partial v_{w_j}^{\prime}h}{\partial h} = \sum_{j=1}^{T(w)-1} (\sigma(v_{w_j}^{\prime\mathrm{T}}h) - t_j) \bullet v_{w_j}^{\prime} \qquad (7.33)$$

Formula (7.33) can be replaced with formula (7.17) for the CBOW model or formula (7.24) for the Skip-Gram model to update the input word vector.

From the preceding information, we can see that the computational cost per training sample is reduced from $O(V)$ to $O(\log(V))$, which is a remarkable improvement in speed. However, we still have the same number of parameters ($V - 1$ inner nodes compared to the original V output units).

2. Negative Sampling

Negative sampling is more straightforward than hierarchical Softmax. It decreases the training time by reducing column vector updates in the weight matrix W' of the output layer per iteration. The column vectors corresponding to ground truth prediction words are updated, whereas the remaining $V - 1$ negative words are sampled and selectively updated according to the probability distribution function $p_n(w)$.

Given the positive sample words $\{w_O, w_I\}$, where w_I is the input context and w_O is the ground truth prediction word, we can maximize the following function:

$$L = \log \prod_{w_j \in \omega_O \cup W_{\text{neg}}} p(w_j|w_I), \; p(w_j|w_I) = \begin{cases} \sigma(v_{w_j}'^{\mathrm{T}} h), & w_j = w_O \\ 1 - \sigma(v_{w_j}'^{\mathrm{T}} h), & w_j \in W_{\text{neg}} \end{cases} \quad (7.34)$$

where

v_{w_j}' is the corresponding output word vector of the ground truth prediction word and

W_{neg} is $\{w_j | j = 1, 2, \ldots, K\}$, which is a set of negative words obtained through sampling according to the probability distribution function $p_n(w)$.

The partial derivative of the loss function L relative to the word vector v_{w_j}' is as follows:

$$\frac{\partial L}{\partial v_{w_j}'} = \frac{\partial L}{\partial v_{w_j}'^{\mathrm{T}} h} \bullet \frac{\partial v_{w_j}'^{\mathrm{T}} h}{\partial v_{w_j}'} = (t_j - \sigma(v_{w_j}'^{\mathrm{T}} h)) h, t_j = \begin{cases} 1, & w_j = w_O \\ 0, & w_j \neq w_O \end{cases} \quad (7.35)$$

The word vector v_{w_j}' is updated as follows:

$$v_{w_j}' = v_{w_j}' + \eta(t_j - \sigma(v_{w_j}'^{\mathrm{T}} h)) h \quad (7.36)$$

Only the ground truth prediction word w_O and the negative words in the set W_{neg} need to be updated, that is, $w_j \in \{w_O\} \cup W_{\text{neg}}$. In order to propagate the error to the hidden layer and update the input word vector, we need to obtain the partial derivative of L relative to the output variable h of the hidden layer. We can achieve this with the following formula:

$$r = \frac{\partial L}{\partial \boldsymbol{h}}$$

$$= \sum_{w_j \in \{w_O\} \cup \boldsymbol{W}_{\text{neg}}} \frac{\partial L}{\partial \boldsymbol{v}_{w_j}'^{\text{T}} \boldsymbol{h}} \bullet \frac{\partial \boldsymbol{v}_{w_j}'^{\text{T}} \boldsymbol{h}}{\partial \boldsymbol{h}}$$

$$= \sum_{w_j \in \{w_O\} \cup \boldsymbol{W}_{\text{neg}}} (t_j - \sigma(\boldsymbol{v}_{w_j}'^{\text{T}} \boldsymbol{h})) \boldsymbol{v}_{w_j}' \qquad (7.37)$$

We can obtain the partial derivative of the input vector in the CBOW model by substituting formula (7.37) into formula (7.17). In the Skip-Gram model, the r value for each word in the context can be calculated and summed up, and the update formula for the input vector can be obtained by substituting the sum into formula (7.24).

7.1.5 Application Scenario

Word2Vec, a tool that converts words into word vectors, is used in almost every NLP task and often used with other language models. It can be replaced by any Item2Vec, such as Book2Vec or Movie2Vec, and is widely used in recommendation systems.

7.1.6 Framework Module

The most common programming languages in GitHub include C and Python. In these programming languages, Word2Vec based on the TensorFlow framework is most widely used.

7.2 GloVe

GloVe is a learning algorithm for obtaining vector representations of words and was widely used prior to proposals for BERT and other networks and algorithms. We can use GloVe concepts such as the co-occurrence matrix and loss function, and its implementation process, as reference. Compared with the more recent networks and algorithms such as BERT, GloVe provides fewer pre-training models based on a global corpus, undermining the convenience and popularity of its use. In the following sections, we will analyze the background, development status, technical principles, and technical difficulties of GloVe.

7.2.1 Background

In 2013, Word2Vec was the most widely used algorithm in NLP. Although it was essentially a language model, its ultimate goal was to obtain word vectors more quickly and more accurately than other approaches. The following year, Jeffrey Pennington, Richard Socher, and Christopher D. Manning from Stanford NLP Group published a paper [1] on EMNLP, in which they presented a word representation tool called GloVe based on global word frequency statistics. This tool converts each word in the corpus into a word vector formed by real numbers and captures semantic features between words. An example of this is the tool's ability to calculate similarity based on the Euclidean distance or cosine similarity.

In general, GloVe is used to construct word vectors based on a global corpus and context, and combines the advantages of latent semantic analysis and Word2Vec.

7.2.2 Development Status

As of July 15, 2019, there were 223 Watches, 3840 Stars, 926 Forks, and 65 Issues (including 42 Closed issues) on the corresponding GitHub page.[5] From the perspective of version development, GloVe has three iterative versions:

(1)   GloVe v.1.0 was released at https://nlp.stanford.edu/projects/glove/ in August 2014.
(2)   GloVe v.1.1 was released at https://github.com/stanfordnlp/GloVe/releases in September 2015.
(3)   GloVe v.1.2 was released at https://github.com/stanfordnlp/GloVe/releases in October 2015.

7.2.3 Technical Principles

1.   GloVe Construction Process

The GloVe construction process is as follows:

(1)   Constructing a co-occurrence matrix based on a corpus. Each element X_{ij} in the matrix represents the number of times that the word i and the context word j appear together in a context window of a specific size (the size of the context window determines how many words are included as context words before and after a given word). If the word i appears in the background window of the word j, the word j also appears in the background window of the word i, that is, $X_{ij} = X_{ji}$. We can express the relationship between the two approximately as follows:

---

[5] See: https://github.com/stanfordnlp/GloVe.

$$w_i^T \tilde{w}_j + b_i + \tilde{b}_j = \log X_{ij} \tag{7.38}$$

where

w_i^T and $\tilde{w}_j$ are word vectors that need to be solved, and
b_i and $\tilde{b}_j$ are, respectively, the bias of w_i^T and the bias of $\tilde{w}_j$.

(2) Constructing an approximate relationship between word vectors and the co-occurrence matrix according to the following objective function:

$$J = \sum_{i,j=1}^{V} f(X_{ij})(w_i^T \tilde{w}_j + b_i + \tilde{b}_j - \log X_{ij})^2 \tag{7.39}$$

where V is the number of words in a corpus. The objective function is the mean square loss of the most basic form, except that only a new weight function $f(X_{ij})$ is added. In any corpus, a word with a high probability is likely to co-occur many times, whereas one with a low probability may co-occur only a few times.

Our expectations are as follows:

① The weight of a word with a high probability is larger than a word with a low probability, so the weight function is non-decreasing.
② The weight should not be too large; that is, it should not be increased after reaching a certain degree.
③ If two words do not appear together, that is, $X_{ij} = 0$, they should not participate in the calculation of the objective function. Specifically, the weight function needs to satisfy $f(X_{ij} = 0) = 0$.

A large number of functions satisfy the preceding conditions. Here, we can use the following piecewise function:

$$f(x) = \begin{cases} (x/x_{\max})^{\alpha}, & x < x_{\max} \\ 1, & \text{else} \end{cases} \tag{7.40}$$

If we assume that $x_{\max} = 100$, we are able to observe that the value of $x_{\max}$ has little effect on the results. However, if we use $\alpha = 3/4$, we can obtain better results than if we use $\alpha = 1$.

Figure 7.5 shows a function image of $f(x)$ when $\alpha = 3/4$. We can see that, for a smaller X_{ij}, the weight is also smaller.

Fig. 7.5 Function image of $f(x)$

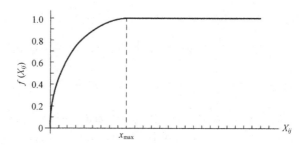

2.   GloVe Training Process

GloVe is based on supervised learning. Though GloVe does not require manual annotation, it has a label: $\log X_{ij}$.

The training process of GloVe, in which vectors w and $\tilde{w}$ are learning parameters, is essentially the same as the training method used in supervised learning. In AdaGrad, the gradient descent algorithm is used to randomly sample all nonzero elements in the matrix X, and the learning rate is set to 0.05. The vector is iterated 50 times if the vector value is less than 300 or 100 times for other values, until convergence is implemented.

Following this, we obtain the two word vectors $\tilde{w}$ and w. Because X is symmetric, $\tilde{\omega}$ and ω are theoretically symmetric, but because their initial values are different, their final values are also different. Both $\tilde{\omega}$ and ω can be used as the final results, but in order to improve the model's robustness, the sum of $w + \tilde{w}$ is selected as the final vector. This is like adding different random noises, despite the initial values being different.

3.   GloVe Loss Function

The most difficult part of the objective function is the following formula:

$$w_i^T w_j = b_i + \tilde{b}_j = \log X_{ij} \tag{7.41}$$

This formula is described in detail in the GloVe paper.

(1) X_{ij} is the number of times that the word j appears in the context of the word i in the same corpus.
(2) X_i is the total number of times that all words in the context of the word i appear in the same corpus.

$$X_i = \sum_{k=1}^{V} X_{ik} \tag{7.42}$$

(3) P_{ij} is the probability that the word j appears in the context of the word i in the same corpus.

Table 7.2 Probability statistics[6]

Probabilities and ratios	$k = $ Solid	$k = $ Gas	$k = $ Water	$k = $ Fashion
$P(k|\text{Ice})$	0.00019	0.000066	0.003	0.000017
$P(k|\text{Steam})$	0.000022	0.00078	0.0022	0.000018
$P(k|\text{Ice})/P(k|\text{Steam})$	8.9	0.085	1.36	0.96

$$P_{ij} = P(j|i) = X_{ij}/X_i \qquad (7.43)$$

Table 7.2 shows a probability statistical table that is defined in the GloVe paper.

We can use Table 7.2 to evaluate and compare the correlation between the words i and k and between the words j and k. The following rules apply here:

(1) The correlation between the words Solid and Ice is stronger than that between Solid and Steam. Table 7.2 shows that $P(\text{Solid}|\text{Ice})/P(\text{Solid}|\text{Steam})$ is much larger than 1.
(2) The correlation between the words Gas and Ice is weaker than that between Gas and Steam. Table 7.2 shows that $(\text{Gas}|\text{Ice})/P(\text{Gas}|\text{Steam})$ is much smaller than 1.
(3) The correlation between the words Water and Ice is similar to that between Water and Steam. Table 7.2 shows that $P(\text{Water}|\text{Ice})/P(\text{Water}|\text{Steam})$ is slightly larger than 1.
(4) There is no correlation between the words Fashion and Ice, nor between Fashion and Steam. Additionally, there is no significant correlation between the two groups of words. Table 7.2 shows that $P(\text{Fashion}|\text{Ice})/P(\text{Fashion}|\text{Steam})$ is close to 1.

Given the information provided in Table 7.2, we can reasonably conclude that a more appropriate approach to learning and obtaining word vectors is to use probability ratios rather than probabilities.

To reflect the probability ratio, the following function is available:

$$f(w_i, w_j, \tilde{w}_k) = \frac{P_{ik}}{P_{jk}} \qquad (7.44)$$

where

the form and parameters of the function f are not determined;
the parameters w_i, w_j, and $\tilde{w}_k$ are word vectors, but w and $\tilde{w}$ are different vectors; and $w_i, w_j, \tilde{w}_k \in R^d$.

Because vector space is linear, we can subtract the two vectors and modify the function f as follows to express the ratio of two probabilities:

---

[6] The data in Table 7.2 is obtained from the GloVe paper (available at https://nlp.stanford.edu/pubs/glove.pdf) and differs slightly from the actual calculation.

$$f(w_i - w_j, \tilde{w}_k) = \frac{P_{ik}}{P_{jk}} \tag{7.45}$$

where the left side of the equal sign are two vectors, whereas the right side is a scalar. In order to change the left side from the two vectors to a scalar, we can calculate the inner product of the two vectors, as follows:

$$f((w_i - w_j)^\mathrm{T} \tilde{w}_k) = \frac{P_{ik}}{P_{jk}} \tag{7.46}$$

The co-occurrence matrix X is a symmetric matrix, and the words and context words in a corpus correspond to each other. This formula should remain valid if we transform $w \leftrightarrow \tilde{w}$ to $X \leftrightarrow \tilde{X}$. However, the function f must first satisfy homomorphism.

$$f((w_i - w_j)^\mathrm{T} \tilde{w}_k) = \frac{f(w_i^\mathrm{T} \tilde{w}_k)}{f(w_i^\mathrm{T} \tilde{w}_k)} \tag{7.47}$$

By combining formula (7.46) and formula (7.47), we can obtain:

$$f(w_i^\mathrm{T} \tilde{w}_k) = P_{ik} = X_{ik}/X_i \tag{7.48}$$

If $f(x) = e^x$, we can obtain:

$$w_i^\mathrm{T} \tilde{w}_k = \log P_{ik} = \log X_{ik} - \log X_i \tag{7.49}$$

There is $\log X_i$ on the right side of formula (7.49), so symmetry is not satisfied. Because $\log X_i$ is independent of k and related only to i, we can add a bias for w_i, that is, b_i. The updated formula is as follows:

$$w_i^\mathrm{T} \tilde{w}_k + b_i = \log X_{ik} \tag{7.50}$$

This formula also fails to satisfy the symmetry, meaning that we need to add a bias for w_k, that is, b_k. The updated formula then becomes:

$$w_i^\mathrm{T} \tilde{w}_k + b_i + b_k = \log X_{ik} \tag{7.51}$$

7.2.4 Technical Difficulties

GloVe is a typical representative of the word embedding model and was proposed after Word2Vec. It uses the mean square loss as the loss function and implements the following three changes in the loss function.

(1) The non-probability distribution variables $P_{ik} = X_{ik}/X_i$ and $\exp(w_i^T \tilde{w}_k) = P_{ik}$ are used to calculate the log:

$$w_i^T \tilde{w}_k = \log P_{ik} = \log X_{ik} - \log X_i \qquad (7.52)$$

(2) A scalar model parameter (i.e., bias b_i) is added for each word w_i; a scalar model parameter (i.e., bias b_j) is added for the background word $\tilde{w}_j$ to obtain the square loss (SquareLoss$_{ij}$).

$$\text{SquareLoss}_{ij} = (w_i^T \tilde{w}_j + b_i + \tilde{b}_j - \log X_{ij})^2 \qquad (7.53)$$

(3) Because the weights of the loss should be different, we set the weight function $f(X_{ij})$, which is a monotonic non-decreasing function within [0, 1]. The goal of the GloVe model is to derive the minimal loss function:

$$\text{Loss} = \sum_{i,j=1}^{V} f(X_{ij})(w_i^T \tilde{w}_j + b_i + \tilde{b}_j - \log X_{ij})^2 \qquad (7.54)$$

Unlike Word2Vec, which fits the asymmetric conditional probability P_{ij}, the GloVe model fits the symmetric $\log X_{ij}$. This means that the word vector w and background word vector $\tilde{w}$ of each word in a corpus are equivalent in the GloVe model. Because their initial values are different (due to the addition of different random noises), the word vector w and background word vector $\tilde{w}$ of each word may be different after learning is complete. When the GloVe model learns to obtain the word vector w and $\tilde{w}$ of each word in a corpus, the model uses the sum of w and $\tilde{w}$ of the word as its final word vector, thereby improving its robustness.

7.2.5 Application Scenario

The word vectors obtained by using GloVe can be used in a wide variety of applications, such as text classification, automatic text summarization, machine translation, automatic question answering, and information retrieval.

7.2.6 Framework Module

The GitHub official homepage and other open-source projects have supported mainstream frameworks such as TensorFlow, PyTorch, and Keras, covering Python, C++, Java, and C in descending order of popularity.

7.3 Transformer

Transformer is a deep machine learning model based on the encoder–decoder network architecture and is used primarily in the field of NLP. It offers many advantages, such as resolving the problem of long-term dependencies, but it also has some disadvantages. For example, it cannot be used in inference scenarios where the character string length or type exceeds the training requirement.

From the perspective of network architecture, Transformer provides several reference substructures, such as positional encoding, multi-head attention, and position-wise feedforward. Due to its advantages, Transformer has gained greater popularity and wider use in the industry compared with algorithms such as GloVe. The following sections provide the background of Transformer and analyze its development status, technical principles, and technical difficulties.

7.3.1 Background

The Transformer model was proposed by Google in its 2017 paper *Attention is All You Need* [3] for solving the Sequence2Sequence problem. Google enables developers to invoke Transformer by providing an open-source third-party library called Tensor2Tensor, which is based on TensorFlow. Transformer was first used in machine translation to reduce the amount of computation while also increasing the parallelization without compromising performance and has achieved significant results.

As mentioned already, Transformer is based on the encoder–decoder network architecture.[7] In a traditional RNN based on the attention mechanism (see Fig. 7.6), processing using the encoder–decoder architecture is performed as follows: (1) The encoder receives a source language sequence, either word by word or token by token. (2) It integrates information in the source language sequence and generates a context vector based on the attention mechanism. (3) The decoder then generates a target language sequence, word by word, based on the context vector. Because the decoder is self-regressive, the output y_t of the current word is based on the output y_{t-1} of the previous word. Transformer uses only the self-attention feature, rather

---

[7] See: Bahdanau D, ChoK, Bengio Y. Neural Machine Translation by Jointly Learning to Align and Translate [EB/OL]. 2014 [2019-11-10] https://arxiv.org/pdf/1409.0473.pdf.

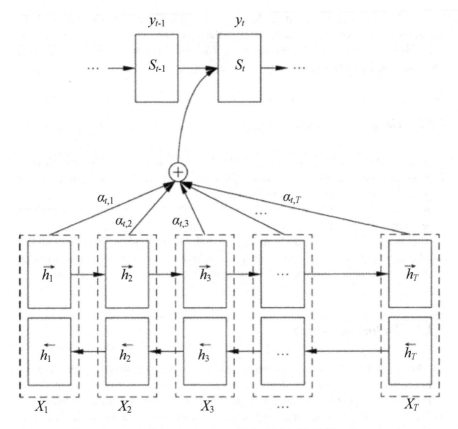

Fig. 7.6 Encoder–decoder network architecture of the traditional RNN based on attention

than architectures such as a CNN, RNN, LSTM, or GRU. Given its capability to realize high parallelization, Transformer offers a significant increase in processing speed compared with traditional architectures. It is also more effective at resolving the problem of long-term dependencies. For example, the CNN needs to increase the number of convolution layers to expand the field of view, and the RNN needs to perform sequential calculations from 1 to n. Because of Transformer's self-attention feature, only one matrix calculation step is required, and any two words (or tokens) can be directly interconnected.

Despite its many advantages, however, Transformer has a number of disadvantages. For example, it is inflexible and cannot be adapted to some tasks that can otherwise be performed easily with RNN models. Another disadvantage is Transformer's inability to replicate a character string or even complete simple logical inference if the length of the string or formula exceeds that observed by the model in training. In theory, Transformer, as well as its BERT model, is a non-RNN model considered as non-Turing complete and unable to accomplish computation tasks such as inference and decision in NLP. To address these issues, Google subsequently proposed the

Universal Transformer network architecture in 2018. For more information about this architecture, you may wish to refer to the paper *Universal Transformers*,[8] the article *Moving Beyond Translation with the Universal Transformer*[9] on Google AI Blog, and the Universal Transformer source code.[10]

7.3.2 Development Status

As mentioned in Sect. 7.3.1, Google provides Tensor2Tensor for developers to invoke Transformer. You can find out more information about Tensor2Tensor in the paper *Tensor2Tensor for Neural Machine Translation*.[11]

As of July 22, 2019, there were 429 Watches, 8394 Stars, 2136 Forks, 420 Open issues, and 611 Closed issues in the corresponding GitHub page.[12]

The proposed datasets and models include mathematical language understanding, story question answering, image classification, image generation, language modeling, sentiment analysis, speech recognition, data summary, and translation.

7.3.3 Technical Principles

As shown in Fig. 7.7, Transformer is based on the encoder–decoder network architecture, with the encoder shown on the left and the decoder on the right.

From the perspective of processing, the input is converted into an input vector for the encoder through embedding, positional encoding, and summation. This input vector then enters the N groups of multi-head attention mechanisms and position-wise feedforward network layers (N is set to 6 here). After the decoder receives the vector, which is converted from the output through embedding and positional encoding, the vector enters N (also set to 6) groups of superposition modules. These modules consist mainly of masked multi-head attention, multi-head attention, and positionwise feedforward layers. The vectors obtained by the N groups of multi-head attention mechanisms and positionwise feedforward network layers in the encoder are also used to predict the output probability based on the linear layer and the activation function.

---

[8] See: Dehghani M, Gouws S, Vinyals O, et al. Universal Transformers [EB/OL]. 2018 [2019-11-10] https://arxiv.org/pdf/1807.03819.pdf.

[9] See: https://ai.googleblog.com/2018/08/moving-beyond-translation-with.html.

[10] See: https://github.com/tensorflow/tensor2tensor/blob/master/tensor2tensor/models/research/universal_transformer.py.

[11] See: Vaswani A, Bengio S, Brevdo E, et al. Tensor2Tensor for neural machine translation [EB/OL]. 2018 [2019-11-10] https://arxiv.org/pdf/1803.07416.pdf.

[12] See: https://github.com/tensorflow/tensor2tensor.

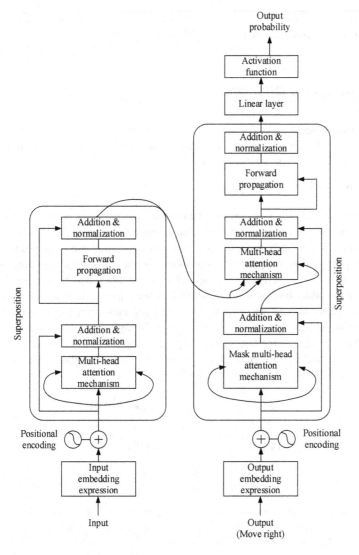

Fig. 7.7 Network architecture of Transformer [3]

A number of documents provide further information that may be of interest. For example, you may wish to read *Transformer: A Novel Neural Network Architecture for Language Understanding*[13] published by Google and two documents written

---

[13] See: https://ai.googleblog.com/2017/08/transformer-novel-neural-network.html.

by Jay Alammar: *The Illustrated Transformer*[14] and *Visualizing Neural Machine Translation Mechanics of Seq2seq Models with Attention.*[15]

7.3.4   Technical Difficulties

The following sections cover several important substructures in the Transformer network architecture, including positional encoding, multi-head attention, and positionwise feedforward network layers.

1.   **Positional Encoding**

In the field of NLP, the position information of each word (or phrase) is extremely valuable. Because the Transformer network architecture does not include any subnetwork of the RNN or CNN, the concept of positional encoding was proposed in order to use the input position information. As the name implies, positional encoding encodes the position information that is input at each moment. For the purpose of summation, positional encoding has the same dimension as the input embedding representation. There are many alternative methods for positional encoding, two of which are as follows: One is to obtain position information through direct training; the other is to use the sine and cosine functions to represent the position information. Both of these methods deliver similar effects; however, the second method was selected. Its specific calculation is as follows:

$$PE_{(pos,2i)} = \sin\left(pos/10{,}000^{2i/d_{model}}\right) \tag{7.55}$$

$$PE_{(pos,2i+1)} = \cos\left(pos/10{,}000^{2i/d_{model}}\right) \tag{7.56}$$

where

"pos" is a token position that indicates the position of the current token;
i is the dimension, where each dimension corresponds to a sine wave; and
d_{model} is the dimension of the input and output.

There are two reasons for selecting the second method: One is due to the possibility of representing a relative position; that is, PE_{pos+k} can be obtained through linear representation of PE_{pos}, which is known from the expressions $\sin(\alpha + \beta) = \sin\alpha\cos\beta + \cos\alpha\sin\beta$ and $\cos(\alpha + \beta) = \cos\alpha\cos\beta - \sin\alpha\sin\beta$. The other is the ability to help the model generalize to a longer sequence than the training sequence.

2.   **Multi-head Attention**

---

[14] See: https://jalammar.github.io/illustrated-transformer/.
[15] See: https://jalammar.github.io/visualizing-neural-machine-translation-mechanics-of-seq2seq-models-with-attention/.

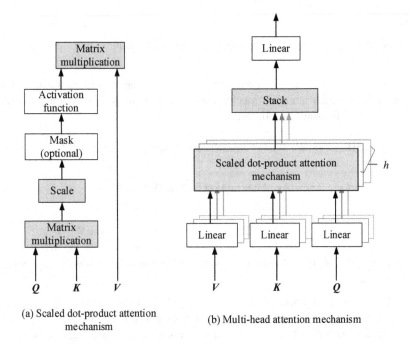

(a) Scaled dot-product attention
mechanism

(b) Multi-head attention mechanism

Fig. 7.8 Structures of the scaled dot product attention mechanism and the multi-head attention mechanism

The multi-head attention mechanism is composed of multiple scaled dot product attention mechanisms, the structures of which are shown in Fig. 7.8.

In encoders and decoders, a query is usually the hidden state of the decoder, a keyword is the hidden state of the encoder, and the corresponding value refers to the weight of the keyword. Q, K, and V each represent matrices with multiple samples.

There are many options for weight calculation, with the most common being "addition" and "dot product." In theory, these two methods have the same level of complexity, but in practice, the latter delivers higher computation speed and spatial utilization, and is therefore the method of choice.

The dot product of the encoder's hidden state K and the decoder's hidden state Q at time t is used as the weight of time t. A scaling operation is then performed to ensure that the dot product is not too large; otherwise, the gradient will be too small when the activation function is used to calculate the weight, potentially leading to gradient disappearance. Due to the operations performed in this process, the attention mechanism is called "scaled dot product attention mechanism." The formula is as follows:

$$\text{Attention}(Q, K, V) = \text{Softmax}\left(\frac{QK^{\text{T}}}{\sqrt{d_k}}\right)V \qquad (7.57)$$

where

Q, K, and V each represent matrices with multiple samples, and d_k is the dimension of the vector K.

In this way, we are able to obtain the multi-head attention mechanism; that is, h scaled dot product attention mechanisms are used for parallel calculation. The calculation formulas are as follows:

$$\text{MultiHead}(Q, K, V) = \text{Concat}(\text{head}_1, \text{head}_2, \cdots, \text{head}_h)W^O \qquad (7.58)$$

$$\text{head}_i = \text{Attention}(QW_i^Q, KW_i^K, VW_i^V) \qquad (7.59)$$

where $W_i^Q \in \mathbb{R}^{d_{model} \times d_k}$, $W_i^K \in \mathbb{R}^{d_{model} \times d_k}$, $W_i^V \in \mathbb{R}^{d_{model} \times d_v}$, and $W^O \in \mathbb{R}^{hd_v \times d_{model}}$. Furthermore, $h = 8$, and $d_k = d_v = d_{model}/h = 64$ at each layer of the network.

From the perspective of overall network architecture, the following points need to be clarified:

(1)   For the self-attention feature of the encoder (or the decoder), Q, K, and V are obtained from the output of the upper layer of encoding/decoding. In the encoder, $Q = K = V$, and they are the results of input embedding representation + positional encoding.

(2)   For the encoder–decoder attention layer, Q is obtained from the upper decoder, and K and V are obtained from the encoder output.

(3)   On both the encoder and decoder, positional encoding (information) is added at the time of input. In other words, the self-attention feature of the encoder and decoder considers the position information of the entire sequence.

(4)   A mask is used at the decoder; that is, there is a mask layer under the activation function in Fig. 7.8a. Because the next word in the decoder is unknown at the current time, the mask is added to prevent incorrect position information from affecting the decoder's self-regressive feature (with all invalid links set to negative infinity). In this way, we are able to ensure that only the first i − 1 words are used for predicting the ith word when using the self-attention feature.

The core idea of Transformer's attention mechanism is to mathematically compute the relationships between each word in a sentence and all the other words in the sentence, and then adjust the importance (weight) of each word based on the relationships. This enables it to obtain a new expression of each word, containing not only the word itself, but also the relationships between the word and other words. As a result, this expression can be considered more comprehensive.

3. **Positionwise Feedforward**

In the Transformer structure (see Fig. 7.7), which is comprised of "linear transformation + activation function," a fully connected layer is superposed behind each attention layer at the encoder and decoder. The mathematical expression is as follows:

$$FFN(x) = \max(0, xW_1 + b_1)W_2 + b_2 \qquad (7.60)$$

According to formula (7.60), we can also understand the positionwise feedforward as a CNN whose convolution kernel is 1. The convolution function convld() is used in code implementation.

7.3.5 Application Scenario

The Transformer model is mainly used in machine translation, machine reading, automatic question answering, emotion analysis, automatic text summarization, and language modeling. To learn more about the applications, you may wish to visit Google's official GitHub page.[16]

7.3.6 Framework Module

By the end of July 2019, Transformer-supported frameworks included Google's official GitHub page and other non-official frameworks and models, such as A TensorFlow Implementation of the Transformer: Attention Is All You Need[17] based on TensorFlow versions 1.2 and 1.12, and PyTorch-based The Annotated Transformer.[18] Visit the related pages for an introduction to invocation and relevant examples.

7.4 BERT

The BERT model, used in language understanding, was proposed by Google in October 2018. It uses the encoder of Transformer as the language model and captures the long-term dependencies more effectively than the RNN does. Two new target tasks—masked language model (MLM) and next sentence prediction—were proposed during pre-training, during which BERT set 11 optimal performance records for NLP tasks.

---

[16] See: https://github.com/tensorflow/tensor2tensor.

[17] See: https://github.com/Kyubyong/transformer.

[18] See: http://nlp.seas.harvard.edu/2018/04/03/attention.html.

7.4.1 Background

Research shows that the pre-trained language model can effectively improve many tasks in NLP, such as automatic question answering, machine translation, topic classification, and token-based tasks (e.g., named entity recognition). We can pre-train an unsupervised general language model by using the semantic context relationship between sentences and words, and then use a supervised fine-tuning language model to deal with specific tasks according to the specific application. Due largely to the concept of transfer learning in the pre-training model, applications of NLP are able to grow at a rapid rate.

In the pre-training model prior to the introduction of BERT, the context-sensitive models include ELMo, Universal Language Model Fine-tuning (ULMFiT) for Text Classification, and GPT. The first of these, the ELMo,[19] uses a bidirectional LSTM (BiLSTM) network for training to predict the maximum likelihood function of the current word according to the context. Compared with the word vector, the ELMo captures semantic information more effectively, provides a character-level representation, and does not limit the size of the vocabulary. However, each token needs to be calculated—this is the main disadvantage in the ELMo and results in a low training speed.

The second model, ULMFiT,[20] uses a three-layer LSTM network, without the attention mechanism and shortcut branch. This model, compared with the ELMo one, is more suitable for non-language tasks with less training data. Although it enables the easy transfer of sequence labeling and classification tasks, it requires a new fine-tuning method to be designed for complex tasks such as automatic question answering. The third of these three models is GPT.[21] This model, proposed by the OpenAI team, uses the Transformer network instead of the LSTM network as the language model, due to the enhanced ability of Transformer's attention mechanism in capturing a long-distance language structure. The objective function of GPT is a unidirectional language model one and uses only the first k words to predict the current word.

Google's paper *BERT: Pre-training of Deep Bidirectional Transformers for Language Understanding*[22] in October 2018 introduced a new language representation model called BERT, which stands for Bidirectional Encoder Representations from Transformers. The overall framework of the BERT model is similar to that of GPT, and both use the encoder of Transformer as the language model. Compared

---

[19] See: Peters M E, Neumann M, Iyyer M, et al. Deep Contextualized Word Representations [EB/OL]. 2018 [2019-11-10] https://arxiv.org/pdf/1802.05365.pdf.

[20] See: Howard J, Ruder S. Universal Language Model Fine-tuning for text classification [EB/OL]. 2018 [2019-11-10] https://arxiv.org/pdf/1801.06146.pdf.

[21] See: Radford A, Narasimhan K, Salimans T, et al. Improving Language Understanding by Generative Pre-training [EB/OL]. 2018 [2019-10-28] https://s3-us-west-2.amazonaws.com/openai-assets/researchcovers/language unsupervised/language understanding paper.pdf.

[22] See: Devlin J, Chang M W, Lee K, et al. Bert: Pre-training of Deep Bidirectional Transformers for Language Understanding [EB/OL]. 2018 [2019-11-10] https://arxiv.org/pdf/1810.04805.pdf.

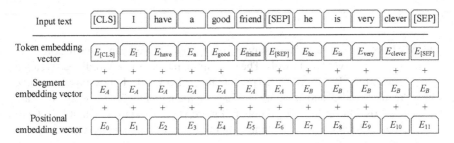

Fig. 7.9 BERT input composition

with GPT, the BERT pre-training model uses the masked language model to capture real bidirectional context information.

7.4.2 Development Status

The Google team provided a set of open-source TensorFlow-based BERT code. As of August 2, 2019, there were 825 Watches, 17,147 Stars, 4339 Forks, 401 Open issues, and 266 Closed issues on the official GitHub page.[23]

The BERT code of PyTorch[24] was also active on GitHub as of August 2, 2019, with 295 Watches, 10,217 Stars, 2480 Forks, 175 Open issues, and 522 Closed issues.

7.4.3 Technical Principles

The primary purpose of BERT is to pre-train the multilayer Transformer network model in order to obtain a language understanding model. The downstream task extracts the word embedding vector from the pre-training network as a new feature, thereby supplementing the downstream task and fine-tuning the entire network. This section describes the input representation, architecture, and two unsupervised pre-training tasks of the BERT model.

1. **Input Representation**

One or a pair of sentences can be converted into a mathematical vector representation, as shown in Fig. 7.9, using the example text "I have a good friend, he is very clever."

The input representation of the text is constructed by summing the corresponding token embedding vector, segment embedding vector, and position embedding vector. These three vectors are described below.

---

[23] See: https://github.com/google-research/bert.

[24] See: https://github.com/huggingface/pytorch-transformers.

(1)   Token embedding vector

The WordPiece model needs to tokenize the original text and can solve the problem of out-of-vocabulary (OOV) words. The main implementation of WordPiece is called byte pair encoding (BPE), which is a process that splits words. For example, the three words "read," "reads," and "reading" all include the meaning of "read," but they are different words. Due to the large number of word variations in English, it is difficult to achieve a high training speed along with effective training results. Consequently, it is necessary to split the words in the corpus. Using the earlier example, the three words are split into "read," "s," and "ing," in order to separate the meaning and tense of the words and effectively reduce the size of vocabulary. In addition, two special tokens, [CLS] and [SEP], are inserted into the beginning and end of the tokenization results, respectively.

The NLP deep learning model sends each word in the text to the token embedding layer, which then converts the one-hot vector obtained through WordPiece into a fixed-dimensional vector. For example, in BERT, each word is converted into a 768-dimensional vector representation.

(2)   Segment embedding vector

The BERT model deals with classification tasks, such as determining whether two texts are semantically similar. In this case, two sentences of the input pair are concatenated and sent to the model. To distinguish between these two sentences, we introduce the concept of segment embedding vector in the BERT model, whereby we mark all words in the first sentence with a segment token "0", and the words in the second sentence with "1". If only one sentence is input, we mark all words with "0". Additionally, the segment token needs to be mapped through linear transformation into a vector that is consistent with the dimension of the token embedding vector, that is, the segment embedding vector.

(3)   Positional embedding vector

The Transformer model (described in Sect. 7.4.2) used in BERT can be considered as a subtle BOW model. In an NLP task, the sequence order is very important: If the order information cannot be obtained, the training effect will be greatly reduced. The use of the "positional embedding vector" was therefore proposed in the BERT model to encode the position information of each token, allowing Transformer to distinguish between words in different positions. In the BERT model, the positional embedding vector is constructed as follows:

$$
\begin{cases}
PE_{2i}(p) = \sin(p/10{,}000^{2i/d_{pos}}) \\
PE_{2i+1}(p) = \cos(p/10{,}000^{2i/d_{pos}})
\end{cases}
\tag{7.61}
$$

where

sin is a sine trigonometric function, and
cos is a cosine trigonometric function.

In the preceding formula, the sequence number p of the token is mapped to a d_{pos}-dimensional position vector, and the value of the ith element of the vector is $PE_i(p)$.

2. Pre-training Task

The BERT model is based on Transformer (see *Attention is All You Need* [3]), whose principles we describe in Sect. 7.3. Note that BERT uses only the encoder of Transformer.

Multiple Transformer layers are stacked in the BERT network architecture. We use L to represent the number of Transformer submodules, H for the size of the hidden layer, and A for the number of self-attention layer heads. If the size of feedforward/filter is set to $4H$, the parameters of two BERT models are as follows:

*BERTbase: $L = 12, H = 768, A = 12$, the total number of parameters $= 110$ M.
*BERTlarge: $L = 24, H = 1024, A = 16$, the total number of parameters $= 340$ M.

The key innovation in BERT is to pre-train it with two unsupervised prediction tasks, namely masked language model and sentence prediction. Figure 7.10 shows the process of the BERT end-to-end pre-training task.

(1) Masked language model

The deep bidirectional model is more effective than the unidirectional shallow connection. To train a deep bidirectional representation and overcome the unidirectional limitations of the GPT model, we use a bidirectional encoder of Transformer and adopt an idea from the cloze task[25]; namely, some of the tokens input into the random mask model are used to predict the original vocabulary of the masked position based on the context.

The masked token is marked with [MASK], and the corresponding vector is input into the output Softmax. However, because [MASK] is not observed during fine-tuning, a mismatch between pre-training and fine-tuning tasks will occur. To solve this problem, we randomly select 15% of the tokens from the sentence (e.g., we select "clever" in the sentence "he is very clever") instead of replacing the masked words completely with [MASK]. This approach has the following effects:

(1) There is an 80% probability that the data generator replaces the word with the [MASK] tag, for example, "he is very [MASK]."
(2) There is a 10% probability that the data generator replaces the word with a random word, for example, "he is very tree."

---

[25] See: Taylor W L, Cloze Procedure: A New Tool for Measuring Readability [J]. Journalism Bulletin, 1953: 415–433.

Fig. 7.10 BERT
pre-training task

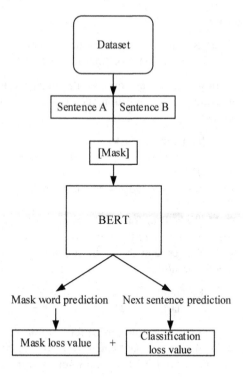

(3)   There is a 10% probability that the data generator retains the original word,
       that is, "he is very clever." The purpose is to indicate a preference for the word
       actually observed.

Because the encoder of Transformer predicts tokens at random, it needs to maintain a distributed context representation of each input token. In terms of its language
understanding ability, the model is relatively robust, with little impact if 1.5% of the
tokens are randomly replaced. For each batch of data, only 15% of the tokens are
predicted; to achieve convergence, more pre-training steps are required. Although
the convergence speed of the masked language model is slightly lower than that of
the unidirectional model, the experimental improvement of the model is much higher
than the increased training cost.

(2)   Sentence prediction

A binary sentence prediction task is pre-trained to understand the model relationship of a sentence. Many important downstream tasks, such as automatic question
answering (QA) and natural language inference (NLI), are based on an understanding
of the relationship between two sentences but cannot be directly obtained through
language modeling. Specifically, when sentences A and B are selected as pre-training
samples, 50% of B is the next sentence of A, and the other 50% is probably a random
sentence from the corpus. For example:

```
Input = [CLS]Jimmy went to the grocery every [MASK][SEP]
He bought a lot of fresh[MASK] and fruit[SEP]
Label = IsNext
Input = [CLS]Jimmy went to the grocery every [MASK][SEP]
There's a [MASK] of adventure to spice up the diving[SEP]
Label= NotNext
```

3. **Fine-tuning Task**

Most NLP tasks can be classified into the following four categories:

(1) Classification tasks. This category includes text classification and sentiment classification, that is, classification of texts with different lengths.

In these tasks, [CLS]—the first token in the sequence—is output as $C \in \mathbb{R}^H$ from the last hidden layer through the BERT network. The prediction value is output after a fully connected layer is added and subsequently connected to the Softmax classification layer $P = \text{Softmax}(CW^\text{T})$.

(2) Sentence relationship judgment tasks. This category includes text entailment, automatic judgment, and natural language inference, that is, determining whether a certain relationship exists between two sentences.

In these tasks, the start and end position tokens need to be added. The hidden-layer sequence of the output part is connected to the predicted start and end positions that are output by the fully connected layer, and is then connected to the Softmax classification layer.

(3) Sequence labeling tasks. This category includes named entity recognition, semantic role labeling, and tokenization, and is characterized by the need for the model to provide a category for each word in the text based on the context.

In sequence labeling tasks, the input part remains unchanged, and each word in the output part corresponds to the output of the last hidden layer of the BERT network.

(4) Generative tasks. This category includes machine translation, text summarization, and automatic poetry composition, and characterizes the need to generate another paragraph after a text is input.

These tasks are sequence-to-sequence (Seq2Seq) ones, where some modifications are needed to use the pre-training result of BERT. Different pre-training data can be selected, and the encoder and decoder can be initialized using BERT.

7.4.4   Technical Difficulties

In BERT, a bidirectional language model is obtained by using the masked language model and sentence prediction as pre-training tasks. Although the BERT model can be easily extended to other downstream tasks and works well, it has several disadvantages:

(1)   BERT assumes that different [MASK] tags are independent of each other and ignores the correlation between them. BERT's training objective is to maximize the joint probability distribution $p(x|x')$, where x is the set of tokens marked with [MASK] and x' is the entire sequence. However, in calculating the probability distribution of words, BERT assumes that the masked tokens are independent of each other, meaning that any correlation between them is lost.

(2)   The distribution of training data in the pre-training phase is inconsistent with that in the fine-tuning phase. BERT uses the [MASK] tag for the corpus during the pre-training phase, but does not use it for any corpus in the fine-tuning phase. This leads to the distribution of training data being inconsistent in the two phases and subsequently affecting the fine-tuning results.

7.4.5   Application Scenario

BERT is widely used in various tasks such as automatic question answering, text summarization, reading comprehension, sentiment analysis, and named entity recognition.

7.4.6   Framework Module

The main programming language of BERT is Python, which supports major computing frameworks such as TensorFlow, PyTorch, Keras, and Chainer.

7.5   Comparison Between Typical Word Vector Generation Algorithms

This section lists some of the key features and disadvantages of the typical word vector generation methods we analyzed in earlier sections, giving you a handy overview of each method arranged neatly in Table 7.3.

Table 7.3 Features and disadvantages of typical word vector generation algorithms

Algorithm	Feature	Disadvantage
Word2Vec	(1) Features are extracted based on a sliding window (2) Unsupervised learning without manual annotation (3) Online learning is supported	The training is based on a local corpus rather than a global context relationship
GloVe	(1) Word vectors are constructed based on the global corpus co-occurrence matrix. GloVe can be regarded as an efficient matrix factorization algorithm that optimizes latent semantic analysis, with AdaGrad being used to optimize the minimum square loss (2) Unsupervised learning, but uses tagging, where a tag indicates the number of co-occurrences (3) Corpus information may be considered as fixed (4) Usually regarded as global Word2Vec with a changed objective function and weight function	The training is based on a global corpus, meaning that the resource consumption is higher than that of Word2Vec
Transformer	(1) The self-attention mechanism is used to increase parallelization, thereby alleviating slow training in the RNN (2) Comprised of an encoding component, a decoding component, and a connection between them (3) Multiple encoders and corresponding decoders can be used (six of each is suggested)	(1) Transformer cannot handle some tasks that the RNN can otherwise implement easily. For example, it is not suitable for scenarios where the length of a character string or a formula exceeds that observed by the model in training (2) Non-Turing complete
BERT	(1) Transformer and the bidirectional language model are used (a real bidirectional text can be captured because the decoder—that is, a complete sentence—is used) (2) Unlike other language representation models, BERT pre-trains deep bidirectional representations based on joint adjustments to the left and right contexts at all layers. With only one output layer added, pre-trained BERT representations can be fine-tuned to create excellent models for more tasks	(1) Non-Turing complete (2) [MASK] will not appear in predictions, and excessive use of it during training will affect performance (3) Only 15% of the tokens are predicted for each batch of data, meaning that BERT converges slower than the left-to-right model

7.6   Application: Automatic Question Answering

In the field of NLP, most scenarios involve specific applications of word vectors. This includes text classification (e.g., people post text on social media platforms), machine translation (e.g., people want to translate text from one language to another), and automatic question answering (e.g., people ask questions on an e-commerce Web site and expect relevant answers). Given that research into automatic question answering is still relatively new, and because there are similarities between how deep learning is used to study automatic question answering and how humans comprehend text, we will focus on automatic question answering in the following sections.

7.6.1   Relevant Concepts of Automatic Question Answering

1.Definition

According to Wikipedia,[26] automatic question answering is a technology in the fields of information retrieval and NLP. It is concerned with building systems that automatically answer questions posed by humans in a natural language. From the application perspective, automatic question answering is an advanced form of information service, because it feeds back accurate answers in natural language to meet people's different requirements.

2.   History

Automatic question answering dates back to 1950, when English mathematician Alan Turing, in his paper *Computing Machinery and Intelligence*, posed the question of whether a machine can be considered intelligent. In the paper, he proposed a method for determining whether a machine can think—it subsequently became known as the Turing test. Over the next 10 years, the study into this topic progressed slowly.

From 1960 to 1970, a number of automatic question answering systems emerged, the most famous of which were BASEBALL, Eliza, SHRDLU, GUS, and LUNAR. BASEBALL (1961) was used to answer questions about the time, place, and scores of baseball games in the USA. Eliza (1966) was used for psychotherapy, playing the role of a psychologist. Using pattern and keyword matching and substitution methods along with heuristic algorithms, it was designed to answer patients' questions and engage them in counseling sessions. SHRDLU (1971) allowed users to converse with the system to move objects in a "block world." GUS (1977) provided tourist information through simple dialogue with users. And LUNAR (1973) used a database from which the system obtained answers to users' questions that were converted into query statements.

---

[26] See: https://en.wikipedia.org/wiki/Question_answering.

Computer scientists made great progress from 1970 to 1990 in their study of natural languages, using mathematical and statistical methods for the first time. They used the statistical language model to determine whether a sentence pattern was reasonable and used SAM—a reading comprehension system developed by Yale University—as the representative system.

After 1990, research and development shifted toward large-scale document-based question answering. For example, in December 1993, a Web-based automatic question answering system known as START went online to answer millions of English questions. In 1999, the technical review on question answering began in Text Retrieval Evaluation Conference (TREC).

Currently, there are a number of automatic question answering systems in use, including START, Watson (IBM), Siri (Apple), Cortana (Microsoft), Duer (Baidu), and Zhihu (a community-based platform).

7.6.2 Traditional Automatic Question Answering Methods

1. Retrieval Question Answering

The development of question answering is closely related to that of Internet search engines. Major milestones occurred in 1999 with the QA Track task of the National Institute of Standards and Technology (NIST) and the formal launch of the retrieval question answering (Retrieval Base, RB) system. Then in 2011, Watson, a question answering system developed by IBM, defeated champion players in the American quiz show Jeopardy!, winning the first place prize of $1 million. At that time, however, the technologies were mainly retrieval and matching, most question types were simple, and the inference ability was not strong. The technologies of that era simply did not break through the limitation of retrieval question answering.

Retrieval question answering mainly includes basic processes such as question analysis, chapter retrieval, and answer extraction, and it can be based on either pattern matching and or statistical information extraction depending on the answer extraction methods used.

For the retrieval question answering based on pattern matching, all types of questions and answers generally need to be obtained through offline calculation. When running online, the question answering system first identifies the type of the question and then extracts a candidate answer for verification. To achieve greater performance, the system uses NLP technology; however, because this technology is not mature, the retrieval question answering is regarded as shallow sentence analysis.

For the retrieval question answering based on statistical information extraction, generally, logical form conversion technology is used to convert questions and answers, and then answer inference verification is performed using a lexical connection technology. A typical representation of this technology is proposed by Language Computer Corporation (LCC) in the USA.

2. Community Question Answering

As the Internet becomes more and more popular, a growing number of Internet-related services based on user-generated content (UGC) have emerged, and the development of community question answering (Community Base, CB) systems has surged. Community question answering involves the following two key points: (1) There are many users in the community question answering system, and new users participate when the system is running online. (2) Participating users provide a large amount of information directly related to goods or user questions, such as user evaluation, voting, scoring, and recommendations, and may provide indirectly related information such as user area, climate, usage scenario, and precautions. This information plays a vital role in the modeling and analysis of questions and answers.

At the heart of the community question answering system is the need to match currently posed questions with ones from the huge number of historical questions and answers, and then provide answers to the current user.

In this system, it is technically challenging to provide accurate answers to current questions by using the traditional retrieval technology based on keyword matching due to the "lexical semantic gap" between the current question and historical questions. To solve this problem, academic and industrial circles have introduced language understanding models into the system by learning the similarity between words in the massive question answering corpora. For example, the words "health," "running," "sleeping," "eating," "organic," "natural," and "travel," among others, are related to the word "healthy."

3. Knowledge Base Question Answering

A knowledge base is formed from the accumulation of pieces of knowledge, such as "Huawei headquarters are in Shenzhen" and "The Forbidden City is in Beijing." Through the Internet, we are able to obtain a great deal of knowledge, using Web sites such as Wikipedia. However, much of this knowledge is in unstructured natural languages, suitable for human reading but not for computer processing. To facilitate computer processing and understanding, researchers proposed the concept of Triple. With Triple, we are able to represent the example sentence "Huawei headquarters are in Shenzhen" in the form of "Entity, Relationship, Entity," namely "Huawei, Headquarters, Shenzhen." If Entity is considered a node, Relationship (including property, category, and more) can be regarded as an edge. In general, the knowledge base consists of large numbers of triples, specifically, nodes and edges.

The terms knowledge base (KB) and knowledge graph (KG) are often used interchangeably by some researchers and can be considered as belonging to the same category. These terms generally refer to a process where a question is given (usually in natural language), it is understood semantically and analyzed by using related technologies, and an answer is then obtained through querying and inference by using a knowledge base (or a KG, topic graph, or knowledge base subgraph). In 2013 and 2014, there was rapid development of knowledge base question answering, yet in 2015, with the breakthrough of deep learning in nature processing, it began to shift toward neural network technology. The following briefly describes the technologies involved in knowledge base question answering during 2013 and 2014.

(1) Semantic parsing. This technology is used to convert a natural language into a logical form (a semantic representation) that can be parsed from the bottom-up and understood by the knowledge base. It enables querying of the knowledge base with query statements in order to obtain an answer. Such query statements are similar to SQL but use semantic parsing syntax and methods such as category compositional grammar (CCG) and dependency-based compositional semantics (DCS). This technology required the use of some manually written vocabulary and rule sets, making it inconvenient in practical use. To learn about the semantic analysis methods, you may wish to read some representative papers such as *Semantic Parsing on Freebase from Question–Answer Pairs* [4] published by Stanford University in 2013. We use one of the graphs from that paper as an example here. In Fig. 7.11, the leaf node statement (where was Barack Obama born) is a given question in a natural language. The bold part of the graph is related to semantic parsing, and the rest is a logical form. The root node of the semantic parsing tree is the semantic parsing result, and the answer can be found in the knowledge base by using the query statement.

(2) Information extraction. This technology extracts the question feature, deleting unimportant information (such as determiners, prepositions, and punctuation), in order to help find an answer to the given question. The process is as follows:

① Simulate human thinking: Identify the topic word in the question, search the knowledge base for relevant knowledge, locate a candidate answer, and extract information (i.e., find the graph node based on the topic word). Then, select the adjacent nodes and edges (usually within one or two hops, and are the candidate answers) as a knowledge base subgraph (called a topic graph).

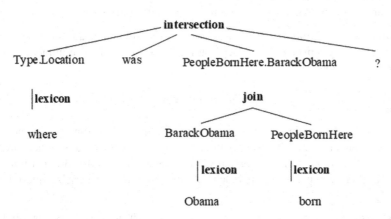

Fig. 7.11 Semantic analysis [4]

② Identify the correct answer from the candidate answers: Extract information according to rules or templates, obtain the eigenvector of the question (each dimension corresponds to one question and one candidate answer feature), and feed it into the classifier for screening or learning to obtain the final answer. This is regarded as binary classification, that is, to determine whether each candidate answer is the correct one.

The following papers provide further details about the method: *Semantic Parsing on Freebase from Question–Answer Pairs* [4] and *Information Extraction over Structured Data: Question Answering with Freebase* [5].

(3) Vector modeling: This method is similar to information extraction. It maps questions and candidate answers to low-dimensional spaces based on the candidate answers in order to obtain their distributed embeddings. Then, it converts existing questions and answers into training data through information extraction, performs training, and ultimately achieves high scores (usually in the form of dot product) for the low-dimensional spatial correlation between the question and the correct answer. For more details about this method, you may wish to refer to *Question Answering with Subgraph Embeddings.*[27]

7.6.3 Automatic Question Answering Method Based on Deep Learning

1. Summary of Algorithm Architecture Generality

For brevity in explaining the automatic question answering algorithm based on deep learning, we use the following conventions:

Q: a given question;
D: a document related to Q; and
A: an answer to Q that can be directly or indirectly found in D.

Mathematical symbols are used to abstract the automatic question answering algorithm (or system) based on deep learning. The function to be implemented or solved is as follows:

$$f(Q, D) = A \qquad (7.62)$$

When faced with an automatic question answering or reading comprehension scenario, humans carefully read Q first, then read D with Q, and either directly extract A if A is found in D, or organize a language to obtain A if A is not found in D. Figure 7.12 compares this approach with that used in deep learning algorithms.

---

[27] See: Bordes A, Chopra S, Weston J. Question Answering with Subgraph Embeddings [EB/OL]. 2014 [2019-11-10] https://arxiv.org/pdf/1406.3676.pdf.

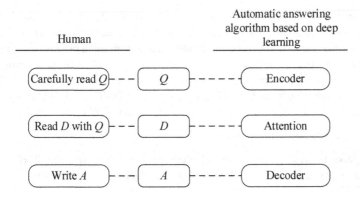

Fig. 7.12 Comparison between human and deep learning algorithms in an automatic question answering or reading comprehension scenario

The design components of the neural network framework can be divided into the following types:

(1) Encoder: It uses a CNN and its variants, or uses an RNN or its variants.

(2) Decoder: In scenarios where A can be directly obtained from D, an extraction generation method such as the Stanford Question Answering Dataset (SQuAD) is used. Conversely, in scenarios where A cannot be obtained directly from D, a generative method such as Microsoft Machine Reading Comprehension (MS-MARCO) is used. Before we can design the decoder, we need to understand the dataset. This is because, given the same dataset (i.e., D), the decoder may change back and forth in the two designs due to different versions.

(3) Architecture: A two-step or end-to-end design is used.

2. **Innovations of Representative Algorithms**

Since 2017, researchers have proposed many innovative algorithms in the field of automatic question answering based on deep learning. There are many exceptional algorithms available, but due to space constraints, we focus on only two papers here. Some other papers you may find of interest include Gated Self-Matching [6], GA-Reader,[28] and R3-Net.[29]

1. Bi-DAF[30]

(1) Introduction to the paper

---

[28] See: Dhingra B, Liu H, Yang Z, et al. Gated-attention Readers for Text Comprehension [EB/OL]. 2016 [2019-11-10] https://arxiv.org/pdf/1606.01549.pdf.

[29] See: Wang S, Yu M, Guo X, et al. R 3: Reinforced Ranker-reader for Open-domain Question Answering [C]. Thirty-Second AAAI Conference on Artificial Intelligence, 2018.

[30] See: Seo M, Kembhavi A, Farhadi A, et al. Bidirectional Attention Flow for Machine Comprehension [EB/OL]. 2016 [2019-11-10] https://arxiv.org/pdf/1611.01603.pdf.

This paper proposes a bidirectional attention flow (Bi-DAF) network, which builds on the attention mechanism widely used in machine understanding and automatic question answering scenarios. Bi-DAF is a multistage hierarchical process that identifies the context of different granularity levels and uses the bidirectional attention flow mechanism to obtain query-aware context representations without earlier digests. This paper shows that Bi-DAF obtained the State-Of-The-Art (SOTA) result in Stanford Question Answering Dataset and CNN/Daily Mail cloze test.

(2)   Network architecture of the model

The paper provides the network architecture of the Bi-DAF method. Here, Q, D, and A are marked in corresponding positions to facilitate understanding, as shown in Fig. 7.13.

In Fig. 7.13, x_i indicates the words of the ith input context paragraph, q_i indicates the words of the ith question, $\boldsymbol{h}_i$ indicates the context vector matrix output from the ith context embedding step, and $\boldsymbol{u}_i$ indicates the question vector matrix output from the ith context embedding step. Based on the combination of context embedding and the attention vector, g_i is generated and represents the query awareness of the ith context vector matrix.

The following explains the Bi-DAF layers shown in Fig. 7.13c.

①   Character embedding layer: It uses a character-level CNN (Char-CNN) and is represented by a square in Fig. 7.13.

②   Word embedding layer: It maps the context and words in the question statement into a semantic space vector. Specifically, it translates the natural language into a digital one understandable by a machine and uses the GloVe algorithm. This layer is represented by a rectangle in Fig. 7.13. If we assume that the word vector dimension is d, we can obtain the context matrix $X \in \mathbb{R}^{d \times T}$ and the question matrix $\boldsymbol{Q} \in \mathbb{R}^{d \times J}$.

③   Context embedding layer: It extracts information at a higher level by using a BiLSTM network. It outputs X and Q to the BiLSTM network and concatenates the forward and backward outputs to obtain the information vector sequence $\boldsymbol{H} \in \mathbb{R}^{2d \times T}$ of the entire article and the comprehensive vector sequence $U \in \mathbb{R}^{2d \times J}$ of the entire question.

④   Attention flow layer: It obtains the answer by combining $\boldsymbol{H}$ and $\boldsymbol{Q}$ in a process that includes matching and fusion. Matching means that the attention mechanism is used to match $\boldsymbol{H}$ and U bidirectionally, and is where Bi-DAF got its name. When the attention mechanism is used, a matching matrix $S \in \mathbb{R}^{T \times J}$ is defined, where S_{tj}, which is equal to $\alpha(H_{:t}, U_{:j}) \in \mathbb{R}$, indicates the similarity between the tth vector in $\boldsymbol{H}$ and the jth vector in U. The similarity is calculated by using a trainable scalar function. $\boldsymbol{h}$ represents a vector in $\boldsymbol{H}$, $\boldsymbol{u}$ represents a vector in U, and $[h; u; h \circ u]$ are concatenated into a six-dimensional vector ($\circ$ represents an inner product). The six-dimensional vector can then be multiplied by a trainable weight vector $\boldsymbol{w}$ to obtain a corresponding s.

The Context2Question attention is calculated as follows: $a_t \in \mathbb{R}^J$ is defined as the importance of J question vectors relative to the tth vector in the context; for

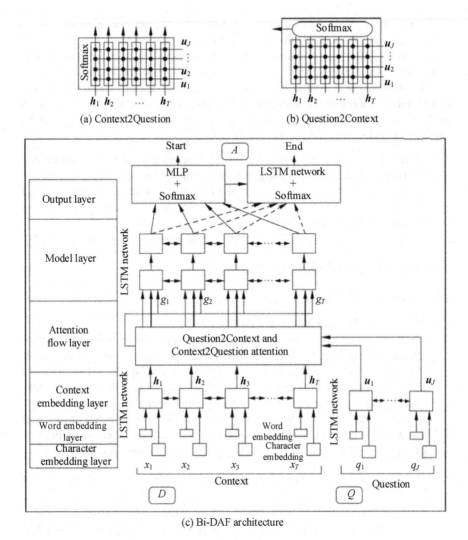

(a) Context2Question   (b) Question2Context

(c) Bi-DAF architecture

Fig. 7.13 Bi-DAF architecture

each t, $\sum a_{tj} = 1$ and $a_t = \text{Softmax}(S_{t:})$, and T different J-dimensional weights of the question vectors are obtained. The weighted question vector sequence $\tilde{U}_{:t} = \sum_j a_{tj} U_{:j}$ is finally obtained based on the attention mechanism. Figure 7.13c uses the architecture shown in Fig. 7.13a.

The Question2Context attention is calculated as follows: $b = \text{Softmax}(\max_{\text{col}}(S))$ $\in \mathbb{R}^T$ is defined as the weight vector of T context vector sequences. Here, we need to determine only whether the context vector is important to a question vector. If one of J dimensions is important, we can conclude that the context vector is important.

From this, we are able to determine the weighted article vector $\widetilde{\boldsymbol{h}} = \sum_t b_t H_{:t} \in \mathbb{R}^{2d}$. Figure 7.13c uses the architecture shown in Fig. 7.13b.

After completing the matching process of the bidirectional attention mechanism, as just described, we are able to obtain two $2d \times T$-dimensional vector sequences.

The fusion process synthesizes these two attention vector sequences and the context information vector sequence $\boldsymbol{H}$ to obtain the query awareness representation on the context vector sequence, which is defined as $G_{:t} = \beta(H_{:t}, \widetilde{U}_{:t}, \widetilde{H}_{:t}) \in \mathbb{R}^{d_G}$, and the dimension of G is $8d \times T$.

⑤   Model layer: The information in G with a dimension of $8d \times T$ is synthesized by using a BiLSTM network to generate M with a dimension of $2d \times T$ (where M contains abundant information). The interaction between the question and the article is reflected and then input to the LSTM network to obtain context information for the interaction.

⑥   Output layer: It can obtain the required output information by using G and M.

(3)   Innovations of the algorithm.

The innovations presented in the paper are as follows:

①   The encoder fuses Q into D and attends to each word in D, that is, the "Context2Question" module in Fig. 7.13. The dot product of $\boldsymbol{h}$ and $\boldsymbol{u}$ is added during attention calculation. Furthermore, the paper proposes to use D to attend to each word in Q, that is, the "Question2Context" module in Fig. 7.13. This is essentially the same as the "Context2Question" module, except that the maximum attention value is obtained and then the weighted averaging is performed on $\boldsymbol{h}$ to obtain a single vector. We can therefore consider that the result of fusing Q into D is used in the input of each time step of the encoder. See the output line of "Question2Context" in Fig. 7.13b. Finally, the following is obtained:

$$G_{:t} = \beta(H_{:t}, \widetilde{U}_{:t}, \widetilde{H}_{:t}) \in \mathbb{R}^{d_G} \tag{7.63}$$

②   The output layer of the encoder performs operation transformation (similar to feature engineering), concatenates vectors such as $\boldsymbol{h}$ and $\boldsymbol{u}$, and then multiplies them by each other. Simple concatenation, as mentioned in the paper, offers good results. The operation is as follows:

$$\beta(\boldsymbol{h}, \widetilde{\boldsymbol{u}}, \widetilde{\boldsymbol{h}}) = [\boldsymbol{h}; \widetilde{\boldsymbol{u}}; \boldsymbol{h} \circ \widetilde{\boldsymbol{u}}; \boldsymbol{h} \circ \widetilde{\boldsymbol{h}}] \in \mathbb{R}^{8d \times T} (i.e.\ d_G = 8d) \tag{7.64}$$

③   The encoder uses Q and D to attend to its output G through the decoder, in order to obtain M for each step. It then uses MLP and Softmax to predict the probability distribution P^1 of the start position, concatenates the MLP and Softmax outputs and M, and uses LSTM and Softmax to predict the probability distribution P^2 of the end position and obtain the loss function (which is a cross-entropy).

$$P^1 = \text{Softmax}\left(\boldsymbol{W}^{\mathrm{T}}_{(P^1)}\right)[G; M] \tag{7.65}$$

$$P^2 = \text{Softmax}\left(W^{\text{T}}_{(P^2)}\right)[G; M^2] \tag{7.66}$$

$$L(\theta) = -\frac{1}{N}\sum_i^N \left(\log(P^1_{y^1_i}) + \log(P^2_{y^2_i})\right) \tag{7.67}$$

2. QA-Net.[31]

(1) Introduction to the paper.

This paper proposes a new architecture, called QA-Net, for the automatic question answering algorithm. QA-Net does not require the RNN, differing from the current end-to-end machine reading and automatic question answering model that achieves lower training and inference speed due to the continuity of the RNN. With QA-Net, the encoder requires only the convolution layer, which involves local interaction, and the self-attention layer, which requires global interaction. While the accuracy of QA-Net on the SQuAD is the same as that of the RNN, the training speed of the QA-Net architecture is increased by 3–13 times, and the inference speed is increased by 4–9 times, allowing more data training models to be "fed" by using QA-Net. This paper combines the QA-Net model with data generated through reverse translation based on the machine translation model. On the SQuAD, by using the enhanced data training model fed by using QA-Net, the F1 score was 84.6 in the test set, which was higher than the previous best score of 81.8.

(2) Network architecture of the model.

The paper provides the network architecture of the QA-Net method. Here, Q, D, and A are marked in corresponding positions to facilitate understanding, as shown in Fig. 7.14.

In Fig. 7.14, the left side is the QA-Net architecture with multiple encoder modules, and the right side is the basic encoder module unit. All the encoders in QA-Net are constructed in this way, and only the number of convolution layers in the module is modified. QA-Net uses layer regularization and residual connection technology between different layers and encapsulates each sublayer of the encoder structure after performing positional encoding (such as convolution, self-attention, and feedforward network) within the residual module. QA-Net also shares context, questions, and some weights between the output encoders to achieve knowledge sharing. The following explains the five layers of QA-Net shown in Fig. 7.14.

The input question $Q = \{q_1, q_2, \ldots, q_m\}$, the context vector $C = \{c_1, c_2, \ldots, c_n\}$, and the output answer span $S = \{c_i, c_{i+1}, \ldots, c_{i+j}\}$ are given. x represents the original word and its embedding.

---

[31] See: Yu A W, Dohan D, Luong M T, et al. QA-Net: Combining Local Convolution with Global Self-attention for Reading Comprehension [EB/OL]. 2018 [2019-11-10] https://arxiv.org/pdf/1804.09541.pdf.

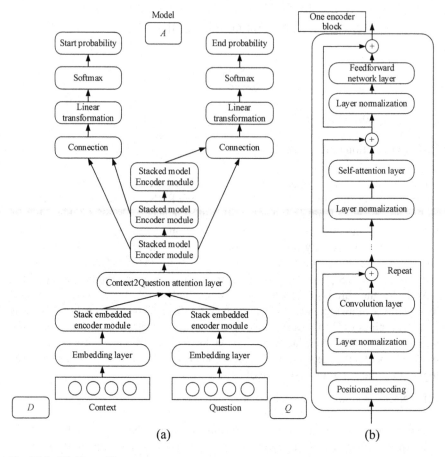

Fig. 7.14 QA-Net architecture

① Embedding layer: It connects character embeddings and word embedding vectors. During training, the word vector remains unchanged, and its dimension is $p_1 = 300$ through GloVe pre-training. The character vector is obtained as follows: (1) Each character can be trained in vector dimension $p_2 = 200$. (2) Each word is truncated or padded to a length of 16. (3) The maximum value of each line is obtained to achieve a fixed vector representation of each word. (4) The final output of the embedding layer is $[x_w; x_c] \in \mathbb{R}^{p_1+p_2}$, where x_w is the word embedding and x_c is the convolution output of the character embedding. (5) Two layers of high-speed networks are added behind the output.

② Embedding encoder layer: It includes two stack embedded encoder modules and uses an encoder block that consists of positional encoding, multiple convolution layers, the self-attention layer, and the feedforward network layer, as shown in Fig. 7.14b. In the same figure, the depthwise separable convolution structure, which has good memory and generalization capabilities, is used for convolution.

The size of the convolution kernel is 7, the number of kernels is 128, and the number of convolution layers in one block is 4. For the self-attention layer, the multi-head attention mechanism is used, employing 8 heads at each layer. For a given input x and an operation f, the calculation result $f(\text{layernorm}(x)) + x$ is the output of the residual block.

③ "Context2Question" attention layer: Like other models, this layer first calculates the similarity between the context and each pair of words in the question. It then forms a matrix $S \in \mathbb{R}^{n*m}$ and normalizes each line of S to obtain $\widetilde{S1}$. The attention of "Context2Question" is calculated as follows:

$$A = \widetilde{S1} * Q^{\mathrm{T}} \in \mathbb{R}^{n*d} \tag{7.68}$$

where

n is the length of the context, and
d is the dimension of the upper layer.

④ Model encoder layer: It includes three connected stack model encoder modules, each of which shares parameters with the others and is formed by stacking seven encoder blocks.

⑤ Output layer: It varies according to the desired task. For example, in the SQuAD task, the paper predicts the probabilities that each position is the start position and end position of the answer span, which are, respectively, denoted as P^1 and P^2.

$$P^1 = \text{Softmax}(W_1[M_0; M_1]) \tag{7.69}$$

$$P^2 = \text{Softmax}(W_2[M_0; M_2]) \tag{7.70}$$

where

W_1 and W_2 are trainable variables, and
M_0, M_1, and M_2 correspond to the outputs of the three stack model encoder modules, from low to high.

Its objective function is the same as those of other models:

$$L(\theta) = -\frac{1}{N} \sum_{i}^{N} \left[\log(P^1_{y^1_i}) + \log(P^2_{y^2_i}) \right] \tag{7.71}$$

where y^1_i and y^2_i are, respectively, the start position and end position of the ith sample.

(3) Innovations of the algorithm

The innovations presented in the paper are as follows:

① The encoder is implemented by using the CNN and several encoder blocks with the same structure, as shown in Fig. 7.14b. Each block includes different layers, among which layer-norm can be regarded as a variant of batch-norm (batch-norm is normalization of x feature in each batch of data, and layer-norm is normalization of x feature output). The depthwise separable convolution structure[32][33] is used for convolution. The convolution method decomposes a convolution kernel of $H \times W \times D$ into two matrices $H \times W \times 1$ and $1 \times D$, which reduces the rank of matrix and the parameter quantity.

② A Context2Question attention layer is added to the decoder, which is similar to Bi-DAF. The paper mentions that the DCN[34] model was referenced, and the dot product of D (i.e., c) and Q (i.e., q) is added to the attention value. The formula is as follows:

$$f(q, c) = \boldsymbol{W}_0[q, c, q \odot c] \tag{7.72}$$

③ The decoder used in QA-Net is similar to that used in Bi-DAF. In addition to the design of the model network, the paper extends the data and uses the English–French and French–English corpora to expand the training datasets. However, if the machine translation model is not sufficiently accurate, errors will be introduced and the expected quality will be reduced, affecting the performance of the QA-Net model.

7.7 Implementing BERT-Based Automatic Answering Using MindSpore

The interfaces and processes of MindSpore may constantly change due to iterative development. For all runnable code, see the code in corresponding chapters at https://mindspore.cn/resource. You can scan the QR code on the right to access relevant resources.

In order to implement BERT-based automatic answering, we can split the implementation process into two parts: dataset preparation and BERT network training.

---

[32] See: Kaiser L, Gomez A N, Chollet F. Depthwise Separable Convolutions for Neural Machine Translation [EB/OL]. 2017 [2019-11-10] https://arxiv.org/pdf/1706.03059.pdf.

[33] See: Chollet F. Xception: Deep Learning with Depthwise Separable Convolutions [C]. Proceedings of the IEEE conference on computer vision and pattern recognition, 2017:1251–1258.

[34] See: Xiong C, Zhong V, Socher R. Dynamic Coattention Networks for Question Answering [EB/OL]. 2016 [2019-11-10] https://arxiv.org/pdf/1611.01604.pdf.s

Dataset preparation involves converting the original set of automatic answering text into the input format required by the BERT network. We start by defining the Bert-ForQuestionAnswer class to construct the network structure, which consists of two fully connected independent layers. These layers are added to the BERT pre-training network to predict the start and end positions of the answer in a paragraph. We then define the BertForQuestionAnswerLoss class to calculate the loss function and construct the QANetworkWithLoss class to integrate the network and loss function into an end-to-end training model.

7.7.1 Preparing the Dataset

Taking the SQuAD 1.0 open dataset as an example, sort the corpus into question–answer pairs, where the first half of each sentence is a question, and the second half is a paragraph containing the answer. Use the tokenize() function in the tokenization package to segment each sentence, where the WordPiece model method is used, [CLS] and [SEP] are used to start and end each sentence, and [SEP] is inserted in the middle as the delimiter between the first half and the second half of the sentence. The word after tokenization is further converted into a unique number by using the convert_tokens_to_ids() function in the tokenization package. In addition, the start_position and end_position of the answer are recorded in each paragraph. The parameter token_type_id indicates whether the word in the corresponding position belongs to the first or second half of the sentence, and input_mask can be used to mask unwanted words in the calculation of the Transformer's attention mechanism. The processed data is stored in a file using the MindSpore data format, with each data entry including attributes such as input_ids, input_mask, token_type_id, start_positions, and end_positions.

Create an NLP dataset using the MindSpore data format API. For details about this API and how to implement the train_dataset() function, see Chap. 14.

7.7.2 Training the BERT Network

Define the BertForQuestionAnswer class of the network structure. Note that mindspore.nn.Cell needs to be inherited, as shown in Code 7.1.

BertModel and BertConfig are built-in modules of MindSpore and can be directly called. The construct function in the BertForQuestionAnswer() class is shown in Code 7.2.

Code 7.1 Defining BertForQuestionAnswer

```
from.bert_model import BertModel, BertConfig
class BertForQuestionAnswer(nn.Cell):
    def __init__(self, config, is_training):
        super(BertForQuestionAnswer, self).__init__()
        self.is_training = is_training
        self.batch_size = config.batch_size
        self.seq_length = config.seq_length
        self.hidden_size = config.hidden_size
        self.weight_init =
        TruncatedNormal(config.initializer_range)
        self.output_weights =
        Parameter(_initializer(self.weight_init, [2,
        config.hidden_size]), name= 'output_weight')
        self.output_bias = Parameter(_initializer('zero', 2),
        name= 'output_bias')
        self.bert = BertModel(config, self.is_training)
        self.reshape = P.Reshape()
        self.matmul = P.MatMul(transpose_b=True)
        self.bias_add = P.BiasAdd()
```

Code 7.2 Constructing a Network Structure Using the Construct Function

```
def construct(self, input_ids, input_mask, token_type_id):
    sequence_output, _, _ = self.bert(input_ids,
    token_type_id, input_mask)
    final_hidden_matrix = self.reshape(sequence_output,
    [self.batch_size*self.seq_length, self.hidden_size])
    start_logits = self.matmul(final_hidden_matrix,
    self.output_weights)
    start_logits = self.bias_add(start_logits,
    self.output_bias)
    end_logits = self.matmul(final_hidden_matrix,
    self.output_weights)
    end_logits = self.bias_add(end_logits, self.output_bias)
    start_logits = self.reshape(start_logits,
    [self.batch_size, self.seq_length])
    end_logits = self.reshape(end_logits, [self.batch_size,
    self.seq_length])
    return start_logits, end_logits
```

The output of the BERT pre-training network is sequence_output, and its dimension is [batch_size, seq_length, hidden_size]. Here, seq_length represents the length of the sequence, and hidden_size represents the dimension of the word vector corresponding to each word obtained through the BERT network. After the two fully connected layers feed information into sequence_output, the prediction outputs of the answer in the start and end positions are obtained, with the dimension being [batch_size, seq_length]. Once the network structure and outputs have been obtained, define the BertForQuestionAnswerLoss class and the loss function, as shown in Code 7.3.

Code 7.3 Defining BertForQuestionAnswerLoss

```
class BertForQuestionAnswerLoss(nn.Cell):
    def __init__(self, config):
        super(BertForQuestionAnswerLoss, self).__init__()
        self.seq_length = config.seq_length
        self.one_hot = P.OneHot()
        self.log_softmax = nn.LogSoftmax(axis=-1)
        self.reduce_mean = P.ReduceMean()
        self.reduce_sum = P.ReduceSum()
    def construct(self, start_logits, end_logits,
                    start_positions, end_positions):
        one_hot_start = self.one_hot(start_positions,
        depth=self.seq_length)
        log_probs_start = self.log_softmax(start_logits)
        loss_start = -
        self.reduce_mean(self.reduce_sum(one_hot_start *
        log_probs_start), -1)
    one_hot_end = self.one_hot(end_positions,
    depth=self.seq_length)
    log_probs_end = self.log_softmax(end_logits)
    loss_end = -self.reduce_mean(self reduce_sum(one_hot_end *
    log_probs_end), -1)
    total_loss =(loss_start+loss_end) / 2.0
    return total_loss
```

The start and end positions of ground truth prediction words are start_positions and end_positions, respectively, which need to be converted into one-hot vectors. The prediction outputs of the BertForQuestionAnswer network are start_logits and end_logits, where the two regression tasks are in the start position and the end position, and the loss functions are loss_start and loss_end. Once the BertForQuestionAnswerLoss class is defined, construct the QANetworkWithLoss class to integrate the network and loss function into an end-to-end training model, as shown in Code 7.4.

Finally, the function for training the network is shown in Code 7.5.

Code 7.4 Defining the Overall Network Structure and QANetworkWithLoss

```
class QANetworkWithLoss(nn.Cell):
    def __init__(self, config, is_training):
        super(QANetworkWithLoss, self).__init__()
        self.is_training = is_training
        self.bert = BertForQuestionAnswer(config, is_training)
        self.loss = BertForQuestionAnswerLoss(config)
        self.cast = P.Cast()
    def construct(self, input_ids, input_mask, token_type_id,
                  start_positions, end_positions):
        start_logits, end_logits = self.bert(input_ids,
        input_mask, token_type_id)
        total_loss = self.loss(start_logits, end_logits,
        start_positions, end_positions)
        return self.cast(total_loss, mstype.float32)
```

Code 7.5 Training the BERT Model for Automatic Answering

```
from mindspore optim import AdamWeightDecay
from mindspore import Model
from mindspore.application.model_zoo.bert import BertConfig,
QANetworkWithLoss,
BertTrainOneStepCell
def train_model():
    dataset = train_dataset()
    config = BertConfig(batch_size=1)
    netwithloss = QANetworkWithLoss(config, True)
    netwithgrads = BertTrainOneStepCell(netwithloss,
    optimizer=AdamWeightDecay(netwithloss.trainable_params()))
    model =
    Model(netwithgrads,optimizer=AdamWeightDecay(netwithloss.tra
    inable_params()))
    model.train(1, dataset)
```

References

1. J. Pennington, R. Socher, C. Manning, GloVe: global vectors for word representation, in *Proceedings of the 2014 Conference on Empirical Methods in Natural Language Processing (EMNLP)* (2014), pp. 1532–154

2. Le, Quoc, Mikolov, et al. Distributed representations of sentences and documents, in *International Conference on Machine Learning* (2014), pp. 1188–1196
3. A. Vaswani, N. Shazeer, N. Parmar, et al., Attention is all you need. Adv. Neural Inform. Proc. Syst. 5998–6008 (2017)
4. J. Berant, A. Chou, R. Frostig, et al., Semantic parsing on freebase from question-answer Pairs, in *Proceedings of the 2013 Conference on Empirical Methods in Natural Language Processing* (2013), pp. 1533–1544
5. X. Yao, B. Van Durme, Information extraction over structured data: question answering with freebase, in *Proceedings of the 52nd Annual Meeting of the Association for Computational Linguistics* (2014), pp. 956–966
6. W. Wang, N. Yang, F. Wei, et al., Gated self-matching networks for reading comprehension and question answering, in *Proceedings of the 55th Annual Meeting of the Association for Computational Linguistics* (2017), pp. 189–198

Chapter 8
Unsupervised Learning: Graph Vector

Graph data involves rich and complex potential relationships and plays an important role in many real-world applications, being used extensively in areas such as
social networks, recommendation systems, science, and NLP. As AI continues to
gain popularity, a growing number of machine learning tasks need to analyze and
process graph data. One effective method for graph analysis is to map a graph's
elements to a low-dimensional vector space while retaining the graph's structure
and property information. This low-dimensional vector is called a graph vector (or
"graph embedding"), which is described below.

8.1 Graph Vector Overview

A graph is a data structure comprising a set of vertices, which are interconnected by
lines called edges, and relationships between the vertices, as shown in Fig. 8.1. The
graph is called a directed graph if each edge has a direction (in this case, the edges
are similarly known as directed edges). Conversely, the graph is called an undirected
graph if the edges have no direction. Two graphs are isomorphic if they have the same
number of vertices and edges and if the second graph can be obtained by permuting
all vertices in the first graph one by one to the names of the vertices in the second
graph. For example, a pentagon with five vertices and a five-pointed star with five
vertices are considered isomorphic. The number of edges associated with the vertex
represents the degree of a vertex. A common storage representation of a graph is the
adjacency matrix, which can be represented by the vertex set V and the edge matrix
E, as shown in Formula (8.1).

© Tsinghua University Press 2021   151
L. Chen, *Deep Learning and Practice with MindSpore*, Cognitive Intelligence
and Robotics, https://doi.org/10.1007/978-981-16-2233-5_8

Fig. 8.1 Common storage
representation of a graph

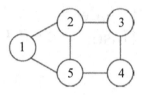

$$V = (v_1, v_2, v_3, v_4, v_5) \, E = \begin{bmatrix} 0 & 1 & 0 & 0 & 1 \\ 1 & 0 & 1 & 0 & 1 \\ 0 & 1 & 0 & 1 & 0 \\ 0 & 0 & 1 & 0 & 1 \\ 1 & 1 & 0 & 1 & 0 \end{bmatrix} \quad (8.1)$$

Graphs are used in all sorts of real-world applications (e.g., in communication networks, social networks, e-commerce networks, and traffic networks). Because they contain rich information, comprising potentially billions of vertices and relationships between the vertices (edges), graph analysis is of particular importance.

However, these graphs are usually high-dimensional ones that contain massive volumes of information, making it difficult to directly process them. An important method for analyzing and processing such graphs is the graph embedding method (GEM), which uses a low dimension, dense vector to represent a graph's vertex and reflect its structure information. The following key features [1] are paramount in a good GEM [1].

1. Neighborhood awareness: The distance between hidden vectors on vertices reflects the distance between the vertices on the graph.
2. Low dimension: This feature is necessary to facilitate subsequent calculations.
3. Adaptation: Adding a vertex (or edge) should not cause all calculation processes to be repeated.
4. Continuity: Continuous representations have smooth decision boundaries and enable refined representations of the graph members.

Depending on the application scenario, the GEM can be divided into vertex embedding, edge embedding, mixed embedding, and whole graph embedding. In the first category, vertex embedding, algorithms such as the classical DeepWalk and Node2Vec, and graph-based neural network ones such as graph convolutional networks (GCNs) and graph attention networks (GATs), are used.

The classical GEMs have two disadvantages: First, during the learning embedding process, parameters are not shared between vertices, and calculation efficiency is low. Second, because learning is directly performed on a particular structure graph, there is a lack of generalization ability, and new or dynamic graphs cannot be processed. Although CNNs are well known for processing Euclidean data, non-Euclidean data is difficult to process. CNNs and GEMs have promoted the development of the graph neural network (GNN) model, which captures the dependence of graphs through message transfer between vertices of graphs. Despite the original GNN being difficult to train and offering suboptimal results, researchers have made significant improvements in its network architecture, optimization methods, and parallel computing, enabling it to achieve good learning capabilities. Over the last few years, GNN has become a popular graph analysis method [2] due to advantages such as excellent performance and high interpretability. In addition, the algorithms represented by GCNs and graph attention networks are gaining significant attention.

This chapter explores the vertex embedding algorithm, with each section centering on the following topics:

1. Section 8.2 focuses on the classical graph embedding method DeepWalk.
2. Section 8.3 examines the classical graph embedding method Large-scale Information Network Embedding (LINE).
3. Section 8.4 discusses the classical graph embedding method Node2Vec.
4. Sections 8.5 and 8.6 cover the algorithms based on graph neural networks, including GCN and GAT.
5. Section 8.7 delves into the application of graph neural networks in the recommendation system.

8.2 DeepWalk Algorithm

The sparsity of graph representation data (such as the adjacency matrix) makes it a challenging task to design algorithms. We need to eliminate the adverse impacts of data sparsity during network application (such as network classification, recommendation, and anomaly detection) in order to develop high-quality machine learning algorithms. Establishing a method to map the complex and high-dimensional sparse graph data to the low-dimensional dense vector is therefore of the utmost importance. Because machine learning cannot directly deal with natural languages, we must convert words into vectors composed of numeric values so that we can subsequently establish models for analysis. In the field of NLP, one of the most prominent algorithms is Word2Vec, which was inspirational in Bryan Perozzi's proposal of the DeepWalk algorithm [1] in 2014. DeepWalk, a classical unsupervised learning algorithm in graph embedding, performs well in the absence of information and is readily usable by statistical models.

8.2.1   Principles of the DeepWalk Algorithm

The DeepWalk algorithm learns the low-dimensional vector representation of a vertex
in a graph by truncating the local information of the random walk (which is often
used as a similarity measure in content recommendation and community discovery).
In the field of natural language, we can consider the vertex as a word, and the
sequence of the vertices obtained through the random walk is like a sentence. The
input of the DeepWalk algorithm is a connected graph (either directed or undirected),
and the output is a vector representation of all vertices in the graph. Figure 8.2
provides an example of low-dimensional vector representation of the DeepWalk
learning vertex, where (a) shows that the input is a graph and (b) shows that the
output is a two-dimensional vector representation of each vertex in the input graph.

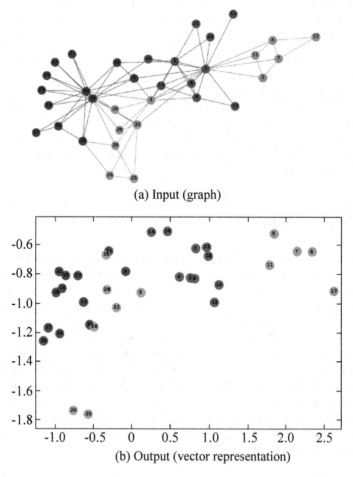

(a) Input (graph)

(b) Output (vector representation)

Fig. 8.2   Example of low-dimensional vector representation of the DeepWalk learning vertex

The vector dimension is determined to be 2 because the two-dimensional vector is easy to visualize. In the figure, the vertices shown in the same color are similar to each other. The more vertices that two vertices have in common, the shorter the distance between the two-dimensional vectors corresponding to the two vertices.

In order to perform model learning using the natural language modeling algorithm, datasets are required, which are the corpus of several sentences and the vocabulary of several words. Conversely, in the DeepWalk algorithm, the corpus is a set of random walk vertex sequences with limited length, and the vocabulary is the vertex of the graph.

The DeepWalk algorithm is divided into two parts—the input (graph) and the output (vector representation)—as shown in the following figure.

1. Generating a vertex sequence through random walk

We define a random walk W_{v_i} with vertex v_i as its root vertex. For graph G, we first perform an even, random sampling on a vertex v_i, which is the root vertex of the random walk W_{v_i}. We then perform uniform sampling on the neighbors of the currently sampled vertex until the number of vertices in the random walk reaches the maximum length t. Note that the lengths of vertex sequences in the random walk can be different. Random walk not only captures community information, but also has the following two advantages:

1. Parallel local exploration for the vertex is easy to implement.
2. Global recalculation is not required when minor changes occur locally, thereby facilitating online learning.

2. Skip-Gram

Skip-Gram is a Word2Vec algorithm in NLP [3] and can learn the random walk W_{v_i} to obtain a vector representation. Given a keyword, Skip-Gram calculates the probability of maximizing the occurrence of surrounding words; that is, it predicts the context. This is explained in more detail in Sect. 7.1. Skip-Gram traverses all possible collocations appearing in the random walk window w. For each collocation, the occurrence probability of neighbor vertices is maximized by each vertex v_i and its representation vector $\Phi(v_j) \in \mathbb{R}^d$. The label dimension is equal to the number $|V|$ of vertices (similar to the one-hot vector), and the number of vertices is generally large. Using Softmax to calculate this probability directly would consume a large amount of computing resources for learning, so instead we can use the hierarchical Softmax [4, 5], which approximates the probability to accelerate the training. Hierarchical Softmax takes the prediction problem and, by assigning vertices to leaf nodes of a binary tree, converts it into maximizing the probability of a path. If we assume that the path to the vertex u_k is a sequence $(b_0, b_1, ..., b_{\lceil \log|V| \rceil})$ regarding the tree node, we can obtain the following:

$$P(u_k|\Phi(v_j)) = \prod_{l=1}^{\lceil \log|V| \rceil} P(b_l|\Phi(v_j)) \qquad (8.2)$$

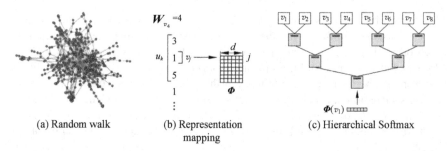

(a) Random walk   (b) Representation   (c) Hierarchical Softmax
                             mapping

Fig. 8.3 Process of the DeepWalk algorithm

where

$P(u_k|\Phi(v_j))$ is the probability that the vertex u_k is the context of the vertex v_j;
$\Phi(v_j)$ is the vector representation of the vertex v_j; and
$P(b_l|\Phi(v_j))$ is the probability that the lth node in the path of the vertex u_k is selected along the binary tree starting from the vertex v_j.

For $P(u_k|\Phi(v_j))$, the calculation of time complexity decreases from $O(|V|)$ to $O(\log|V|)$.

Figure 8.3 and the subsequent description provide details about the process used in the DeepWalk algorithm.

1. In Fig. 8.3a, a random walk sequence W_{v_4} with v_4 as the root vertex is obtained.
2. In Fig. 8.3b, a sample is generated on a sequence W_{v_4} by continuously sliding the window (with a length of $2w + 1$). If we assume that the vertex in the window is [1, 3, 5] and the sample is {(1, 3), (1, 5)}, we can conclude that the center vertex v_1 is mapped to its vector representation $\Phi(v_1)$.
3. In Fig. 8.3c, Hierarchical Softmax decomposes $P(v_3|\Phi(v_1))$ and $P(v_5|\Phi(v_1))$ into probability distribution that corresponds to the path from the root to v_3 and v_5. It maximizes the two probabilities by updating Φ, which is the vertex representation matrix that needs to be calculated.

8.2.2 Implementation of the DeepWalk Algorithm

This section builds on the theoretical information provided earlier by outlining the pseudocode necessary to implement DeepWalk and Skip-Gram.

Algorithm 8.1 Pseudocode for Implementing DeepWalk

Input: Graph $G(V, E)$, window size w, embedding size d, number γ of times that each vertex is walked, and walk length t

Output: Vertex representation matrix $\Phi \in \square^{|V| \times d}$

(1) Initialization: Sample Φ from $U^{|V| \times d}$

(2) Establish a binary tree T from V

(3) For each iteration $i = 0$ to γ, execute:

(4)   Disorder the vertex sequence $O = $ Shuffle(V)

(5)   For each vertex $v_i \in O$, execute:

(6)   Generate random walk with v_i as the root vertex, where $W_{v_i} = $ RandomWalk

            (G, v_i, t)

(7)   Learn embedding by using Skip-Gram (Φ, W_{v_i}, w)

(8) End

Algorithm 8.2 Pseudocode for Implementing Skip-Gram

Input: Vertex representation matrix Φ, random walk sequence W_{v_i}, and window size w

Output: New vertex representation matrix Φ

(1) For each vertex $v_j \in W_{v_i}$ execute:

(2)   For each vertex in the window $u_k \in W_{v_i}[j - w: j + w]$, execute:

(3)   Calculate $J(\Phi) = -\log P(u_k | \Phi(v_j))$

(4)   Update vector representation $\Phi = \Phi - \alpha * \frac{\partial J}{\partial \Phi}$

(5)   End

(6) End

8.3   LINE Algorithm

DeepWalk performs well on many datasets because it is a graph embedding method based on random walk. However, the DeepWalk algorithm considers the similarities between points based on only the explicit connections between such points (e.g., points 6 and 7 in Fig. 8.4); it ignores the possibility that similarities may exist between points that are not connected in the information network. In Fig. 8.4, for example, there is no direct connection between points 5 and 6. But there are similarities between them, because they share points 1, 2, 3, and 4.

We can use an analogy here: If two people have many mutual friends, we can assume that those two people probably have common hobbies and habits. By carefully

Fig. 8.4 Information
network[1]

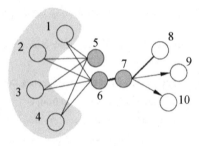

designing the loss function and considering the similarities between points 6 and 7 as well as those between points 5 and 6, we can ensure that the vector representation obtained by the LINE algorithm [6] retains information about both the local and global network architectures.

The LINE algorithm has strong universality and can be used for both directed and undirected graphs. Furthermore, it can be used for both weighted and unweighted graphs. The following sections provide a brief overview of the LINE algorithm and pseudocode for its implementation.

8.3.1   Principles of the LINE Algorithm

Directly connected points always exhibit similarities between them. If there is a direct connection between two vertices, the weight w_{ij} of the edge connecting the two vertices represents a first-order similarity, which is a direct similarity between the pairs of vertices. Conversely, if no direct connection exists between two vertices, the first-order similarity is 0. Figure 8.4 shows a first-order similarity, between points 6 and 7.

The first-order similarity applies only to undirected graphs. For each undirected edge (i, j) in an information network, the joint probability between the vertices v_i and v_j is defined as follows:

$$p_1(v_i, \ v_j) = \frac{1}{1 + \exp(-\mathbf{\Phi}(v_i)^{\mathrm{T}} \bullet \mathbf{\Phi}(v_j))} \tag{8.3}$$

where

$p_1 \ (v_i, v_j)$ is the joint probability between the vertices v_i and v_j;
$\mathbf{\Phi} \ (v_i)$ is the low-dimensional vector representation of the vertex v_i, and $\mathbf{\Phi} \ (v_i) \in \mathbb{R}^d$.

---

[1] Source: http://www.www2015.it/documents/proceedings/proceedings/p1067.pdf.

This formula defines probability distribution p ($\bullet, \bullet$) in $|V| \times |V|$, where V denotes the number of vertices. $\hat{p}_1 = \frac{w_{ij}}{W}$ is the empirical probability, where $W = \sum_{(i,j)\in E} w_{ij}$. To preserve the first-order similarity, we can use Kullback–Leibler (KL) divergence to define the following objective function:

$$D_{KL}\left(\hat{p}_1(\bullet, \bullet), p_1(\bullet, \bullet)\right) = \sum_{(i,j)\in E} \hat{p}_1(v_i, v_j)(\log \hat{p}_1(v_i, v_j) - \log p_1(v_i, v_j)) \quad (8.4)$$

where

$D_{KL}(\hat{p}_1 (\bullet, \bullet), p_1(\bullet, \bullet))$ is the KL divergence of the empirical joint probability distribution and the ground truth joint probability distribution;
$\hat{p}_1 (\bullet, \bullet)$ is the empirical joint probability distribution between vertices; and
$p_1 (\bullet, \bullet)$ is the ground truth joint probability distribution between vertices.

After removing constant terms from Formula (8.4), we can obtain the first-order similarity objective function:

$$O_1 = - \sum_{(i,j)\in E} w_{ij}\log p_1(v_i, v_j) \quad (8.5)$$

where

O_1 is the first-order similarity objective function of the LINE algorithm;
w_{ij} is the edge weight between the vertices v_i and v_j; and
$p_1(v_i, v_j)$ is the ground truth joint probability between the vertices v_i and v_j.

As mentioned earlier, the first-order similarity represents the similarity between the points that have direct connections. However, the information network may contain many other points that have no direct connections. For such cases, the second-order similarity is defined to cover the similarity between the neighbor network architectures of the vertices u and v. If we use $\boldsymbol{p}_u = \left(w_{u,1}, w_{u,2}, \ldots, w_{u,|V|}\right)$ to indicate the first-order similarity between the vertex u and all other vertices, we can conclude that the similarity between $\boldsymbol{p}_u$ and $\boldsymbol{p}_v$ is the second-order similarity between the vertices u and v. Similar to the first-order similarity, the second-order similarity between the vertices u and v is 0 if no vertex is connected to both u and v. Figure 8.4 shows a second-order similarity, between points 5 and 6.

For the second-order similarity, each vertex exists not only as itself but also as the context of other vertices, meaning that two additional vectors are required: $\boldsymbol{\Phi}(v_i)$ and $\boldsymbol{\Phi}(v_i)'$. $\boldsymbol{\Phi}(v_i)$ is the vector representation of the vertex v_i when it is regarded as itself, and $\boldsymbol{\Phi}(v_i)'$ is the vector representation of the vertex v_i when it is regarded as the context of other vertices. The second-order similarity can be used for both directed graphs and undirected graphs. In the information network, one undirected edge can be regarded as two directed edges, so for any directed edge (i, j), the probability that the vertex v_j becomes the context of v_i is defined as:

$$p_2(v_j|v_i) = \frac{\exp(\Phi(v_j)^{'T} \bullet \Phi(v_i))}{\sum_{k=1}^{|V|} \exp(\Phi(v_k)^{'T} \bullet \Phi(v_i))} \qquad (8.6)$$

where

$p_2(v_j \mid v_i)$ is the probability that the vertex v_j becomes the context of v_i;
$\Phi(v_i)^{'T}$ is the low-dimensional vector representation of v_j as the context; and.
$|V|$ is the number of vertices in the information network.

For each vertex v_i, Formula (8.6) defines conditional distribution $p_2(\bullet \mid v_i)$. Its empirical distribution $\hat{p}_2(\bullet \mid v_i)$ is defined as $\hat{p}_2\left(v_j|v_i\right) = \frac{w_{ij}}{d_i}$, where $d_i = \sum_{k \in N(i)} w_{ik}$ (which is the out-degree of the vertex v_i). To preserve the second-order similarity, we can use KL divergence to define the following objective function:

$$D_{KL}\left(\hat{p}_1(\bullet, \bullet), p_1(\bullet, \bullet)\right) = \sum_{(i,j) \in E} d_i \hat{p}_2(v_j|v_i)(\log \hat{p}_2(v_j|v_i) - \log p_2(v_j|v_i)) \quad (8.7)$$

where

$D_{KL}\left(\hat{p}_1(\bullet, \bullet), p_1(\bullet, \bullet)\right)$ is the KL divergence of the empirical joint probability distribution and the ground truth probability distribution between the vertices used as contexts;
$\hat{p}_2(v_j \mid v_i)$ is the empirical probability that the vertex v_j becomes the context of the vertex v_i; and.
d_i is the out-degree of the vertex.

After removing constant terms from Formula (8.7), we can obtain the second-order similarity objective function:

$$O_2 = -\sum_{(i,j) \in E} w_{ij} \log p_2(v_j|v_i) \qquad (8.8)$$

To preserve both the first- and second-order similarities, the LINE algorithm minimizes O_1 and O_2 and then concatenates the low-dimensional vectors obtained based on O_1 and O_2. This makes it possible to obtain the low-dimensional vector representation $\Phi(v_i)$ of each vertex v_i.

If O_2 is minimized directly, we must calculate the sum of all vertices when calculating the conditional distribution $p_2(\bullet \mid v_i)$, resulting in the time complexity of minimizing O_2 reaching $O(|V|^2)$. Here, the objective function that defines negative sampling becomes:

$$\log \sigma(\Phi(v_j)^{'T} \bullet \Phi(v_i)) + \sum_{n=1}^{K} E_{n \sim P_n(v)}[\log \sigma(-\Phi(v_n)^{'T} \bullet \Phi(v_i))] \qquad (8.9)$$

where

σ is the sigmoid function, and $\sigma(x) = \frac{1}{1+\exp(x)}$;
K is the number of negative samples in each data sampling; and
$P_n(v) \propto d_v^{3/4}$.

If we replace $\log p_2(v_j | v_i)$ with the objective function for negative sampling, the objective function of the second-order similarity becomes:

$$O_2 = -\sum_{(i,j) \in E} w_{ij} \left\{ \log\sigma(\Phi(v_j)'^T \bullet \Phi(v_i)) + \sum_{n=1}^{K} E_{v_n j P_n (v)}[\log\sigma(-\Phi(v_n)'^T \bullet \Phi(v_i))] \right\}$$
(8.10)

In addition, when O_1 is minimized directly, $u_{ik} = \infty$, where $i = 1, 2, ..., |V|$; and $k = 1, 2, ..., d$. To avoid $u_{ik} = \infty$, we need to change the objective function by performing negative sampling:

$$O_1 = -\sum_{(i,j) \in E} w_{ij} \left\{ \log\sigma(\Phi(v_j)^T \bullet \Phi(v_i)) + \sum_{n=1}^{K} E_{v_n \sim P_n (v)}[\log\sigma(-\Phi(v_n)^T \bullet \Phi(v_i))] \right\}$$ (8.11)

Regardless of whether O_1 or O_2 is minimized, the objective function includes w_{ij}, which appears in the gradient when we use the gradient descent method for minimization. For different edges, w_{ij} may vary significantly, making it difficult to select an appropriate learning rate. If we select a higher learning rate, gradient explosion may occur on the edge with a larger w_{ij}. Conversely, if we select a lower learning rate, gradient disappearance may occur on the edge with a smaller w_{ij}. To overcome this conundrum, we therefore need to perform edge sampling for optimization, by using the Alias method to sample the original weighted edges. The probability of each sampled edge is proportional to the weight of the edge in the original graph, and the sampled edge weight is used as a binary edge (the weight is 0 or 1). This solves the problem of w_{ij} differing for different edges.

8.3.2 Implementation of the LINE Algorithm

This section builds on the theoretical information provided earlier by outlining the pseudocode necessary to implement the LINE algorithm.

Algorithm 8.3 Pseudocode for Implementing the LINE Algorithm

Input: Graph $G(V, E)$, embedded dimension d, negative sample number K, and initial learning rate lr

Output: Dimension is $\Phi^{|V| \times d}$ low-dimensional dense vector representation

(1)   Minimize the first-order similarity loss function O_1:

(2)   Initialize the representation vector $\Phi(v_i)$, $i = 1, 2, ..., |V|$, where $\Phi(v_i) \in R^d$

(3)   Establish an edge sampling table based on graph $G(V, E)$ by using the Alias method

(4)   Establish a negative sample table based on negative sample number K and graph $G(V, E)$

(5)   When $(i, j) \in E$, cyclically execute:

(6)   Perform edge sampling based on the edge sampling table

(7)   Perform negative sampling based on the negative sampling table

(8)   End of cyclic execution

(9)   Optimize O_1 by using the asynchronous gradient descent

(10) Minimize the second-order similarity loss function O_2

(11) Initialize the representation vectors $\Phi(v_i)$ and $\Phi(v_i)'$, where $i = 1, 2, ..., |V|$, $\Phi(v_i) \in R^d$, and $\Phi(v_i)' \in R^d$

(12) Repeat steps (2) to (8)

(13) Optimize O_2 by using the asynchronous gradient descent

(14) Concatenate $\Phi(v_i)$ obtained based on O_1 and $\Phi(v_i)$ obtained based on O_2 to obtain the low-dimensional vector representation of the graph

8.4   Node2Vec Algorithm

The DeepWalk and LINE algorithms described in Sects. 8.2 and 8.3, respectively, depend on the strict concept of network neighborhood and both are insensitive to the network-specific connection mode. The DeepWalk algorithm samples the vertex neighborhood by using depth-first search (DFS) random walk, whereas the LINE algorithm samples vertices by using breadth-first search (BFS). As shown in Fig. 8.5, the Node2Vec algorithm—a graph embedding method and an extension of the Deep-Walk algorithm—integrates both DFS and BFS. In Fig. 8.5, the neighborhood for DFS is composed of vertices sampled in ascending order of distance to the source vertex u (e.g., s_4, s_5, and s_6), whereas that for BFS is limited to the vertices adjacent to the source vertex u (e.g., s_1, s_2, and s_3).

Fig. 8.5 DFS and BFS
policies from source vertex
u^2

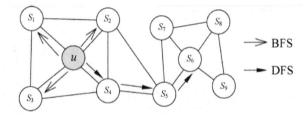

8.4.1 Principles of the Node2Vec Algorithm

The Node2Vec algorithm, proposed by Aditya Grover in 2016 [7], is used to learn
the continuous vector representations of a graph's vertices. Compared with both the
DeepWalk and LINE algorithms described earlier, Node2Vec can effectively explore
different neighborhoods (homogeneity and structural equivalency) by designing a
biased random walk process for vertices, allowing it to learn more comprehensive
representations of the vertices. The Node2Vec algorithm functions in a similar way
to the DeepWalk algorithm and can be divided into two processes: biased random
walk and learning vector representations.

1. **Biased random walk**

The biased random walk process is implemented by assigning different sampling
probabilities to different vertices. If we assume that the source vertex is u, the random
walk length is l, the *ith* vertex is c_i, and the start vertex is $c_0 = u$, we can use the
following formula to calculate the sampling probability of the vertex c_i:

$$P(c_i = x | c_{i-1} = v) = \begin{cases} \frac{\pi_{vx}}{Z}, & (v, x) \in E \\ 0, & \text{else} \end{cases} \tag{8.12}$$

where

π_{vx} is the unnormalized transition probability between the vertex v and the vertex
x; and
Z is a normalization constant.

To implement the biased random walk process, Node2Vec introduces p and q—
two parameters that are used in calculating the transition probability in Formula
(8.12). If we assume that the walk is performed through edge (t, v) to the vertex v, we
can calculate the transition probability of the edge (t, v) on the basis of v, allowing
us to determine the next vertex for the walk. We use the following unnormalized
transition probability:

---

[2] Source: https://cs.stanford.edu/~jure/pubs/node2vec-kdd16.pdf.

Fig. 8.6 Example of random walk

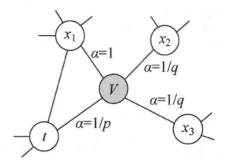

$$\pi_{vx} = \alpha_{pq}(t, x) \bullet w_{vx}\alpha_{pq}(t, x) = \begin{cases} \frac{1}{p} & d_{tx} = 0 \\ 1 & d_{tx} = 1 \\ \frac{1}{q} & d_{tx} = 2 \end{cases} \tag{8.13}$$

where d_{tx} is the shortest path distance from the vertex t to the vertex v.

d_{tx} must be one of $\{0, 1, 2\}$ so that the two parameters p and q can adequately control the walk process, as shown in Fig. 8.6. The return parameter p controls the probability of subsequently accessing the vertex in the previous step. If the current vertex is v, and p is greater than $\max(q, 1)$, the probability of accessing the vertex t in the previous step will decrease. Conversely, the probability will increase if p is less than $\min(q, 1)$. The "in–out" parameter q controls whether the walk process is more like BFS or DFS. A larger q indicates that the vertex for the random walk is closer to the vertex t, meaning that the walk process is more like BFS. Conversely, a smaller q indicates that the vertex is farther away, which is more like DFS.

Each sampling step in biased random walk is based on the transition probability π_{vx}. We can pre-calculate this probability by using the Alias sampling method [8, 9] and then use it directly in the sampling process. In this case, the sampling complexity is $O(1)$, meaning that the walk process of the algorithm is faster.

2.   **Vector representations of vertices**

The biased random walk process enables us to obtain a set of vertex sequences for random walk. Now we will introduce learning vector representations of vertices.

For a given graph $G = (V, E)$, the mapping function from a vertex to a vector representation is $f: V \rightarrow \mathbb{R}^d$, where d is the dimension of a representation vector. For each vertex $u \in V$, an algorithm is used to learn the vertex vector representation. This enables us to subsequently optimize the following formula of the objective function:

$$f^* = \underset{f}{\text{argmax}} \sum_{u \in V} \log P(N_s(u)|f(u)) \tag{8.14}$$

where

$f(u)$ is the vector representation of the vertex u; and
$N_S(u)$ is the neighborhood of the vertex u under the neighborhood sampling strategy S.

However, due to the complexity involved in solving the optimization problem, we introduce the following two assumptions:

1. Conditional independence assumption:

$$P(N_S(u)|f(u)) = \prod_{n_i \in N_S(u)} P(n_i|f(u)) \tag{8.15}$$

where n_i is the vertex in the neighborhood of the vertex u under the neighborhood sampling strategy S.

2. Feature space symmetry assumption:

$$P(n_i|f(u)) = \frac{\exp(f(n_i) \bullet f(u))}{\sum_{v \in V} \exp(f(v) \bullet f(u))} \tag{8.16}$$

Given these two assumptions, we can simplify the objective function in Formula (8.14) as follows:

$$\frac{\partial E}{\partial u_j} = t_j - y_j = e_j f^*$$
$$= \operatorname*{argmax}_f \sum_{u \in V} [-\log Z_u + \sum_{n_i \in N_S(u)} f(n_i) \bullet f(u)] \tag{8.17}$$

where Z_u is the partition function of each vertex, and $Z_u = \sum_{v \in V} \exp(f(u) \bullet (f(v)))$.

By using negative sampling, we are able to minimize the calculation costs of the partition function. And to optimize Formula (8.17), we can use SGD—similar to training a neural network—in order to continuously learn the parameters of mapping f to obtain the vector representation of each vertex.

8.4.2 Implementation of the Node2Vec Algorithm

Similar to the DeepWalk algorithm, the Node2Vec algorithm is mainly used to generate random walk sequences and learn vector representations. In this section, we describe how to implement the Node2Vec algorithm through pseudocode.

Algorithm 8.4 Pseudocode for Implementing Node2Vec

Input: Graph G (V, E, W), embedding dimension d, number of times γ that each vertex is walked, walk length l, window size w, return parameter p, and in-out parameter q

Output: Embedded mapping function f

(1)   Calculate the transition probability π = PreprocessModifiedWeights (G, p, q)

(2)   Initialize walk to null

(3)   For each iteration iter = 1 to γ, execute:

(4)   For each vertex $u \in V$

(5)   Generate random walk = node2vecWalk (G', u, l)

(6)   Save the random walk to "walks"

(7)   Learn mapping f = stochastic gradient descent (w, d, walks)

node2vecWalk (graph G' = (V, E, π), start vertex u, walk length l)

(1)   Initialize walk to [u]

(2)   For the walk from the source vertex walk_iter = 1 to l, execute:

(3)   Obtain the current vertex curr = walk[-1]

(4)   Obtain the neighbor of the current vertex V_curr = GetNeighbors (curr, G')

(5)   Sample vertex s = AliasSample (V_{curr}, π)

(6)   Save the sampled vertex s to the end of walk

(7)   Return walk

8.5   GCN Algorithm

In the field of computer vision, CNNs achieve good results because discrete convolution can effectively extract spatial features. For low-dimensional matrices (such as images or videos) where pixels are ordered, CNNs calculate weighted summation of center and adjacent pixels to extract spatial features. But when given high-dimensional graph data that lacks an ordered structure, CNNs find it difficult to process the data. In order to solve this problem, Bruna et al. proposed GCNs, which aggregate the vertex information of irregular graph data.

The approaches that apply convolution to graph domain can be divided into spectral and non-spectral. The GCN is a spectral approach that, by leveraging the spectral graph theory, implements convolution operations on topologies, and uses the Laplacian matrix to move convolution operations in the spatial domain to the spectral domain. By representing any vector on a graph as a linear combination of Laplacian eigenmatrices, the features of the graph can be extracted in the spectral domain. This results in the GCN being more effective than the non-spectral approach, which directly extracts the features in the spatial domain. Furthermore, because the GCN model can extract information about the entire graph in one go, and the parameters of the filter can be shared at all positions in the graph [10], there is no need to calculate the parameters of the filter for each vertex. This in turn significantly reduces the complexity of the model.

Building on the first generation of GCN, Defferranrd et al. proposed to replace the convolution kernel with the Chebyshev polynomial summation [11]. This method enables us to obtain a smooth filter in the frequency domain while reducing the model complexity. Subsequently, numerous approaches for replacing the convolution kernel with mathematical transformation have emerged. In the model described in the following section, Kipf and Welling limit the filter to run in the first-order neighborhood around each vertex, thereby reducing the calculation costs, increasing the network efficiency, and improving the model accuracy.

8.5.1 Principles of the GCN Algorithm

The formula of the two-layer GCN model selected by Kipf and Welling is as follows:

$$Z = f(\mathbf{X}, \mathbf{A}) = \text{Softmax}\left(\hat{A}\,\text{ReLU}\left(\hat{A}\mathbf{X}\mathbf{W}^{(0)}\right)\mathbf{W}^{(1)}\right) \tag{8.18}$$

where $\hat{A} = \tilde{\mathbf{D}}^{-\frac{1}{2}}\tilde{A}\tilde{\mathbf{D}}^{-\frac{1}{2}}$, $\tilde{\mathbf{D}}_{ii} = \sum_j \tilde{A}_{ij}$, and $\tilde{A} = A + \mathbf{I}_N$;

$\mathbf{A}$ is the adjacency matrix of a graph;
$\mathbf{W}^l$ represents $\mathbf{W}^{(0)}$ and $\mathbf{W}^{(1)}$, which are weight parameters; and
$\mathbf{X}$ is the vertex eigenmatrix of the graph.

The following explains the origin of Formula (8.18), starting with the formula:

$$L = \mathbf{I}_N - \mathbf{D}^{-1/2}L\mathbf{D}^{-1/2} \tag{8.19}$$

We use this formula to define the symmetric normalized Laplacian matrix, where $\mathbf{D}$ is the vertex degree matrix.

The Laplacian matrix is then decomposed to obtain the following:

$$L = \mathbf{U}\Lambda\mathbf{U}^{\mathsf{T}} \tag{8.20}$$

where

$\mathbf{U}$ is the normalized Laplacian eigenvector matrix (i.e., a spectral matrix), and
Λ is the corresponding eigenvalue matrix (a diagonal matrix).

The spectral convolution on the graph may be defined as the product of the signal $x \in \mathbb{R}$ and the filter $\text{diag}(\theta)$ $(\theta \in \mathbb{R})$ in the Fourier domain, that is:

$$q_\vartheta \star x = U q_\vartheta \, U^T \, x \qquad (8.21)$$

where

$U^T x$ is the graph Fourier transform of x; and
g_θ is the function of the eigenvector $\mathcal{L}$, that is, $g_\theta(\Lambda)$.

Computing the Laplacian eigenmatrix involves substantial overheads if the graph data is large, so to reduce the calculation complexity, we can use the K-order truncation of Chebyshev polynomial and thereby approximate $g_\theta(\Lambda)$.

$$g_{\theta'}(\Lambda) \approx \sum_{k=0}^{K} \theta_k' T_K(\tilde{\Lambda}) \qquad (8.22)$$

where

$\tilde{\Lambda}$ is the eigenvector matrix after scaling is performed based on the maximal eigenvalue λ_{max}, of $\mathcal{L}$, and $\tilde{\Lambda} = 2/\lambda_{max} \bullet \Lambda - I_N$; and
θ' is the Chebyshev parameter vector, where $\theta' \in \mathbb{R}^K$. The Chebyshev polynomial is defined by recursion: $T_k(x) = 2xT_{k-1} - T_{k-2}(x)$, where $T_0(x) = 1$ and $T_1(x) = x$.

By replacing g_θ with $g_{\theta'}$, we can obtain:

$$g_{\theta'} \star x \approx_z U \sum_{k=0}^{K} \theta' T_k(\tilde{\Lambda}) U^T x$$

$$= \sum_{k=0}^{K} \theta' U T_k(\tilde{\Lambda}) U^T x \qquad (8.23)$$

$T_k(\tilde{\Lambda})$ is a k-order polynomial of Λ, and $U \, \tilde{\Lambda}^{\,k} U^T = (U \, \tilde{\Lambda} \, U^T)^k = \tilde{L}^k$, where $\tilde{L} = \frac{2}{\lambda_{max}} L - I_N$. Formula (8.22) can therefore be expressed as follows:

$$g_{\theta'} \star x \approx \sum_{k=0}^{K} \theta' T_k(\tilde{L}) x \qquad (8.24)$$

With the Chebyshev polynomial approximation, the spectral convolution is no longer dependent on the entire graph. Instead, it is related to only the k-order vertices (i.e., the kth-order neighborhood) of the center vertex.

After we perform the Chebyshev polynomial approximation, we can consider each convolution operation as aggregating the k-order neighbor information for each center vertex. Even so, the calculation amount remains high after approximation because the graph structure data is large. In order to reduce the calculation costs, we can further simplify the calculation by letting $k = 1$, meaning that the information of only first-order neighbors is aggregated at any given time. In this case, the spectral convolution can be approximated as a linear function of $\tilde{L}$. As mentioned earlier, only the dependence between the center vertex and the first-order neighbor is established. In order to solve this problem, a stacked GCN must be used to establish the dependence of k-order neighbors. We are able to obtain the first-order neighbor information of the second-order graph convolution after superimposing the first-order neighbor of the second-order graph convolution. This means that the center vertex will obtain the second-order neighbor information through the first-order neighbor of the second-order graph convolution, and so on. Furthermore, the Chebyshev polynomial does not limit the dependence of k-order neighbors when this dependence is established.

We can further simplify the calculation. In the linear model of the GCN, we can obtain the following first-order linear approximate expression of spectral convolution by defining $\lambda_{max} \approx 2$:

$$g_{\theta'} \star x \approx \theta_0' x + \theta_1' (L - I_N) x$$
$$= \theta_0' x - \theta_1' D^{-\frac{1}{2}} A D^{-\frac{1}{2}} x \tag{8.25}$$

Formula (8.25) includes only two parameters: θ_0' and θ_1'. So to establish the dependence of k-order neighbors, we can use a k-layer filter.

We limit the number of parameters to avoid overfitting and minimize the matrix multiplication of each layer to reduce the calculation complexity. If we let $\theta = \theta_0' = -\theta_1'$, we can express Formula (8.25) as follows:

$$g_\theta \star x \approx \vartheta \left(I_N + D^{-\frac{1}{2}} A D^{-\frac{1}{2}} \right) x \tag{8.26}$$

The eigenvalue range of $I_N + I_N + D^{-\frac{1}{2}} A D^{-\frac{1}{2}}$ is [0, 2], meaning that when the operation is repeated continuously (in very deep networks), gradient explosion or disappearance may occur. To avoid this problem, the renormalization trick is introduced:

$$I_N + D^{-\frac{1}{2}} A D^{-\frac{1}{2}} \rightarrow \tilde{D}^{-\frac{1}{2}} \tilde{A} \tilde{D}^{-\frac{1}{2}} \tag{8.27}$$

where $\tilde{\mathbf{A}} = \mathbf{A} + \mathbf{I}_N$, $\tilde{\mathbf{D}}_{ii} = \sum_j \tilde{\mathbf{A}}$ When the representation of each vertex in a graph is not a separate scalar but is instead a vector of size C, we can use its variants for processing:

$$\mathbf{Z} = \tilde{\mathbf{D}}^{-\frac{1}{2}} \tilde{\mathbf{A}} \tilde{\mathbf{D}}^{-\frac{1}{2}} \mathbf{X} \boldsymbol{\vartheta} \tag{8.28}$$

where

$\boldsymbol{\theta}$ is a parameter matrix, and $\boldsymbol{\theta} \in \mathbb{R}^{C \times F}$; and
$\mathbf{Z}$ is the corresponding convolution result, and $\mathbf{Z} \in \mathbb{R}^{N \times F}$

In this case, the vertex representation of each vertex is updated to a new F-dimensional vector that includes the information of the corresponding first-order neighbor.

We are now able to obtain the layer-by-layer propagation expression of the graph CNN:

$$\mathbf{H}^{(l+1)} = \sigma \left(\tilde{\mathbf{D}}^{-\frac{1}{2}} \tilde{\mathbf{A}} \tilde{\mathbf{D}}^{-\frac{1}{2}} \mathbf{H}^{(l)} \mathbf{W}^{(l)} \right) \tag{8.29}$$

where the input of the l-layer network is $\mathbf{H}^{(l)}$, and $\mathbf{H}^{(l)} \in \mathbb{R}^{N \times F}$ (initial input is $H^{(0)} = X$);

N is the number of vertices in the graph, and each vertex is represented by a d-dimensional eigenvector;
$\mathbf{W}^{(l)}$ is the weight parameter that needs to be trained, and $\mathbf{W}^{(l)} \in \mathbb{R}^{d \times d}$; and
σ is the activation function.

Through this derivation, we are able to obtain the GCN architecture:

$$\mathbf{Z} = f(\mathbf{X}, \mathbf{A}) = \text{Softmax} \left(\hat{\mathbf{A}} \text{ReLU} \left(\hat{\mathbf{A}} \mathbf{X} \mathbf{W}^{(0)} \right) \mathbf{W}^{(1)} \right) \tag{8.30}$$

8.5.2 Implementation of the GCN Algorithm

This section describes how to implement the GCN algorithm through pseudocode.

Algorithm 8.5 Pseudocode for Implementing GCN

Input: Graph G (V, E), vertex eigenmatrix X, adjacency matrix A, learning rate lr, and labeled vertex set y_L

Output: Output eigenmatrix Z

(1)   Randomly initialize the weight parameter W

(2)   Input the vertex feature X and the adjacency matrix A

(3)   Extract the vertex degree matrix D

(4)   Calculate the Laplacian matrix $\hat{A}$ based on the matrix D and the matrix A

(5)   Perform a graph convolution operation on X using $\hat{A}$ and W to obtain a feature map

(6)   Use the ReLU function for activation to obtain the output matrix Z_0

(7)   Perform the graph convolution operation based on the output Z_0 of the upper layer to obtain a new feature map

(8)   Use the Softmax function for activation to obtain the new output eigenmatrix Z

(9)   Use the loss function to calculate the loss between the output eigenmatrix Z and y_L

(10) Update the weight parameter W by using gradient descent

(11) Repeat steps (4) to (9)

(12) End

8.6 GAT Algorithm

For the spectral approaches represented by the GCN, each calculation relies on the Laplacian matrix eigenvector and graph structure. This makes it difficult to apply a GCN model on other graphs once it has been trained on a particular graph structure. Furthermore, because the GCN model lacks the inductive ability, it has a limited scope for application.

For the non-spectral approaches, convolution is defined directly on the graph to operate adjacent vertices in space. However, such approaches are problematic, in that it is challenging to define an operation that can handle neighbors of different sizes while also ensuring that CNN parameters can be shared. To address this challenge, researchers have made a series of improvements [12–15]. For example, in 2017, Hamilton et al. proposed a classical inductive learning algorithm called GraphSAGE. In GraphSAGE, sampling is performed based on the neighborhood of a fixed size, and each vertex is represented by an aggregate of its neighbors. This means that a vertex not present during the training can still be appropriately represented by its neighbor vertices if it subsequently appears at a later stage. GraphSAGE has shown promising results in several large-scale induction benchmark tests.

In practice, however, the impacts of neighbor vertices on the target vertices are different. The methods referred to earlier do not take into account that fact that different neighbors are of the same importance. In 2018, Petar et al., taking inspiration from the attention mechanism widely used in deep learning models, proposed the graph attention network (GAT) [16], a graph data vertex classification model based on the attention mechanism [16]. The attention mechanism imitates human intuition, focusing on salient parts helpful for the target task while ignoring other invalid information. Similarly, the GAT pays attention to its neighbors and determines the weights of the neighbor vertices through the self-attention strategy. Different neighbor vertices have different impacts on the target vertices, allowing the hidden representation of each target vertex to be calculated more effectively.

8.6.1 Principles of the GAT Algorithm

This section focuses on the graph attention layer, which is an important component of the graph attention network. Here we make the following assumptions:

- The input of the current attention layer is a set of vertex features: $h = \{\vec{h}_1, \vec{h}_2, ..., \vec{h}_N\}$, $\vec{h}_i \in \mathbb{R}^F$, where N is the number of vertices, and F is the number of features of each vertex.
- The output of the attention layer is a new set of vertex features: $h' = \{\vec{h}'_{1\,1}, \vec{h}'_2, ..., \vec{h}'_N\}$, $\vec{h}'_i \in \mathbb{R}^{F'}$.

Because we need at least one nonlinear transformation so that we can convert input features into higher-level features, we perform linear transformation on each vertex, and then use the self-attention mechanism a to calculate the attention correlation coefficient e_{ij}. This coefficient indicates the importance of the feature of vertex j to vertex i.

$$e_{ij} = a\left(W\vec{h}_i, W\vec{h}_j\right) \tag{8.31}$$

where

W is the weight matrix, and $W \in \mathbb{R}^{F' \times F}$; and
a is the self-attention mechanism $a: \mathbb{R}^{F'} \times \mathbb{R}^{F'} \to \mathbb{R}$.

We then introduce the attention mechanism into the graph structure through masked attention: e_{ij} is calculated only for vertices of $j \in N_i$, where N_i is a neighbor vertex of vertex i (and includes vertex i itself). To normalize all neighbor vertices j of vertex i, making it easier to compare the coefficients of different vertices, we use the Softmax function:

$$a_{ij} = \text{Softmax}_j(e_{ij}) = \frac{\exp(e_{ij})}{\sum_{k \in N_i} \exp(e_{ik})} \tag{8.32}$$

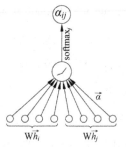
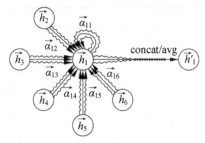

(a) Calculation of the attention coefficient

(b) Aggregation of the multi-head graph attention layer ($K = 3$)

Fig. 8.7 Network architecture of the attention mechanism[3]

The attention mechanism a may be a single-layer feedforward neural network, which is determined by $\vec{a} \in \mathbb{R}^{2F'}$ and LeakyReLU nonlinear activation function (slope $a = 0.2$ when the input is negative). Figure 8.7a shows the network architecture of the attention mechanism.

In order to calculate the attention coefficient, we use the following formula:

$$a_{ij} = \frac{\exp(\text{LeakyReLU}(\vec{a}^T[\boldsymbol{W}\vec{h}_i \| \boldsymbol{W}\vec{h}_j]))}{\sum_{k \in N_i} \exp(\text{LeakyReLU}(\vec{a}^T[\boldsymbol{W}\vec{h}_i \| \boldsymbol{W}\vec{h}_k]))} \tag{8.33}$$

where $\bullet^T$ indicates the transpose operation, and $\|$ indicates the concatenation operation.

By performing the preceding calculation, we are able to obtain the normalized attention coefficient, which we can subsequently use to calculate the output features of each vertex.

$$\vec{h}'_i = \sigma\left(\sum_{j \in N_i} a_{ij} \boldsymbol{W}\vec{h}_j\right) \tag{8.34}$$

Similar to the Transformer model proposed by Vaswani et al., extending the self-attention mechanism to the multi-head attention mechanism improves the calculation stability. The calculation process involves performing K calculations separately based

---

[3] Source: https://arxiv.org/pdf/1710.10903.pdf.

on the self-attention mechanism, and then concatenating the obtained features to obtain the final vertex representation:

$$\vec{h}_i^{'} = ||_{k=1}^{K} \sigma \left(\sum_{j \in N_i} a_{ij}^k \, \mathbf{W}^k \vec{h}_j \right) \tag{8.35}$$

where

a_{ij}^k is the normalized attention coefficient obtained through the *Kth* calculation based on the self-attention mechanism; and
W^k is the corresponding input weight matrix for linear transformation.

When the multi-head attention mechanism is used at the last layer of the network, concatenation is less effective and so is replaced with an averaging operation. After nonlinear activation, the vertex representation of the multi-head attention layer is obtained:

$$\vec{h}_i^{'} = \sigma \left(\frac{1}{K} \sum_{k=1}^{K} \sum_{j \in N_i} a_{ij}^k \, \mathbf{W}^k \vec{h}_j \right) \tag{8.36}$$

Figure 8.7b illustrates the aggregation process of the multi-head graph attention layer ($K = 3$). Different arrow styles in the graph represent separate attention calculation processes. The representation of a target vertex in the graph attention network is the weighted sum of its first-order neighbor vertices including the target vertex, which is a calculation process on a local graph.

The GAT has a number of advantages, such as high efficiency, flexibility, and portability. To achieve high efficiency, the GAT implements parallel calculation for the local graph vertex neighbor pair. To realize flexibility, it assigns different weights to vertices of different degrees. And in terms of portability, the model can be extended to unknown graphs, representing the ability of inductive learning. The GAT considers the different importance of neighbor vertices to target vertices and has achieved good results in some practical scenarios.

8.6.2 Implementation of the GAT Algorithm

This section describes how to implement the GAT algorithm through pseudocode.

Algorithm 8.6 Pseudocode for Implementing the GAT Algorithm

Input: Graph G (V, E), vertex feature h, vertex label y, learning rate lr, and number K of the units in the multi-head attention mechanism

Output: Weight parameter W and $\vec{a}$

(1)   Randomly initialize the weight parameter matrix W and $\vec{a}$

(2)   Repeatedly execute:

(3)   For the input layer and the hidden layer:

(4)   Execute the self-attention mechanism for each iteration iter = 0 to K

(5)   Calculate the attention cross-correlation coefficient α_{ij}

(6)   Calculate the output feature h' of the vertex under the self-attention mechanism

(7)   Concatenate K output eigenvectors to obtain the output feature h' of the vertex under the multi-head attention mechanism

(8)   Use the output feature h' as the input feature at the next layer

(9)   For the output layer:

(10)   Repeat steps (3) to (5)

(11)   Average K output eigenvectors to obtain the output feature h' of the vertex under the multi-head attention mechanism

(12)   Update the weight parameter matrix W and $\vec{a}$ based on the difference between the vertex label y and the output feature h'

(13)   Proceed until the stop condition is met

8.7 Application: Recommendation System

We are currently in the midst of an information boom driven by the unprecedented popularity of the Internet and the near-ubiquitous use of mobile terminals. In today's fast-paced world, people want information at their fingertips. But given the vast amounts of information now available, it has become critical to ensure that people can obtain what they want, when they need it. In order to meet such demands, the recommendation system is developed.

The existing recommendation systems employ collaborative filtering, indicating that similar users like the same items and, conversely, the same user likes similar items. This type of filtering is divided into memory-based methods and model-based methods.

Memory-based methods can be further divided into user-based and item-based collaborative filtering. User-based collaborative filtering recommends items to similar users, whereas item-based collaborative filtering recommends similar items to users. In order to implement these two methods, we need to define the similarity between items or users. Although these methods are simple, easy to understand, and easy to implement, a significant amount of time is required to calculate the similarities between each pair of items or users, and to find similar items or users, especially when there are a huge number of items or users.

For highly efficient recommendation systems, one of the most successful methods for implementing collaborative filtering is the model-based matrix factorization. In this model, a user and an item (a user-item pair) are modeled as implicit vectors in the same space based on interactions between the user and item. For an unknown user-item pair, the preferences are calculated based on the vectors of the corresponding user and item (usually through the vector inner product operation). Two popular models in the matrix factorization family are SVD and SVD + + . The SVD model, which is based on the general matrix factorization, improves the stability of the model training by introducing user bias, item bias, and global bias variables. SVD ++ , as an extension of SVD, improves the effectiveness by introducing an auxiliary feature: the interaction history between the user and the item.

8.7.1 Recommendation System in Industry Applications

The recommendation system dates back to as early as the twentieth century, but it wasn't until the last decade when the industry began adopting it more widely. For example, it is estimated that Amazon sells more than 35% of its listed items through recommendation systems. In addition, by using recommendation systems, Google generated revenue of $43 billion in Internet advertising in 2014, and in 2015, Google Play and Apple's App Store earned $10 billion and $21 billion, respectively. Huawei—ranked highly in the Fortune Global 500 list—also applies the recommendation system throughout its business operations. The recommendation system involves an extensive range of content, so extensive in fact that we could write an entire book dedicated exclusively to this topic. So, given the space limitations in this book, we will focus on the recommendation system only from the perspective of industry researchers.

Industry recommendation systems consist of three steps: candidate set generation, matching prediction, and sorting. The number of items that these systems recommend may be millions or more, but matching predictions and sorting on such large candidate sets cannot be performed within an acceptable timeframe. As a result, it is necessary to generate a smaller candidate set (typically ranging from hundreds to thousands) based on the current recommendation scenario, the features of the item, and even the user's preferences. After the candidate set is generated, the matching prediction model predicts the current user's preference for each item in the candidate set. Ultimately, the sorting step combines the results of the matching prediction model with business rules to generate the final sorting results.

An important part of industry recommendation systems is click through rate (CTR) prediction, which first appeared in online advertisement scenarios and belongs to the matching prediction step described earlier. In online advertisement scenarios using the cost per click (CPC) model, revenue is generated for the platform each time a user clicks on an advertisement. The amount of revenue is specified in a contract between the advertiser and platform. In most cases, the platform uses CTR × bid sorting rules for candidate advertisements, where CTR is an estimate of the current user's CTR for the advertisement, and bid represents the amount of money the advertiser will pay to the platform if the user clicks on the advertisement. The sorting rules arrange candidate advertisements according to the expected benefits; that is, they are sorted based on the revenue they generate for the platform each time they are displayed. Such rules are also used for real-time bidding advertisements, and similar rules are used in game and video sorting scenarios. Game sorting is generally based on CTR × LTV, where life time value (LTV) is the average fee a user pays for the game. Video sorting generally uses CTR × WT, where watch time (WT) is the average time a user spends watching the video. Given its wide scope of application, CTR prediction is extremely important in the industry recommendation system.

The recommendation system models used by most enterprises have evolved from the wide model—using logistic regression (LR) or factorization machine (FM)—to the deep learning model, and then to the reinforcement learning model in addition to the deep learning model where the graph structure is considered.

To understand the graph neural network-based model, we first need to understand the input data form used in the recommendation system. This input data form differs significantly from that used in NLP and computer vision. The recommendation system covers many discrete features, such as gender, city, and day of the week. Because these features have no numerical meaning, they are typically represented by one-hot encoding. In this encoding method, all possible values are represented by a high-dimensional vector with a value of 0–1, where the corresponding bit is 1 and all other bits are 0. The dimension of the one-hot vector is the number of all possible values. For example, "Friday" can be represented as [0, 0, 0, 0, 1, 0, 0], the gender "male" can be represented as [0, 1], and the city "Shanghai" can be represented as [0, 0, 1, ..., 0]. From the preceding information, we can see that the input data of the recommendation system is usually high-dimensional and sparse.

8.7.2 Graph Neural Network Model in a Recommendation System

Ultra-large recommendation systems face several challenges due to the high-dimensional and sparse nature of their input data:

1. Storage: The data is structured and all features are arranged in a certain order, with many of them duplicated. For example, if there are 10,000 male users, the

system needs to store 10,000 male-represented vectors, such as [0, 1]. As the number of features, users, and items increases, the amount of duplicated data becomes larger.

2. Sparsity: For movie-recommending scenarios like MovieLens [17], the data is usually represented by a "user-item" score matrix. As the number of users and items increase, the dimensions and sparsity of the score matrix also increase. This is because most users do not score most items, and the collaborative filtering algorithm relies on the score matrix.

3. Scalability: The ability to process ever-increasing volumes of data and the exponential growth of collaborative filtering calculation make it extremely difficult for recommendation systems to scale easily [18].

The graph data structure makes it possible to address these challenges.

1. For repeated storage of features, male can be represented as a vertex on a graph, with all male users having an edge from the user's vertex to the male vertex. This means that information about only the edge needs to be maintained. For higher-dimensional features, the effectiveness of graph structure storage is more pronounced.

2. In response to the sparsity challenge, graph structure storage is vertex-centric, and only the in-edge and out-edge are maintained.

3. To facilitate scalability, the graph structure makes it easy to add new vertices and edges, requiring the model to be updated only for the new additions.

PinSage [18], jointly published by Pinterest and Stanford University, is the industry's first commercial end-to-end recommendation model based on the graph neural network. Pinterest, an image-based social networking site, displays images in the form of a waterfall stream, where new images are automatically loaded at the bottom of the page without needing users to change the current page. Users can pin images of interest on the pinboard and can save and share the images, while other users can follow and forward the images. The main items recommended on Pinterest are images (called Pins), which may include images of food, clothes, products, etc. Users group images they like into Boards. Pinterest data can be modeled to construct a bipartite graph, which includes two types of vertices (Pins and Boards). In the bipartite graph, shown in Fig. 8.8, there is no connection edge between vertices of

Fig. 8.8 Pinterest bipartite graph

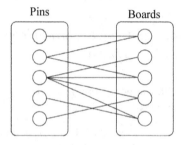

the same type, and the vertex features include images and textual annotations (title and description).

In the traditional GCN, the entire graph is used for training. However, in industrial recommendation scenarios such as Pinterest, there are billions of vertices and tens of billions of edges, making it difficult to perform operations if the entire graph is used for training. To solve this problem, PinSage took inspiration from GraphSage to make improvements to the GCN. GraphSage can be considered as a GCN based on random walk and is an inductive variant of the GCN. It learns the vertex representation by sampling the neighbor information of the aggregated vertex in order to avoid operating the entire Laplacian matrix of the graph. This means that GraphSage can be generalized to an unknown vertex if one exists, and its neighbor information can be used to learn the representation of the vertex. The key improvements PinSage made to the GCN are as follows:

1. Local graph convolution is performed by dynamically constructing a new computational graph through random walk (short random walks) sampling of vertex neighbors. Because the importance of different neighbors to the target vertex is different, the neighbor will have an importance score during the information aggregation.
2. Distributed training is performed based on mini-batch. The CPU is used to sample vertex neighbors to obtain the features required for defining local convolution. Through tensor calculation and hardware acceleration, the distributed stochastic gradient descent calculation is performed for each pre-calculated small graph. The convolution operation can be performed separately, and the parameters of each convolutional layer are shared.
3. Repeated calculation of vertex neighbors is eliminated by using related technologies during inference.

The PinSage algorithm uses the local graph convolution to learn the vertex embedding of the web-level graph containing billions of objects, whereby high-quality vertex embedding facilitates subsequent recommendations. The PinSage algorithm can be summarized into two parts.

The first part is convolution, which is shown in Algorithm 8.7. The vertex embedding calculation, vertex neighbors, weights of the vertex neighbors, and aggregate function are used as the input. Through information aggregation, the neighbor embedding (line 1 of the pseudocode) is calculated. Then, the neighbor and vertex embeddings are used to update the current vertex embedding (line 2 of the pseudocode). Finally, the resulting vertex embedding is normalized (line 3 of the pseudocode).

The method for sampling vertex neighbors during information aggregation has two advantages: (1) the number of neighbors is fixed and the memory used for calculation is controllable; and (2) different importance of the neighbors to the vertex is used for information aggregation. Each time the convolution operation (Algorithm 8.7) is used to obtain the new embedding of a vertex, more information about the local graph structure around the vertex can be obtained by superposing several such convolutions.

Algorithm 8.7 Convolution.

Input: Embedding $\mathbf{z}_u$ of the current vertex u, neighbor embedding set $\{\mathbf{z}_v | v \in N(u)\}$, neighbor weight set α, and aggregate function $\gamma(\bullet)$

Output: New embedding $\mathbf{z}_u^{NEW}$ of the vertex u.

(1) Aggregate neighbor information

$$\mathbf{n}_u \leftarrow \gamma\left(\{\text{ReLU}(\mathbf{Q}\mathbf{h}_v + q) | v \in N(u)\}, \alpha\right)$$

(2) Calculate and update the vertex embedding

$$z_u^{NEW} \leftarrow \text{ReLU}\left(\mathbf{W} \bullet \text{Concat}(z_u, \mathbf{n}_u) + \mathbf{w}\right)$$

(3) Normalize the vertex embedding

$$z_u^{NEW} \leftarrow z_u^{NEW} / \left\| z_u^{NEW} \right\|_2$$

The second part of the PinSage algorithm is mini-batch, shown in Algorithm 8.8, which stacks convolutions into a mini-batch of vertices M to generate the embedding. The mini-batch vertex neighbor sampling process is performed to obtain the neighbor of each vertex (lines 2–8 of the pseudocode). Then, K convolutions are used to iteratively generate K representations of the target vertex (lines 9–16 of the pseudocode). Finally, the vertex embedding is obtained through learning (based on the previously obtained embedding) by using a fully connected neural network (lines 17–19 of the pseudocode). G_1, G_2, and g are the parameters of the fully connected layer.

Algorithm 8.8 Mini-batch.

Input: Small-batch vertex set $M \subset V$, depth parameter K, and neighbor function $N: V \rightarrow 2^V$

Output: Embedding z_u, where $\forall u \in M$

(1)   Mini-batch1: Neighbor sampling of mini-batch vertices

(2) $S^{(K)} \leftarrow M$

(3)   For each depth parameter $k = K, K-1, ..., 1$, execute:

(4) $S^{(k-1)} \leftarrow S^{(k)}$

(5)   For each vertex $u \in S^{(k)}$, execute:

(6) $S^{(k-1)} \leftarrow S^{(k-1)} \cup N(u)$

(7)   End

(8)   End

(9)   Generate the vertex embedding

(10) $h_u^{(0)} \leftarrow x_u, \forall u \in S^{(0)}$

(11) For each depth parameter $k = 1, 2, ..., K$, execute:

(12)   For each vertex $u \in S^{(k)}$, execute:

(13) $\mathcal{H} \leftarrow \{h_v^{(k-1)}, \forall v \in N(u)\}$

(14) $h_u^{(k)} \leftarrow \text{Convolve}^{(k)}(h_u^{(k-1)}, \mathcal{H})$

(15)   End

(16) End

(17) For each vertex $u \in M$, execute:

(18) $z_u \leftarrow G_2 \cdot RELU(G_1 h_u^{(K)} + g)$

(19) End

PinSage has achieved positive results and encouraged the use of the graph convolution algorithm in commercial recommendation systems. In the future, graph neural networks can be expanded to solve the learning problems of other large-scale graph representations and generate greater value in real-world scenarios.

References

1. B. Perozzi, R. Al-Rfou, S. Skiena, DeepWalk: online learning of social representations, in *Proceedings of the 20th ACM SIGKDD International Conference on Knowledge Discovery and Data Mining,* 20, 701–710
2. J. Zhou , G. Cui, Z. Zhang et al., *Graph Neural Networks: A Review of Methods and Applications* [EB/OL]. (2019–07–10) [2019–10–28]. https://arxiv.org/pdf/1812.08434.pdf
3. T. Mikolov, K. Chen, G. Corrado et al., *Efficient Estimation of Word Representations in Vector Space* [EB/OL]. (2013–09–07) [2019–10–28] https://arxiv.org/pdf/1301.3781.pdf%5D

4. A. Mnih, G.E. Hinton, A scalable hierarchical distributed language model. Adv. Neur. Inf. Proc. Syst. 1081–1088 (2009)
5. F. Morin, Y. Bengio, Hierarchical probabilistic neural network language model, in *Proceedings of the International Workshop on Artificial Intelligence and Statistics, 5,* 246–252
6. J. Tang, M. Qu, M. Wang et al. Line: large-scale information network embedding, in *Proceedings of the 24th International Conference on World Wide Web. International World Wide Web Conferences Steering Committee,* vol. 24 (2015), pp. 1067–1077.
7. A. Grover, J. Leskovec, Node2Vec: scalable feature learning for networks, in *Proceedings of the 22nd ACM SIGKDD International Conference on Knowledge Discovery and Data Mining,* vol. 22 (2016), pp. 855–864
8. J.R. Norris, *Markov Chains* (Cambridge University Press, Cambridge, 1998)
9. A.J. Walker, New fast method for generating discrete random numbers with arbitrary frequency distributions. Electron. Lett. **10**(8), 127–128 (1974)
10. D.K. Duvenaud, D. Maclaurin, J. Iparraguirre et al., Convolutional networks on graphs for learning molecular fingerprints. Adv. Neu. Inf. Proc. Syst. 2224–2232 (2015)
11. T.N. Kipf, M. Welling, Semi-supervised classification with graph convolutional networks, in *International Conference on Learning Representations* (2017)
12. J. Atwood, D. Towsley, Diffusion-convolutional neural networks. Adv. Neu. Inf. Proc. Syst. 1993–2001 (2016)
13. M. Niepert, M. Ahmed, M. Kutzkov, Learning convolutional neural networks for graphs, in *Proceedings of The 33rd International Conference on Machine Learning,* vol. 48 (2016) 2014–2023
14. F. Monti, D. Boscaini, J. Masci et al., Geometric deep learning on graphs and manifolds using mixture model CNNs, in *Proceedings of the IEEE Conference on Computer Vision and Pattern Recognition,* (2017), pp. 5115–5124
15. W. Hamilton, Z. Ying, J. Leskovec, Inductive Representation Learning on Large Graphs. Adv. Neu. Inf. Proc. Syst. 1024–1034 (2017)
16. F.M. Harper, J.A. Konstan, The movieLens datasets: history and context. Acm Trans. Interact. Intell. Syst. **5**(4), 19 (2016)
17. L. Sharma, A. Gera, A survey of recommendation system: research challenges. Int. J. Eng. Trends Technol. **4**(5), 1989–1992 (2013)
18. R. Ying, R. He, K. Chen et al. Graph convolutional neural networks for web-scale recommender systems, in *Proceedings of the 24th ACM SIGKDD International Conference on Knowledge Discovery & Data Mining* (ACM, 2018), pp. 974–983

Chapter 9
Unsupervised Learning: Deep Generative Model

9.1 Variational Autoencoder

Variational autoencoders (VAEs), proposed by Kingma and Welling in 2013,[1] allow us to design complex generative models of data, which can then be trained to generate fictional images such as celebrity faces and high-resolution digital artworks.

9.1.1 Background

An autoencoder consists of an encoder and a decoder, which are both neural networks connected to each other. The encoder receives an input and converts it into code (usually a low-dimensional representation vector), whereas the decoder receives the code and converts it into an output similar to the original input. Figure 9.1 illustrates the autoencoder framework, where (a) is the input, and (c) is the output. An autoencoder network is usually trained as a whole, whereby the constructed loss function (called reconstruction loss) is the mean square error or cross-entropy between the output and the input. In this way, the input is approximated and copied in a controlled manner, forcing the network to determine which input data needs to be copied first and ensuring useful features of the input data are learned.

Although an autoencoder network can learn how to generate compact representation features and reconstruct the input, a problem exists in how the latent space of the network is interpolated: Only simple interpolation is performed after the input is converted into a coding vector, leading to discontinuity. For example, after an autoencoder is trained on an MNIST dataset and visualized in a two-dimensional latent space, and as shown in Fig. 9.2, we can see that different categories of images are distributed over different clusters.

---

[1] See: Kingma D P, Welling M. Auto-Encoding Variational Bayes [EB/OL]. 2013 [2019–11–10] https://arxiv.org/pdf/1312.6114.pdf.

L. Chen, *Deep Learning and Practice with MindSpore*, Cognitive Intelligence and Robotics, https://doi.org/10.1007/978-981-16-2233-5_9

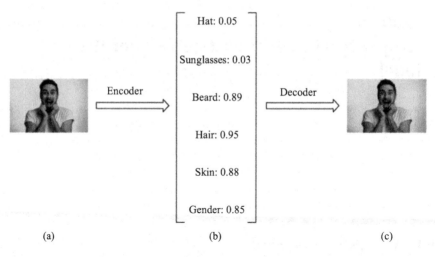

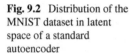

(a)   (b)   (c)

Fig. 9.1 Autoencoder framework

Fig. 9.2 Distribution of the MNIST dataset in latent space of a standard autoencoder

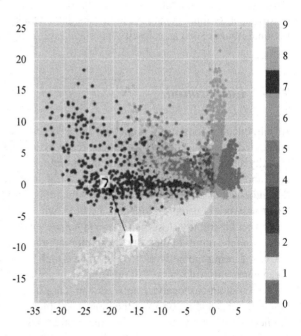

This is because different categories of images have different code, allowing us to obtain an image identical to the input through decoding by using the decoder. However, in scenarios where we want to randomly perform sampling in a latent space or produce an output different from the input image from a continuous latent space, the decoder will produce an unexpected output if the space is discontinuous (such as a gap between different clusters) and sampling is performed in this space.

The reason for this is simple: The decoder does not know how to handle distribution in the latent space because the network has never observed a coding vector from a latent space during training.

To address the problem of discontinuous latent space evident with autoencoders, a VAE that allows differential and random sampling has emerged.

9.1.2 Development Status

The VAE describes the observation of latent space in a probabilistic manner, meaning that a VAE network outputs the probability distribution for each potential property, rather than outputting code for each potential state property as a standard autoencoder does. Figure 9.3 shows the VAE's framework: For an input image, the VAE model outputs statistical distribution of possible values in latent space. The model randomly samples the eigenvalues in the output to obtain a new vector, which it then provides to the subsequent decoder model. Through this process, the VAE is able to implement a continuous and smooth representation of latent space. We expect the decoder to accurately reconstruct the input from the vector comprising all sampling values in the latent space distribution after training, so adjacent features in the latent space should correspond to similar reconstructions.

As of August 1, 2019, a large number of projects implementing the VAE were available on GitHub. Taking Google Brain's Magenta Music VAE [1] as an example, there were 813 Watches, 13,641 Stars, 2714 Forks, 181 Open states, and 396 Closed issues.

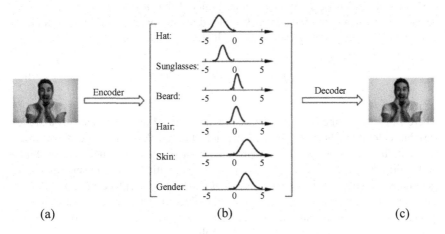

(a)   (b)   (c)

Fig. 9.3 Framework of the VAE

9.1.3   Technical Principles

As alluded to in Sect. 9.1.2, the difference between a standard autoencoder and a VAE is that the former outputs the state value in the latent space whereas the latter outputs the parameter describing the distribution of each dimension in the latent space.

This parameter is represented as z, which the decoder module of the VAE uses to generate observed data x, as shown in Fig. 9.4.

The VAE network provides us with only the output x, so we need to calculate $p(z|x)$ in order to deduce the features of z. We can achieve this by using Bayes' theorem to obtain the following formula.

$$p(z|x) = \frac{p(x|z)p(z)}{p(x)} \tag{9.1}$$

where

$p(z|x)$ is the occurrence probability of z under the condition x;
$p(x|z)$ is the occurrence probability of x under the condition z;
$p(z)$ is the occurrence probability of z; and
$p(x)$ is the occurrence probability x.

Following this, we need to calculate $p(x)$, which is the overall distribution of data samples. Assume that we can obtain a batch of data outputs $\{x_1, x_2, ..., x_n\}$ through the VAE network, where the data samples are collectively represented by X. If we can obtain the overall distribution $p(x)$ of the data samples based on $\{x_1, x_2, ..., x_n\}$, we can obtain all the possible data (the data other than $\{x_1, x_2, ..., x_n\}$) through $p(x)$ sampling. This is an ideal generative model, but it is difficult to implement because the distribution of local data samples does not match that of the overall data. Therefore, we can rewrite the probability distribution as

$$p(x) = \int p(x|z)p(z)dz \tag{9.2}$$

where $p(x|z)$ describes a model for generating x based on z. Because z is a hidden variable, calculating Formula (9.2) is extremely difficult. As such, we need to estimate the value by using variational inference. With variational inference, we can find a probability distribution $q(z)$, which is easier to work with. We then ensure that $q(z)$ is as close as possible to $p(z|x)$ and subsequently use $q(z)$ to replace $p(z|x)$ so that we can approximate the complex probability distribution. The Kullback–Leibler (KL) divergence, used to measure the difference between two probability distributions, also comes into play here and is defined as follows:

Fig. 9.4   Decoder module

$$\text{KL}(q \, \| p) = \int q(t) \log \frac{q(t)}{p(t)} \mathrm{d}t = E_q(\log q - \log p)$$

$$= E_q[\log q] - E_q[\log p]$$

(9.3)

where

$q(t)$ is the probability distribution q;
$p(t)$ is the probability distribution p;
$\log q$ is the logarithm of q; and
$E_q[\log q]$ is an expected $\log q$ under the probability distribution q.

KL divergence meets the following condition:

$$\text{KL}(q\|p) \geq 0 \text{ and } \text{KL}(q\|p) = 0 \leftrightarrow q = p$$

(9.4)

To ensure that $q(z)$ is as close as possible to $p(z|x)$, we can minimize the KL divergence between the two probability distributions by using the following formula:

$$\min \text{KL}(q(z)\|p(z|x))$$

(9.5)

According to the definition of KL divergence and $p(z|x) = \frac{p(z,x)}{p(x)}$, we can obtain

$$\text{KL}(q(z)\|p(z|x)) = E[\log q(z)] - E[\log p(z,x)] + \log p(x)$$

(9.6)

If we assume that the evidence lower bound objective (ELBO) is a lower bound of $p(x)$ likelihood, then

$$\text{ELBO}(q) = E[\log p(z,x)] - E[\log q(z)]$$

(9.7)

According to the non-negative property of KL divergence, we can combine Formulas (9.6) and (9.7) to obtain the following:

$$\log p(x) = \text{KL}(q(x)\|p(z|x)) + \text{ELBO}(q) \geq \text{ELBO}(q)$$

(9.8)

Because $p(x)$ is a constant for a given dataset, minimizing $\text{KL}(q(x) \, \| \, p(z|x))$ in Formula (9.8) is equivalent to maximizing $\text{ELBO}(q)$, which is denoted as L to emphasize the parameters that need to be optimized. After simple transformation is performed according to the multiplication formula of probability, maximizing $\text{ELBO}(q)$ can be written as

$$\max L(\theta, \Phi; x^{(i)}) = E_{q_\Phi(z|x)}[\log p_\theta(x^{(i)}|zz)] - \text{KL}(q_\Phi(z|x^{(i)})\|p_\theta(z))$$

(9.9)

where the first term $E_{q_\Phi(z|x)}[\mathrm{logp}_\theta(x^{(i)}|z)]$ represents the possibility of reconstruction, and the second term $\mathrm{KL}(q_\Phi(z|x^{(i)})||p_\theta(z))$ ensures that the learned distribution q is similar to the real prior distribution p.

By using the optimized Formula (9.9), we can obtain the distribution q (which is as close as possible to the real prior distribution p) and then use q to infer the hidden variable z in the latent space. When we know the hidden variable, we can use it to generate observed data $\tilde{x}$. For the purpose of intuitionism, the observed data is constructed into a neural network structure, in which the encoder model learns the mapping from the real data x to the hidden variable z, and the decoder model learns the mapping from the hidden variable z to the observed data $\tilde{x}$, as shown in Fig. 9.5.

Once the network is established, the loss function needs to be constructed. As mentioned earlier, the loss function punishes any reconstruction error between the real and observed data, while also encouraging the learned distribution $q(x|z)$ to approach the real prior distribution $p(z)$. We can use the following loss function:

$$\mathcal{L}(x, \tilde{x}) + \sum_j \mathrm{KL}(q_j(z|x)||p(z)) \tag{9.10}$$

where

j	is each dimension of the latent space;
$\mathcal{L}(x, \tilde{x})$	is the reconstruction error between the real and observed data; and.
$\mathrm{KL}(q_j(z|x) \parallel p(z))$	is the KL divergence of probability distribution $q_j(z|x)$ and probability distribution $p(z)$ under the dimension j.

To gain a better understanding of how the VAE functions, we first need to understand how it is implemented. As mentioned earlier, the learned probability distribution $q(x|z)$ is subject to the normal distribution, and the latent space outputs two vectors to describe the mean and variance of the potential state distribution. According to these two vectors, the decoder model performs sampling from the pre-defined normal distribution in order to generate a potential vector and start reconstructing the original input.

Fig. 9.5 Structure of the VAE

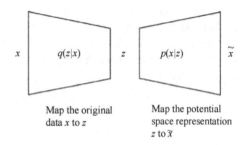

Map the original
data x to z

Map the potential
space representation
z to $\tilde{x}$

Fig. 9.6 Network
architecture of the VAE

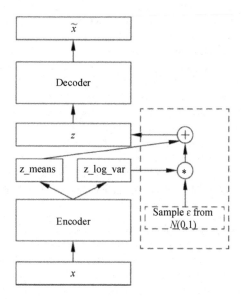

Figure 9.6 shows the network architecture of the VAE, in which two encoder modules are used—one to calculate the mean, and the other to calculate the variance, of the samples.

The encoder for calculating the mean of the samples adds Gaussian noise to the output result, so that the decoder module that decodes the result can acquire robustness to noise. Furthermore, the encoder uses the additional KL loss (described earlier) with a mean of 0 and a variance of 1 as a regularization term, ensuring that the encoder's mean output approximates 0.

The second encoder, used for calculating the variance of the samples, dynamically adjusts the noise intensity. If the decoder is not well trained (meaning that the reconstruction error far exceeds the KL loss), the noise is reduced appropriately (i.e., the KL loss increases). This is performed in order to make the fitting easier, due to the reconstruction error beginning to decrease. Conversely, if the decoder is well trained (meaning that the reconstruction error is less than the KL loss), the noise is increased (i.e., the KL loss is reduced), making the fitting more difficult as the reconstruction error starts to increase. In this case, we need to improve the generation capability of the decoder.

Subsequently, we need to train the VAE model, using backpropagation to calculate the relationship between each parameter in the network and the loss function. However, we cannot calculate the relationship between each parameter and the loss function during the backpropagation, because random sampling is needed in the VAE. To overcome this limitation, the VAE introduces a method called the reparameterization trick, as shown in the dashed box in Fig. 9.6.

As shown in Figs. 9.7 and 9.8, which illustrate forward propagation and backpropagation in the reparameterization trick, respectively, this method begins with

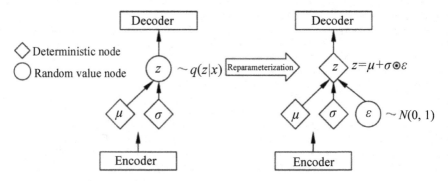

Fig. 9.7 Forward propagation in the reparameterization trick

Fig. 9.8 Backpropagation in
the reparameterization trick

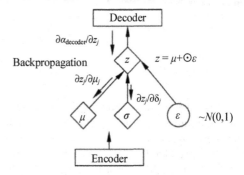

the random sampling ε of unit Gaussian distribution. The reparameterization trick then changes the random sampling ε through the potential distribution mean μ and subsequently scales it based on the potential distribution variance σ. The reparameterization trick effectively overcomes the limitation mentioned earlier, and as a result, it optimizes the distribution parameters while maintaining the ability to perform random sampling on this distribution.

Figure 9.9 shows the distribution of latent space that experiences two-dimensional visualization after training is performed using the VAE on the MNIST dataset. Compared with the standard autoencoder in Fig. 9.2, which produces uneven distribution of clusters in latent space (some areas of the latent space do not represent any data), the VAE can learn to convert input data into a smooth potential feature that maintains local similarity of adjacent code by clustering. This feature ensures balanced distribution through the cluster formation properties of the reconstruction loss and the dense packaging properties of the KL loss, thereby enabling the decoder to decode different clusters. As such, if a vector is sampled from the same distribution of the coding vector, the decoder will successfully decode it; the decoder can understand and decode the cluster as a smooth combination feature, without sudden gaps, after the vector is inserted.

Fig. 9.9 Distribution of the MNIST dataset in latent space of the VAE

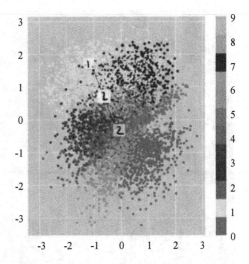

9.1.4 Technical Difficulties

The VAE is a generative model that obtains latent space through the encoder, performs sampling in the latent space, and then generates new data similar to the input data through the decoder. It can be used to process distinct types of data, such as sequential or non-sequential data, continuous or discrete data, and tagged or untagged data. A central part of the VAE is the loss function, which has two purposes: (1) to punish any reconstruction error between the real and observed data and (2) to encourage the learned distribution to approach the real prior distribution. In order to strike a balance between these two purposes while also ensuring the accuracy of the results, we need to verify the effects by conducting large numbers of experiments. Furthermore, although the VAE explicitly defines probability distribution, it approximates probability distribution with the lower bound, meaning that it is unable to solve probability distribution completely. As such, the resulting samples are more ambiguous than those in the generative adversarial network [2]. Solving this problem is therefore a topic of interest for researches in the future, as too is the possibility of combining the VAE with the generative adversarial network.

9.1.5 Application Scenarios

The VAE has been used extensively in fields such as virtual image and video generation as well as reinforcement learning, achieving good results. For example, we can construct LSTM "encoder–decoder" pairs to train a VAE for generating synthetic text, by combining the Magenta Music VAE mentioned in Sect. 9.1.2 with LSTM

Fig. 9.10 Generating fictitious faces by using the VAE

networks based on the VAE model. In addition to text and sound generation, a "convolutional–deconvolutional encoder–decoder" in place of the standard fully connected "encoder–decoder" can achieve good results in generating fictitious facial images, as shown in Fig. 9.10 [3].

9.2 Generative Adversarial Network

The generative adversarial network (GAN)—both a generative model and an unsupervised learning method—was proposed by Goodfellow et al. in 2014 [2]. It is comprised of two neural networks, one called a generator network and the other called a discriminator network, that contest with each other in order to achieve training. The generative adversarial network is used extensively in fields such as computer vision and image processing to generate fictitious images and augment data and has become a hot topic of research in the field of AI, attracting a growing number of researchers.

9.2.1 Background

Development of AI can be summarized into two important stages: perception and cognition. In the perception stage, external signals (such as those involved in image and speech recognition) are received and discriminated, whereas in the deeper cognition stage, such signals are discriminated and understood to a certain extent. In the generative adversarial network, generators can generate new data samples after understanding the input data, thereby facilitating exploration of AI in the cognition stage and allowing AI to gain a deeper understanding of data [4].

AlexNet, which was proposed by the Hinton team in 2012, spurred widespread attention in deep learning and neural networks following its success at the 2012 ImageNet Large Scale Visual Recognition Challenge. Deep learning has since developed at a rapid pace in fields such as vision, language, and speech recognition, and thanks to the improvement of computational power, we have been able to partly overcome the difficulties involved in training a neural network with many parameters. In terms of training, the neural network can be easily trained and can be optimized through the general backpropagation. Its structure is both simple and flexible, while its modeling ability is extremely strong, allowing it to theoretically approach any kind of function. The DNN and its development lay a crucial foundation on which the generative adversarial network is built.

We can divide supervised learning into a generative method and a discriminative method, which are used to obtain their respective models. With the generative method, we can obtain a joint probability distribution $P(X, Y)$ based on data and obtain the conditional probability distribution $p(Y|X) = \frac{P(X,Y)}{P(X)}$ based on Bayes' theorem. We then use $P(Y|X)$ as the prediction input of the model in order to obtain the generative model. With the discriminative method, we obtain the corresponding model by first obtaining the prediction output, which is the decision function $f(X)$ or the conditional probability distribution $P(Y|X)$, based on data.

The generative method involves the data distribution hypothesis and parameter learning. In most cases, we hypothesize the distribution of the data's explicit and implicit variables, use training data to fit the distribution parameters, and obtain the distribution model through training. In order to fit the generative model, we typically use the maximum likelihood estimation method and the Markov chain method. Different from the general generative method, in which distribution parameters are learned and fitted based on the explicit data distribution hypothesis, the generative adversarial network does not need to directly hypothesize the data distribution. Instead, it learns the essential characteristics of real data by using an unsupervised generative model. In this way, it can reflect the distribution characteristics of sample data and generate new data similar to training samples. Of note is the fact that the generative model typically has fewer parameters than the amount of training data, meaning that the model can learn to discover the main characteristics of the data and generate new data similar to the original input.

Due to the development of deep learning, theories on the generative method and model have become increasingly mature, leading to the introduction of adversarial learning in the field of AI. As deep learning continues to gain widespread recognition, the generative adversarial network has become central in the development of deep learning across fields such as vision, language, and speech recognition. The generative adversarial network is derived from the two-person zero-sum game in game theory, where the generative model G and the discriminative model D act as the two players. The generative model G continuously learns the probability distribution of the real data in the training dataset and attempts to convert the input noise data z to approximate the real data. Its opponent, the discriminative model D, attempts to distinguish between the generated data and the real data and is continuously optimized during the training in order to judge the source of input data more accurately. The ensuing game between the two models ensures that they are trained simultaneously, resulting in the generative model G generating the data while the discriminative model D identifies the data source.

9.2.2   Development Status

Various derivatives of the generative adversarial network have emerged, making improvements to the objective function and model structure as well as solving [5] some issues that affected the original.

The generative model's objective is to ensure that the distribution $p_g(x)$ of the generated data is as close as possible to the distribution $p_{\text{data}}(x)$ of the real data. The model's training is therefore heavily dependent upon minimizing the difference between the two probability distributions. In order to minimize $(p_{\text{data}} \parallel p_g)$, which is the Jensen–Shannon divergence (JSD), the standard generative adversarial network uses a discriminative model. Researchers found that, by replacing the distance calculation method or divergence, they were able to enhance the performance of the generative adversarial network. Such replacements include f-GAN [6] and Least Square GAN (LSGAN) [7], which are based on the f divergence, and Wasserstein GAN (WGAN),[2] WGAN with Gradient Penalty (WGAN-GP) [8], Fisher GAN [9], and Maximum Mean Discrepancy GAN (MMDGAN) [10], which are based on integral probability metric (IPM).

The structure of the generative model and that of the discriminative model is extremely important because they affect the training stability and final training results of the generative adversarial network. Some common techniques used to modify

---

[2] See: Arjovsky M, Chintala S, Bottou L. Wasserstein GAN [EB/OL]. 2017 [2019–11–10] https://arxiv.org/pdf/1701.07875.pdf.

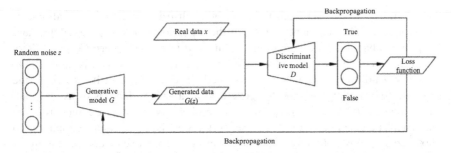

Fig. 9.11 Generative adversarial network

model structures include batch normalization, stacked structure, and multiple generative and discriminative models. Additionally, deep convolutional GAN (DCGAN),[3] a well-known class of CNNs, provides a good reference for other GAN models and offers a stable training GAN model. Hierarchical GANs are also common, and examples of such include StackedGAN [11], which uses multiple GANs and progressive GAN,[4] which uses a single GAN. Also of interest are boundary equilibrium GAN (BEGAN)[5] and margin adaptation GAN (MAGAN) [12].

Training the generative adversarial network dynamically involves some theoretical and practical problems, the most prominent of which is mode collapse. Once mode collapse occurs, it is difficult to obtain the probability distribution of real data by using the generative model. In order to solve this problem, researches have proposed two solutions: unrolled GAN[6] based on the objective function and multi-agent diverse (MAD) GAN [12] based on the network structure.

9.2.3 Technical Principles

The generative adversarial network, as shown in Fig. 9.11, estimates the generative model in an adversarial mode and includes two training processes: (1) using the generative model G to obtain the probability distribution of the real training data and (2) using the discriminative model D to determine whether the input data is from the real training sample or from the generative model G. In process (1), the discrimination error probability of the discriminative model D is maximized. Before

---

[3] See: Radford A, Metz L, Chintala S. Unsupervised Representation Learning with Deep Convolutional Generative Adversarial Networks [EB/OL]. 2015 [2019–11–10]. https://arxiv.org/pdf/1511.06434.pdf.

[4] See: Karras T, Aila T, Laine S, et al. Progressive Growing of GANs for Improved Quality, Stability, and Variation [EB/OL]. 2017 [2019–11–10]. https://arxiv.org/pdf/1710.10196.pdf.

[5] See: Berthelot D, Schumm T, Metz L. BEGAN: Boundary Equilibrium Generative Adversarial Networks [EB/OL]. 2017 [2019–11–10]. https://arxiv.org/pdf/1703.10717.pdf.

[6] See: Metz L, Poole B, Pfau D, et al. Unrolled Generative Adversarial Networks [EB/OL]. 2016 [2019–11–10]. https://arxiv.org/pdf/1611.02163.pdf.

the generative model can learn the probability distribution p_g of the real data x, the prior probability distribution $p_z(z)$ of the input noise must first be defined, and the prior probability distribution must be mapped to the data space $G(z; \theta_g)$. Here, G is a differentiable function composed of an MLP with θ_g as a parameter. On the other hand, the discriminative model is defined as $D(x; \theta_d)$. It uses either the real data (whose label is 1) or the generated data (whose label is 0) as an input, where the output scalar $D(x)$ represents the probability that data x comes from the real data. The generative adversarial network trains the discriminative model D to maximize the output of correct labels and trains the generative model G to minimize the output of correct labels from the discriminative model D.[7] In other words, the two models obtain the results by optimizing the objective function of the following "minimax two-player game" problem, which can be considered as summarizing the entire optimization process of the generative adversarial network.

$$\min_{G} \max_{D} V(D, G) = E_{x \sim p_{\text{data}}(x)}[\log D(x)] + E_{z \sim p_x(z)}[\log(1 - D(G(z)))] \quad (9.11)$$

where

G	is the generative model;
D	is the discriminative model;
$V(D, G)$	is the value function of D and G;
x	is the sample data;
$p_{\text{data}}(x)$	is the real data distribution;
z	is the noise data; and
$p_z(z)$	is the noise data distribution.

The objective function may lack the ability to provide a gradient sufficient for the generative model G to achieve effective learning. During the early stage of training when the generative model G has yet to converge, the discriminative model D can distinguish the generated data from the training sample data with a higher confidence, resulting in the saturation of $\log(1\text{-}D(G(z)))$. Consequently, to train the generative model G to minimize $\log(1\text{-}D(G(z)))$, we must train it to maximize $\log(D(G(z)))$. Because training is performed for $\log(D(G(z)))$, the gradient provided during the early stage of learning is more sufficient. Algorithm 9.1 shows the training algorithm used in the generative adversarial network.

Algorithm 9.1 Training of the Generative Adversarial Network

Input: For the GAN mini-batch stochastic gradient descent training, the discriminative model training step k is a hyperparameter (set to 1 here), and the training iteration number is T.

Output: Parameter updating result θ_{dkT} of the adversarial model D, and parameter updating result θ_{gT} of the generative model G

---

[7] See: Jahanian A, Chai L, Isola P. On the "Steerability" of Generative Adversarial Networks [EB/OL]. 2019 [2019–11–10] https://arxiv.org/pdf/1907.07171.pdf.

(1) Let $t \in \{1, 2, ..., T\}$

(2) Obtain m noise samples $\{z^{(1)}, z^{(2)}, ..., z^{(m)}\}$ from the noise prior probability distribution. $p_g(z)$

(3) Obtain m samples $\{x^{(1)}, x^{(2)}, ..., x^{(m)}\}$ from the data generation probability distribution $p_{\text{data}}(x)$.

(4) Let $r \in \{1, 2, ..., k\}$

(5) Update the discriminative model through the stochastic gradient ascent:

$$\theta_{d_{tr}} \leftarrow \theta_{d_{t(r-1)}} + \nabla_{\theta_d} \frac{1}{m} \sum_{i=1}^{m} [\log(D(x^{(i)})) + \log(1 - D(G(z^{(i)})))] \quad (9.12)$$

(6) Obtain m noise samples $\{z^{(1)}, z^{(2)}, ..., z^{(m)}\}$ from the noise prior probability distribution $p_g(z)$.

(7) Update the generative model through the stochastic gradient descent:

$$\theta_{g_t} \leftarrow \theta_{g_{t-1}} - \nabla_{\theta_g} \frac{1}{m} \sum_{i=1}^{m} \log(1 - D(G(z^{(i)}))) \quad (9.13)$$

(8) Output: Gradient-updated adversarial model D and generative model G

(9) Maximize the value function $V(D, G)$ for any generative model G during training of the discriminative model D:

$$V(G, D) = \int_x p_{\text{data}}(x) \log(D(x)) dx + \int_z p_z(z) \log(1 - D(g(z))) dz \tag{9.14}$$

$$= \int_x p_{\text{data}}(x) \log(D(x)) + p_g(x) \log(1 - D(x)) dx \tag{9.15}$$

(10) Maximize the function $a\log(y) + b\log(1-y)$ for y at $\frac{a}{a+b}$ for any $(a, b) \in \mathbb{R}^2$ \\{0, 0\}.

When the generative model G is fixed, the optimal discriminative model D is

$$D_G^*(x) = \frac{p_{\text{data}}(x)}{p_{\text{data}}(x) + p_g(x)} \tag{9.16}$$

(11) The process of training the discriminative model D can be interpreted as maximizing the likelihood estimation conditional probability function $P(Y = y|x)$, where Y represents that x is from p_{data} (when $y = 1$) or from p_g (when $y = 0$). The objective function can be transformed into

$$C(G) = \max V(G, D)$$
$$= E_{x \sim p_{\text{data}}}[\log(D_G^*(x))] + E_{x \sim p_z}[\log(1 - D_G^*(G(z)))]$$
$$= E_{x \sim p_{\text{data}}}[\log(D_G^*(x))] + E_{x \sim p_g}[\log(1 - D_G^*(x))]$$

$$= E_{x \sim p_{\text{data}}} \left[\log \left(\frac{p_{\text{data}}(x)}{p_{\text{data}}(x) + p_g(x)} \right) \right] + E_{x \sim p_g} \left[\log \left(\frac{p_g(x)}{p_{\text{data}}(x) + p_g(x)} \right) \right]$$

$$(9.17)$$

(12) $C(G)$ can be optimized in the form of KL divergence:

$$C(G) = -\log(4) + \text{KL} \left(p_{\text{data}} \middle\| \frac{p_{\text{data}} + p_g}{2} \right) + KL \left(p_g \middle\| \frac{p_g + p_g}{2} \right)$$

$$(9.18)$$

$C(G)$ can be rewritten to the form of JSD, that is

$$C(G) = -\log(4) + 2\text{JS} \left(p_{\text{data}} \middle\| p_g \right) \tag{9.19}$$

The JSD between two distributions is always non-negative, and the minimum value of 0 is obtained only when $p_{\text{data}} = p_g$. Therefore, when the discriminative model D is fixed and the generative model G is updated, the objective function obtains the global minimum value only when $p_{\text{data}} = p_g$.

(13)   The result of the preceding process is that the generative model G can generate data $G(z)$. However, the discriminative model D has trouble determining whether the generated data is real data.

$$D^*(x) = \frac{p_{\text{data}}(x)}{p_{\text{data}}(x) + p_g(x)} = \frac{1}{2} \tag{9.20}$$

For each round of parameter update during the training of the GAN, the parameters of the discriminative model D are updated through k gradient ascents, whereas those of the generative model G are updated through one gradient descent.

9.2.4   Technical Difficulties

The GAN solves some of the problems associated with the generative model, while adversarial learning has inspired the development of machine learning. However, some new problems have been identified in the GAN, whose greatest advantage—the rule of adversarial learning—is also its biggest challenge. In order to achieve good training results in adversarial learning, it is necessary to train both the generative and discriminative models synchronously while also maintaining a balance between them. However, in real-world applications, this is a difficult objective to achieve, where theoretically determining whether the model converges or whether a balance point exists is problematic. Furthermore, because both the generative and discriminative models adopt the MLP neural network model, they inherit the problem of poor interpretability from the neural network model. Although a trained GAN can produce a wide variety of samples, it may also produce many slightly different samples due to the possible mode collapse.

9.2.5 Application Scenarios

The GAN offers strong performance in terms of data generation, finding favor in data augmentation where it can be directly applied. It can generate data samples—such as images and videos—that are consistent with real data distribution and can be used to solve learning problems that arise when labeled data is insufficient. Furthermore, it can be applied to both semi-supervised and unsupervised learning and can be used in fields such as language and speech recognition to perform tasks including dialog and text-to-image generation.

The GAN is used extensively in the image and computer vision fields. Prominent algorithms include

- Pix2Pix [13], PAN [14], CycleGAN [15], and DiscoGAN [16] in the image migration field (where an image is converted from domain X to domain Y)
- SRGAN [17] in the image super-resolution field
- SeGAN [18] and perceptual GAN [19] in the object detection field
- GeneGAN[8] in the object deformation field
- CoupledGAN in the joint image generation field
- Video GAN [20], Pose-GAN [21], and MoCoGAN [22] in the video generation field
- Stack GAN [23] in the text-to-image generation field
- AGE-GAN [24] in the field of changing facial properties.

The GAN is also popular in sequential data generation, where SeqGAN,[9] RankGAN [25], and VAW-GAN[10] are some prevalent examples used for generating music, generating text, and converting speech, respectively.

In other fields, SSLGAN [26] and Triple-GAN [27] are used for semi-supervised learning, UPLDA [28] is used for adaptation, and DI2IN [29] and SeGAN [30] are used for medical image segmentation.

An increasing amount of attention is being paid to the GAN, which, as we can see, has found use most extensively in the vision, speech recognition, and language fields.

---

[8] Zhou S, Xiao T, Yang Y, et al. GeneGAN: Learning Object Transfiguration and Attribute Subspace From Unpaired Data [EB/OL]. 2017 [2019–11–10] https://arxiv.org/pdf/1705.04932.pdf.

[9] See: Yu L, Zhang W, Wang J, et al. SeqGAN: Sequence Generative Adversarial Nets with Policy Gradient [C]. Thirty-First AAAI Conference on Artificial Intelligence, 2017.

[10] See: Hsu C C, Hwang H T, Wu Y C, et al. Voice Conversion from Unaligned Corpora Using Variational Autoencoding Wasserstein Generative Adversarial Networks [EB/OL]. 2017 [2019–11–10]. https://arxiv.org/pdf/1704.00849.pdf.

9.2.6   Framework Module

Mainstream frameworks such as TensorFlow, PyTorch, and Keras are available on GitHub and supported by open-source code, covering such programming languages as Python, C++ , Java, and C.

9.3   Application: Data Augmentation

As its name implies, data augmentation augments data, or adds it, and as the meaning of augmentation is somewhat related to generation, it can be regarded as a typical application direction of the DNN generative model. The following sections explain what data augmentation is with reference to real-world scenarios in the image field.

9.3.1   Definition of Data Augmentation

Data augmentation is also known as data amplification or data expansion. In deep learning, overfitting may occur if we do not have a sufficient amount of data. This in turn might result in a small training error, but it would also result in a large test error. To address such a shortfall in data, we would ideally obtain more labeled data. However, this is not always possible, so the next best solution is to generate new data, that is, to manually increase the size of the training set. Data augmentation is a method of generating new data based on existing (limited) data.

9.3.2   Purpose of Data Augmentation

Data augmentation has two main objectives: One is to expand the data scale based on existing data, and the other is to increase the variety of data by using old and new data in order to reduce overfitting of the network model.

9.3.3   Conventional Data Augmentation Methods

Conventional data augmentation methods have matured over the years. This section describes some of the classic and commonly used ones.

1. **Space geometry transformation operations**

    (1)   Flip

Flip includes two types: horizontal flip and vertical flip. Figure 9.12a is the original image, and Fig. 9.12b is the flipped image.

(2) Crop

Crop means that the useful area of an image, or that of interest, is retained while the remainder is discarded. Figure 9.13 shows the result of random crop, which is typically used in training.

(3) Rotation/reflection

Rotation/reflection means that the orientation of an image is changed. Random rotation is usually used in training. Figure 9.14 shows the result of rotation/reflection.

(4) Zoom

Zoom means that an image is zoomed in or out either in its entirety or on a certain part.

Zoom includes two types: One is to zoom the entire image to a certain size, and the other is to zoom a part of the image to the size of the original image. Figure 9.15 shows the effects of zooming the image shown in Fig. 9.14a.

2. **Pixel color transformation operations**

(1) Noise addition

Noise addition means that some noise is randomly superimposed on an image. During training, salt and pepper noise or Gaussian noise is usually added. Figure 9.16 shows the effect of randomly adding Gaussian noise twice on the image shown in Fig. 9.14a.

(2) Coarse dropout

Coarse dropout means that a rectangular or circular region in an image is randomly selected for implementing information loss transformation. In the selected region, a black block is generated if all the channel information is lost, whereas a color block is generated if only some of the channel information is lost. Figure 9.17 shows the effect of coarse dropout based on the image shown in Fig. 9.14a.

(a) Original image   (b) Flip effect

Fig. 9.12 Flip

(a) Original image   (b) Effect of random crop 1

(c) Effect of random crop 2   (d) Effect of random crop 3

Fig. 9.13 Crop effects

(3) Fuzzy transformation

Fuzzy transformation means that the difference between the pixel values of the image is reduced to achieve pixel smoothing and image blurring. Figure 9.18 shows the effect of fuzzy transformation based on the image shown in Fig. 9.14a.

(4) Contrast transformation

Contrast transformation means that the saturation S and the luminance component V of each pixel are changed while retaining the original hue H in the image HSV color space. Figure 9.19 shows the effect of contrast transformation based on the image shown in Fig. 9.14a.

(5) Random erasure

Random erasure means that a region in an image is randomly selected for deletion. Each pixel in the deleted region is usually filled with random noise. Figure 9.20 shows the effect of random erasure based on the image shown in Fig. 9.14a.

(6) Invert

Invert means that the pixel value m of some or all channels is converted to 255-m according to a given probability. Figure 9.21 shows the effect of inversion based on the image shown in Fig. 9.14a.

(7) Sharpen

(a) Original image	(b) Rotation/reflection effect 1
(c) Rotation/reflection effect 2	(d) Rotation/reflection effect 3

Fig. 9.14   Rotation/reflection effects

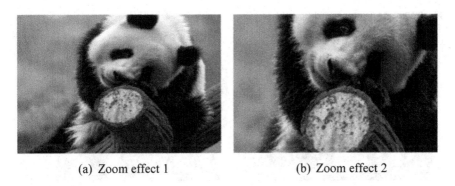

(a) Zoom effect 1	(b) Zoom effect 2

Fig. 9.15   Zoom effects

Sharpen means that the contour of an image is compensated to highlight the edge of an object in the image and the part with the grayscale jump change. This process aims to improve the contrast between the edge of the ground object and the surroundings, thereby making the image clearer. Figure 9.22 shows the effect of sharpening based on the image shown in Fig. 9.14a.

(a) Effect of adding Gaussian noise 1   (b) Effect of adding Gaussian noise 2

Fig. 9.16 Effects of noise addition

(a) Effect of coarse dropout 1   (b) Effect of coarse dropout 2

Fig. 9.17 Effects of coarse dropout

(a) Effect of fuzzy transformation 1   (b) Effect of fuzzy transformation 2

Fig. 9.18 Effects of fuzzy transformation

(a) Effect of contrast transformation 1 (b) Effect of contrast transformation 2

(c) Effect of contrast transformation 3 (d) Effect of contrast transformation 4

Fig. 9.19 Effects of contrast transformation

(8) Emboss
Emboss means that an object in an image is raised on the plane where the object is located. Figure 9.23 shows the effect of embossing based on the image shown in Fig. 9.14a.

3. **Unsuitable Scenarios**
Conventional data augmentation methods preclude the use of certain transformation operations in some task scenarios, such as number recognition. For example, the numbers 6 and 9 cannot be distinguished in an image after rotation. For an image that shows a side view of a face, left and right cannot be distinguished after the flip transformation.

9.3.4 Data Augmentation Methods Based on Deep Learning

In recent years, we have seen the emergence of some exceptional data augmentation methods based on deep learning. This section focuses on some of the typical methods and their applications, attempting to classify them roughly for reference purposes.

1. **Image Enhancement Based on a Convolutional Network**

(a) Effect of random erasure 1

(b) Effect of random erasure 2

(c) Effect of random erasure 3

(d) Effect of random erasure 4

Fig. 9.20   Effects of random erasure

(a) Effect of inversion 1

(b) Effect of inversion 2

Fig. 9.21   Effects of inversion

1)   Real-time Image Enhancement[11]
    (1)   Applicable scenario. This method is typically used to enhance images in real time on mobile terminals. It can be user-selected for image adjustment or can be embedded in the image processing pipeline.

[11] See: Gharbi M, Chen J W, Barron J T, et al. Deep Bilateral Learning for Real-time Image Enhancement [J]. ACM Transactions on Graphics (TOG), 2017, 36(4): 118.

Fig. 9.22 Effect of
sharpening

Fig. 9.23 Effect of
embossing

(2)   Solution. The neural network structure is designed based on the
concept of bilateral grid processing and local affine color transformation. The model is fed with a pair of input and output images,
and the CNN is trained to predict the coefficients of the local affine
model in the bilateral space. The model learns how to make local,
global, and content-dependent decisions to approximate the desired
image transformation.
In offline model training, a low-resolution image is used as input in
the neural network, and a set of affine transformations is generated
in the bilateral space. These transformations are upsampled in edge-
preserving mode by using new slice nodes and are then applied to
the full-resolution image.

(3)   Innovations. This method introduces a new neural network architecture inspired by bilateral grid processing and local affine color
transformation. It also implements real-time enhancement of 1080P
images within milliseconds. In Figure 9.24, (a) is the original image

(a) Original image   (b) HDR + hue drawing   (c) Processing results

Fig. 9.24 Results of real-time image enhancement

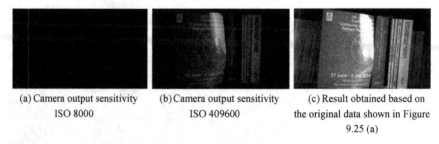

(a) Camera output sensitivity   (b) Camera output sensitivity   (c) Result obtained based on
        ISO 8000   ISO 409600   the original data shown in Figure
                                                                             9.25 (a)

Fig. 9.25 Effects of low-light image enhancement

with 12 million pixels and a 16-bit linear input hue-mapped to facilitate visualization; (b) shows HDR + hue drawing, which takes 400–600 ms; and (c) shows the processing result of the algorithm, which takes 61 ms and achieves a peak signal-to-noise ratio of 28.4 dB.

2) Low-light Image Enhancement[12]

    (1) Applicable scenario. This method is typically used to enhance dark, stationary images in low-light environments but is not suitable for handling humans or dynamic objects.

    (2) Solution. The See-in-the-Dark (SID) dataset, comprised of 5094x2 raw short-exposure images, each with a corresponding long-exposure reference image, is an open-source dataset used to develop an end-to-end training pipeline based on a fully convolutional network.

    (3) Innovations. The open-source SID dataset is useful for enhancing images taken in low-light environments, as can be seen in Figure 9.25.

3) Image Style Transfer [31]

    (1) Applicable scenario. This method is used to convert an existing photo to a specific style of a reference photo while keeping the photo realistic.

---

[12] See: Chen C, Chen Q F, Xu J, et al. Learning to See in the Dark [C]. Proceedings of the IEEE Conference on Computer Vision and Pattern Recognition. 2018: 3291–3300.

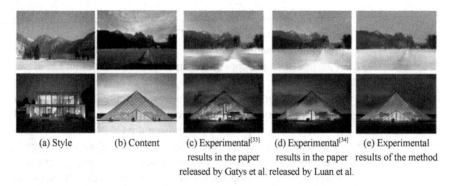

(a) Style   (b) Content   (c) Experimental[33]   (d) Experimental[34]   (e) Experimental
                                       results in the paper   results in the paper   results of the method
                                    released by Gatys et al. released by Luan et al.

Fig. 9.26 Effects of style transfer and content transfer

(2)   Solution. The encoder–decoder architecture is used to implement photo-level style transfer. Two steps are used in this method: The stylization step transfers the style of the reference photo to the content photo, and the smoothing step ensures spatially consistent stylizations.

(3)   Innovations. The two-step approach used in this method overcomes the issues observed in other photorealistic image stylization methods that tend to generate spatially inconsistent stylizations with noticeable artifacts. Specifically, smooth transformation makes the style transfer more realistic, and both the style transfer and smooth transfer steps can be separately implemented. Figure 9.26e shows the experimental results of the method.

2.   **Image Enhancement Based on GAN**

1)   Using Fewer Labels to Generate High-Fidelity Images[13]

(1)   Applicable scenario. This method is used to generate high-fidelity images when only a small amount of labeled data is available.

(2)   Solution. This method involves pre-training and co-training approaches, both of which are split into unsupervised and semi-supervised approaches.

- Pre-training—unsupervised: These approaches (proposed by Gidaris et al. in 2018[14] and Kolesnikov et al. in 2019[15]) are used to extract the feature representation from the real training data. They then perform clustering, using the cluster as an alternate

[13] See: Lucic M, Tschannen M, Ritter M, et al. High-Fidelity Image Generation With Fewer Labels [EB/OL]. 2019 [2019–11–10]. https://arxiv.org/pdf/1903.02271.pdf.

[14] See: Gidaris S, Singh P, Komodakis N. Unsupervised Representation Learning by Predicting Image Rotations [C]. In International Conference on Learning Representations, 2018.

[15] See: Kolesnikov A, Zhai X, Beyer L. Revisiting Selfsupervised Visual Representation Learning [C]. In Computer Vision and Pattern Recognition, 2019.

identifier for the label, in order to minimize the corresponding hinge loss function to train the GAN.

- Pre-training—semi-supervised: This approach (proposed by Zhai et al. in 2019[16]) adapts the unsupervised loss function for use in semi-supervised scenarios. It assumes that only one subset of the training set is used. It obtains the feature representation through training based on unsupervised learning and a linear classifier and uses the feature representation to train the GAN.

- Co-training—unsupervised: This approach, unlike the unsupervised pre-training approaches, does not extract feature representations before training the GAN. Instead, it directly deduces the label in the GAN training process. One approach sets the same label for both the real and generated samples after removing the real label and removes the mapping layer from the discriminator. Another approach maps random labels to real unlabeled images (this part of the data does not provide valid information to the discriminator, whereas the sampled labels help the generator provide additional random information).

- Co-training—semi-supervised: This approach combines both feature representation extraction and GAN training.

(3) Innovations. The semantic feature extractor used with training data can be obtained through self-supervised learning,[17] and the feature representation can be used to guide the GAN training process. In addition, the label of the training set can be deduced from its subset and used as conditional information for GAN training.

2) Using a Small Amount of Data to Quickly Generate High-resolution Images[18]

(1) Applicable scenario. This method is used to quickly generate high-resolution images when only a small amount of labeled data is available.

(2) Solution. Measuring the probability that the generated data is more real than the labeled real value data in the discriminator of the standard GAN may be feasible.

Figure 9.27 illustrates the theoretical analysis of prior knowledge, where (a) shows the minimization of the Jensen–Shannon divergence (JSD) to obtain the optimal solution, (b) shows the use of the standard GAN to train the generator in order to minimize the loss function, and (c) shows the ideal process of training the generator to minimize the

[16] See: Zhai X, Oliver A, Kolesnikov A, et al. S4L: Selfsupervised Semi-Supervised Learning [EB/OL]. 2019 [2019–11–10]. https://arxiv.org/pdf/1905.03670.pdf.

[17] See: Lucic M, Tschannen M, Ritter M, et al. High-fidelity image generation with fewer labels [EB/OL]. 2019 [2019–11–10]. https://arxiv.org/pdf/1903.02271.pdf.

[18] See: Jolicoeur-Martineau A. The relativistic discriminator: a key element missing from standard GAN [EB/OL]. 2018 [2019–11–10]. https://arxiv.org/pdf/1807.00734.pdf.

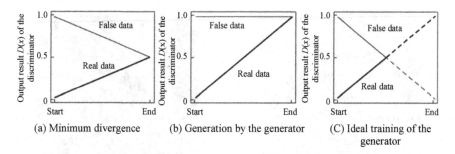

Fig. 9.27   Training convergence effects of the generator and the discriminator

loss function (the dashed line indicates that the subsequent iteration is optional after the balance is reached at the intersection point).

When the minimization of divergence is analyzed, the loss function of the discriminator is set to JSD [2]. The experimental results show that minimizing the saturation loss of the standard GAN only increases the output result of the discriminator for the real data—it does not increase the result of the discriminator for the false data, as shown in Fig. 9.27b. This means that the dynamic of the standard GAN differs significantly from the minimization of the JSD. Analysis indicates that both the real and false data contribute the same to the gradient of the discriminator loss function in the GAN based on the integral probability metrics. Conversely, in the standard GAN, the real data is ignored in the gradient if the discriminator is optimal.

Of note too is the proposal relativistic standard GAN, relativistic GAN, and relativistic average GAN.

(3)   Innovations. In general, the conventional GAN measures the real probability of the generated data. The proposed relativistic GAN, on the other hand, measures the probability that the generated data is more real than the labeled real data. To measure this "relative authenticity", a new distance is constructed. The experimental data shows that the relativistic GAN can generate a high-resolution image (256×256) based on the 2011 labeled samples, but the conventional GAN cannot do this, as shown in Figure 9.28.

3.   **Adaptive Image Enhancement Based on Data**

As of June 2019, there were two representative articles in this field: *AutoAugment: Learning Augmentation Strategies From Data*[19] by Google Brain and

---

[19] See: Cubuk E D, Zoph B, Mane D, et al. AutoAugment: Learning Augmentation Strategies From Data [C]. Proceedings of the IEEE Conference on Computer Vision and Pattern Recognition. 2019: 113–123.

(a) Cat images (256×256) through GAN   (b) Cat images (256×256) through RaSGAN
training (5000 iterations)   training (indicator FID = 32.11)

Fig. 9.28 Generation effect of the relativistic GAN

Fast AutoAugment[20] by Kakao Brain. We focus on the former, as the latter is derivative work.

(1) Applicable scenario. This method is used to automatically augment data based on the existing data. Conventional data augmentation requires a pre-defined strategy for each image, whereas automatic augmentation selects an appropriate one from a pre-designed automatic augmentation strategy library for each image.

(2) (2) Solution. Google Brain defines the search for the optimal enhancement strategy as a discrete search problem, which predominantly consists of two parts: search algorithm and search space. From a high-level perspective, the search algorithm (implemented by the controller RNN) samples the data augmentation strategy S. Here, S indicates the possibility and intensity of the preprocessing operation to be performed on the image in each batch process. S is then used to train the neural network with a fixed architecture, and the verification accuracy R is fed back to update the controller. Because R is not differentiable, the controller is updated based on the policy gradient. Specifically:

① Search space: Each data augmentation strategy includes five substrategies, each of which includes two image operations (Google Brain specifies the selection of 16 operations).

② Search algorithm: Reinforcement learning is used in the experiment, which is composed of two parts: RNN-based controller and near-end strategy optimization algorithm.

(3) Innovations. Google Brain proposes AutoAugment, which searches for or selects a data augmentation strategy automatically. Additionally, each

---

[20] See: Lim S, Kim I, Kim T, et al. Fast AutoAugment [EB/OL]. 2019 [2019–11–10]. https://arxiv. org/pdf/1905.00397.pdf.

Table 9.1 Comparison of top 1 error rate (%) between the baseline and AutoAugment in the Inception v4 model

Dataset	Training scale	Category	Baseline value	AutoAugment
Oxford 102 Flowers [32]	2040	102	6.7	4.6
Caltech-101 [33]	3060	102	19.4	13.1
Oxford-IIIT Pets [34]	3680	37	13.5	11.0
FGVC Aircraft[①]	6667	100	9.1	7.3
Stanford Cars[②]	8144	196	6.4	5.2

[①]See: Maji S, Rahtu E, Kannala J, et al. Fine-Grained Visual Classification of Aircraft [EB/OL]. 2013 [2019–11–10]. https://arxiv.org/pdf/1306.5151.pdf.
[②]See: Krause J, Deng J, Stark M, et al. Collecting a Large-Scale Dataset of Fine-Grained Cars [J]. In Second Workshop on Fine-Grained Visual Categorization, 2013,2:7.

strategy in the search space includes several substrategies, each of which includes processing functions (such as translation and rotation) and uses probability and intensity. AutoAugment has delivered promising results that exceed the baseline. Of note is the state-of-the-art accuracy achieved with AutoAugment: It realized a lower error rate on the Stanford Cars dataset (5.2%, compared with 5.9% for the previous best result), as shown in Table 9.1.

9.4 Implementing GAN-Based Data Augmentation Using MindSpore

The interfaces and processes of MindSpore may constantly change due to iterative development. For all runnable code, see the code in corresponding chapters at https://mindspore.cn/resource. You can scan the QR code on the right to access relevant resources.

References

1. A. Roberts, J. Engel, D. Eck, Hierarchical variational autoencoders for music, in *NIPS Workshop on Machine Learning for Creativity and Design* (2017)
2. I. Goodfellow, J. Pouget-Abadie, M. Mirza, et al., Generative adversarial nets. Adv. Neural Inf. Process. Syst. 2672–2680 (2014)
3. X. Hou, L. Shen, K. Sun, et al., Deep feature consistent variational autoencoder, in *2017 IEEE Winter Conference on Applications of Computer Vision (WACV)*. (IEEE, 2017), pp. 1133–1141
4. K. Wang, C. Gou, Y. Duan et al., Research progress and prospect of generative adversarial network GAN. IEEE/CAA J. Automatica Sinica (JAS) **43**(3), 321–332 (2017)
5. A. Creswell, T. White, V. Dumoulin et al., Generative adversarial networks: an overview. IEEE Sig. Process. Mag. **35**(1), 53–65 (2017)

6. S. Nowozin, B. Cseke, R. Tomioka, f-GAN: training generative neural samplers using variational divergence minimization, in *Advances in Neural Information Processing Systems*, pp. 271–279

7. X. Mao, Q. Li, H. Xie, et al., Least squares generative adversarial networks, in *Proceedings of the IEEE International Conference on Computer Vision* (2017), pp. 2794–2802

8. I. Gulrajani, F. Ahmed, M. Arjovsky, et al., Improved training of Wasserstein GANs, in *Advances in Neural Information Processing Systems* (2017), pp. 5767–5777

9. Y. Mroueh, T. Sercu, Fisher GAN, in *Advances in Neural Information Processing Systems* (2017), pp. 2513–2523

10. C.L. Li, W.C. Chang, Y. Cheng, et al., MMD GAN: towards deeper understanding of moment matching network, in *Advances in Neural Information Processing Systems* (2017), pp. 2203–2213

11. H. Zhang, T. Xu, H. Li, et al., StackGAN: text to photo-realistic image synthesis with stacked generative adversarial networks, in *Proceedings of the IEEE International Conference on Computer Vision* (2017), pp. 5907–5915

12. A. Ghosh, V. Kulharia, V.P. Namboodiri, et al., Multi-agent diverse generative adversarial networks, in *Proceedings of the IEEE Conference on Computer Vision and Pattern Recognition* (2018), pp. 8513–8521

13. P. Isola, J.Y. Zhu, T. Zhou, et al., Image-to-image translation with conditional adversarial networks, in *Proceedings of the IEEE Conference on Computer Vision and Pattern Recognition* (2017), pp. 1125–1134

14. C. Wang, C. Xu, C. Wang et al., Perceptual adversarial networks for image-to-image transformation. IEEE Trans. Image Process. **27**(8), 4066–4079 (2018)

15. J.Y. Zhu, T. Park, P. Isola, et al., Unpaired image-to-image translation using cycle-consistent adversarial networks, in *Proceedings of the IEEE international Conference on Computer Vision* (2017), pp. 2223–2232

16. T. Kim, M. Cha, H. Kim, et al., Learning to discover cross-domain relations with generative adversarial networks, in *Proceedings of the 34th International Conference on Machine Learning-Volume 70*. JMLR.org. (2017), pp. 1857–1865

17. C. Ledig, L. Theis, F. Huszár, et al., Photo-realistic single image super-resolution using a generative adversarial network, in *Proceedings of the IEEE Conference on Computer Vision and Pattern Recognition* (2017), pp. 4681–4690

18. K. Ehsani, R. Mottaghi, A. Farhadi, SeGAN: segmenting and generating the invisible, in *Proceedings of the IEEE Conference on Computer Vision and Pattern Recognition* (2018), pp. 6144–6153s

19. J. Li, X. Liang, Y. Wei, et al., Perceptual generative adversarial networks for small object detection, in *Proceedings of the IEEE Conference on Computer Vision and Pattern Recognition* (2017), pp. 1222–1230

20. C. Vondrick, H. Pirsiavash, A. Torralba, Generating videos with scene dynamics, in *Advances In Neural Information Processing Systems* (2016), pp. 613–621

21. J. Walker, K. Marino, A. Gupta, et al., The pose knows: video forecasting by generating pose futures, in *Proceedings of the IEEE International Conference on Computer Vision* (2017), pp. 3332–3341

22. S. Tulyakov, M.Y. Liu, X. Yang, et al., MocoGAN: decomposing motion and content for video generation, in *Proceedings of the IEEE Conference on Computer Vision and Pattern Recognition* (2018), pp. 1526–1535

23. X. Huang, Y. Li, O. Poursaeed, et al., Stacked generative adversarial networks, in *Proceedings of the IEEE Conference on Computer Vision and Pattern Recognition* (2017), pp. 5077–5086

24. G. Antipov, M. Baccouche, J.L. Dugelay, Face aging with conditional generative adversarial networks, in *17th IEEE International Conference on Image Processing (ICIP)* (2017), pp. 2089–2093

25. K. Lin, D. Li, X. He, et al., Adversarial ranking for language generation, in *Advances in Neural Information Processing Systems* (2017), pp. 3155–3165

26. T. Salimans, I. Goodfellow, W. Zaremba, et al., Improved techniques for training GANs, in *Advances in Neural Information Processing Systems* (2016), pp. 2234–2242

27. C. Li, K. Xu, J. Zhu, et al., Triple generative adversarial nets, in *Advances in Neural Information Processing Systems* (2017), pp. 4088–4098

28. K. Bousmalis, N. Silberman, D. Dohan, et al., Unsupervised pixel-level domain adaptation with generative adversarial networks, in *Proceedings of the IEEE Conference on Computer Vision and Pattern Recognition* (2017), pp. 3722–3731

29. D. Yang, T. Xiong, D. Xu, et al., Automatic vertebra labelling in large-scale 3D CT using deep image-to-image network with message passing and sparsity regularization, in *International Conference on Information Processing in Medical Imaging.* (Springer, Cham, 2017), pp. 633–644

30. Y. Xue, T. Xu, H. Zhang et al., SeGAN: Adversarial network with multi-scale L_1 loss for medical image segmentation. Neuroinformatics **16**(3–4), 383–392 (2018)

31. Y. Li, M.Y. Liu, X. Li, et al., A closed-form solution to photorealistic Image stylization, in *Proceedings of the European Conference on Computer Vision (ECCV)*, pp. 453–468 (2018)

32. M.E. Nilsback, A. Zisserman, Automated flower classification over a large number of classes, in *2008 6th Indian Conference on Computer Vision, Graphics and Image Processing.* (IEEE, 2008), pp. 722–729

33. L. Fei-Fei, R. Fergus, P. Perona, Learning generative visual models from few training examples: an incremental bayesian approach tested on 101 object categories, in *2004 Conference on Computer Vision and Pattern Recognition Workshop.* (IEEE, 2004), pp. 178–178

34. Y. Em, F. Gag, Y. Lou, et al., Incorporating intra-class variance to fine-grained visual recognition, in *2017 IEEE International Conference on Multimedia and Expo (ICME).* (IEEE, 2017), pp. 1452–1457

Chapter 10
Deep Reinforcement Learning

This chapter starts by covering the basic concepts involved in reinforcement learning and then describes how to solve reinforcement learning tasks by using basic and deep learning-based solutions. It also provides a brief overview of the typical algorithms central to the deep learning-based solutions, namely DQN, DDPG, and A3C.

10.1 Basic Concepts of Reinforcement Learning

Deep reinforcement learning, as its name implies, combines the principles used in deep learning and reinforcement learning, covering a wide range of knowledge and, in particular, mathematical knowledge such as Markov property, Markov decision process, Bellman equation, and optimal control. This section therefore focuses on the basic mathematical concepts involved in reinforcement learning in order to provide a greater understanding of deep reinforcement learning.

10.1.1 Basic Concepts and Theories

As mentioned earlier, we are better able to understand deep reinforcement learning once we have a firm grasp of the basic concepts and mathematical theories behind reinforcement learning. In this section, we focus on the concepts of policy π, action a, value v, reward r, and the relationships between them.

1. **Fundamental theory**

   We can understand reinforcement learning through the concepts of agents, environments, states, rewards, and actions, as shown in Fig. 10.1. The agent interacts with the environment, performing actions that are rewarded (or punished). In the figure, the state of the agent at time t is s_t. According to this state, the agent performs action a_t in the environment. The environment moves to a new state

© Tsinghua University Press 2021

L. Chen, *Deep Learning and Practice with MindSpore*, Cognitive Intelligence and Robotics, https://doi.org/10.1007/978-981-16-2233-5_10

Fig. 10.1 Basic architecture
for reinforcement learning

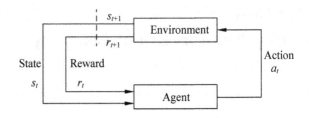

s_{t+1} and gives the reward r_{t+1} corresponding to the new state after sensing the new action of the agent. The agent interacts with the environment repeatedly according to this process, which is central to reinforcement learning.

2. **Reward**

    Reward is a mechanism by which to define the agent's learning objective. Each time the agent interacts with the environment, the environment feeds back the reward signal r to the agent. The reward indicates the quality of action a and can be regarded as a reward or punishment mechanism to evaluate the success or failure of the agent's actions.

    The goal of reinforcement learning is not to maximize the current reward but rather to maximize cumulative reward R, the sum of all rewards, as shown in Formula (10.1):

$$R = r_1 + r_2 + \ldots + r_n \tag{10.1}$$

Because the environment is generally either stochastic or unknown, the next state s may be stochastic. This means that we are unable to determine the agent's next-step action nor its reward. As the agent explores further into the future, the results of the agent's actions become less certain. In order to account for this fact, we can replace the cumulative future reward with the cumulative future discounted reward G_t:

$$G_t = R_t + \gamma R_{t+1} + \ldots + \gamma^{n-t} R_n, \gamma \in [0, 1] \tag{10.2}$$

By multiplying the reward with the discount factor γ, this formula ensures that future rewards have less impact on the cumulative future discounted reward the further away they are from the current time step t. The cumulative future discounted reward G_t for the time step t can be represented by using the cumulative future discounted reward G_{t+1} for the time step $t + 1$:

$$\begin{aligned} G_t &= R_t + \gamma \left[R_{t+1} + \gamma (R_{t+2} + \ldots) \right] \\ &= R_t + \gamma G_{t+1} \end{aligned} \tag{10.3}$$

In conclusion, the ultimate goal of reinforcement learning is to ensure that the agent selects a policy that maximizes the cumulative future discounted reward G_t.

3. **Policy**

Policy, defined as π, refers to the rules that determine how the agent selects actions according to the state s_t and reward r_t, where the value function v is the expected cumulative reward E (G). In reinforcement learning, the optimal policy π^* is obtained through trial-and-error learning that utilizes feedback from the environment and corresponding state adjustments.

In general terms, we can classify policy π as either a deterministic or a stochastic policy.

(1) Deterministic policy: The action a is selected according to the state s, that is, $a = \pi(s)$. The selection process is deterministic, with no probability, and does not require the agent to make a selection.

(2) Stochastic policy: An action is selected according to the random probability P_{sa}, as defined by $\pi(a|s) = P[a_t = a|s_t = s]$ (note that $\Sigma\pi(a|s) = 1$). In state s, the agent selects the probability of action a according to the probability of each action $\pi(a|s)$.

4. **Value**

The value function is used to evaluate the state s_t of the agent at time step t, that is, to evaluate the immediate reward r for a given interaction. It is called the state value function $v(s)$ when the input of the algorithm is the state s; the action value function $q(s,a)$ when the input is the state-action pair $< s,a >$; and the value function v when the input is not distinguished.

The state value function $v(s)$ is a prediction of the cumulative future discounted reward, representing the expected reward that the agent can obtain by performing the action a in the state s.

$$v(s) = E[G_t|s_t = s] \tag{10.4}$$

The action value function $q(s,a)$ is typically used to evaluate the quality of the action a selected by the agent in the state s. This function and the state value function $v(s)$ are similar, but the difference between them is that the former one considers the effect of performing action a at the current time step t.

$$q(s, a) = E[G_t|s_t = s, a_t = a] \tag{10.5}$$

Formula (10.5) shows that the result of the action value function $q(s,a)$ is the mathematical expectation value, that is, the expected cumulative discounted reward.

10.1.2   Markov Decision Process

The Markov decision process (MDP) is a central aspect of deep reinforcement learning. In this section, we describe not only the MDP itself, but also the Markov property (MP), in order to lay a solid foundation for understanding deep reinforcement learning.

1. **Markov property**

    The Markov property indicates that a process is memoryless. Specifically, after the action a_t is performed in state s_t, the state s_{t+1} and reward r_{t+1} of the next time step are associated with only the current state s_t and action a_t. They are associated with neither the state of a historical time step nor an earlier time step. This means that the next state of the system is related to only the current state and not to the previous or earlier state—in essence, the Markov property has no aftereffect. However, in real-world applications, the feedback of the time step $t + 1$ does not necessarily depend on only the state and action of the time step t. Consequently, the task that the agent needs to accomplish does not completely satisfy the Markov property. But, to simplify the process of solving a reinforcement learning task, it is assumed that the task does indeed satisfy the Markov property—this is achieved by restricting the state of the environment.

2. **Markov decision process**

    The memoryless characteristic of the Markov property, as mentioned earlier, simplifies the Markov decision process considerably. This process is represented as a four-tuple:

$$\text{MDP} = (S, A, P, R) \tag{10.6}$$

where S is a set of states called the state space, and $S = \{s_1, s_2, ..., s_n\}$. Here, s_i denotes the state of the agent's environment at the time step i;

A is a set of actions called the action space, where $A = \{a_1, a_2, ..., a_n\}$. Here, a_i denotes the action performed by the agent at the time step i;

P is the state transition probability. It is the probability that action a in state s at time t will lead to state s' at time $t+1$ and is denoted as $p(s'|s,a)$. If the feedback signal r of the environment is received, the state transition probability is denoted as $p(s',r|s,a)$;

R is the reward function. It is the reward r received by the agent after transitioning from state s to state s' upon performing action a, where $r = R(s,a)$.

The Markov decision process is central to learning and solving most—if not all—reinforcement learning tasks. Because the process takes into account both the action a and state s, the next state in a reinforcement learning task is related to both the current state s and action a.

By converting reinforcement learning tasks into the Markov decision process, we can significantly reduce the difficulty and complexity and thereby increase the efficiency and accuracy, in solving such tasks.

10.1.3 Bellman Equation

Solving a deep reinforcement learning task is, to some extent, equivalent to optimizing the Bellman equation.

Because the Bellman equation represents the relationship between the current time t and the next time $t + 1$ (specifically, the values of their states), we can use it to represent both the state value function $v(s)$ and the action value function $q(s,a)$.

For both of these functions, the substitution of Formula (10.2) includes two parts: the immediate reward r_t and the discount value $\gamma v(s_{t+1})$ of a future state. An example of the state value function $v(s)$ represented by the Bellman equation is as follows:

$$v(s) = E[G_t|s_t = s] = E[r_t + \gamma v(s_{t+1})|s_t = s] \tag{10.7}$$

We can therefore express the Bellman equation of the state value function $v(s)$ as follows:

$$v(s) = R_s + \gamma \sum_{s' \in S} P_{ss'} v(s') \tag{10.8}$$

Using Formula (10.8), we can obtain the value function of the current state s by adding the reward R_s of the current state to the product of the state transition probability $P_{ss'}$ and the state value function $v(s')$ of the next state, where γ is the future discount factor. We can also use linear algebra to reduce Formula (10.8) as follows:

$$v = \mathbf{R} + \gamma \mathbf{P} v' \tag{10.9}$$

10.2 Basic Solution Method

Section 10.1 covered the basic concepts of reinforcement learning that allow us to abstract reinforcement learning tasks through the Markov decision process and express such tasks through the Bellman equation. Building on that understanding, this section describes the solution methods of reinforcement learning.

We can consider the process of solving a reinforcement learning task to be the same as finding the optimal policy, which we can obtain by first solving the optimal value function. This means that the solution of the optimal value function and, in turn, the reinforcement learning task is optimization of the Bellman equation.

For a small-scale Markov decision process, we can solve the value function directly; but for a large-scale process, we need to optimize the Bellman equation by using methods such as dynamic programming, Monte Carlo, or temporal difference.

These methods enable us to solve the Bellman equation according to the Markov decision process, allowing us to obtain the reinforcement learning model.

10.2.1   Dynamic Programming Method

The dynamic programming method splits a complex problem into several subproblems that can be solved individually. "Dynamic" means that the problem includes a series of states and can change gradually over time, whereas "programming" means that each subproblem can be optimized.

With this method, we use the value function of all subsequent states (denoted as *s')* of the current state *s* to calculate the value function and calculate the subsequent state value function according to *p(s'|s,a)* of the MDP in the environment model. The formula for calculating the value function is as follows:

$$v(s) \leftarrow \sum \pi(a|s) \sum p(s'|s, a)[r(s'|s, a) + \gamma v(s')] \qquad (10.10)$$

1. **Policy evaluation**

   Given a known environment model, we can use policy evaluation to estimate the expected cumulative reward of a policy and accurately measure the policy. Policy evaluation enables us to evaluate the policy π by calculating the state value function $v_\pi(s)$ corresponding to this policy. In other words, given a policy π, we can calculate the expected state value $v(s)$ of each state s under the policy and subsequently evaluate the policy according to the obtained values.

2. **Policy improvement**

   Policy improvement allows us to act on the results we obtain through policy evaluation, namely to find a better policy. After we calculate the state value $v(s)$ of the current policy by using policy evaluation, we then use the policy improvement algorithm to further solve the calculated state value $v(s)$ in order to find a better policy.

3. **Policy iteration**

   Policy iteration encompasses both policy evaluation and policy improvement. In order to describe the policy iteration process, let us take policy π_0 as an example. We first use policy evaluation to obtain the state value function $v_{\pi_0}(s)$ of the policy and then use policy improvement to obtain a better policy π_1. For this new policy, we again use policy evaluation to obtain the corresponding state value function $v_{\pi_0}(s)$, and then, through policy improvement, we again obtain a better policy π_2. By performing these steps repeatedly, the policy iteration algorithm nears the optimal state value $v(s)$, enabling us to eventually obtain the optimal policy π^* and its corresponding state value function $v_{\pi^*}(s)$.

4. **Value iteration**

The value iteration algorithm, in essence, is a more efficient version of the policy iteration algorithm we just described. With this efficiency-optimized algorithm, all states s are updated in each iteration according to the following formula:

$$v_{k+1}(s) = \max_a \sum_{s',r} p(s', r|s, a)[r + \gamma v_k(s')] \qquad (10.11)$$

where $p(s', r \mid s, a)$ is the probability that the environment transitions to the state s' and the reward r is obtained when the action a is performed in the state s.

The objective of value iteration is to maximize the probability of the state value. After $k + 1$ rounds of iterations are performed, the maximum state value $v(s)$ can be assigned to $v_{k+1}(s)$ through the value iteration until the algorithm ends. We can then obtain the optimal policy based on the state value v.

By using Formula (10.11), we are able to obtain the local optimal state value after iteration of all states and subsequently obtain the local optimal policy based on the local optimal state value. This iterative process continues until the local optimal state value converges to the global optimal state value.

10.2.2 Monte Carlo Method

The Monte Carlo method is suitable for model-free tasks because it needs only to collect the experience episode from the environment rather than requiring complete knowledge of the environment. With this method, we use the calculated data of the experience episode in order to obtain the optimal policy. Specifically, the Monte Carlo method estimates the state value function based on the experience episode mean, which refers to the cumulative discount return value G at the state s in a single experience episode. Its value function is calculated according to the following formula:

$$v(s_t) \leftarrow v(s_t) + a[G_t - v(s_t)] \qquad (10.12)$$

The Monte Carlo method is notable for the following four characteristics:

(1) It can learn the experience episode directly from the environment, that is, the sampling process.
(2) It does not need to know the state transition probability P of the MDP in advance, making this method suitable for model-free tasks.
(3) It uses a complete experience episode for learning and is an offline learning method.
(4) It uses a simpler process to solve model-free reinforcement learning tasks based on the assumption that the expected state value is equal to the average reward of multiple rounds of sampling.

10.2.3   Temporal Difference Method

The temporal difference method is mainly based on the difference data of time series and includes an on-policy, represented by the Sarsa algorithm, and an off-policy, represented by the Q-Learning algorithm.

1. **Sarsa algorithm**

    The Sarsa algorithm is used to estimate the action value function $q(s,a)$. Specifically, it estimates the action value function $q_\pi(s,a)$ for all possible actions in any state s in policy π. The expression for this function is as follows:

    $$q(s_t, a_t) \leftarrow q(s_t, a_t) + a[\underbrace{r_{t+1} + \gamma q(s_{t+1}, a_{t+1})}_{\text{Target}} - q(s_t, a_t)] \qquad (10.13)$$

    $$\underbrace{\qquad\qquad\qquad\qquad\qquad\qquad\qquad}_{\text{Error}}$$

    where $\theta = r_{t+1} + \gamma q(s_{t+1}, a_{t+1})$ is the temporal difference target, and.

$\theta - q(s_t, a_t)$ is the temporal difference error.

The name Sarsa is derived from the five variables needed for each update of the action value function: current state s, current action a, environment feedback reward r, state s' of the next time step, and action a' of the next time step. The algorithm flow is as follows:

Algorithm 10.1 Sarsa algorithm

Input: Random state s

Output: Action value function $q(s,a)$

(1)   **Initialization:**

(2)   Set $q(s,a)$ to any value for any state s

(3)   **Repeat** the experience episode

(4)   Initialize the state s

(5)   Perform the action a in state s according to the action value q

(6)   **Repeat** the time step t in the experience episode

(7)   Perform the action a in state s according to the action value q

(8)   Update the action value function: $q(s,a) \leftarrow q(s,a) + \alpha [r + \gamma q (s', a') - q(s,a)]$

(9)   Record the new state and the new action: $s \leftarrow s', a \leftarrow a'$

(10)   **Proceed until** the state s ends

(11) **Output** the action value function $q(s,a)$.

The Sarsa algorithm starts by initializing the action value function q with a random value and then samples the experience episodes iteratively. In collecting an experience episode, the agent first selects and performs the action a in state s according to the greedy policy. It then learns the environment and updates the action value function $q(s,a)$ until the algorithm ends.

2. Q-Learning algorithm

In updating the action value function $q(s,a)$, the Q-Learning algorithm adopts a policy that differs from one used for selecting an action. The action value function $q(s,a)$ is updated as follows:

$$q(s_t, a_t) \leftarrow q(s_t, a_t) + a[\underbrace{r_{t+1} + \gamma \max_a q(s_{t+1}, a_t)}_{\text{Target}} - q(s_t, a_t)] \qquad (10.14)$$

$$\underbrace{\phantom{q(s_t, a_t) \leftarrow q(s_t, a_t) + a[r_{t+1} + \gamma \max_a q(s_{t+1}, a_t) - q(s_t, a_t)]}}_{\text{Error}}$$

When the Q-Learning algorithm updates the Q value, the temporal difference target is the maximum value $\max_a q(s_{t+1}, a_t)$ of the action value function, which is independent of the policy used in the current selected action. This approach is different from the Sarsa algorithm and means that the action value Q is usually optimal.

In many aspects, the Q-Learning algorithm is similar to Sarsa. However, once the Q-Learning algorithm enters the cycle of repeating the experience episode and initializes the state s, it directly enters the iteration phase of the experience episode and then selects the action a' in the state s' according to the greedy policy. The algorithm flow is shown in Algorithm 10.2.

Algorithm 10.2 Q-Learning algorithm

Input: Random state s

Output: Action value function $q(s,a)$

(1) **Initialization:**

(2) Set $q(s,a)$ to any value for any state s

(3) **Repeat** the experience episode

(4) Initialize the state s

(5) **Repeat** the time step t in the experience episode

(6) Perform the action a in state s according to the action value q

(7) Perform action a to obtain the reward and the state s' of the next time step

(8) Update the action value function: $q(s,a) \leftarrow q(s,a) + a[r + \gamma \max_a q(s',a) - q(s,a)]$·

(9) Record the new state: $s \leftarrow s'$

(10) **Proceed until** the time step T_s ends

(11) **Output** the action value function $q(s,a)$.

Although the dynamic programming method can adequately represent the Bellman equation, most reinforcement learning tasks in real-world applications are model-free tasks, that is, only limited environmental knowledge is provided. The Monte Carlo method based on sampling can solve the problem of reinforcement learning tasks to some extent, and both the Monte Carlo and temporal difference methods are similar in that they estimate the current value function based on the sampled data. The difference between them lies in how they calculate the current value function: The former performs calculation only after the sampling is completed, whereas the latter uses the boosting algorithm in the dynamic programming method for calculation.

10.3   Deep Reinforcement Learning Algorithm

In order to improve the performance of reinforcement learning agents in practical tasks, we need to employ all of the advantages deep learning offers, especially its strong representation ability. As mentioned earlier, deep reinforcement learning is the combination of both deep learning and reinforcement learning, and this combination lends itself to ensuring the agent has strong perception and decision-making abilities.

10.3.1   DQN Algorithm

The deep Q-Learning network (DQN) algorithm, proposed by Minh et al. at Google DeepMind in 2013, was the first deep reinforcement learning algorithm to achieve human-level performance playing a number of classic Atari 2600 games. For some games, the DQN algorithm even exceeded human performance. Figure 10.2 compares the effects of the DQN algorithm, which spawned a surge in research into deep reinforcement learning.

The DQN algorithm introduces three key technologies: objective function, target network, and experience replay. Through these technologies, the DQN algorithm can implicitly learn the optimal policy based on the action value function.

1.   **Objective function**

The DQN algorithm introduces a DNN, which is used to approximate the action value function $q(s,a)$ in high-dimensional and continuous state. However, before using this approximation, we need to define the optimization objective of the network (that is, the objective function of optimization, also called the loss function). We also need to update the weight parameter of the model by using other parameter learning methods.

In order to obtain an objective function that the DNN model can learn, the DQN algorithm uses the Q-Learning algorithm to construct the loss function that the network model can optimize. Using formula (10.14) as the basis, the loss function of the DQN algorithm is as follows:

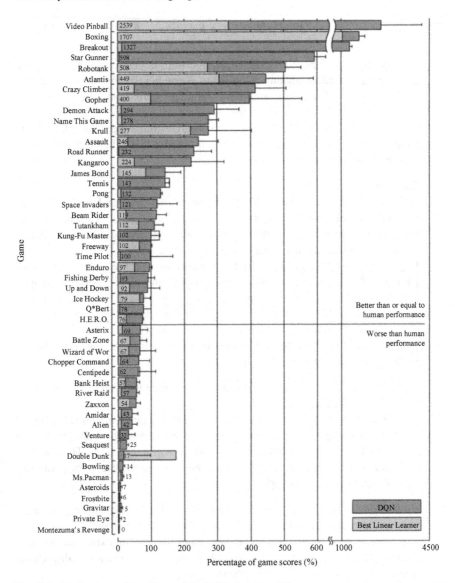

Fig. 10.2 Comparison of the effects of the DQN algorithm [1]

$$L(\boldsymbol{\theta}) = E\big[(\text{Target}\,\boldsymbol{Q} - q(s, a, \boldsymbol{\theta}))^2\big] \qquad (10.15)$$

where $\boldsymbol{\theta}$ is the weight parameter of the DNN model; and target $\boldsymbol{Q}$ is the target action value, where

$$\text{Target } Q = r + \gamma \max_{a'} q(s', a', \theta) \tag{10.16}$$

Because the loss function in the DQN algorithm is determined based on the Q-Learning algorithm update, the effect of Formula (10.14) is the same as that of Formula (10.15); specifically, both formulas approximate the target value based on the current prediction value.

After obtaining the loss function of the DQN algorithm, we can solve the weight parameter θ of the DNN model's function $L(\theta)$ by using the gradient descent algorithm in deep learning.

2. **Target network**

As we can see from Formula (10.15), the prediction value and target value use the same parameter model in the Q-Learning algorithm. This means that the prediction value increases with the target value, increasing the probability of model oscillation and divergence.

In order to solve this problem, the DQN algorithm uses the historical network parameter θ^- to evaluate the value of the next time step of an experience sample. It updates the historical network parameter θ^- only in the offline multi-step time interval to provide a stable training target for the network to be evaluated and allows sufficient training time to mitigate any estimation errors.

Furthermore, the DQN algorithm uses two CNNs for learning: a prediction network and a target network.

(1)   Prediction network $q(s, a, \theta_i)$: used to evaluate the value function of the current state-action pair.

(2)   Target network $q(s, a, \theta_i^-)$: used to generate the target action value (target Q). The algorithm updates parameter θ belonging to the prediction network according to the loss function in Formula (10.15). Then, after N rounds of iterations, the algorithm copies this parameter to the parameter θ^- in the target network

By introducing the target network, the DQN algorithm ensures that the target value remains unchanged for a certain period of time. It also reduces the correlation between the prediction and target values to a certain extent and reduces the possibility of oscillation and divergence occurring in the loss value during training, thereby improving algorithm stability.

3. **Experience replay**

In deep learning tasks, each input sample data is independent of other samples, meaning that there is no direct relationship between them. For example, images A and B used as input in an image classification model are not directly related. Conversely, in reinforcement learning tasks, the samples are often strongly correlated and non-static. If we were to use correlated data directly to train the DNN, the loss value would fluctuate continuously during training, making it difficult to achieve model convergence.

To solve this problem, the DQN algorithm introduces the experience replay mechanism. This mechanism allows experience sample data—obtained through interaction between the agent and environment at each time step—to be stored in an experience pool. Subsequently, when network training needs to be performed, a mini-batch of data is selected from the experience pool for retraining. Such a mechanism offers a number of advantages: (1) facilitates the backing up of reward data; (2) helps remove the correlation and dependence between samples, because mini-batches of random samples can be obtained; (3) reduces the deviation of value function estimation after function approximation; (4) solves the problems of data correlation and non-static distribution; and (5) facilitates network model convergence.

Due to the use of this mechanism, the DQN algorithm stores a large amount of historical experience sample data, using the following quintuple format for storage:

$$(s, a, r, s', T) \tag{10.17}$$

This quintuple indicates that the agent performs action a in state s, enters the new state s', and obtains the corresponding reward r. Here, T is a Boolean value that indicates whether the new state s' is the end state.

After performing any time step in the environment, the agent stores the obtained experience data in the experience pool. Subsequently, the agent randomly selects a mini-batch of experience sample data from this pool after performing N steps. Based on the experience sample data, the DQN Formula (10.15) is executed to update the Q function.

The experience replay mechanism, despite its simplicity, effectively removes the correlation and dependence between samples. In so doing, it allows the DNN to obtain an accurate value function in reinforcement learning tasks.

4. **Algorithm flow**

The DQN algorithm uses a deep CNN with the weight parameter θ as the network model of the action value function and simulates the action value function $q_\pi(s, a)$ by using the CNN model $q(s, a, \theta)$, that is,

$$q(s, a, \theta) \approx q_\pi(s, a) \tag{10.18}$$

This means that we can define the object function, based on the mean square error, as the loss function of the deep CNN.

$$L_i(\theta_i) = E[(r + \gamma \max_{a'} q(s', a', \theta_i) - \max_a q(s, a, \theta_i)^2] \tag{10.19}$$

where a' is the action value of the next time step, and
s' is the state value of the next time step.

From Formula (10.19), we can see that the Q-Learning algorithm mainly uses the updated Q value as the target value for training. Conversely, in the DQN algorithm, the target Q value is predicted by the target network, and the current Q value is predicted by the prediction network. Subsequently, the mean square error algorithm is used to calculate the temporal difference error in the Q-Learning algorithm.

Using Formula (10.19) as the basis, we calculate the gradient of the deep CNN model parameter θ as follows:

$$\nabla_{\theta_i} L_i(\theta_i) = E[(r + \gamma \max_{a'} q(s', a', \theta_i) - \max_a q(s, a, \theta_i))\nabla_{\theta_i}(s, a, \theta_i)]$$

$$(10.20)$$

To optimize the objective function, we implement the CNN model by using the mini-batch stochastic gradient descent algorithm. The CNN then calculates ∇_{θ_i} (s, a, θ_i) in order to obtain the optimal action value (Q value).

The application scope of the DQN algorithm is limited, as it can deal with only discrete-control reinforcement learning tasks. In order to overcome these limitations, a number of DQN algorithm variants, such as Double DQN and Dueling DQN, have been proposed.

The specific flow of DQN algorithm version 2015 is described below.

Two CNNs are used: The prediction network $q(s, a, \theta_i)$ is used to evaluate the current action function, and the target network $q(s, a, \theta_i^-)$ is used to calculate the target value. The DQN algorithm updates the parameters of the target network according to the loss function and after C rounds of iterations assigns the relevant parameters of the prediction network to the target network.

Algorithm 10.3   DQN algorithm version 2015

Input: Prediction network and target network

Output: Target network

(1)   **Initialize** the experience pool $\mathcal{D}$, which stores a maximum of N experience samples

(2)   **Initialize** the prediction network with the weight parameter $\boldsymbol{\theta}$

(3)   **Initialize** the target network with the weight parameter $\boldsymbol{\theta}^- = \boldsymbol{\theta}$

(4)   **Repeat** the experience episodes 1 to M times

(5)   Initialize the state s_1, and calculate the input sequence $\phi_1 = \phi(s_1)$

           Repeat the time steps from 1 to T in the experience episode

(6)   Select the random action a_t based on the probability ε

                Select the action a_t based on the probability 1-ε according to
                $$a_t = \max_a q^{\bullet}(\phi(s_1), a, \boldsymbol{\theta})$$

(7)   Perform action a_t to obtain the reward r_t and the state image frame x_{t+1}

(8)   Let $s_{t+1} = s_t, x_{t+1}$, and calculate the input sequence for the next time step:
                $$\phi_{t+1} = \phi(s_{t+1}) \tag{1.21}$$

(9)   Store the experience samples $(\phi_t, a_t, r_t, \phi_{t+1})$ in the experience pool $\mathcal{D}$

(10)   Obtain a mini-batch of random sample data $(\phi_t, a_t, r_t, \phi_{t+1})$ from the experience pool $\mathcal{D}$

(11)   Set y_i:
                $$y_i = \begin{cases} r_j \\ r_j + \gamma \max_{a'} q^-(\phi_{j+1}, a', \boldsymbol{\theta}^-) \end{cases} \tag{1.22}$$

(12)   Update the network parameter $\boldsymbol{\theta}$ in the loss function $(y_i - q\ (\phi_j, a_j, \boldsymbol{\theta}))^2$ by using the gradient descent algorithm

(13)   Re-assign $q^- = q$ every C steps.

10.3.2   DDPG Algorithm

The deep deterministic policy gradient (DDPG) [2] algorithm, proposed by Lillicrap et al. in 2015, widens the application scope of the DQN algorithm, allowing it to be used for reinforcement learning tasks with continuous action spaces rather than only those tasks with discrete actions. To better understand the DDPG algorithm, we must first explore its constituent parts.

1.   **Policy gradient algorithm** [3]
     The policy gradient (PG) algorithm explicitly expresses the optimal policy of each time step by using the policy gradient probability distribution function $\pi_\theta(s_t \mid \boldsymbol{\theta}^\pi)$. To obtain the optimal action value a_t^* of the current time step,

the agent samples the action at each time step t according to the probability distribution.

$$a_t^* \sim \pi_\theta(s_t | \boldsymbol{\theta}^\pi) \qquad (10.23)$$

The optimal action is generated through a random process, meaning that the policy distribution function $\pi_\theta(s_t | \boldsymbol{\theta}^\pi)$ learned by the policy gradient algorithm is a stochastic policy.

2. **Deterministic policy gradient algorithm** [4]

    One of the major weaknesses in the policy gradient algorithm is its inefficiency in terms of policy evaluation. Once the algorithm learns the stochastic policy, the agent can obtain a specific action value only after sampling actions at each time step according to the optimal policy probability distribution function. This consumes a great deal of computing resources, because the agent performs sampling in high-dimensional action space at each time step.

    To address this inefficiency, David Silver—in 2014—explored the possibility of using the deterministic policy gradient (DPG) algorithm to quickly and efficiently solve reinforcement learning tasks with continuous actions. For the action of each time step t, the action value is determined by the function μ.

$$a_t^* \sim \mu_\theta(s_t | \boldsymbol{\theta}^\mu) \qquad (10.24)$$

    where μ is the optimal action policy, which is a stochastic policy obtained without sampling.

3. **Deep deterministic policy gradient algorithm**

    In 2016, Lillicrap et al. pointed out that the DDPG algorithm fuses the DNN with the DPG algorithm and uses the actor-critic algorithm as the basic architecture of the algorithm. The DDPG algorithm makes the following improvements over the DPG algorithm:

    (1) Uses the DNN as a function approximation

         The DNN is used as an approximation of the policy function $\mu(s; \boldsymbol{\theta}^\mu)$ and of the action value function $q(s, a; \boldsymbol{\theta}^q)$. To train the parameters in these two neural network models, the stochastic gradient descent algorithm is used. With the accuracy, efficiency, and convergence of nonlinear approximation policy functions, deep reinforcement learning can deal with deterministic policy problems.

    (2) Introduces an experience replay mechanism

         When actors interact with the environment, the resulting state transition sample data is chronologically correlated. With the experience replay mechanism of the DQN algorithm, the correlation and dependence between samples are removed. Furthermore, the deviation of value function estimation is reduced after the approximation of function. This effectively solves the problem of independently identically distribution (i. i. d) and allows the algorithm to converge more easily.

(3)   Uses a dual-network architecture

For both the policy function and value function, the dual-DNN architecture is used, which includes the policy target network $\mu'(s;\theta^{\mu'})$, policy online network $\mu(s; \theta^{\mu})$, value online network $q(s; \theta^{q})$, and value target network $q'(s;\theta^{q'})$. Such an architecture speeds up the algorithm's convergence and achieves a stable learning process.

10.3.3   A3C Algorithm

Based on the idea of asynchronous reinforcement learning, Minh et al. proposed a lightweight deep reinforcement learning framework called asynchronous advantage actor-critic (A3C) [5]. This framework uses the asynchronous gradient descent algorithm to optimize the deep network model and employs several reinforcement learning algorithms in order to perform fast, CPU-based policy learning during deep reinforcement learning. The A3C algorithm is a combination of the advantage actor-critic algorithm and the asynchronous algorithm, both of which are described as follows.

1. **Advantage actor-critic algorithm**
    The actor-critic algorithm combines the advantages of two algorithms: value-based reinforcement learning, which is used as a critic, and policy-based reinforcement learning, which is used as an actor. When the critic network is updated, the concept of advantage function is introduced to evaluate the output action of the network model. In so doing, deviation in the evaluation of the policy gradient is reduced.
    The A3C algorithm combines the advantage function and the actor-critic algorithm and uses two network models: one to approximate the value function $v(s)$, used to judge the quality of a state; the other to approximate the policy function $\pi(s)$, used to estimate the probability of a set of output actions.
(1)   Value-based learning—critic
    In reinforcement learning based on value function approximation, the DNN can be used as the approximation function of the value function, where w is the weight parameter of the network model.

$$q(s, a) \approx q(s, a; w) \qquad (10.25)$$

The loss function of the DQN algorithm is as follows:

$$L(w_i) = E[(\text{Target}Q - q(s, a; w_i))^2] \qquad (10.26)$$

where target Q is the target action value:

$$\text{Target } Q = r + \gamma \max_{a'} Q(s', a'; w_i^-) \qquad (10.27)$$

The loss function in Formula (10.25) is based on the single-step Q-Learning algorithm. This means that only the state of the next time step is considered during calculation of the target action value, having an adverse effect directly or indirectly. Specifically, it only directly affects the value of the state-action pair that produces the reward r and can only indirectly affect other state-action pairs based on the action value function. The result of this is a decrease in the algorithm's learning rate.

In order to quickly propagate the reward, we can use the multi-step Q-Learning algorithm, where "multi-step" refers to the states of the subsequent n steps.

$$\text{Target } Q = r_t + \gamma r_{t+1} + \dots + \gamma^{n-1} r_{t+n-1} + \gamma^n \max_a Q(s_{t+n}, a)$$

The main advantages of this approach are that the previous n state-action pairs can be directly affected by the reward r, the historical experience can be better simulated, and the learning efficiency of the algorithm can be significantly improved.

(2)   Policy-based learning—actor

In policy-based reinforcement learning, the DNN is used as the approximation function of the policy function, where θ is the weight parameter of the policy network model.

$$\pi(s, a) \approx \pi(a|s; \theta) \tag{10.29}$$

The A3C algorithm uses policy iteration to update the weight parameter θ in the network. Because the goal of the policy function is to maximize the reward, we can calculate the expected reward by using the gradient ascent algorithm. The formula for updating the policy gradient is as follows:

$$\nabla_\theta E[r_t] = \nabla_\theta \log \pi(a_t|s_t; \theta) r_t \tag{10.30}$$

where $\pi(a_t \mid s_t; \theta)$ is the probability of selecting action a_t in state s_t; and $\nabla_\theta \log \pi(a_t \mid s_t; \theta) r_t$ means that the logarithm of the probability is multiplied by the reward r_t of the action, and the weight parameter θ is updated by using the gradient ascent algorithm.

Formula (10.28) indicates that an action with a higher reward expectation is more likely to be selected. However, assuming that each action has a positive reward, the probability of outputting each action will increase continuously with the gradient ascent algorithm, leading to a significant reduction in the learning rate while increasing the gradient variance. In order to reduce the gradient variance, we can standardize Formula (10.30) as follows:

$$\nabla_\theta \log \pi(a_t|s_t; \theta)(r_t - b_t(s_t)) \tag{10.31}$$

where $b_t(s_t)$ is a baseline function, which is set to the estimated reward r_t. The gradient is calculated to update the parameter θ. When the total reward exceeds the baseline, the probability of the action increases; conversely, the probability decreases when the reward falls below the baseline. In both cases, the gradient variance will be reduced.

The estimated variance can be reduced and kept unbiased by deducting the baseline function $b_t(s_t)$ from the reward r_t in order to learn the policy function.

(3)   Advantage function.

The advantage function is modified based on the loss function of the actor-critic algorithm, allowing it to estimate the action value more accurately according to the reward.

During a policy gradient update, the agent learns which actions are good and which ones are bad based on the discounted reward r_t used in the update rule. Subsequently, the network is updated to determine the quality of the action. The function is the advantage function $A(s_t, a_t)$:

$$A(s_t, a_t) = q(s_t, a_t) - v(s_t) \tag{10.32}$$

Referring back to Formula (10.31), we can regard the discounted reward r_t as an estimate of the action value function $q(s_t, a_t)$ and regard the baseline function $b_t(s_t)$ as an estimate of the state value function (s_t). This means that we can replace $r_t - b_t(s_t)$ with an action advantage function, as follows:

$$r_t \approx q^\pi(s_t, a_t) \tag{10.33}$$

$$b_t(s_t) \approx v^\pi(s_t) \tag{10.34}$$

From Formula (10.32), we can use $q(s_t, a_t) - v(s_t)$ to evaluate the value of the current action value function relative to the mean value. This is because the state value function $v(s_t)$ is the expected action probability of all the action value functions in the state of the time step t, and the action value function $q(s_t, a_t)$ is the value corresponding to a single action.

Although the A3C algorithm does not directly determine the action value Q, it uses the discounted cumulative reward R as the estimate of the action value Q. As a result, we are able to obtain the advantage function, as follows:

$$A(s_t, a_t) = R(s_t, a_t) - v(s_t) \tag{10.35}$$

2.   Asynchronous algorithm

The DQN algorithm uses an agent, represented by a single DNN, to interact with the environment, whereas the A3C algorithm uses multiple agents to interact with the environment and thereby achieve greater learning efficiency. As shown in

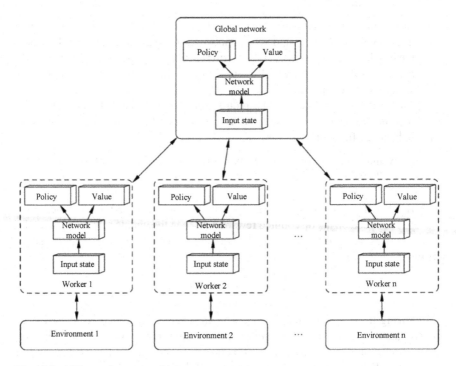

Fig. 10.3 A3C asynchronous architecture

Fig. 10.3, the main components of the A3C asynchronous architecture are environments, workers, and a global network, where each worker functions as an agent
to interact with an independent environment and uses its own DNN model. In this
architecture, different workers simultaneously interact with the environment, and
executed policies and learned experiences differ among the workers. As a result, this
multi-agent asynchronous approach offers faster and more effective operation along
with greater diversity than a single worker approach.

The flow of the A3C algorithm is asynchronous, as shown in Fig. 10.4. From the
figure, we can see that each worker replicates the global network as a parameter of
its own DNN model (1). Then, each agent uses multiple CPU threads to allocate
tasks, and different workers use the greedy policy with different parameters in order
to ensure that they obtain different experiences (2). Next, each worker calculates its
own value and policy loss (3). Based on the calculation results, each worker then
calculates the gradient by using the loss function (4). Finally, each worker updates the
parameters of the global network, that is, each thread updates the learned parameters
to the global network (5). This flow is repeated until the ideal network parameters
are learned.

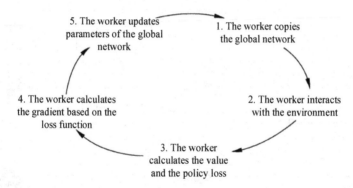

Fig. 10.4 Flow of the asynchronous algorithm

10.4 Latest Applications

10.4.1 Recommendation System

In recent years, Internet companies such as Facebook, Alibaba, JD.com [6], and Tencent have begun to explore how they can use and implement deep reinforcement learning in their recommendation systems. For example, Zheng et al. [7] used deep reinforcement learning to address the recommendation variability problem in the news field, and Chen et al. [8] from Alibaba used model-based deep learning in recommendation systems, the latter of which we discuss below.

Those who implement recommendation systems typically do so using a loss function to evaluate a model that can minimize the difference between the model's prediction result and the user's immediate response. In other words, the typical recommendation system model does not explicitly consider users' long-term interests, which may vary over time depending on what they see. Furthermore, such changes may have a significant influence on the behavior of the recommenders.

Chen pointed out that, in the recommendation system, solving high sample complexity of a model-free task is performed more reliably by using model-based deep reinforcement learning. As shown in Fig. 10.5, the recommendation system framework uses a unified minimax framework to learn a user behavior model and related reward functions and subsequently uses this model to learn the policy of deep reinforcement learning.

Specifically, this framework uses the generative adversarial learning network to simulate the dynamic behavior of users and learn its reward function. User behavior and rewards can be evaluated using the minimax algorithm. As a result, we are able to obtain a more accurate user model, as well as a method for learning a reward function that is consistent with the user model. Such a reward function can also strengthen the learning task compared with an artificially designed one. Furthermore, this user model enables researchers to execute model-based reinforcement learning tasks for new users, thereby achieving better recommendation results.

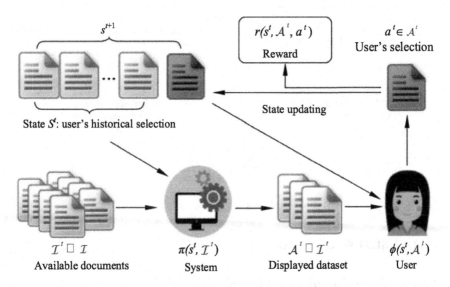

Fig. 10.5 Interaction between a user and a recommendation system

To obtain a combined recommendation policy, researchers developed a cascading DQN algorithm that not only identifies the optimal subset of objects from many potential candidates, by using the cascading design of the action function, but also significantly reduces the computational difficulty because the time complexity of the cascading function is linearly related to the number of candidates. Figure 10.6 compares such effects of the DQN algorithm.

In terms of held-out likelihood and click prediction, experimental results show that the GAN model is a better fit for user behavior. Based on the user model and the reward learned, researchers found that evaluating the recommendation policy provides users with better long-term cumulative rewards. Furthermore, in the case of model mismatch, the model-based policy can quickly adapt to the dynamic changes of user interests.

10.4.2   Gambling Game

In 2018, Wu et al. [9] from Tencent released the Honor of Kings AI based on reinforcement learning for group gaming. The algorithm used five independent Honor of Kings agents, pitted against five human players, to play 250 games, 48% of which the algorithm won.

StarCraft is another game that also uses reinforcement learning. Because it involves a large observation space, huge action space, partial observations, simultaneous multi-player moves, and long-term local decision-making, researchers have found this game to be of significant interest. For example, Sun et al. [10] in Tencent

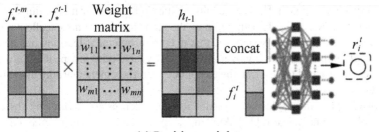

(a) Position weights

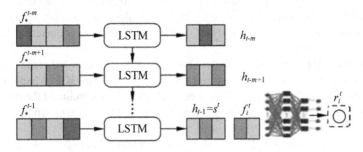

(b) LSTM parameterization model architecture

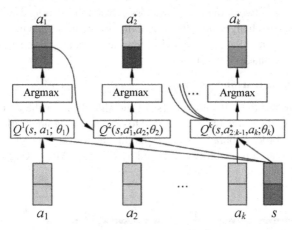

(c) Cascading Q network

Fig. 10.6 Comparison of the effects of the DQN algorithm

AI Lab developed an AI agent capable of defeating the built-in AI agents in the full game of StarCraft II, including the cheating agents at levels 8, 9, and 10, by using reinforcement deep learning. Of note is that the built-in AI at level 10 is estimated to be equivalent to the top 30–50% of human players according to the Battle.net League ranking system. DeepMind has also explored StarCraft, using the meta-reinforcement learning (Meta-RL) [11] algorithm to play the game and achieving excellent results.

Against this backdrop, we can see that deep reinforcement learning has become increasingly popular in gaming over the past few years. Taking AlphaGo Zero as an example, we proceed to describe the use of deep reinforcement learning in the board game Go.

AlphaGo [12], the predecessor to AlphaGo Zero, learns how to play by observing human play. AlphaGo Zero [13] skips this step. Instead, it learns by playing itself, starting from scratch. The AlphaGo Zero algorithm begins with a DNN that, except for the game rules, lacks any understanding of how to play Go. It proceeds to learn the game by combining the DNN with the search algorithm to play against itself, during which the DNN continuously adjusts and upgrades its parameters in order to predict the probability of each move as well as the final winner.

As mentioned already, AlphaGo Zero has no background knowledge of Go, except the rules. It uses only one neural network, differing from AlphaGo, which includes two DNNs: One, called the policy network, evaluates the possibility of the next move based on numerous human games, and the other, called the value network, evaluates the current situation.

AlphaGo Zero uses the Monte Carlo tree search algorithm to generate games that it uses as training data for the DNN. A 19 × 19 Go board is used as the input in the DNN, while the output is based on the probability of the next move and the win rate (the difference between the two is the loss). Through ongoing execution of the Monte Carlo tree search algorithm, the probability of the move and the win rate will eventually stabilize, and the accuracy will increase as training continues. Next, we will describe the AlphaGo Zero algorithm.

1.   Reinforcement learning process

Figure 10.7 shows the self-play process of the algorithm for the time steps s_1 to s_T. In each state s_t, the last network f_θ is used to execute the Monte Carlo tree search algorithm once in order to obtain the corresponding action a_θ. The action is selected according to the search probability calculated by using the Monte Carlo tree search

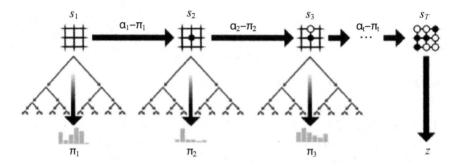

Fig. 10.7   Self-play process of AlphaGo Zero

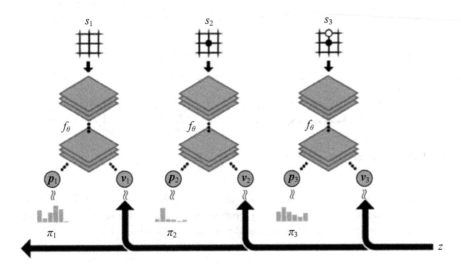

Fig. 10.8 Neural network training process of AlphaGo Zero

algorithm, that is, a_t to π_t. After reaching the end state s_T, the algorithm determines the winner z and the reward according to the rules of the game.

Figure 10.8 shows the neural network training process of AlphaGo Zero. The network uses the original Go board state s_t as the input and outputs two channels of data through multiple convolution operations. One of these channels is vector p_t, which indicates the probability distribution of the moves in the Go game; the other channel is scalar v_t, which represents the win rate of the player in the current game s_t. The error between the predicted winner v_t and the actual winner z is calculated based on the similarity between the maximization policy vector p_t and the search probability π_t. The neural network model parameter θ is updated automatically, and the new parameters will be applied to the next round of self-play.

2. **Monte Carlo tree search process**

As already mentioned, AlphaGo Zero uses the Monte Carlo tree search algorithm. Figure 10.9 shows the algorithm process, which is subsequently described.

(1) For each branch selected through simulation, the largest $Q + U$ is selected, where Q is the action value, and U is the upper confidence limit. U depends on the priority probability p stored on the branch and the number of access times N to the branch of the search tree.

(2) The leaf node is extended, the neural network $(p, v) = f_\theta$ is used to evaluate the state s, and the value of vector p is stored on the extended edge corresponding to the state s.

(3) The action value Q is updated based on the value v and reflects the mean value of the subtrees of all actions.

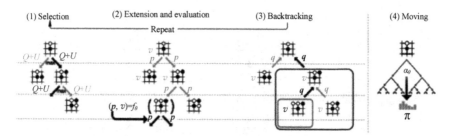

Fig. 10.9 Monte Carlo tree search process of AlphaGo Zero

(4)   Once the search is completed, the search probability π is returned. The number of remaining searches is directly proportional to $N^{1/\tau}$, where N is the number of access times to each branch, and τ is the control parameter.

10.5   Implementing DQN-Based Game Using MindSpore

The interfaces and processes of MindSpore may constantly change due to iterative development. For all runnable code, see the code in corresponding chapters at https://mindspore.cn/resource. You can scan the QR code on the right to access relevant resources.

References

1. V. Mnih, K. Kavukcuoglu, D. Silver et al., Playing atari with deep reinforcement learning, (2013). [2019–11–10] https://arxiv.org/pdf/1312.5602.pdf
2. T.P.Lillicrap, J.J. Hunt, A. Pritzel et al., Continuous control with deep reinforcement learning, (2015). [2019–11–10] https://arxiv.org/pdf/1509.02971.pdf
3. R.S. Sutton, D.A. McAllester, S.P.Singh et al., Policy gradient methods for reinforcement learning with function approximation. in *Advances in Neural Information Processing Systems* (2000), pp. 1057–1063
4. D. Silver, G. Lever, N. Heess et al., Deterministic policy gradient algorithms, (2014). [2019–11–10] http://xueshu.baidu.com/usercenter/paper/show?paperid=43a8642b8 1092513eb6bad1f3f5231e2&site=xueshu_se
5. V. Mnih, A.P. Badia, M. Mirza et al., Asynchronous methods for deep reinforcement learning. in *International Conference on Machine Learning* (2016), pp. 1928–1937

6. X. Zhao, L. Zhang, Z. Ding et al., Deep reinforcement learning for list-wise recommendations, (2017). [2019–11–10] https://arxiv.org/pdf/1801.00209.pdf

7. G. Zheng, F. Zhang, Z. Zheng et al., DRN: a deep reinforcement learning framework for news recommendation. in *Proceedings of the 2018 World Wide Web Conference. International World Wide Web Conferences Steering Committee*, (2018), pp. 167–176

8. X. Chen, S. Li, H. Li et al., Generative adversarial user model for reinforcement learning based recommendation system. in *International Conference on Machine Learning* (2019), pp. 1052–1061

9. B. Wu, Q. Fu, J. Liang et al., Hierarchical macro strategy model for MOBA game AI, (2018) [2019–11–10] https://arxiv.org/pdf/1812.07887.pdf

10. P. Sun, X. Sun, L. Han et al., TStarBots: defeating the cheating level builtin AI in starCraft II in the full game, (2018). [2019–11–10] https://arxiv.org/pdf/1809.07193.pdf

11. J.X. Wang, Z. Kurth-Nelson, D. Kumaran et al., Prefrontal cortex as a meta-reinforcement learning system. Nat. Neurosci. **21**(6), 860 (2018)

12. D. Silver, A. Huang, C.J. Maddison et al., Mastering the game of go with deep neural networks and tree search. Nature **529**(7587), 484 (2016)

13. D. Silver, J. Schrittwieser, K. Simonyan et al., Mastering the game of go without human knowledge. Nature **550**(7676), 354 (2017)

Chapter 11
Automated Machine Learning

Over the past few decades, machine learning has been the subject of extensive research and application. In fields such as speech recognition [1], image recognition, and machine translation [2, 3], for example, deep learning has witnessed significant achievements. Yet despite this, the application of machine learning in real-world scenarios remains a challenging feat. Conventional machine learning [4–6] relies heavily on human expertise to preprocess data, extract effective features, and select suitable algorithms and hyperparameters for model training. And although deep learning does not require manual extraction of features, it too relies on human expertise. Specifically, experts need to account for different hardware devices (GPU, TPU, and NPU) and different performance constraints (latency and memory) when designing neural network architectures. In order to reduce the dependence on expertise and avoid manual deviation, automated machine learning (AutoML) emerges.

11.1 AutoML Framework

AutoML automates the end-to-end process of applying machine learning to real-world scenarios, automating data annotation, data preprocessing, feature engineering, model selection, and hyperparameter tuning, as shown in Fig. 11.1. Significant differences exist between conventional machine learning and deep learning in terms of data preprocessing, feature engineering, and model selection. For example, conventional machine learning needs to preprocess original data into a standardized structure through data cleaning, integration, and transformation. Conversely, deep learning does not require data preprocessing (but still needs data annotation), because it uses homogeneous unstructured data, such as images and audio. In conventional machine learning, feature engineering includes extraction, cleaning, selection, and dimension reduction, and model selection selects optimal models from numerous algorithms or generates enhanced hybrid models by using an ensemble learning method.

© Tsinghua University Press 2021

L. Chen, *Deep Learning and Practice with MindSpore*, Cognitive Intelligence and Robotics, https://doi.org/10.1007/978-981-16-2233-5_11

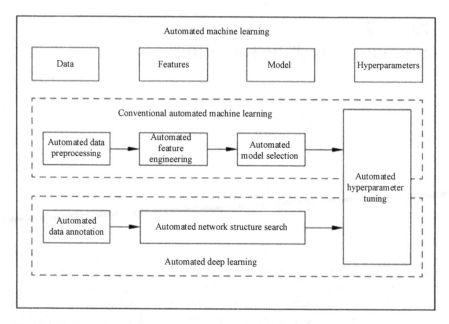

Fig. 11.1 Basic framework for automated machine learning

Feature engineering and model selection are independent of each other in conventional machine learning, whereas they are combined in deep learning, where they mainly depend on the structural design of the neural network, including the use of operators and spatial arrangement.

AutoML also employs NAS and automated hyperparameter tuning. The NAS algorithm automates the design of neural network architectures that meet specific requirement through reinforcement learning [7–9], evolution of algorithms [10, 11], and gradient methods [12–14]. Used extensively in fields such as computer vision (including image classification, object detection [15], semantic segmentation [16, 17], and image super resolution [18]), NLP [19], and graph neural networks [20], this algorithm can determine the neural network architecture. However, the resulting architecture requires many hyperparameters to be set in advance, including the learning rate, weight decay, and number of training cycles. As research has shown, the settings of these hyperparameters directly affect the accuracy of the model as well as the training and inference speed. In order to automate the search and tuning of hyperparameters in a given scenario, we can use the grid search, random search, or Bayesian optimization algorithm.

The commercial application of AutoML has been successful, with companies such as Google, Microsoft, Oneclick, Baidu, 4Paradigm, and WISUTECH launching a range of AutoML products. For example, Google's use of AutoML in its cloud platform enables users with limited expertise to train high-quality deep learning

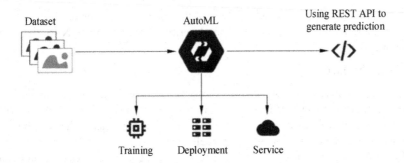

Fig. 11.2 Operating principle of Google AutoML[1]

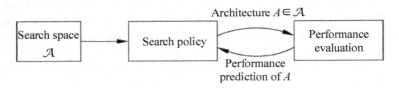

Fig. 11.3 Basic flow of the NAS algorithm

models, as shown in Fig. 11.2. As mentioned earlier, the NAS algorithm and automated hyperparameter tuning are key technologies in AutoML. This section focuses on these two technologies.

11.1.1 NAS Algorithm

The NAS algorithm consists of three components, namely search space, search policy, and performance evaluation, as shown in Fig. 11.3. The search space defines the types of neural networks that the algorithm can design and optimize; the search policy defines how to generate the optimal network structure in the search space; performance evaluation analyzes performance metrics, such as the precision and latency of the identified neural network architecture, based on training and validation datasets.

Through an ongoing process of optimizing the search policy based on results of performance evaluation, we are able to obtain an optimal network structure. Yet our pursuit of optimal performance is limited by computing resources and time costs. In recent years, researchers have focused on optimizing the NAS algorithm in order to minimize resource consumption while ensuring performance. Such optimizations include narrowing the search space for specific tasks based on prior knowledge. In addition, we can employ weight sharing to avoid the need for standard training

---

[1] Reference website: https://cloud.google.com/automl/.

and validation processes, thereby reducing the time costs of performance evaluation. In the remainder of this section, we describe each of the three NAS algorithm
components in turn.

1. **Search space**

The search space not only defines the types of neural networks that the NAS
algorithm can design and optimize, as mentioned earlier, but also restricts the network
architecture and affects the result of the algorithm. In most cases, the search space
is based on either an entire network or a cell.

In the search space based on an entire network, the common types of architecture
are chain and multi-branch networks. A chain network is the simplest of the two,
where the output of one layer is used as the input of the subsequent layer, as shown in
Fig. 11.4a. Before establishing a chain network, we first need to define the network
size (that is, the number of layers) and then define the operations at each layer,
for example, 3×3 convolution or 3×3 pooling. For a simple chain network, the
search space is small and easy to examine, but this compromises the algorithm's
ability to search freely. In order to address this problem, the NAS algorithm adds the

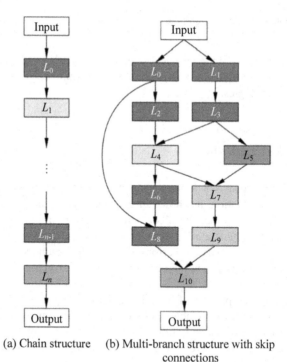

(a) Chain structure   (b) Multi-branch structure with skip
                            connections

Fig. 11.4 Neural network architectures with different connection types[2]

---

[2] Source: https://arxiv.org/pdf/1808.05377.pdf.

multi-branch network architecture to the search space. This architecture, as shown in Fig. 11.4b, involves skip connections, making it more complex. Similar to a chain network, a multi-branch network uses the output of one layer as the input of the subsequent layer, but it also allows one layer to establish a skip connection with a previous layer and use its output as the input. Furthermore, each layer in the search space can accept more than one input. To define the search space, it is first necessary to add parameters such as anchor points (which are used to indicate skip connections) defining how the network is connected. While the multi-branch network increases the search space of the algorithm, it also inevitably increases the search complexity.

In the cell-based search space (see Fig. 11.5), the algorithm determines the network architecture by stacking cells (normal and reduction cells, which generally include operations such as convolution and pooling) according to a predefined structure. In a normal cell, the input dimension remains unchanged, whereas in a reduction cell, this is reduced for output. The cell-based search space improves the network's ability to migrate to different tasks and datasets in addition to reducing the search space and the search complexity. For example, Zoph et al. successfully migrated the

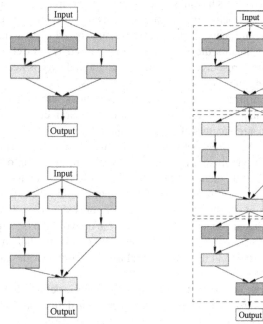

(a) Two different cell structures: normal cell (top) and reduction cell (bottom)

(b) Neural network architecture constructed by stacking cells sequentially

Fig. 11.5 Cell-based search space[3]

---

[3] Source: https://arxiv.org/pdf/1808.05377.pdf.

cell structure used on CIFAR-10 to ImageNet and achieved results that surpassed the previous best at that time on the ImageNet dataset. The cell-based search method is also used in other fields such as object detection [15] and semantic segmentation [17]. Ghiasi et al. [15], for example, generated the object detection network based on the cell structure used in the feature pyramid network (FPN), and Liu et al. [17] generated the semantically segmented network by searching for the cell structure of atrous spatial pyramid pooling (ASPP).

2. **Search policy**

Since both network-wide and cell-based search spaces are large, it is impractical to traverse the entire search space. Even in the same search space, the results from different search policies, which also affect the algorithm result, may vary due to limited computing resources. In order to address these concerns, we need to update the search framework and quickly find the globally optimal solution, rather than a locally optimal one. The key to this hinges on us using the feedback information effectively.

Zoph et al. [7] took a novel approach by using reinforcement learning on CIFAR-10 and PTB datasets. The NAS has subsequently become an area of focused research in machine learning after achieving competitive results, driving the use of reinforcement learning, evolutionary learning, and gradient-based approaches in neural network search. Yet despite this, the NAS algorithm proposed by Zoph et al. consumes a great deal of computing resources, something that the industry is keen to address in addition to improving the accuracy of network models.

In reinforcement learning, an agent performs continuous sampling in the operation space to sequentially generate network architecture parameters. The algorithm determines the network architecture after sampling is complete, and the validation set returns the accuracy of the current network architecture to the agent as a bonus value, thereby updating agent parameters in order to improve the selection of operations during sampling. Zoph et al. achieved this by using an RNN as an agent to control the generation of network architectures, so that we can simplify the explanation. Let us take the generation of a neural network including only the convolution layer as an example. An RNN agent sequentially generates the convolution hyperparameters for each layer, including the number of convolution kernels, the height and width of each convolution kernel, and the longitudinal and horizontal strides, as shown in Fig. 11.6.

Specifically, the network generation process of the RNN is defined as a continuous action $a_{1:T}$, and the reward value $J(\theta_c)$ of the algorithm is defined as follows:

$$J(\theta_c) = E_{P(a_{1:T}; \theta_c)}[R] \tag{11.1}$$

where θ_c is an RNN parameter;
P is the probability that the RNN selects the current network architecture after T steps; and
R is the accuracy of the current network architecture in the validation set.

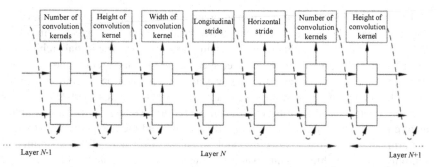

Fig. 11.6 Network sequence generated by the RNN agent[4]

Because R is indifferentiable, the policy gradient $\nabla_{\theta_c} J(\theta_c)$ is used in the algorithm to update θ_c:

$$\theta_{c'} = \theta_c + \eta \nabla J(\theta_c) \tag{11.2}$$

$$\nabla_{\theta_c} J(\theta_c) = \sum_{t=1}^{T} E_{P_{(a_{1:T};\theta_c)}} \left[\nabla_{\theta_c} \log P\left(a_t | a_{(t-1):1}; \theta_c\right) R \right] \tag{11.3}$$

where η is the learning rate.

In different reinforcement learning NAS algorithms, the definition and optimization methods of search policies are different. For example, Zoph et al. used the policy gradient to update RNN parameters, whereas Baker et al. used the Q-Learning method to control the generation of the network architecture.

In the approach used by Zoph et al., the network architecture is searched from scratch. To address this, Cai et al. proposed the concept of network morphism, in which the algorithm uses the existing network architecture as the starting point to obtain the new architecture through morphism. Because network morphism reuses existing parameters, it can reduce the training time significantly. To define the agent, the network morphism algorithm uses reinforcement learning. Specifically, the operation space of the agent is defined as follows: changing the depth and width of the network and using the accuracy of the network architecture in the validation set as the reward value to update the agent's parameters. The main advantages of the network morphism algorithm are its enhanced usage of the high-quality artificially designed network and its reduced consumption of computing resources compared with the from-scratch search approach. But although the algorithm proposed by Cai et al. offers a number of benefits, it is limited to supporting only hierarchical network morphism. Klein et al. took this a step further by proposing an algorithm that adds multiple branches in order to modify the network topology, resulting in improved algorithm freedom and expanded search space.

---

[4] Source: https://arxiv.org/pdf/1611.01578.pdf.

Unlike the algorithms used in reinforcement learning, those in evolutionary learning regard the generation of the network architecture as a process in which the initial architecture gradually evolves with the algorithm. The initial architecture can be randomly generated, or to meet specific performance requirements, it can be manually designed. In evolutionary learning, the population corresponds to the network architecture pool. Sampling enables us to obtain parent architectures, but different evolutionary algorithms differ in parent architecture sampling and architecture pool maintenance; for example, Real et al. used the competition method to perform sampling in the architecture pool, whereas Gao et al. used Pareto optimality sampling. By using high-quality parent architectures, we are able to obtain mutated child architectures, to which we can assign the reproduction permission and add them to the architecture pool. In order to ensure that the number of architecture pools remains unchanged in the algorithm, we need to remove one architecture from the pool after generating each child architecture. The architecture we elect to remove can be either the one with the worst performance of the two sampled parent architectures or the one not updated for the longest period. Removing the former ensures that the best evolutionary algorithm is kept, while removing the latter ensures diversity of the architecture pool in order to prevent the pool containing mostly descendants of the same architecture. Research shows that both reinforcement learning and evolutionary learning perform slightly better than a random algorithm, but that evolutionary learning offers faster search times and can find smaller networks.

Optimization of the NAS based on reinforcement learning and evolutionary learning is always performed in a discrete space following an approximate accuracy-based direction rather than a specific direction. For example, instead of using the gradient-free algorithm, Luo et al. found the gradient descent direction based on the continuity of architecture representations. In this approach, the neural architecture optimization (NAO) algorithm includes three parts: an encoder, a predictor, and a decoder. The encoder maps neural network architectures into a continuous space. The predictor, which is defined as a common regression network, takes as training labels the representations obtained by the encoder and the accuracy of the network architecture in the corresponding dataset in order to predict the accuracy of representations in the continuous spaces. The decoder maps the representations in the continuous spaces back into the normal network architecture. After the encoding–prediction–decoding architecture is trained, the algorithm can find a better architecture along the gradient direction of the predictor.

The NAO uses the representations in the continuous spaces to find the direction of gradient descent, thereby improving the search efficiency. However, to train the predictor requires a great deal of computing resources, because the NAO must first obtain the data labels of the architecture accuracy. Unlike the NAO, the differentiable architecture search (DARTS) proposed by Liu et al. finds the gradient descent direction by loosening the continuity of the cell-based search space. In the DARTS algorithm, the cell-based search space is defined as a directed acyclic graph (DAG). The operation set in the entire search space is defined as $\mathcal{O}$, where a convex combination of operations is used in the entire $\mathcal{O}$ rather than single operations at each layer.

A weight is set for each operation as a network architecture parameter. The input of any intermediate node j is defined as the sum of the outputs of all its previous nodes i.

$$x^{(j)} = \sum_{i<j} o^{(i,j)}\left(x^{(i)}\right) \tag{11.4}$$

where $o^{(i,j)}$ is the operation between the ith node and the jth node.

The DARTS algorithm aims to optimize the operation weight α and the network parameter w, that is:

$$\min_{a} \mathcal{L}_{\text{val}}\left(w^*(\alpha), \alpha\right) \tag{11.5}$$

$$\text{s.t. } w^*(\alpha) = \text{argmin}_w \mathcal{L}_{\text{train}}(w, \alpha) \tag{11.6}$$

where $\mathcal{L}_{\text{val}}$ is the loss function in the validation set, and $\mathcal{L}_{\text{train}}$ is the loss function in the training set.

The validation set is used to optimize the network architecture parameter α, whereas the training set is used to optimize the general network parameter w. Because it is difficult to implement two-level optimization, the algorithm uses approximate optimization. After the training, the operation with the highest weight α between every two nodes is used as an operation in the final cell:

$$O^{(i,j)} = \arg\max_{o \in \mathcal{O}} \alpha_O^{(i,j)} \tag{11.7}$$

Both NAO and DARTS consider only the model accuracy and ignore other objectives such as the latency and model size. However, such objectives are important considerations when designing a neural network suitable for use on mobile phones and other devices with limited resources. An example of a high-quality network designed manually for devices such as mobile phones is Mobilenet, a multi-objective algorithm that delivers high accuracy and considers the model inference latency. Mobilenet V2, together with the super-core search space, forms the basis on which single path—an efficient search algorithm—is constructed. This search algorithm, implemented in the MindSpore framework, is described below.

The single-path algorithm uses the same search space as Mobilenet V2, where the space is a cell-based chain structure with a fixed number of layers. Mobile inverted bottleneck convolution (MBconv) is used as the internal structure of a cell. In the search space, shown in Fig. 11.7, the search is performed on only the convolution kernel size $k \times k$ ($3 \times 3/5 \times 5$) and the expansion rate e (3/6) for controlling the number of convolution kernels (that is, MBconv-$k \times k$-e).

In order to obtain a large feature map in the cell operation, we first use a 5×5 convolution kernel with an expansion rate of 6. We can then capture the desired feature map according to the size and expansion rate of the convolution kernel selected in the

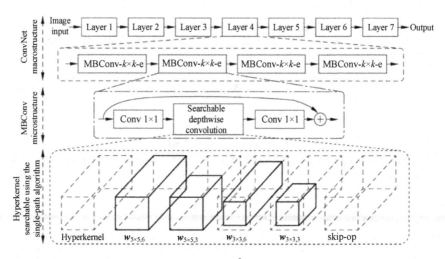

Fig. 11.7 Search space of the single-path algorithm[5]

search process. This process uses only a single path and cancels an operation branch in addition to significantly reducing the number of feature maps and the amount of consumed memory.

In the single-path search process, the network architecture is determined by comparing the L2 norm (Euclidean norm) of the weight value and the threshold. Note that the threshold is also defined as a parameter of the neural network and updated through gradient descent. Single path, as mentioned earlier, is an end-side multi-objective algorithm that considers not only the model accuracy but also the model inference latency. We can therefore determine its loss function as follows:

$$\text{Loss} = \min_{w} \text{CE}(w|t_k, t_e) + \lambda \bullet \log(R(w|t_k, t_e)) \tag{11.8}$$

where CE $(w \mid t_k, t_e)$ is cross-entropy, and
$R (w \mid t_k, t_e)$ is the model inference latency.

This loss function can directly update the network parameter w and the threshold parameter t through gradient descent. Of particular importance is the fact that the single-path algorithm simultaneously updates both the network parameters and network architecture parameters with the data in the training set, differing from DARTS and other algorithms that use the training set to train the network parameters and use the validation set to train the network architecture parameters. The approach taken in the single-path algorithm facilitates training to some extent while also ensuring the effectiveness of the algorithm, but we should still consider whether network overfitting might occur.

3.   **Performance evaluation**

Performance evaluation aims to increase the generalization ability of the neural network architecture found by the NAS. Typically, we would train and validate the network structure on the training and validation sets, respectively. However, this approach requires the NAS algorithm to generate more network structures in the search process, consuming a large amount of computing resources if we need to train each network structure from scratch. In order to address this issue and accelerate performance evaluation, the industry has proposed a number of different methods, such as low fidelity estimation, learning curve extrapolation, weight inheritance, and weight sharing.

Low fidelity estimation is the most direct way to speed up performance evaluation because it extracts only some subsets of data during the training process, reducing image resolution and the number of convolution channels and cells in addition to accelerating evaluation. Theoretically, this method is effective as long as the relative ranking between the NAS-generated network structures remains unchanged. However, the latest research calls this into question by showing that the relative ranking of the network structures obtained using low fidelity estimation does not produce accurate results.

Using the learning curve extrapolation method, we obtain the performance curve in a similar way to machine learning in order to promptly terminate unsatisfactory use cases. For example, Domhan et al. accelerated the evaluation process by basing trend predictions on the performance of the initial training. Similarly, Liu et al. were able to predict a large network model by training a surrogate model based on the existing network structure.

Weight inheritance and weight sharing reuse existing weights in order to accelerate performance evaluation. In weight inheritance, the weights of other networks (e.g., a parent model) are inherited. Conversely, the weights of the common edges can be shared in weight sharing, because the sub-networks generated by the one-shot algorithm can be considered as subgraphs in the hypergraph, as shown in Fig. 11.8. A typical example of weight inheritance is the network morphism model, which reduces the training time (GPU/day) by modifying the network structure without changing the function. There are many examples of weight sharing, including the reinforcement learning-based efficient neural architecture search (ENAS) algorithm proposed by Pham et al. and the DARTS algorithm proposed by Liu et al. Although weight sharing accelerates the evaluation significantly, it cannot ensure that the relative ranking of performance evaluation obtained by different sub-networks reflects the actual situation accurately. Furthermore, it restricts the subgraph search space to the range of the hypergraph, limiting the solution space of the network structure. Because the original weight sharing method saves the hypergraph in GPU memory, it supports only cell-based search and cannot directly search large datasets. To address these issues, the ProxylessNAS algorithm binarizes the network weights and activates the candidate operator on only one path during training.

In Fig. 11.8, 0 represents the input of the neural network; 1, 2, and 3 are different hidden layers; and 4 is the output layer.

Significant developments have been made in the NAS algorithm, which has been used extensively in fields such as image classification, object detection, semantic

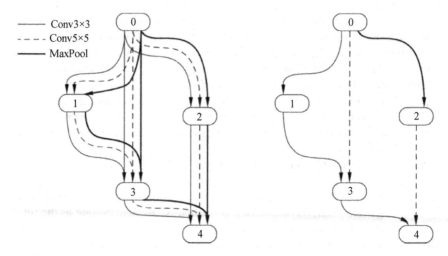

Fig. 11.8 One-shot method[6]

segmentation, and image super resolution. However, published results are often difficult to reproduce, because they depend on data augmentation and hyperparameter
settings as well as the network structure, all of which determine the performance
of the neural network model. To improve network performance on the CIFAR-10
dataset, for example, researchers often use methods such as pre-learning rate policies,
CutOut data enhancement, MixUp, and Shake-Shake regularization. Using hyperparameter tuning and data augmentation for optimizing the NAS algorithm may
therefore become an area of focused research in the future.

11.1.2 Hyperparameter Tuning

In deep learning, tuning hyperparameter settings appropriately can deliver substantial results in model optimization, and this has therefore become a subject of much
research. Model training usually involves two types of parameters: weights (parameters) of the model itself and hyperparameters (such as the learning rate, weight
decay, and number of training rounds) that determine the training process. In the
DNN, each node has a weight, which represents the impact of the node on the final
prediction result. Because we need to obtain the weights by using training data, the
parameters will change dynamically during the training process. On the other hand,
hyperparameters are configuration variables that we need to set before the training
process starts, many of which remain static during training.

Hyperparameter tuning generally involves the following operations: (1) define a
possible range of values for all hyperparameters; (2) define a method to sample a set

---

[6] Source: https://arxiv.org/pdf/1808.05377.pdf.

of hyperparameter values within a specified range of values; (3) define evaluation criteria and evaluate the results of the current model through cross-validation; and (4) tune the hyperparameters based on the current results. We repeat these operations until we find a better set of parameters for handling the current training tasks. Hutter et al. described hyperparameter tuning as follows: Given a machine learning model A with N parameters, after it is defined that the Nth hyperparameter is from space Λ_N, the entire hyperparameter space is $\Lambda = \Lambda_1 \times \Lambda_2 \times \ldots \times \Lambda_N$. A set of hyperparameters $\lambda^* \in \Lambda$ is found on the given dataset D so that:

$$\lambda^* = \arg\min_{\lambda \in \Lambda} E_{(D_{\text{train}}, D_{\text{valid}}) \sim D} V(\mathcal{L}, \mathcal{A}_\lambda, D_{\text{train}}, D_{\text{valid}}) \tag{11.9}$$

where $\mathcal{L}$ is the loss function for model training;
$\mathcal{A}_\lambda$ is a set of parameters λ of given algorithm A;
D_{train} is the training data i for cross-validation;
D_{valid} is the validation data i for cross-validation; and
$V(\mathcal{L}, \mathcal{A}_\lambda, D_{\text{train}}, D_{\text{valid}})$ is to measure the loss function of model A that is based on the training set D_{train} in the validation set D_{valid} under hyperparameter configuration λ.

Hyperparameters play a crucial role in model training because of their significant impact on model performance. For example, the learning rate determines the speed at which weights are updated: set it too high, and the optimal value may be missed; set it too low, and local optimum will occur. Many other hyperparameters in addition to the learning rate determine the model training process. Consequently, we face the following problems when trying to obtain a set of hyperparameters that enable optimal performance:

(1) The hyperparameter space is a complex high-dimensional space in which multiple hyperparameters affect each other and multiple types may exist.
(2) Because of the many evaluation tests, we need to perform on the training operations in hyperparameter tuning, it is essential that we track and analyze them.
(3) For deep learning, the costs per evaluation process are high.
(4) It is often difficult to obtain gradient information such as certain enumerated or discrete hyperparameters.

Tuning hyperparameters manually is often a difficult and cumbersome process, especially when faced with the preceding problems. A number of automatic hyperparameter tuning methods and tools have therefore been proposed, not only to reduce the labor costs, but also to produce better results than manual tuning and further improve the performance, allowing us to compare and reproduce different hyperparameter tuning methods more fairly. Given the large number of automatic hyperparameter tuning methods, Hutter et al. divided them into model-independent and model-dependent black-box optimization methods. Similarly, we divide them into trial-independent and trial-dependent methods, due to some methods (such as grid search and random search) validating different sets of configurations independently.

Specifically, such methods do not explicitly use other validation results for each validation, whereas most of the other methods (such as Bayesian optimization) explicitly use the existing validation results for the next validation.

1. **Trial-independent methods**

Grid search and random search are typical trial-independent methods. Grid search is an all-factor test design that defines a limited set of test values for each hyperparameter and validates each parameter combination. It has the following features:

(1) The number of hyperparameters has a significant impact on efficiency, and the number of validations increases exponentially with the number of parameters, resulting in a dimension disaster.

(2) Increasing the number of search points for each hyperparameter significantly increases the number of validations. For example, let us assume that there are n hyperparameters: If each hyperparameter has two values, the total number of configurations is 2^n; however, if each hyperparameter has three values, this increases to 3^n. Grid search is therefore suitable only for a small number of configurations.

(3) Validations do not affect each other and can be performed concurrently.

Another trial-independent method is random search. Random search presets the number of searches and then samples the hyperparameter combinations randomly for validation. The main advantage of random search over grid search is that it can validate more parameter points for each hyperparameter. For example, let us assume that N hyperparameters are given for C times of validation: Grid search validates only $C^{\frac{1}{N}}$ points for each hyperparameter, whereas random search can validate C different points for each hyperparameter. This advantage is of particular significance when we need to handle certain hyperparameters that are especially important to the model. Figure 11.9 illustrates this point.

Random search is often used as a baseline search method because it offers the following features:

(1) The algorithm does not make any assumptions about the model. As long as sufficient resources are available, random search can reach any approximation of the optimal solution. This method can be combined with other more complex search methods (such as the methods proposed by Ahmed[7] and Hutter) in order to expand the exploration space and improve the search effect and can also be used in the initial search process.

(2) It often takes longer than model-based search algorithms. In a scenario where the hyperparameter space includes N independent Boolean parameters and the value of each parameter corresponds to one good and one poor parameter, random search requires 2^{N-1} validations to find the optimal solution. Conversely, by optimizing a single hyperparameter each time, only $N + 1$ validations are required to find the optimal solution.

---

[7] See: https://www.cs.ubc.ca/~schmidtm/Documents/2016_NIPSw_FOBO.pdf.

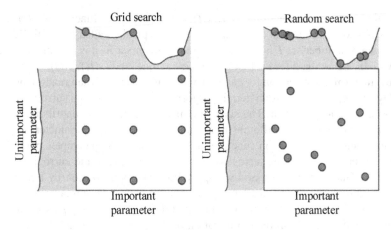

Fig. 11.9 Parameter search comparison between grid search and random search

(3) Parallel validation is possible without relying on other configurations.

2. **Trial-dependent methods**

By establishing the relationship between hyperparameter configurations and performance, trial-dependent methods approximate the optimal solution of hyperparameter configuration with prior knowledge and sampling points. These methods generally have the following features:

(1) Prior knowledge about the configuration space needs to be artificially formed in order to guide the optimization process. Generally, there is a surrogate model for this purpose.

(2) Multiple configurations need to be collected for validation. To reduce the number of validations, the next trial configuration is inferred from prior knowledge. The optimization process is sequential—typically sequential model-based optimization (SMBO).

Bayesian optimization, a model-related method, is one of the best methods for global optimization of the "black-box" function. In particular, hyperparameter optimization (HPO) in deep learning offers exceptional results and has been used in tasks such as image classification, speech recognition, and NLP. Bayesian optimization is especially suitable for continuous variables with fewer than 20 dimensions and is feasible for objective functions that require long-term validation. To facilitate a better understanding of Bayesian optimization, let us first briefly introduce the Gaussian process, which is a common model in Bayesian optimization. You may wish to explore the articles written by Brochu [21] and Shahriari [22] for a more in-depth understanding.

For a sequence number set T and a variable set $x = (x_t)_{t \in T}$ on a general probability space, x is called a Gaussian process. It is assumed that for any $t_1, t_2, \ldots, t_n \in T$, vectors $(x(t_1), x(t_2), \ldots, x(t_n))$ are subject to normal distribution, which is uniquely determined by a mean function $t \rightarrow E[x(t)]$ and a covariance function $K(x(t), x(s))$: $= \text{cov}[x(t), x(s)]$, where the covariance matrix is typically called a kernel. Because the sequence number set T is defined as a real number set $\mathbb{R}$, it is conceivable that x is a variable set defined for each point on the timeline, and $(x(t_1), x(t_2), ..., x(t_n))$ is subject to normal distribution for each point, that is, x is a Gaussian random process.

Bayesian optimization is an iterative algorithm that consists of a surrogate model and an acquisition function. The surrogate model describes the distribution of the objective function under different parameters (such as hyperparameters in deep learning), and the acquisition function determines the next parameter point to be validated under the current surrogate model. In most cases, the surrogate model selects the Gaussian process, and we apply Bayesian optimization by treating the hyperparameter configuration (denoted by λ) as a sequence number set T. If we assume that $f(\lambda)$ is the objective function and define $f = (f(\lambda))_{\lambda \in T}$ as a Gaussian process, we can transform the optimization of the objective function (e.g., the test accuracy of the model on the test set) into the sampling and fitting of the Gaussian process—the optimal solution of λ is a prediction result of the fitting. As alluded to earlier, the Gaussian process is uniquely determined by the mean function $m(\lambda)$ and the covariance function $k(\lambda, \lambda')$. In most cases, we can assume that the mean function is a constant function, so the effectiveness of the Gaussian process depends only on the covariance function. A typical covariance function is Matérn covariance, in which the Matérn 5/2 Kernel is commonly used. Note that the covariance depends only on the distance between two points. If no noise is present in the observed value, the predictions of the mean value $\mu(\bullet)$ and the covariance $\sigma^2(\bullet)$ are as follows:

$$\mu(\lambda) = k_*^T K^{-1} y, \sigma^2(\lambda) = k(\lambda, \lambda) - k_*^T K^{-1} k_* \qquad (11.10)$$

where k_* is the covariance vector between λ and all observed values;
K is the covariance matrix of all observed values; and
y is the predicted target value under the λ configuration.

Because the search space is relatively closed in most cases, it is generally safe to set the prior mean of the Gaussian process to 0 in the mean formula. However, the prediction of a new point is highly dependent on a kernel, meaning that the prior mean being 0 is almost impossible.

In such a framework, the sampling process is particularly important. If the objective function is unsuitable for the Gaussian process due to insufficient collected points, the fitted Gaussian process cannot predict an optimal solution. Currently, many acquisition functions are available, one of which is expected improvement (EI):

$$E[I(\lambda)] = E[\max(f_{\min} - y, 0)] \qquad (11.11)$$

where $I(\bullet)$ is an indicative function;
$f_{\min}$ is the best observed value at present; and
y is the predicted target value under the λ configuration.

When y is subject to normal distribution under hyperparameter configuration λ, the function can be calculated in closed form:

$$E[I(\lambda)] = (f_{\min} - \mu(\lambda))N\left(\frac{f_{\min} - \mu(\lambda)}{\sigma}\right) + \sigma\phi\left(\frac{f_{\min} - \mu(\lambda)}{\sigma}\right) \qquad (11.12)$$

where $N(\bullet)$ is the density function for the standard normal distribution;
$\Phi\,(\bullet)$ is the standard normal distribution function;
μ is the predicted mean value of target values under λ configuration; and
σ is the predicted standard deviation of the target values under λ configuration.

Both $f_{\min}$ and y have the same meanings as those in Formula (11.11). Figure 11.10 shows the Bayesian optimization process, where the objective is to use the Gaussian process to minimize the value indicated by the dashed line (the objective function). In the figure, the black solid line represents the predicted value of the model, the interval marked with ① represents uncertainty, and the curve marked with ② represents the values of the acquisition function. Based on the observation points, the algorithm

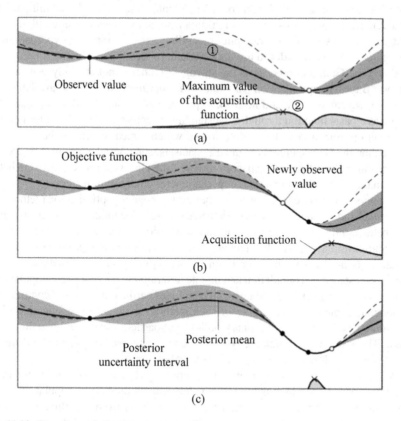

Fig. 11.10 Bayesian optimization process

obtains the next sampling point by maximizing the value of the acquisition function, as shown in Fig. 11.10a. The value of the acquisition function corresponding to the observation point is smaller than the value predicted at the point corresponding to the maximum value of the acquisition function, which is on the left side of the observation point. In this case, the uncertainty is high, and the predicted value may be better than that obtained at the observation point. As shown in Fig. 11.10b, after the Gaussian process update is complete, the predicted value on the right side of the observation point is the smallest, the value of the acquisition function is the largest, and the sampling is performed on the right side. Subsequently, the uncertainty predicted in Fig. 11.10c is very low, and re-validation is performed once according to the value of the acquisition function.

One disadvantage of the standard Gaussian process is that the calculation amount increases by $O(n^3)$ with the number of data points. Fitting in the Gaussian process is therefore limited if we have a large number of acquisition data points. The sparse Gaussian process enables quick fitting, effectively resolving this disadvantage by using only some inducing points to construct the covariance matrix; however, this approach may lead to inaccurate estimation of uncertainty. Another disadvantage is that it cannot process high-dimensional data points effectively. We can mitigate this disadvantage by preprocessing the high-dimensional hyperparameter configuration. One way to do so is to use random embedding and separate the hyperparameter configuration space in order to use the Gaussian process.

Using the Gaussian process as the surrogate model is not the only way we can perform Bayesian optimization—a number of other methods are also available. For example, we can use a neural network to preprocess the input and then process the output as a basis function through Bayesian linear regression. Another alternative to Bayesian optimization is the random forest, which typically delivers better performance than the Gaussian process in large datasets, categorical configuration spaces, and conditional configuration spaces; however, the Gaussian process delivers better performance in smaller numerical hyperparameter configuration spaces.

The population-based method is another trial-dependent optimization method, but it is model-independent. In hyperparameter tuning, a population is a set of hyperparameter configurations. Each time the population is updated, the hyperparameter configuration is partially mutated, and the configurations are combined—the update lasts until a specified condition is met. Population-based methods, as the name suggests, keep a population and update it iteratively to obtain new populations. Note that a general iterative update method includes partial mutation and combination of population members. Examples of such methods include the genetic algorithm, evolutionary algorithm, evolutionary policy, and particle swarm optimization algorithm. These methods, which are typically easy to understand, can handle different data types and allow for simple parallelized validation.

We would be amiss not to mention the covariance matrix adaptation evolution strategy (CMA-ES), which is the most widely known method in population-based optimization. It samples hyperparameter configurations from a multivariate Gaussian distribution and updates the mean value and the covariance of the hyperparameter configurations based on the validation results of the members in each iteration.

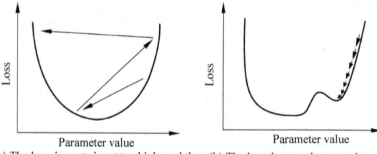

(a) The learning rate is set too high, and the model misses the optimal point   (b) The learning rate is set too low, and the model falls into the local optimum

Fig. 11.11 Inappropriate learning rates

CMA-ES is one of the most effective black-box optimization methods and delivers exceptional performance in the black-box optimization benchmark test.[8]

3. Tricks in hyperparameter tuning

Neural network training includes many hyperparameters, such as the learning rate, momentum, weight decay rate, batch size, and number of training steps. Many methods exist for automatic hyperparameter tuning, and numerous tricks are available for selecting the hyperparameters. Here, we introduce two tricks: setting the learning rate and early stopping. Smith [23] and Goodfellow [24] go into greater detail in their respective articles explaining the hyperparameter selection method.

The methods most commonly used for training a neural network are stochastic gradient descent and its variants (such as Adam and RMSProp). These optimization methods require the input of learning rate, which has a significant impact on neural network training. For example, if the learning rate is set too low, the network will converge too slowly, delaying the removal of the local optimal solution—especially when local optimum occurs. Conversely, if the learning rate is set to high, the learning process will be unstable. The loss function will fluctuate significantly, and the optimal point may be missed or the convergence may fail. Figure 11.11 shows the effects of setting inappropriate learning rates.

In most cases, we determine the learning rate manually based on experience, often achieving good results. However, because this approach usually requires many trials, it is cumbersome and consumes many resources. To determine the learning rate more effectively, Leslie N. Smith [25] proposed a method of cyclical learning rates (CLRs).

In the CLR method, we set a boundary between the minimum and maximum learning rates. In addition, we set the step size, which is the number of steps that describe the change in the learning rate (i.e., the number of training iterations or epochs). Each cycle lasts for two steps, as shown in Fig. 11.12. The learning rate increases linearly from the minimum value to the maximum value in the first step

---

[8] See: http://numbbo.github.io/workshops/index.html.

Fig. 11.12 CLR method

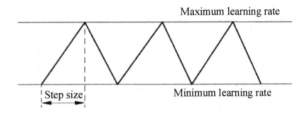

and decreases linearly from the maximum value to the minimum value in the second step. Other methods for determining the learning rate change were experimented with, but because the results were equivalent, the simplest linear change method is recommended.

In order to test an available learning rate interval, Leslie N. Smith obtained the maximum and minimum learning rates by setting the number of learning iterations or steps, setting a low learning rate at the beginning of the training, and then increasing the learning rate step by step (linearly or exponentially) in each iteration. This change in the learning rate provides us with valuable information from which we can determine the learning rate. When the learning rate is low, the network will begin to converge, but as it increases beyond a certain range, the value of the network loss function will increase, and the validation accuracy will decrease. According to this concept, we determine the maximum learning rate as either the newly observed validation loss or the point where the accuracy begins to decrease. Conversely, to determine the minimum learning rate, we can use the following methods:

(1)   Use the rule of thumb that the optimal minimum learning rate is 1/3 or 1/4 of the maximum learning rate.
(2)   Set the minimum learning rate as 1/10, 1/20, or a smaller proportion of the maximum learning rate.
(3)   Experiment by running hundreds of iterations with a set of initial learning rates, and then, select the highest learning rate that reflects the convergence trend.
(4)   Use the minimum learning rate allowed by the training framework for interval testing, and then, select a point where the increase in precision begins to slow down. As shown in Fig. 11.13, the learning rate increases slowly at about 0.001, so we would select 0.001 as the minimum learning rate. Conversely, as described earlier, we could select 0.006 as the maximum learning rate.

Another of the tricks available in hyperparameter tuning is early stopping, which is used to promptly stop tests on evidently inappropriate hyperparameter configurations. It is also used extensively to prevent overfitting in neural network training.

A simple way to prevent overfitting is to observe errors that occur when the neural network uses the training and validation sets. If errors start to increase using the validation set while errors decrease using the training set, we may need to terminate the model training. In hyperparameter tuning, the early stopping method relies on performance curves, two of which we describe briefly: the model performance curve stopping rule and the median stopping rule. You can see Google Vizier for details.

Fig. 11.13 Interval test of learning rates in CIFAR-10

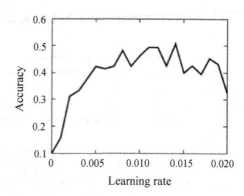

The model performance curve stopping rule performs regression on the model performance curve, which is the test error or precision of the model on the validation set. This stopping rule uses the performance measurements already obtained by the model as the basis for predicting the next measurement. Using the validation set as an example, this stopping rule predicts the error value of the 11th epoch based on the error values of the first through tenth epochs. If the predicted value has a sufficiently low probability of exceeding the optimal observed value, model training ends. Vizier is based on the nonparametric Bayesian regression method. To keep this description brief, we do not describe the parametric Bayesian regression method here.

The median stopping rule is a model-independent early stopping rule. For brevity, let us assume that each epoch is a stage for determining early stopping and that the target measured value at step s in epoch i is x_s^i. This stopping rule determines whether the mean value $\hat{x}_{1:s}^i$ of the target values of steps 1–s in the current epoch i is significantly lower than median $(x_{1:s}^1, x_{1:s}^2, \ldots, x_{1:s}^{i-1})$ of the mean value of the target values in the completed epochs for the same period. Here, $x_{1:s}^i$ represents the mean value of the target values at the current stage. Because this rule does not rely on the parameterization model, it is applicable to a wider range of performance curves.

11.2 Existing AutoML Systems

AutoML systems come in many flavors and can be implemented using closed-source methods, such as Google Vizier and oneclick.ai, and open-source methods, such as AutoWeka, Auto-Sklearn, HyperOpt, and Microsoft NNI. This section focuses on systems used for conventional machine learning (such as AutoWeka) and those used for deep learning (Microsoft NNI).

11.2.1 Auto Weka, Auto-Sklearn, and HyperOpt

Conventional machine learning includes processes such as data acquisition/cleaning, feature extraction, model selection, hyperparameter tuning, and model deployment. Of these, model selection and hyperparameter tuning pose the biggest obstacles for non-experts using machine learning and require data scientists to perform a great deal of repeated tests in various scenarios. Overcoming these obstacles is therefore vitally important.

In the artificial modeling process, we typically select one or more algorithms according to target and dataset characteristics and then adjust the related parameters to meet our requirements. Note that different algorithms involve different hyperparameter dimensions. In AutoML, model selection and hyperparameter tuning are two interdependent optimization problems, which we can solve as a joint optimization problem in order to obtain an optimal combination of models and hyperparameters. Given the algorithm set $\mathcal{A} = \{A^{(1)}, A^{(2)}, ..., A^{(k)}\}$ and associated hyperparameter space $\Lambda^{(1)}, \Lambda^{(2)}, ..., \Lambda^{(k)}$, we can express this joint optimization problem as follows:

$$A^*_{\lambda*} \in \operatorname*{argmin}_{A^{(j)} \in A, \lambda \in \Lambda^{(j)}} \frac{1}{k} \sum_{i=1}^{k} \mathcal{L}\left(A^{(j)}, \mathcal{D}^{(i)}_{\text{train}}, \mathcal{D}^{(i)}_{\text{valid}}\right) \tag{11.13}$$

where $A^{(j)}_{\lambda}$ is a parameter set λ of the given algorithm A;

$\mathcal{D}^{(i)}_{\text{train}}$ is the training data i for cross-validation;

$\mathcal{D}^{(i)}_{\text{valid}}$ is the validation data i for cross-validation;

$\mathcal{L}(A^{(j)}_{\lambda}, \mathcal{D}^{(i)}_{\text{train}}, \mathcal{D}^{(i)}_{\text{valid}})$ is the loss function value, on the validation data i, that is obtained after a set of hyperparameters in a given algorithm are trained based on the training data i; and.

$A^*_{\lambda*}$ is a set of algorithms and hyperparameters in a hyperparameter space that minimize the loss function.

The joint optimization problem is modeled as simple joint hierarchical hyperparameter optimization on the parameter space $\Lambda = \Lambda^{(1)} \cup ... \cup \Lambda^{(k)} \cup \{\lambda_r\}$. Here, λ_r is a new root hyperparameter used to select an algorithm among $A^{(1)}, A^{(2)}, ..., A^{(k)}$, and each hyperparameter subspace $\Lambda^{(i)}$ is generated when the corresponding algorithm $A^{(i)}$ is selected by the root hyperparameter λ_r. The objective of optimization is to minimize the loss value of K-fold cross-validation when the training is performed on the training set $\mathcal{D}_{\text{Train}}$ by using the model and the hyperparameter and when the validation is performed on the validation set $\mathcal{D}_{\text{valid}}$.

SMBO is a Bayesian optimization method that effectively solves the joint hierarchical optimization problem in Formula (11.13). It not only deals with discrete and continuous hyperparameters simultaneously, but also fully explores the hierarchical structure on which the hyperparameter space depends. The SMBO algorithm is implemented as follows: Model $\mathcal{M}_{\mathcal{L}}$ is constructed to capture the dependency of the loss function $\mathcal{L}$ on the hyperparameter setting λ; model $\mathcal{M}_{\mathcal{L}}$ determines a candidate parameter λ; the loss c of parameter λ on the dataset is evaluated; and model $\mathcal{M}_{\mathcal{L}}$ is updated by using the new data point (λ, c).

This can be illustrated in the following pseudocode:

(1) Initialize model $\mathcal{M}_{\mathcal{L}}$ data point $\mathcal{H} \leftarrow \emptyset$.
(2) While the optimization time is below the upper limit.
(3) $\lambda \leftarrow$ Obtain candidate parameters from model $\mathcal{M}_{\mathcal{L}}$.
(4) Calculate the loss $c = \mathcal{L}(A_{\lambda}^{(j)}, \mathcal{D}_{train}^{(i)}, \mathcal{D}_{valid}^{(i)})$.
(5) $\mathcal{H} \leftarrow \mathcal{H} \cup \{(\lambda, c)\}$
(6) Update model $\mathcal{M}_{\mathcal{L}}$ by using the data point $\mathcal{H}$.
(7) End the search.
(8) Return the parameter λ that minimizes c.

SMBO defines an obtaining function according to model $\mathcal{M}_{\mathcal{L}}$ in order to obtain hyperparameter λ for the next step. It evaluates the benefits of hyperparameter λ and then determines which hyperparameter λ maximizes the obtaining function in the search space Λ each time. An improvement of hyperparameters based on a given loss value c_{min} is defined as follows:

$$I_{c_{min}}(\lambda) = \max\{c_{min} - c(\lambda), 0\} \qquad (11.14)$$

where λ *is* a set of hyperparameters;
$c(\lambda)$ is the loss of the given hyperparameter λ;
c_{min} is the baseline loss value; and
$I_{c_{min}}(\lambda)$ is the improvement or gain of the given hyperparameter λ compared with the baseline loss value.

After factoring model $\mathcal{M}_{\mathcal{L}}$ into the preceding formula, we can calculate the EI of the obtaining function by using the following expression:

$$E_{\mathcal{M}_{\mathcal{L}}}\left[I_{c_{min}}(\lambda)\right] = \int_{-\infty}^{c_{min}} \max\{c_{min} - c(\lambda), 0\} \bullet \rho_{\mathcal{M}_{\mathcal{L}}}(c|\lambda)dc \qquad (11.15)$$

where $\rho_{\mathcal{M}_{\mathcal{L}}}(c|\lambda)$ is the probability distribution of the loss function for a given hyperparameter; and
$E_{\mathcal{M}_{\mathcal{L}}}[I_{c_{min}}(\lambda)]$ is the expected improvement in the loss of the given hyperparameter.

In different algorithms, the dependency of the loss function c on the hyperparameter λ is modeled $(\rho(c|\lambda))$ in different ways. For example, the sequential model-based algorithm configuration (SMAC) algorithm uses the Gaussian approximation process and random forest model and assigns default values to hierarchical dependent parameters not activated in λ during model training and prediction. By using the random forest model, SMAC obtains the mean μ_{λ} and variance δ_{λ}^2 of the predicted distribution parameters for a group of loss functions c and models $\rho_{\mathcal{M}_{\mathcal{L}}}(c|\lambda)$ as Gaussian distribution $\mathcal{N}(\mu_\lambda,\delta_\lambda^2)$. Furthermore, it uses the loss of the optimal parameters, up to the current iteration, as $c_{\min}$, and factors the model into Formula (11.15) in order to obtain the closed expression of the obtaining function:

$$\mathrm{E}_{\mathcal{M}_{\mathcal{L}}}[I_{c_{\min}}(\lambda)] = \sigma_\lambda \bullet [\mu \bullet \phi(\mu) + \varphi(\mu)] \qquad (11.16)$$

where μ is the normalized value of the loss improvement of the given hyperparameter, and $\mu = \frac{c_{\min}-\mu_\lambda}{\delta_\lambda}$;
φ is the probability density function of standard normal distribution; and
ϕ is the cumulative distribution function of standard normal distribution.

By using the optimal parameter for each iteration and evaluating the parameter performance with a high level of certainty, SMAC is resistant to noise caused by function evaluation. It has found extensive use in AutoML tools such as AutoWeka, Auto-Sklearn, and NNI.

AutoWeka, developed by Chris Thornton et al. [26, 27] in 2013, is based on the open-source Weka, which was developed by the University of Waikato in New Zealand. AutoWeka supports various data mining algorithms and tools, including data preprocessing, clustering, classification, regression, visual interaction, and feature selection. Using the feature selection and machine learning algorithm provided by Weka as the search space, AutoWeka uses the SMAC algorithm to automatically select learning algorithms and set parameters according to user-provided data.

Auto-Sklearn, developed by Matthias Feurer et al. [28] in 2015 at the University of Freiburg in Germany, supports the ensemble model based on Sklearn and implements partial machine learning automation. Sklearn is an open-source machine learning library for Python and supports conventional algorithms such as classification, regression, clustering, dimension reduction, model selection, and data preprocessing for data mining and analysis. In addition to using SMAC to perform model and hyperparameter search, Auto-Sklearn uses meta-learning to accelerate the convergence of SMAC by setting the historical optimization result as the initial value and uses the ensemble model to increase the generalization ability.

HyperOpt, developed by James Bergstra et al. [10] in 2013, is an open-source Python library for machine learning model selection and hyperparameter tuning. It provides an optimization interface for users to customize objective functions, search spaces, storage of search process results, and search algorithms. In terms of the search space, HyperOpt supports conditional variables with specified distribution rather than supporting only a simple vector space and can be combined with a machine learning library (such as Sklearn) to perform a model search. It supports trials to accelerate the search process, using search algorithms such as random search and tree of Parzen estimators (TPE). TPE is an SMBO algorithm and differs from SMAC, which uses a simple piecewise function to predict the distribution of loss functions.

AutoWeka, Auto-Sklearn, and HyperOpt—some common selection and hyperparameter tuning tools—have different implementation languages and search algorithms, access different machine learning algorithms, and use Bayesian optimization to automate conventional machine learning algorithms. However, because they support only a small hyperparameter space and model space for searches, these tools are unsuitable for deep learning with large-scale hyperparameter or model structure searches.

11.2.2 Microsoft NNI

Microsoft's neural network intelligence (NNI) is an open-source AutoML tool that abstracts the hyperparameter or model structure search process into three layers: front-end interaction, search algorithm, and underlying training platform. Each layer is scalable and flexible and supports multiple options and implementations. The NNI framework is shown in Fig. 11.14.

At layer 1, front-end interaction is performed through either the command line interface or the Web user interface (WebUI) to define items such as the test, search space, and trial. The following describes the test, search space, configuration, and trial used in the NNI framework:

Test: a task for finding the best hyperparameter or neural network structure of a model and consists of two parts: trial and the AutoML algorithm.
Search space: a feasible area for model tuning, such as the value range of each hyperparameter.
Configuration: a sample in the search space, that is, a set of specific values of adjustable hyperparameters.
Trial: a single attempt to apply a set of hyperparameters or a specific network structure, which the trial code must support in order to run successfully.

At layer 2, the NNI kernel implements the search algorithm through two modules (a tuner and an assessor) to complete one test search process. In the two modules,

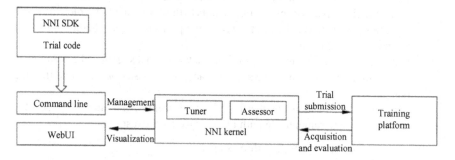

Fig. 11.14 NNI framework

the NNI supports user-defined algorithms and many built-in ones for different test scenarios. These two modules are defined as follows.

Tuner: an AutoML algorithm that generates a set of new parameters for the next trial, based on which a new trial can be run. The tuner can search both hyperparameters and deep learning model structures and includes the built-in algorithms described in Table 11.1.

Assessor: analyzes the immediate trial results, such as the periodic accuracy evaluation on test datasets and then determines whether to stop the trial early.

At layer 3, the training platform implements each trial, which depends on the parameters of the test, using a variety of mechanisms. It can be a local machine, a remote server, or a large training platform such as OpenAI or Kubernetes.

During tests run by NNI, the interaction between the involved modules is as follows:

(1) The user defines a search space and a trial and calls the trial interface.
(2) The tuner obtains the search space generation parameters defined at the front end.
(3) The generation parameters are transmitted to the training platform to execute trials.
(4) The trial results are transmitted to the assessor, which then evaluates the results and determines whether to end the trial.

If the trial is permitted to continue, the evaluation results are returned to the tuner, and steps (2) to (4) are repeated.

The front-end interface makes it easy to complete a hyperparameter tuning or model structure search trial, requiring only four simple steps:

(1) Define a search space, including parameter names, sampling policies, and related parameters, in a JSON file.
(2) Update the model code. Specifically, define the code to be executed for a trial (several code lines need to be added based on the original training code). The NNI software package needs to be included in the trial code, and the parameter acquisition interface is then called to obtain the parameters required for each execution from the tuner. Next, the result reporting interface is called to feed back the periodic evaluation results to the assessor, after which the result reporting interface is called to feed back the performance evaluation results of the model to the tuner.
(3) Define a test by using an execution parameter file that specifies the parameters related to modules such as the search space, tuner, assessor, trial, and training platform.
(4) Start the test, and then, invoke the **NNI test create** command to specify the test execution parameter file path in order to run the test.

Figure 11.15 illustrates the first three steps.

Table 11.1 Built-in algorithms for the tuner

Algorithm	Description	Recommended scenario
TPE	A sequence model-based optimization method, in which the Gaussian process is used to model the distribution of hyperparameters in different model performance segments, and a new hyperparameter value is selected according to the updated distribution in historical trials.	A black-box optimization algorithm, which is applicable to various scenarios When the computing resources are limited, only a few trials show better performance It has proven to be better than random search.
Random search	A simple and effective method, in which hyperparameters are randomly generated	Used as a baseline when the prior hyperparameter distribution is unknown; Computing resources are sufficient. Trials can be completed quickly
Anneal	A simple variant of random search, which samples from a prior solution, searches its neighborhood, and gradually converges to obtain an optimal solution	Computing resources are sufficient. Trials can be completed quickly. Search space variables can be sampled from prior distribution.
Naïve evolution	Genetic algorithm, in which a certain number of initial populations are set, and new hyperparameters are generated through mutation. Natural screening is then performed to select high-quality models, which are used as parent models for further mutation.	Computing resources are sufficient. Trials can be completed quickly. An assessor can be used for early stopping. Weight migration is supported.
SMAC	A sequence model-based optimization method, in which the Gaussian random process is used to simulate the relationship between hyperparameters and model performance, and the random forest model is used to predict the next hyperparameter.	A black-box optimization algorithm, which is applicable to various scenarios Computing resources are limited, and hyperparameters are discrete.
Batch tuner	It enables users to directly list the required trial parameter groups, run the trial, and end the trial.	Determined by the parameter list
Grid search	It performs exhaustive search on the search space and determines the sampling values based on the specified sampling distribution.	Small search space

(continued)

Table 11.1 (continued)

Algorithm	Description	Recommended scenario
Hyperband	An exploration-only algorithm that explores as many parameters as possible given the available resources, it uses limited resources during a trial to find potential parameters for the next trial.	The obtained intermediate results sufficiently reflect the final performance. Computing resources are limited, but the search space is large.
Network morphism	It automatically searches the structure of the deep learning model. Each sub-network inherits the parameters of its parent network, and network morphism is performed in terms of the depth, width, and residual structure. The sub-network performance is evaluated using historical trial data in order to select the most promising structure for test.	A deep network structure needs to be designed.
Metis tuner	It predicts the best parameters of the next trial according to the current results and determines the performance loss caused by parameter tuning. The trial is run only if the predicted parameters can achieve sufficient optimization.	A black-box optimization algorithm, which is applicable to various scenarios Providing guidance for continuous trials
BOHB	Based on the Hyperband algorithm, it overcomes the inability of Hyperband to use historical trial data for randomly generating the parameter combination and uses the Bayesian optimization algorithm to generate new parameters for the trial. This algorithm can converge to obtain a better set of parameters than Hyperband.	The obtained intermediate results can sufficiently reflect the final performance. Computing resources are limited, but the search space is large.
GP tuner	The Gaussian process (GP) tuner is a Bayesian optimization method based on sequential model-based optimization. The Gaussian process model is used to model the relationship between hyperparameters and model performance, fit historical trial data, and provide new parameters.	Resources are limited, but the objective function is difficult to model and optimize. Only a few trials are required.

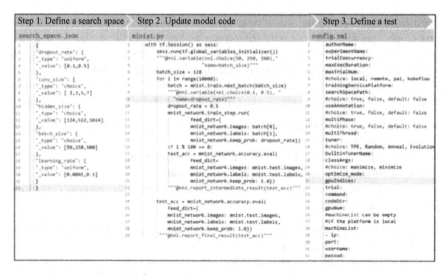

Fig. 11.15 User test procedure

NNI provides a greater number of functions and supports more scenarios than other AutoML services and tools due to the high-quality design of its framework. It has the following features:

Easy to use: The front-end interface provides both the command line and WebUI to meet the expectations of different users, allowing them to quickly create a test based on the original training code.

Scalability: The training platform interface is abstracted to support different computing resources, including local machines, remote servers, and large training platforms such as OpenAI and Kubernetes. Distributed scheduling is supported, and resources can be planned according to availability.

Flexibility: Users can customize hyperparameter search algorithms, model structure search algorithms, and early stopping algorithms or use and freely combine the built-in module algorithms. In addition to the supported training platforms, users can add extensions to access more training platforms, such as virtual machines and Kubernetes cloud services, and even access external environments for applications and model parameter adjustment.

High efficiency: The hyperparameter and model structure search methods used at the system and algorithm layers offer greater efficiency. For example, an early feedback mechanism is used to accelerate parameter adjustment.

11.3 Meta-learning

Meta-learning, also called "learning to learn", systematically observes how different machine learning methods work on a wide range of learning tasks in order to learn from the experiential knowledge (or metadata) and subsequently learn new tasks more quickly. This not only accelerates and improves the design of machine learning methods and neural network structures, but also replaces manually designed algorithms with a data-driven method, making it easier to learn new tasks.

In the meta-learning process, metadata or meta-knowledge describing previous learning tasks and models needs to be collected. This includes

- Algorithm configuration, such as hyperparameter settings, algorithm flow, and network architecture,
- Model evaluation, such as accuracy rate and training time,
- Model parameters, such as neural network weights,
- Measurable task properties, such as meta-features (including sample categories and missing values).

The collected tasks are then learned to extract and transfer knowledge in order to guide the search for an optimal model in a new task.

Prior experience is useless if the new and previous tasks differ significantly; however, if the tasks are similar, we can use more metadata, thereby enhancing the knowledge transfer effects.

There has been a number of meta-learning algorithms proposed [29–31] in the fields of conventional machine learning and deep learning—this section focuses only on those recently proposed in the field of deep learning, such as the learning optimizer, learning parameter initialization, learning loss function, and learning metric.

It is worth noting here that the learning neural network structure is also a common meta-learning method. For details, see the related sections above.

11.3.1 Learning Optimizer

The selection of an optimizer is essential to deep learning—selecting a good one can significantly accelerate model training. The effects of different optimizers on different models vary according to the scenarios in which the optimizers are used. Researchers in the field of deep learning often invest a great deal of time and energy in manually selecting and adjusting optimizers. However, a better way is to use the deep learning model to learn an optimizer [32–34]. Andrychowicz [33], Ravi [34] et al. used the LSTM trained on multiple previous tasks as the optimizer of new tasks. In this approach, the loss of the meta-learner (optimizer) is defined as the sum of the loss of the learner (the model, that is, the optimized object) and is optimized by using the gradient descent method. In each step, the meta-learner updates weights based on previously learned model weights and current gradients in order to minimize model errors. The training and using process of the LSTM-based meta-learner [34] is shown in Fig. 11.16.

A model can be generated in one complete LSTM process, and each unit in the LSTM-Optimizer (meta-learner) corresponds to one training iteration (learner).

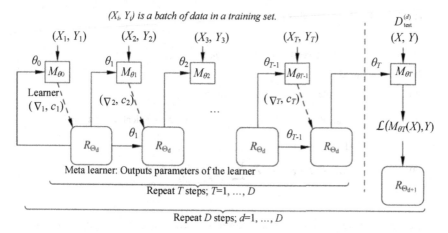

Fig. 11.16 Training and using process of the LSTM-based meta-learner[9]

(1) Use the LSTM-Optimizer to train different recommendation models on different datasets.
(2) Evaluate models, and update the meta-learner based on the evaluation results.
(3) Repeat (1) and (2) until the model generated using the LSTM-Optimizer meets requirements.
(4) Use the LSTM-Optimizer during inference to quickly generate a recommendation model based on new user data.

11.3.2 Learning Parameter Initialization

Good weight initialization can accelerate model training and even improve the model convergence accuracy. In a training set with a large number of similar tasks, the general model initialization parameter W_{init} is used as the basis from which to quickly train a deep learning model for new tasks by using only a few training samples. Learned weight initialization allows us to train a new model much faster than if we were to use random parameter initialization. The methods of parameter initialization based on meta-learning include Meta-SGD [30], MAML [31], and the methods proposed by Nichol et al. [35] The following describes the Model-Agnostic Meta-Learning (MAML) algorithm.

Algorithm 11.1 Pseudocode for parameter initialization in MAML
Input: Task distribution $p(T)$, learning rates α and β, error definition L, and model f

Output: Model initialization parameter θ

---

(1)   Randomly initialize θ

(2)   while:

(3)   Extract several batch tasks $T_i - p(T)$

(4)   for all T_i:

(5)   Evaluate $\nabla_\theta L_{T_i}(f_\theta)$ on K samples

(6)   Calculate $\theta_i' = \theta - \alpha \nabla_\theta L_{T_i}(f_\theta)$ using the gradient descent method

(7)   End

(8)   Update $\theta \leftarrow \theta - \beta \nabla_\theta \sum_{T_i \sim p(T)} L_{T_i}(f_{\theta'_i})$

(9)   End

Before training can commence, certain preparations are necessary: We need to randomly select N categories in the training set, where each category includes K training samples (support set) and K' validation samples (query set) to form a task. A task can be analogous to a sample in the training process of an ordinary deep learning model. Then, we repeatedly extract several tasks from the training set to form a task set. In MAML, an iterative process includes two parameter updates, and α and β are learning rates.

Once the preparations are complete, we can start the training process:

(1) Initialize the model parameter θ.
(2) Extract a batch of tasks from the task set.
(3) For each task in this batch, calculate the error on its support set; obtain the expected parameter on the current task by performing one gradient descent based on the learning rate α; validate the error based on this expected parameter with the query set to obtain the error on the query set; and calculate the sum of errors of all tasks in this batch on the query set, using the sum as the meta-loss.
(4) Derive the original parameter θ of the model based on the meta-loss, and optimize the parameters of the model.
(5) Repeat the preceding steps on all batches until the initialization parameters of the model are obtained.

11.3.3 Learning Loss Function

The loss function is a model evaluation index used to estimate the difference between the predicted and real values of a model, and this difference subsequently guides the model update through backpropagation. Depending on the scenario and model, researchers in the field of deep learning typically use different loss functions, such as the log loss, mean square loss, cosine proximity, and triplet loss. Different loss functions can change the direction in which the model is updated, so defining a suitable loss function is extremely important to the training process. A better loss function can dramatically accelerate the learning process—a good solution to this

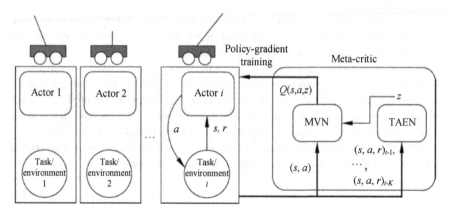

Fig. 11.17 Meta-critic network framework[10]

is to construct the loss function by learning the previous task experience. Sung [36] proposed to migrate the meta-critic network framework from reinforcement learning to supervised learning in order to obtain the loss function, as shown in Fig. 11.17.

In reinforcement learning, an actor network is constructed for each training task, and a meta-critic network is trained with multiple tasks at the same time. The meta-critic network includes a meta-value network and a task-actor encoder, which uses an RNN structure. During training, a triplet set (that is, state, action, and reward) is input, and a task representation z is output. Subsequently, the representation z, state, and action are input into the meta-value network. The θ of the actor network and ϕ and ω of the meta-critic network are obtained through training based on the following formula. The training method is similar to that of actor-critic [37] in reinforcement learning, as shown below.

$$\theta^{(i)} \leftarrow \underset{\theta^{(i)}}{\arg\max}\, Q_\phi\left(s_t^{(i)}, a_t^{(i)}, z_t^{(i)}\right), i \in \{1, 2, ..., M\} \qquad (11.17)$$

$$\phi, \omega \leftarrow \underset{\phi,\omega}{\arg\min} \sum_{i=1}^{m} \left(Q_\phi\left(s_t^{(i)}, a_t^{(i)}, z_t^{(i)}\right) - r_t^{(i)} - \gamma Q_\phi\left(s_{t+1}^{(i)}, a_{t+1}^{(i)}, z_{t+1}^{(i)}\right)\right)^2$$

$$(11.18)$$

where θ, ϕ, and ω correspond to the parameters of the actor network, meta-value network, and task-actor encoder, respectively;
s, a, z, and r correspond to the state, action, representation of an encoded task, and reward, respectively;
Q is the output of meta-critic;
i and t denote the ith task and tth step, respectively; and
γ denotes the decay.

---

[10] Source: https://arxiv.org/pdf/1707.09835.pdf.

When a new task occurs, a new actor network is created, whereas the meta-critic network remains unchanged. The actor-critic method is used for training, and the actor network of the current task can be learned quickly.

We can obtain a loss function by applying the meta-critic framework to supervised learning, in which the actor network corresponds to the model to be learned, its input is feature x (corresponding to the state), and its output is the predicted target value $\hat{y}$ (corresponding to the action). The negative value $-l$ of the loss function $(\hat{y}, y)$ corresponds to the reward r. Supervised learning is equivalent to a step in the reinforcement learning process and does not include a subsequent step. This means that we can train the network according to the following formulas:

$$\theta^{(i)} \leftarrow \underset{\theta^{(i)}}{\arg\max}\, Q_\phi\left(x^{(i)}, \hat{y}^{(i)}, z^{(i)}\right), i \in \{1, 2, ..., M\} \tag{11.19}$$

$$\phi, \omega \leftarrow \underset{\phi,\omega}{\arg\min} \sum_{i=1}^{M} \left(Q_\phi\left(x^{(i)}, \hat{y}^{(i)}, z^{(i)}\right) - r_t^{(i)}\right)^2 \tag{11.20}$$

where x is the input feature, and.
$\hat{y}$ is the predicted value that is output by the model.

By maximizing $-r$ (that is, the negative value of the loss function) estimated by meta-critic, the model (actor network) is trained, and the meta-critic network learns the real loss of each task. Meta-critic includes information about multiple tasks—for each new task, it can generate a loss, that is, $-r$.

11.3.4   Learning Metric

Learning metric can be used in fields such as NLP and CV, for example, to measure the similarity between samples [38–40] for classification tasks.

The Siamese network [38–40] learns a similarity metric from the data and compares this metric with a sample from a known category in order to determine the category of a sample from an unknown category. The Siamese neural network consists of two identical networks, which share the same weight. Corresponding eigenvectors are obtained by using two inputs through embedding, allowing the distance metric (e.g., a Euclidean distance) similarity between the vectors to be calculated. During training, for samples of the same category in the training set, the distance between the vectors is minimized. Conversely, the distance between the vectors is maximized for samples of different categories in the training set.

Koch [38] proposed to perform one-shot image classification by using the Siamese neural network, as shown in Fig. 11.18. That is, a model is obtained through training, one to-be-classified image and one image in the training set are input, and the probability that the two images are of the same category is output. The image is then

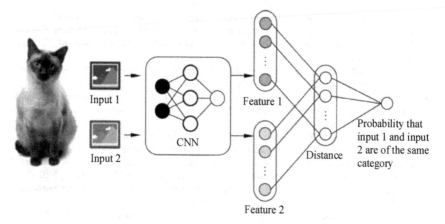

Fig. 11.18 Image classification using the convolutional Siamese network[11]

compared with all images in the training set to find the most likely image—the category of this most likely image is the category of the to-be-classified image.

11.4 Implementing AutoML Using MindSpore

The interfaces and processes of MindSpore may constantly change due to iterative development. For all runnable code, see the code in corresponding chapters at https://mindspore.cn/resource. You can scan the QR code on the right to access relevant resources.

References

1. G. Hinton, L. Deng, D. Yu et al., Deep neural networks for acoustic modeling in speech recognition. IEEE Signal Process. Mag. **29**(6), 82–97 (2012)
2. I. Sutskever, O. Vinyals, Q.V. Le, Sequence to sequence learning with neural networks, in *Advances in Neural Information Processing Systems* (2014), pp. 3104–3112
3. D. Bahdanau, K. Cho, Y. Bengio, *Neural Machine Translation by Jointly Learning to Align and Translate.* (2016-05-19) [2019-10-26] https://arxiv.org/pdf/1409.0473.pdf
4. D.W. Hosmer, S. Lemeshow, *Applied Logistic Regression* (Wiley, New York, 2000)

---

[11] See: https://lilianweng.github.io/lil-log/2018/11/30/meta-learning.html.

5. C. Cortes, V. Vapnik, Support-vector networks. Mach. Learn. **20**(3), 273–297 (1995)
6. J. Ye, J.H. Chow, J. Chen, et al., Stochastic gradient boosted distributed decision trees. *Proceedings of the 18th ACM Conference on Information and Knowledge Management* (ACM, 2009), pp. 2061–2064
7. B. Zoph, Q.V. Le, *Neural Architecture Search with Reinforcement Learning.* (2017-2-15) [2019-10-26] https://arxiv.org/pdf/1611.01578.pdf
8. B. Zoph, V. Vasudevan, J. Shlens, et al., Learning transferable architectures for scalable image recognition, in *Proceedings of the IEEE Conference on Computer Vision and Pattern Recognition* (2018), pp. 8697–8710
9. H. Pham, M. Guan, B. Zoph, et al., Efficient neural architecture search via parameter sharing, in *International Conference on Machine Learning* (2018), pp. 4092–4101
10. E. Real, S. Moore, A. Selle, et al., Large-scale evolution of image classifiers, in *Proceedings of the 34th International Conference on Machine Learning*, vol. 70 (JMLR.org, 2017), 2902–2911
11. E. Real, A. Aggarwal, Y. Huang, et al., Aging evolution for image classifier architecture search, in *AAAI Conference on Artificial Intelligence* (2019)
12. H. Liu, K. Simonyan, Y. Yang, *Darts: Differentiable Architecture Search.* (2019-04-23) [2019-10-26] https://arxiv.org/pdf/1806.09055.pdf
13. S. Xie, H. Zheng, C. Liu, et al., *SNAS: Stochastic Neural Architecture Search.* (2019-01-12) [2019-10-26] https://arxiv.org/pdf/1812.09926.pdf
14. H. Cai, L. Zhu, S. Han, *Proxyless NAS: Direct Neural Architecture Search on Target Task and Hardware.* (2019-02-23) [2019-10-26] https://arxiv.org/pdf/1812.00332.pdf
15. G. Ghiasi, T.Y. Lin, Q.V. Le, NAS-FPN: learning scalable feature pyramid architecture for object detection, in *Proceedings of the IEEE Conference on Computer Vision and Pattern Recognition* (2019), pp. 7036–7045
16. L.C. Chen, M. Collins, Y. Zhu, et al., Searching for efficient multi-scale architectures for dense image prediction, in *Advances in Neural Information Processing Systems* (2018), pp. 8699–8710
17. C. Liu, L.C. Chen, F. Schroff, et al., Auto-Deep Lab: hierarchical neural architecture search for semantic image segmentation, in *Proceedings of the IEEE Conference on Computer Vision and Pattern Recognition* (2019), pp. 82–92
18. X. Chu, B. Zhang, H. Ma, et al., *Fast, Accurate and Lightweight Super-resolution with Neural Architecture Search.* (2019-01-24) [2019-10-26] https://arxiv.org/pdf/1901.07261.pdf
19. D. So, Q. Le, C. Liang, The evolved transformer, in *International Conference on Machine Learning* (2019), pp. 5877–5886
20. Y. Gao, H. Yang, P. Zhang, et al., *Graph NAS: Graph Neural Architecture Search with Reinforcement Learning.* (2019-08-20) [2019-10-26] https://arxiv.org/pdf/1904.09981.pdf
21. E. Brochu, V.M. Cora, N. De Freitas, *A Tutorial on Bayesian Optimization of Expensive Cost Functions, with Application to Active User Modeling and Hierarchical Reinforcement Learning.* (2010-12-12) [2019-10-26] https://arxiv.org/pdf/1012.2599.pdf
22. B. Shahriari, K. Swersky, Z. Wang et al., Taking the human out of the loop: a review of bayesian optimization. Proc. IEEE **104**(1), 148–175 (2015)
23. L.N. Smith, *A Disciplined Approach to Neural Network Hyper-Parameters: Part 1—Learning Rate, Batch Size, Momentum, and Weight Decay.* (2018-04-24) [2019-10-26] https://arxiv.org/pdf/1803.09820.pdf
24. I. Goodfellow, Y. Bengio, A. Courville, *Deep Learning* (MIT Press, 2016)
25. L.N. Smith, Cyclical learning rates for training neural networks, in *2017 IEEE Winter Conference on Applications of Computer Vision (WACV)* (IEEE, 2017), pp. 464–472
26. J.S. Bergstra, R. Bardenet, Y. Bengio, et al., Algorithms for hyper-parameter optimization, in *Advances in Neural Information Processing Systems* (2011), pp. 2546–2554
27. J. Bergstra, D. Yamins, D.D. Cox, HyperOpt: a python library for optimizing the hyperparameters of machine learning algorithms, in *Proceedings of the 12th Python in Science Conference* (2013), pp. 13–20
28. J. Bergstra, Y. Bengio, Random search for hyper-parameter optimization. J. Mach. Learn. Res. **13**(2), 281–305 (2012)

29. K. Hsu, S. Levine, C. Finn, *Unsupervised Learning via Meta-Learning*. (2019-03-21) [2019-10-26] https://arxiv.org/pdf/1810.02334.pdf

30. Z. Li, F. Zhou, F. Chen, et al., *Meta-SGD: Learning to Learn Quickly for Few-Shot Learning*. (2017-09-28) [2019-10-26] https://arxiv.org/pdf/1707.09835.pdf

31. C. Finn, P. Abbeel, S. Levine, Model-agnostic meta-learning for fast adaptation of deep networks, in *Proceedings of the 34th International Conference on Machine Learning*, vol 70 (JMLR.org, 2017), pp. 1126–1135

32. I. Bello, B. Zoph, V. Vasudevan, et al., Neural optimizer search with reinforcement learning, in *Proceedings of the 34th International Conference on Machine Learning*, vol. 70 (JMLR.org, 2017), pp. 459–468

33. M. Andrychowicz, M. Denil, S. Gomez, et al., Learning to learn by gradient descent by gradient descent, in *Advances in Neural Information Processing Systems* (2016), pp. 3981–3989

34. S. Ravi, H. Larochelle, Optimization as a model for few-shot learning, in *International Conference on Learning Representations (ICLR)* (2017)

35. A. Nichol, J. Achiam, J. Schulman, *On First-Order Meta-Learning Algorithms*. (2018-10-22) [2019-10-26] https://arxiv.org/pdf/1803.02999.pdf

36. F. Sung, L. Zhang, T. Xiang, et al., *Learning To Learn: Meta-Critic Networks for Sample Efficient Learning*. (2017-06-29) [2019-10-26] https://arxiv.org/pdf/1706.09529.pdf

37. A.G. Barto, R.S. Sutton, C.W. Anderson, Neuronlike adaptive elements that can solve difficult learning control problems. IEEE Trans. Syst. Man Cybern. **5**, 834–846 (1983)

38. G. Koch, R. Zemel, R. Salakhutdinov, Siamese neural networks for one-shot image recognition, in *ICML Deep Learning Workshop* (2015), pp. 2

39. F. Sung, Y. Yang, L. Zhang, et al., Learning to compare: relation network for few-shot learning, in *Proceedings of the IEEE Conference on Computer Vision and Pattern Recognition* (2018), pp. 1199–1208

40. O. Vinyals, C. Blundell, T. Lillicrap, et al., Matching networks for one shot learning, in *Advances in Neural Information Processing Systems* (2016), pp. 3630–3638

41. S. Falkner, A. Klein, F. Hutter, *BOHB: Robust and Efficient Hyperparameter Optimization at Scale*. (2018-07-04) [2019-10-26] https://arxiv.org/pdf/1807.01774.pdf

42. J. Vanschoren, *Meta-Learning: A Survey*. (2018-10-08) [2019-10-26] https://arxiv.org/pdf/1810.03548.pdf

43. J. Bromley, I. Guyon, Y. Lecun, et al., Signature verification using a "Siamese" time delay neural network, in *Advances in Neural Information Processing Systems* (1994), pp. 737–744

Chapter 12
Device–Cloud Collaboration

We are currently witnessing a rapid increase in the popularity of mobile and wearable devices. In order to use deep learning technologies more extensively in mobile device scenarios, the industry has proposed lightweight models and deep learning frameworks that are more suitable for mobile devices. In such scenarios, however, the application of deep learning is challenging because it relies heavily on big data. On one hand, the amount of device data is typically small and the distribution of such data differs among different devices, making it infeasible to implement pure on-device learning. On the other hand, as regulators and users pay more attention to data privacy, privacy laws typically prohibit the direct collection of personal data, making it difficult to use device data. To overcome these problems, the industry has extensively explored and applied different stages of collaboration, namely on-device inference, transfer learning, and federated learning. This chapter covers these three stages and analyzes the device–cloud collaboration framework that streamlines the entire device–cloud process.

12.1 On-Device Inference

AI is implemented on mobile devices through the cloud, which opens up AI capabilities—for tasks such as image classification and translation—by way of application programming interfaces (APIs). This approach, however, involves uploading user data, long latencies, unavailability after network disconnection, and inadequate user experience. In order to address these problems, TensorFlow Lite,[1] Paddle-Lite,[2] MNN,[3] PyTorch Mobile,[4] and MindSpore on-device inference frameworks have

---

[1] https://www.tensorflow.org/lite.

[2] https://github.com/PaddlePaddle/Paddle-Lite.

[3] https://github.com/alibaba/MNN.

[4] https://pytorch.org/mobile/home.

© Tsinghua University Press 2021
L. Chen, *Deep Learning and Practice with MindSpore*, Cognitive Intelligence and Robotics, https://doi.org/10.1007/978-981-16-2233-5_12

emerged. These frameworks optimize and convert a cloud model into an on-device inference model and provide the capabilities to load the model and infer the local data.

On-device inference requires lightweight, or compressed, models due to the limited computing power and energy of devices. Table 12.1 lists the common techniques used to achieve lightweight models for on-device inference.

Efficient structure design can be performed manually or combined with the AutoML technology (before model training) for automation. Model pruning is usually done either during or after model training. Knowledge distillation, a model training method, is usually performed in conjunction with the preceding two techniques but does not make the model lightweight. These three techniques aim to produce a lighter model structure, reducing the latency or size of the model without sacrificing accuracy. Network structure fusion is usually carried out during model compilation and computing graph optimization. It involves the inference model or graph rather than model training. Model quantization, comprised of weight quantization, quantization aware training, and quantization without training, differs from gradient quantization, which is used in distributed training scenarios. Together with network structure fusion, model quantization is usually performed when the cloud model is converted into an on-device model.

After models are converted to lightweight model files, the on-device inference framework loads and execute them, performing hardware-accelerated processing based on the device's hardware specifications. For example, the framework may invoke an NPU, graphical processing unit (GPU), ARM NEON,[5] or other hardware-based methods to accelerate operator execution. It may also use static memory management, memory pool, and shared memory in order to reduce the time required for memory application, copy, and release.

12.2 Device–Cloud Transfer Learning

Due to the inherent differences between real device data and a dataset used in cloud pre-training models, on-device training is needed to utilize the real device data necessary for achieving an accurate, personalized experience. Training a model from scratch is impractical because devices are limited in terms of computing power, energy, and data volume; consequently, transfer learning technology is used to simplify on-device learning. The industry has yet to reach consensus on a consistent definition of transfer learning, so this section focuses on the general concept of transfer learning, covering incremental training, online learning, and weighted transfer learning. We discuss only cloud-to-device transfer learning in device–cloud collaboration scenarios—this is referred to as device–cloud transfer learning.

As shown in Fig. 12.1, a typical device–cloud transfer learning process is as follows:

---

[5] https://developer.arm.com/architectures/instruction-sets/simd-isas/neon.

Table 12.1 Common techniques for achieving lightweight models

Technique	Description	Example
Efficient structure design	Improves the neural network convolution mode (e.g., separable convolution) and designs models to be more refined and efficient in order to minimize computation and parameters	MobileNet series, ShuffleNet series, and SequeezeNet
Model pruning	Deletes parameters that have a slight impact on accuracy. It learns connections through normal training (which does not need to be performed from scratch) and prunes those that fall below the threshold. It then retrains the weights of the remaining sparse connections	One-shot pruning, iterative pruning, unstructured pruning, and structured pruning
Knowledge distillation	Trains a compact model to distill knowledge from large models. The effect of this technique depends on the usage scenario and network structure. Training needs to be performed from scratch and can be used only for classification tasks with the Softmax loss function	"Student–Teacher" paradigm
Network structure fusion	Performs vertical operator or horizontal structure fusion on the network	Fusion of convolution, batch normalization, and activation function: horizontal fusion of the inception network
Weight quantization	Quantizes only model weights and reduces the number of bits occupied by each weight to downsize original models. It restores Float32 during computation	Value truncation, and clustering-based quantization
Quantization aware training	Quantizes both model weights and activations, and simulates quantization effects during training to ensure that the resultant models can be directly used. Training from scratch and pre-training are both supported	TensorFlow Lite and TensorRT
Quantization without retraining	Quantizes both model weights and activations asymmetrically, and uses a calibration set (e.g., 100 images) to learn the distribution of activations	TensorFlow Lite and outlier channel splitting (OCS)

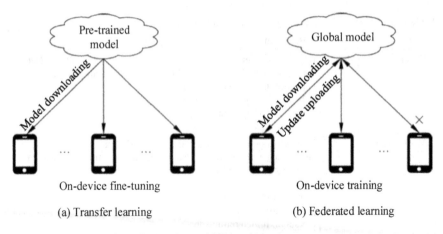

(a) Transfer learning   (b) Federated learning

Fig. 12.1 Device–cloud transfer learning and federated learning

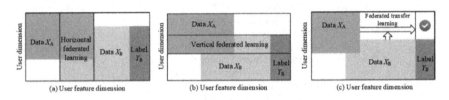

(a) User feature dimension   (b) User feature dimension   (c) User feature dimension

Fig. 12.2 Federated learning defined by Yang et al. [1]

(1) The cloud selects a pre-trained model or trains a new model based on the task on the device.
(2) The cloud delivers the model to the device.
(3) The device optimizes the model based on local data.
(4) The device uses the optimized model for inference.

Transfer training is typically achieved by either training the entire network of the model with device data or training only the last several layers of the model. The latter method is used mainly in image-type tasks, which typically use CNNs. In general, the first several layers (called shallow layers) of the CNN learn rudimentary details and simple features common to different images, for example, horizontal stripes, oblique stripes, corners, and colors. The last several layers (called deep layers) learn advanced and abstract features, which differ for different tasks and include faces, animals, cars, and more. By training only the last several layers, we can accelerate the training process significantly, but this approach depends on the level of accuracy we hope to achieve. For language models such as those used in translation tasks, the complexity of the transfer strategies is higher because the languages themselves are more complex and have different semantic structures.

Incremental training and incremental learning sound like similar concepts—and are frequently used interchangeably—but they differ from each other. In incremental training, the device uses a small amount of data to incrementally train a model pre-trained on the cloud. The datasets used to pre-train this model must be similar to those on the device; specifically, the cloud- and device-based datasets must be of the same categories. However, samples of certain categories on devices are richer than those on the cloud. The main benefit of incremental training is that it can improve overfitting of the device data in the pre-trained model.

Learning can be performed in either online or offline mode. Incremental learning, which is an online learning method, relies on the ongoing generation of data. As the distribution of data changes, new data is used to continuously train the model. Central to this is the ability of the model to remember what it learned from previous data; that is, it avoids catastrophic forgetting (also called catastrophic interference). The opposite of online learning is, naturally, offline learning, which is favored for most model training tasks. It requires all data to be available during training and ensures the uniform distribution of data by shuffling the data samples. In cases where data is generated over time and the distribution of data changes gradually, the online learning method—rather than the offline one—is used. Online, continual, and life-long learning share many similarities in terms of concepts and methods, but given the limited space in this book we do not describe them in detail here. As alluded to earlier, catastrophic forgetting is the tendency to forget previously learned information after learning new information. In device–cloud collaboration, which relies on additional training of the model by using device data, catastrophic forgetting may occur if the device data is unbalanced or only a small volume is available—the trained model may identify only the sample categories that appear on the device, but lose the capabilities learned from the cloud. To overcome this problem, three types of methods are available:

(1) Regularization methods, such as elastic weight consolidation (EWC) and synaptic intelligence (SI);
(2) Methods based on dynamic architecture, such as neurogenesis deep learning (NDL) and dynamically expanding network (DEN);
(3) Complementary learning systems and memory replay, such as deep generative replay (DGR), learning without forgetting (LwF), and gradient episodic memory (GEM).

A simple yet effective memory replay method involves downloading small datasets (memory) from the cloud for joint training with the device data (replay).

Weighted transfer learning is extremely popular today in academia and industry circles. Many of the prominent models currently in use, such as ResNet50, MobileNetV2, BERT, YOLOV3, and SSDLite-MobileNetV2, have released pre-trained model files. Developers and researchers can search model libraries to obtain a pre-trained model that meets their requirements, and then adapt it to their task by modifying the model's output layer or last several layers. Subsequently, they can then further train the modified model by using local data. In essence, adapting pre-trained models for specific use cases is typical in transfer learning. Cloud-to-device transfer learning offers a number of tangible benefits, especially its high effectiveness in device–cloud collaboration. However, although it is theoretically possible to modify any layer of a pre-trained model in transfer learning, only the last several layers of the model are usually modified in practice. For example, when modifying the fully connected (FC) layer in a classification model, we can adjust the number of categories.

After a pre-trained model is modified, partial or dynamic training can be performed. Typically, we do not change the weight parameters of the unmodified layer (the frozen layer), and train only the weight parameters of the modified layer, or train the last several layers in addition to the modified layer. Alternatively, we could adopt a stage-by-stage approach for learning: train the modified layer first, then fine-tune the entire network, and repeat these two steps until the model converges. We must also consider how to minimize computation while also accelerating model training. We can achieve this by using the following technique: First, split the frozen layer and modified layer of the model into two submodels, which we will refer to as model A and model B. Model A is inferred based on local data, and the inferred feature map is saved as a dataset for training model B. Model B is then trained based on the saved feature map until model B converges. After training is completed, models A and B are concatenated to produce a complete model. By using this technique, we avoid repeated computation of model A because its weight does not need to be trained, which in turn accelerates the training process.

In conclusion, device–cloud transfer learning offers two key advantages over the direct use of device data in model training: It not only avoids model overfitting when only a small amount of device data is available (fine-tuning usually requires a small learning rate), but also minimizes the time and resources needed for on-device training.

12.3 Device–Cloud Federated Learning

Device–cloud joint learning methods and frameworks enable us to fully utilize device data and on-device training capabilities by combining the power of multiple devices, while also ensuring privacy on the devices. Back in 2006, Google proposed a federated learning framework and conducted extensive research into gradient aggregation, gradient compression, privacy protection, and device availability. Subsequently, Yang et al. proposed horizontal federated learning, vertical federated learning, federated transfer learning, and federated reinforcement learning, as well as their corresponding frameworks, and defined federated learning as being comprised of the first three methods in a general sense, as shown in Fig. 12.2. This section focuses on horizontal federated learning, specifically, device–cloud federated learning.

Device–cloud federated learning aims to combine multiple users (devices) with a common training model while ensuring privacy. Those looking to implement this method typically raise the following questions:

(1) How can we combine multi-device data and training capabilities?

- Federated averaging, described later, is typically used to combine multiple devices. To increase the computation/communication ratio, methods such as gradient compression are used (which is also described later).
(2) How can we ensure device privacy?
- Differential privacy, homomorphic encryption, security aggregation, and other mechanisms are used to ensure device privacy.
(3) How can we ensure the personalization of each device model while combining multiple devices for joint model training?
- Technologies such as federated meta-learning and federated incremental training are used for personalized on-device models.
(4) How can we prevent uncontrollable factors (such as malicious user attacks) caused by learning process decentralization?
- Technologies such as meta-learning, consensus algorithms, and malicious sample detection are used to address malicious attacks and uncontrollable factors.

12.3.1 Federated Averaging

Google proposed the federated averaging method to increase the computation/communication ratio, which rises with the number of epochs trained on devices. It shows a reduction in required communication rounds by 10–100x as compared to synchronized stochastic gradient descent. In each round of federated training, devices perform multi-epoch training, and the cloud subsequently aggregates weights of multiple devices and obtains a weighted average. Algorithm 12.1 shows the basic flow of the federated averaging algorithm.

Algorithm 12.1 Federated averaging

Input: Number of devices (K), device index (k), mini-batch data on devices (B), number of epochs on devices (E), learning rate on devices (a), and loss function (l)
Output: Weight W
Cloud operations:

(1) Initialize weight W_0
(2) In each round of $t = 1, 2, \ldots$, perform (3) to (5):
(3) S_t = Randomly selected K devices
(4) Trigger on-device training for each device $k \in S_t$ in parallel according to the following Formula:

$$W_{t+1}^k = \text{ClientUpdate}(k, W_t)$$

(5) Aggregate device weights according to the following Formula:

$$W_{t+1} = \sum_{k=1}^{K} \frac{n_k}{n} W_{t+1}^k$$

On-device training ClientUpdate (k, W):

(1) B = mini-batches divided from device data
(2)   In each generation e = 1, 2, ..., E, execute (3):
(3)   Compute gradients and update weights for each mini-batch data $b \in B$ according to the following Formula:

$$W = W - a\, \nabla l\ (W, b)$$

(4)   Return W to the cloud

12.3.2   Gradient Compression

Another technology used to improve the communication efficiency is gradient compression. This technology compresses downloaded or uploaded gradient data to not only reduce communication costs, but also reduce energy and bandwidth consumption of mobile devices. The common methods that adopt gradient compression are as follows:

(1)   Gradient quantization. Typical examples of gradient quantization include Tern-Grad, SignSGD, and QSGD. These methods quantize each element in the gradient tensor or simultaneously utilize the sparsity brought by quantization. Table 12.2 lists the communication costs of these methods, the basic principles of which are as follows:

①   TernGrad: quantizes each element into one of $\{-1, 0, 1\}$. For example, $g = [0.1, -0.8, 0.5, 0, 0.05]$ can be quantized to $Q(g) = [0, -1, 1, 0, 0]$. The approximate value of the quantized gradient is unbiased and can ensure convergence of the training process. The communication costs of TernGrad reach $O(d\ \log 3)$, that is, the compression ratio is $32/\log 3$. However, for gradient compression in federated learning, TernGrad is not a competitive choice, as gradient compression methods such as SignSGD and QSGD offer superior compression.

Table 12.2   Several gradient compression algorithms

	Algorithm			
	SGD	TernGrad	SignSGD	QSGD
Communication costs	32d	$d$log3	d	$\sqrt{d}$ log$d$

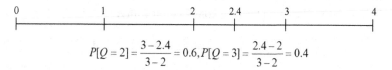

$$P[Q=2] = \frac{3-2.4}{3-2} = 0.6, P[Q=3] = \frac{2.4-2}{3-2} = 0.4$$

Fig. 12.3 Schematic diagram of QSGD (P indicates the probability that a gradient element is quantized into Q, and Q indicates the quantization result)

② SignSGD: takes only the sign of each element. For example, $g = [0.1, -0.8, 0.5, -0.1, 0.05]$ can be quantized into $Q(g) = [1, -1, 1, -1, 1]$ by using SignSGD. The communication costs of SignSGD reach $O(d)$, that is, the compression ratio is 32. In terms of compression, SignSGD is outperformed by QSGD. Furthermore, because SignSGD selects only the sign of each gradient element, the convergence accuracy of the model is reduced.

③ QSGD: quantizes each element by randomized rounding to a discrete set of values. For example, 4-bit quantization has 16 (2^4) discrete values. As shown in Fig. 12.3, [0, 4] is evenly divided into four intervals, and then each element is quantized to the endpoint of the interval. For example, 2.4 is quantized to 2 or 3 at a certain probability. Because many gradient elements may be quantized to zero values, the gradient tensors are sparse. QSGD utilizes this sparsity to further compress the gradient by using the nonzero elements and indexes of the nonzero elements. The communication costs of QSGD reach $O(\sqrt{d} \log d)$, the gradient compression ratio is $32/\sqrt{d} \log d$, and the upper bound of the gradient variance is approximated as $\sqrt{d}$. Although it is almost always necessary to strike a balance between the communication efficiency and gradient accuracy, the communication costs can be reduced by transmitting lower-accuracy gradients. However, if QSGD quantization uses fewer than 4 bits, the convergence accuracy is significantly decreased. Usually, 4-bit or 8-bit QSGD is used, delivering communication costs of $O(4d)$ or $O(8d)$, respectively.

In the table, d denotes the dimension of the gradient vector, and SGD algorithms do not use a compression algorithm.

(2) Gradient sparsity. With the sparsity brought by quantization or a random subset taken from a gradient through downsampling, devices only need to upload the nonzero elements of the sparse tensor as well as the index or random seed for downsampling.

(3) Structured updates. Google proposed a structured gradient compression method that limits the structure of the gradient tensor—instead of conducting quantization or sparsity on the computed gradient—in order to train and update a smaller structure. In this method, the following two concepts are of particular note:

① Low rank: As shown in Formula (12.1), weight W is decomposed into low-rank matrices. Tensor A remains unchanged, whereas tensor B is trained. During each iteration, devices upload only the update of B, and then normal weight W

is restored on the cloud through computation with A.

$$W\left(d_1^* d_2\right) = A(d_1^* k)^* B(k^* d_2), \; k < d_1 \tag{12.1}$$

where

W Weight tensor
d_1 Size of the first dimension of the weight
d_2:   Size of the second dimension of the weight
A Low-rank matrix
B Low-rank matrix

: .

②   Random mask: A random seed is used to generate a specific sparsity pattern, which is used to initialize and update weights, before each round of training begins. During each round, devices upload only the nonzero elements and random seeds of the sparsity tensor.

Figure 12.4 shows the position of gradient compression in the federated learning system, which is deployed on a distributed system covering devices and the cloud. Gradient compression device (2) is deployed on the devices, whereas gradient restoration device (4) is deployed on the cloud. After each round of training begins, the device generates the gradient—several such rounds may occur. The gradient compression device compresses the gradient and uploads it to the cloud through the communication module, after which the normal gradient data is obtained through the gradient restoration device on the cloud. The gradient aggregation module performs gradient aggregation and then delivers the new model to the device for the next round

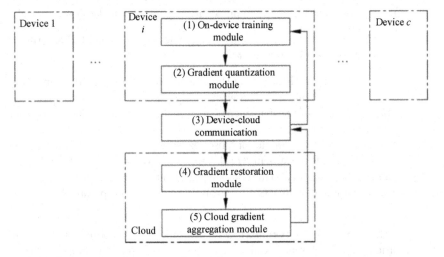

Fig. 12.4 Federated learning system using gradient compression

of training. The weights delivered from the cloud-to-the device can be compressed in the same way as the gradient uploaded in the federated learning scenario. For the same model, the gradient tensors and weight tensors are identical in terms of number, shape, dimension, compression method, and restoration method. It is worth mentioning that compressing the delivered weights will affect the convergence accuracy of the model.

12.4 Device–Cloud Collaboration Framework

AI involves a multitude of devices and service scenarios, with its focus gradually shifting toward a balance of performance and costs rather than outright accuracy. Different models differ in size, memory occupancy, and latency, while different devices vary significantly in storage space, memory size, and chip performance. Given all of these differences, there is an urgent need to optimize the long and complex process involved in developing models for different devices, covering the design, training, and deployment. Existing open-source frameworks are currently unsuitable, and so a device–cloud collaboration framework—one oriented to device service scenarios—is required to not only streamline the entire cloud-to-device process, spanning model generation, optimization, training, deployment, and application, but also improve R&D efficiency and iteration speed.

The main objectives of the device–cloud collaboration framework are as follows:

(1) Rapid deployment in multiple scenarios. The framework constructs a diversified model library by using NAS technology so that models can be quickly adapted to different types of hardware on multiple devices. In this way, we can search the library for a model that satisfies the performance constraints of a given application and use the model directly without additional training.

(2) Full-stack performance optimization. The framework enables users to optimize the precision, size, and latency of models in order to achieve ultimate performance through methods such as NAS, model compression (pruning, distillation, and quantization), and compilation optimization (operator fusion, constant folding, and hardware acceleration).

(3) High flexibility and ease of use. The framework supports a combination of multiple strategies, including model generation, model compression, and compilation optimization, and not only streamlines the entire device–cloud process, but also centrally manages the strategies and configurations throughout the process, delivering tangible benefits in terms of improved ease of use.

(4) Various learning patterns. The framework supports advanced learning patterns that require on-device training capabilities, including transfer learning and federated learning, as well as basic patterns such as on-device inference. (Support for different learning patterns is being added gradually.)

This section focuses on the theoretical aspects and logical architecture involved in building the device–cloud cooperation framework, rather than covering the cloud platform, device–cloud communication, or device software development kit (SDK).

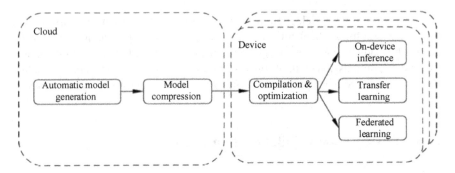

Fig. 12.5 Modules in the device–cloud collaboration framework

As shown in Fig. 12.5, the device–cloud collaboration framework includes cloud-based automatic model generation and model compression modules, and device-based compilation and optimization and learning modules. On the cloud side, the automatic model generation module is used to construct a model library, while the model compression module is used to prune and quantize models in the library. On the device side, the compilation and optimization module is used to compile and optimize the computational graph and accelerate the operator execution. The learning module, also on the device side, includes three learning patterns (listed in ascending order of complexity): on-device interference, device–cloud transfer learning, and device–cloud federated learning. These patterns differ in terms of implementation difficulty and correspond to the three stages of device–cloud collaboration.

Automatic model generation is critical to the entire device–cloud collaboration framework. By establishing an offline model library, we can directly select models from it to use in various application scenarios, but we need the ability to retrieve optimal models that satisfy application-specific constraints without performing additional training. This means that it is necessary to generate different models with different sizes, latency, and accuracy by combining multiple tasks (classification and object detection), multiple datasets (open source and private), multiple architectures (MobileNetV2, one-stage detection model, and two-stage detection model), and multiple network configurations (input shape, number of channels, depth, and kernel size). In general, we can generate only one model based on only one set of constraints at a time by using automatic machine learning or NAS technology. To enrich the model library, we must therefore perform multiple processes based on different combinations, but this usually requires a great deal of time spent in performing search and training processes each time. Such models include ENAS, mobile neural architecture search (MNAS), AmoebaNet (based on evolutionary algorithms), differentiable architecture search (DARTS), neural architecture optimization (NAO), progressive neural architecture search (PNAS), and efficient multi-scale architectures.

Another method we can use for generating a model library quickly is by training a supernet, which consists of trained subnets with different channel numbers, depths, and kernel sizes. Each subnet extracted from the supernet is pre-trained and can be directly used for inference. In the online state, we can search the subnet for a model that satisfies our specific constraint requirements and then use the model directly without additional training. For instance, Han Cai et al. used this approach to fully train each subnet of the supernet. The implementation process, using image classification as an example, is as follows:

(1) Determine the basic network structure. Here we use MobileNetV2. There are 5 stages, with each stage containing a maximum of 4 blocks to give us a potential total of 20 blocks. Each block is implemented by using depthwise separable convolutions (including two pointwise convolutions and one depthwise convolution).

(2) Define the search space. The value range of the image size is [128, 224], and the sampling interval is 4. The value range of the depth (i.e., the number of blocks) in each stage is [4, 3, 2], that of the width is [6, 5, 4] (representing the channel expansion ratio of the depthwise convolution), and that of the kernel size is [7, 5, 3].

(3) Build a supernet. Use the maximum value of each dimension in the search space. Specifically, in each stage, the depth is 4, the kernel size of the depthwise convolution of each block is 7, and the channel expansion ratio is 6.

(4) Train the supernet. To eliminate interference among subnets during the training process, which must cover the entire network, it is necessary to adopt an effective supernet training strategy, such as progressive shrinkage training. Select one dimension and fix the others, gradually decrease the value of the selected dimension, and use the knowledge distillation method for training until the value ranges of all dimensions are traversed. In this way, we are able to generate the supernet parameter file.

(5) Sample subnets. Obtain the subnet structure and parameters from the supernet according to the values of the different dimensions. Sequentially select corresponding blocks based on the depth of each stage, for example, the first two blocks of the stage are represented by a depth value of 2. Then, select corresponding channels based on the width of each block, and select the weight parameters of the corresponding part based on the kernel size. After selecting all the necessary items, generate and output the subnet model file and the corresponding weight file according to the network structure.

The generated model determines the task type, input shape, accuracy, size, and output format, but does not determine the latency on different device models. As such, we need to build latency models for different device models so that the latency can be used directly. Specifically, we need to deliver all operators in the NAS space (those that may be used by all models in the library) to all target device models. Then we need to calculate the latency of each device through repeated inference, and subsequently build the latency model of each device model (we can use the latency model to calculate the latency of each model in the library). The search space of operators should factor in the operator type (such as convolution, full connection,

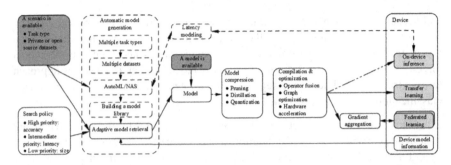

Fig. 12.6 Flow of the device–cloud collaboration framework

batch normalization, or Softmax) and parameters (kernel size, stride, input dimension, and output dimension) and should be determined based on the desired search algorithm.

In addition to model generation and latency modeling, another critical task is creating index tables for the model library, where the combination of each task type and a dataset corresponds to an index table. Each entry in a table records indicators such as model, input shape, accuracy, size, output format, and latency for different device models. The latency indicator will be expanded as the number of supported device models continues to increase.

Figure 12.6 shows the procedural flow of the device–cloud collaboration framework. The dashed boxes indicate items that can be completed in advance offline, whereas boxes with a dark gray background indicate two situations: a scenario and model are both available; and a scenario is available, but a model is not. The boxes with a light gray background represent three learning patterns: on-device inference, transfer learning, and federated learning. After generating or customizing a model, we can use it in the three on-device learning patterns. For on-device inference, the model is usually compressed (e.g., pruned, distilled, and quantized), and compiled and optimized (e.g., operator fusion, graph optimization, and hardware acceleration). For both transfer and federated learning, the model can be pruned, distilled (transfer learning only), graph optimized, and hardware-accelerated. Federated learning also involves gradient aggregation and gradient compression.

The following uses an object detection application as an example to describe the process of using the device–cloud collaboration framework. Assuming that only a scenario but no model is available, the process is as follows:

(1) Set the scenario: Set the task type (such as object detection), and provide a private dataset (this is optional, but enables us to produce a model better suited to the scenario). If no private dataset is available for the scenario, select an open-source dataset (such as COCO 2017).

(2) Build a model library: This step is usually performed offline before application development. To generate private model libraries using private datasets for automatic model generation, we first need to set the scenarios, datasets, and base models and then perform training using the automatic model generation

module. If the latency model does not cover the target device model, we need to provide the target device model and perform latency modeling for it by using the latency modeling module.

(3) Set a search policy: The model index table is determined based on the task type (object detection) and training dataset (COCO 2017), but we still need to determine the search policy. We are more likely to obtain a model with lower latency and smaller size if we set the search priority as follows (listed in descending order of priority): model latency > model size > model accuracy.

(4) Obtain device model information: To determine the latency of each model in the library, we need to automatically obtain information about the target device model by using the device SDK. If the target device model is not included in the list of modeled devices, the latency modeling process is started, ensuring that all operators in the NAS space are delivered to the target device model. Furthermore, the latency of each device model is calculated through repeated inference, and then the latency model of the target device model is built. Subsequently, we can use the latency model to calculate the latency of each model in the model library.

(5) Retrieve the model: Based on our search criteria, device model information, and search policy, we can adaptively retrieve the optimal model from the model library.

(6) Perform model compression and compilation and optimization: Compress (prune and distill) the retrieved model to make it as lightweight as possible, without compromising accuracy, and then perform operator fusion, constant folding, and quantization when converting it for on-device inference.

(7) Perform on-device learning: For the three learning patterns, the on-device framework performs hardware acceleration based on the device's current hardware configurations. For example, we can accelerate operator execution by using methods such as the NPU, GPU, and ARM NEON.

As we have discussed in this section, MindSpore's device–cloud collaboration framework is unique among its competitors in terms of the benefits it brings to users and the speed and accuracy at which it delivers these benefits.

Reference

1. Q. Yang, Y. Liu, T. Chen et al., Federated machine learning: concept and applications. ACM Trans. Intell. Syst. Technol. (TIST) **10**(2), 12 (2019)

Chapter 13
Deep Learning Visualization

13.1 Overview

In recent years, deep learning has developed at a rapid pace, gaining a great deal of popularity. Although deep learning models excel in handling classical problems, these models are often complex, with a nonlinear internal structure, making it difficult for us to understand the decision process or explain why certain models excel on specific problems. Consequently, locating errors that occur in the models, and performing the subsequent code debugging, is a difficult process. Developers and model users alike therefore urgently need a method to help them explain, debug, and optimize deep learning models.

A powerful tool for addressing such needs is visualization. Visualization technologies for deep learning are becoming increasingly mature, due in part to the focused development of explainable artificial intelligence (XAI). This section starts by introducing the process of a deep learning task, as shown in Fig. 13.1, and then describes different visualization methods from four aspects: data analysis, model building, training, and evaluation. The section concludes by describing the problems that developers can solve by using these methods.

13.1.1 Data Analysis

As shown in Fig. 13.1, the data engineering stage is comprised of three steps: data acquisition, data analysis, and data processing. If we detect a problem at any step, we can return to the previous step to rectify the problem. By performing data analysis during the data engineering stage, we are able to gain a preliminary understanding of the collected data in order to optimize the data processing method. Visualization of data analysis is therefore a vital tool that enables us to gain insights into datasets.

© Tsinghua University Press 2021
L. Chen, *Deep Learning and Practice with MindSpore*, Cognitive Intelligence and Robotics, https://doi.org/10.1007/978-981-16-2233-5_13

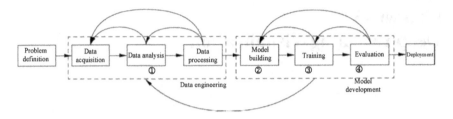

Fig. 13.1   Process of a deep learning task

This section describes the application of visualization in data analysis from three aspects: statistical analysis, dimension reduction, and dataset diagnosis.

1.   **Statistical analysis**

Statistical analysis provides us with a basic understanding of datasets by summarizing their statistical features, such as the global distribution of data, the mean value of a statistical feature, a standard deviation, and a confidence interval. Typical visualization methods used in statistical analysis employ charts such as box plot, histogram, and violin plot. In Fig. 13.2, (a) shows the main characteristics of the box plot, (e) shows the sampling size and confidence interval, and (f) through (i) show the distribution of the data.

2.   **Dimension reduction**

As mentioned earlier, statistical analysis gives us insights into the basic features of datasets. However, this may involve analyzing hundreds or even thousands of charts, adding to the already high workload. To reduce the potential workload, we can use dimension reduction before analyzing high-dimensional data. Some typical examples of the methods used for dimension reduction include principal components analysis (PCA), t–distributed stochastic neighbor embedding (t-SNE), and linear discriminant analysis (LDA). Through dimension reduction, we can visualize the distribution of high-dimensional data in two- or three-dimensional space, making it easier to identify clusters, outliers, and data points that would otherwise be difficult to distinguish by classifiers.

Figure 13.3 shows an MNIST dataset that has been reduced to two-dimensional space. At the boundary of each cluster, several sample points of different clusters exist—such sample points may increase the difficulty in classification. By identifying these sample points in advance, we can preprocess the datasets to ensure that they do not compromise the model's performance.

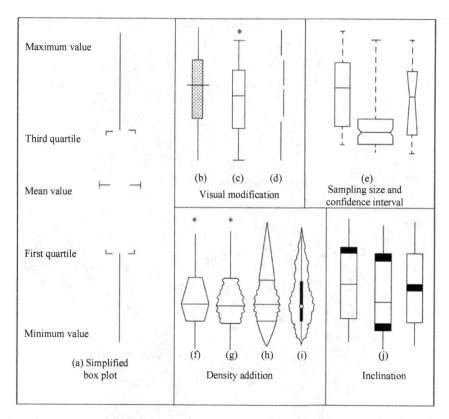

Fig. 13.2 Statistical analysis charts[1]

3. Dataset diagnosis

Dataset diagnosis allows us to detect problems in a dataset through visualization. For example, we can perform dataset diagnosis to identify missing or abnormal values of a feature from a histogram, or to identify data imbalance in multiclass classification from a bar chart. In Fig. 13.4, which shows a dataset for news classification, we can see that the numbers of samples in different categories are imbalanced. For categories that include a large number of samples, the classifier may produce effective results; but for those with fewer samples, the effectiveness may be compromised. Compounding this is the inability of the classification accuracy index to adequately reflect the classifier's ability. To illustrate this point, let us assume that there are three categories of samples in a dataset: A, B, and C. Category A includes 80 samples, B includes 10 samples, and C includes a further 10 samples. Given these samples, the classifier classifies all those in category A correctly, but classifies those in categories B and C incorrectly. This produces an overall classification accuracy of 80%, but because the accuracy is 0% for categories B and C, the classifier is unsuitable. From this, we can see that the

---

[1] Source: https://arxiv.org/pdf/1807.06228.pdf.

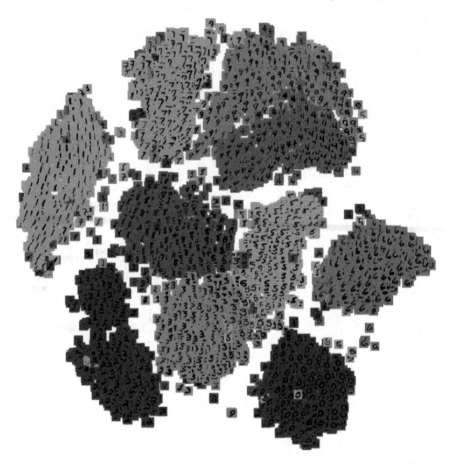

Fig. 13.3 *t*-SNE for MNIST datasets[2]

impact of data imbalance in deep learning classification tasks is not something that we can ignore. Again, visualization can help us detect such problems in advance—it also helps us to lower requirements on computing resources.

In addition to addressing sample imbalance, visualization facilitates our selection of a suitable data processing method. For example, by analyzing the correlation between different features and between features and categories based on heat maps, we can select or construct category-specific features in order to improve the training effect of deep learning models.

---

[2] Source: https://www.cse.ust.hk/~huamin/explainable_AI_yao.pdf.

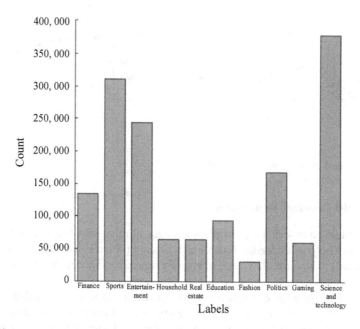

Fig. 13.4 Samples of different categories in datasets used for news classification

13.1.2 Model Building

After data preprocessing, the next step in a deep learning project is to build a model. Deep learning models are typically more complex and involve more layers than traditional machine learning models such as the SVM and logistic regression. Table 13.1 shows the complexity of two popular network structures in computer vision and NLP.

When working with deep learning models, we need to understand their structure clearly and intuitively, detect problems quickly, and communicate effectively. We can use visualization to achieve these goals.

In general, a deep learning model consists of its structure and its parameters. The following describes how we can use visualization to address problems that might occur during model building.

Table 13.1 Complexity of popular network structures

Network	Number of network layers	Application field	Model feature
ResNet-50	50	Computer vision	A large number of layers
BERT	12 (small) 24 (large)	NLP	The computational unit is a transformer that consists of multiple layers

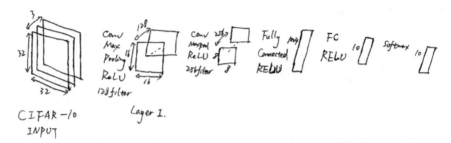

Fig. 13.5 Hand-drawn network structure[3]

1. Model structure visualization

When building a model, we generally rely on an intuitive visual representation of its structure to help us understand the model, detect problems, and explain the model functionality. The most direct way to visually represent a model structure is to draw it by hand.

Figure 13.5 shows an example of a hand-drawn structure. We can see that the input dataset is CIFAR-10. Layer 1 indicates the first layer of neurons, Conv indicates the convolution kernel, and MaxPool (max-pooling) indicates the maximum pooling layer. The activation function of the rectified linear unit is ReLU, and the number of channels of the convolution kernel is 128 (as indicated by 128 filter). Furthermore, Fully Connected indicates the fully connected layer, and Softmax indicates the normalized exponential activation function in multiclass classification.

Although a hand drawing provides a convenient representation of a model's structure, it reveals only subjective ideas rather than verifying the structure in terms of code workability. This approach also makes it impossible to present the microcosmic information of the model, such as the specific operation and data size, which are critical during troubleshooting. The following explains how to solve such problems with a particular focus on using visualization.

Many of the deep learning frameworks in use today typically have a complex structure and numerous layers. So, in order for computers to understand and run deep learning models, they translate the user-written code into a computational graph and then rely on the kernel of the framework to perform computation.

The computational graph, as its name implies, contains all the information necessary for the computer to compute the model. It specifies the flow of input data and a series of operations to be performed on the data, similar to the continuous flow of water in an agricultural drainage network. Figure 13.6 shows an example of a computational graph, where the tensor represents the format of the data flow.

Computational graphs are either static or dynamic. A static computational graph does not change after the training procedure starts, whereas a dynamic one can be adjusted by the training framework as needed during the training process. This means

---

[3] Source: https://idl.cs.washington.edu/files/2018-TensorFlowGraph-VAST.pdf.

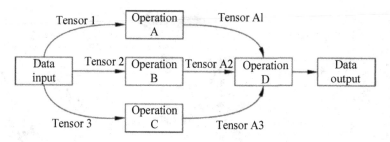

Fig. 13.6 Example of the computational graph

Table 13.2 Mainstream image visualization methods

Visualization method	Operation node	Data information (tensor size, etc.)	Name field	Product cases
Visible hierarchical computational graph	✓	✓	✓	TensorBoard (by Google)
Visible tiled computational graph	✓	–	–	VisualDL (by Baidu), Open Neural Network Exchange (ONNX)

that we can visualize the model structure by using the computational graph translated from user-written code.

In a visualized graph, a node represents an operation such as scalar addition or matrix multiplication, and an edge represents the direction of the data. Table 13.2 lists the two visualization types commonly found in today's mainstream visualization methods.

2. Computational unit visualization

Computational graph-based visualization of a deep learning model, as described earlier, involves many specific tensor computations and operations. Based on this, each node in the graph structure can be represented as a computational unit, also called a neuron, mimicking the trigger mechanism of neurons in the human brain. Specifically, each neuron is triggered to propagate the information forward once a certain threshold is reached after performing a series of computations and processing. In computational unit visualization, the main visualized components are the activations value and the gradient of the loss function.

Visualization of activations can help us understand how input data is converted and processed in the neural network. The activations are computed by using an activation function such as sigmoid, ReLU, or Tanh. For example, Fig. 13.7 shows three different layers of a neural network model. In the figure, each point represents the dimension-reduced activations vector of a data sample at these layers. As the input data samples flow through the network, the activations vectors belonging to

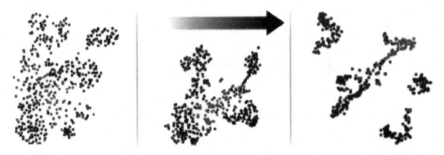

Fig. 13.7 Activation unit visualization[4]

different classes of data samples gradually form clusters. Consequently, the model can classify the original datasets more effectively in the inference process.

By visualizing activations, we are also better able to understand and explain the model. Figure 13.8 shows an example of an image classification model.

In this example, a CNN model is used to classify objects in the image. Because the image contains multiple objects (such as sunglasses and bow tie), the classification results contain multiple labels. Here, we analyze the label "sunglasses". It is easy for us, as humans, to determine that the object on the man's face is a pair of sunglasses. But how does the model arrive at the same conclusion? To explain this, we first need

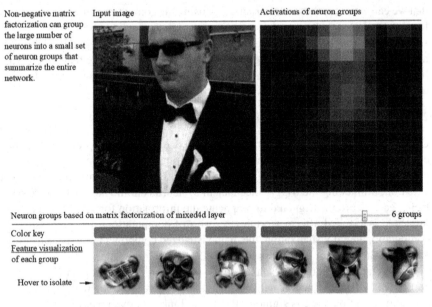

Fig. 13.8 Visualization of activation units helping explain the model[5]

---

[4] Source: https://arxiv.org/pdf/1801.06889.

[5] Source: https://distill.pub/2018/building-blocks/.

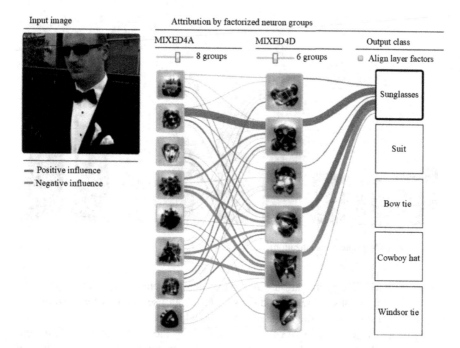

Fig. 13.9 Influence between neuron groups during model classification[6]

to divide the neurons at the intermediate layer of the model into different neuron groups [1]. In this way, we can describe the decision-making process using the pattern (in this case, the "glasses" pattern) learned by different neuron groups, where we represent the pattern through an image by using the feature visualization method [2]. In Fig. 13.8, the lower six images (the feature visualizations) correspond to six neuron groups, and each image corresponds to one pattern. Note that the second of the six images contains the "glasses" pattern. When we hover over the second of the six images, we can see that the activation value of the neuron group containing the "glasses" pattern is the highest among the six neuron groups, meaning that this neuron group has learned the "glasses" pattern in the sunglasses region of the original image.

Figure 13.9 shows the influence between neuron groups at different layers when the model recognizes that the input image contains the label "sunglasses". Note that the thickness of the connecting lines represents the influence level. We can see from this figure that the neuron group with the "glasses" pattern has the greatest influence on the classification results.

For the computational unit, we can also visualize the gradient of the loss function. The most common training method of the deep learning model is the backpropagation of errors. This method adjusts the network parameters by using gradient descent to propagate the gradient of the loss function from back to front, layer by layer, in the

6 Source: https://distill.pub/2018/building-blocks/.

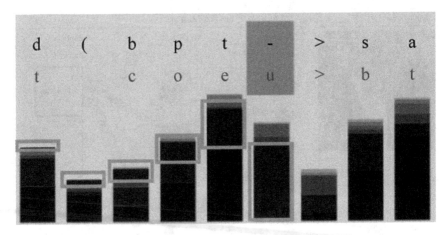

Fig. 13.10 RNN gradient visualization[7]

neural network. The propagation direction of the gradient is the exact opposite to that of the activations value. This means that we can use gradient visualization to help us better understand the features of the model structure.

Figure 13.10 is an example of predicting code in the C programming language by using an RNN. The first line of code is real code in the training sample, whereas the second line is the code predicted by the model. We can see in the figure that a prediction error occurs at the position where the real code is "-" and the predicted code is "u"—the parts marked in boxes under the code lines correspond to the error gradient propagation. Through gradient visualization, we can see the influence of previous characters on subsequent prediction results.

3.   **Model parameter visualization**

In deep learning, all layers of the neural network model are formed by neurons, which are connected at different layers by different weights (parameters) and function as edges to propagate information. The model training process mainly involves the adjustment of these weights by using the error backpropagation algorithm. Visualization of these weights is extremely useful in this case, as shown in Fig. 13.11, because it helps us to not only understand the model structure and explain the training results, but also promptly detect any anomalies that occur during the training.

Figure 13.11 shows a fully connected feed forward neural network. The thickness of the connection edges shown in the figure represents the absolute values of the node weights (parameters) for connecting different layers after the training process is completed—the thicker the line, the larger the absolute value. From this, we can see which neurons at a previous layer have noticeable influence on a particular neuron node. We can also observe the change of parameter distribution during training, for layers with many neuron nodes, based on the distribution graph.

---

[7] Source: https://vadl2017.github.io/paper/vadl_0107-paper.pdf.

Fig. 13.11 Model parameter
visualization

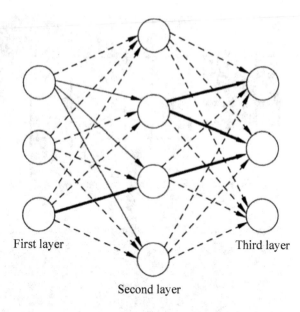

First layer   Third layer

Second layer

Compared with a normal feedforward neural network, the neuron layer in the CNN has a unique feature: The weights (parameters) corresponding to the convolution kernel are shared. With the convolution mechanism, different convolution kernels in the network can extract different features from the training data. This means that, by visualizing the weights of the convolution kernel, we can observe which features are extracted during and after the training, as shown in Fig. 13.12.

Figure 13.12 shows an example of image classification by using the CNN. At each convolution layer, each 3×3 grid on the left with a gray background represents a specific convolution kernel. With the deconvolution method, each grid shows the features extracted by the convolution kernel from each of the nine images whose value of the convolution kernel activation unit is maximized in the validation set. Corresponding original images are displayed on the right. From the figure, we can see a significant difference between the image features extracted by the convolution kernels at different layers. The features extracted at a deeper layer are more complex, while the differences between those extracted by the same kernel from different images are less noticeable. This helps us to better understand the roles that different convolution kernels play in the model inference process.

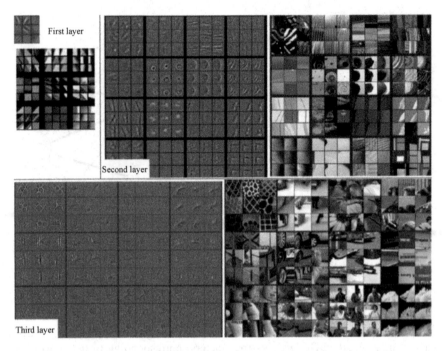

Fig. 13.12   Visualization of the weights of the CNN convolution kernel[8]

13.1.3   Training

Visualization is also crucial to model training. In this case, by visualizing the variation curve of parameters at the intermediate layer of the model, we are able to detect abnormal model performance. For example, we can visualize indexes such as the model loss or accuracy in order to monitor the model training process more effectively in real time. In Fig. 13.13, which shows how the loss curves change during the model training process, we can see that the loss of both the training and validation sets decrease rapidly and converge as the training iteration continues, indicating that the model is normal during the training process. Conversely, a loss curve that changes significantly or rises sharply at a given point indicates that the training process is unstable or abnormal. In this case, we may elect to terminate the training process immediately in order to avoid wasting resources unnecessarily.

---

[8] Source: https://cs.nyu.edu/~fergus/papers/zeilerECCV2014.pdf.

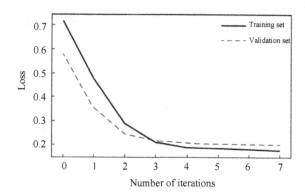

Fig. 13.13 Error changes in the training set and validation set

13.1.4 Evaluation

After training the model, we need to evaluate it. By evaluating a trained model, we can:

1. Determine whether it meets our criteria;
2. Select the best model if we trained more than one; and
3. Gain a deeper understanding of how the model works as well as its decision-making process. For example, when handling a BERT-based text classification task, we can utilize case analysis and visualization to help us intuitively detect words that play a decisive role in the classification result at the text level.

This section describes the role of visualization in model evaluation from two aspects: model evaluation and comparison, and case analysis.

1. **Model evaluation and comparison**

Model evaluation is based on common model indexes such as accuracy, precision, recall, and F1 score. But because a single index is unable to comprehensively measure the model's effectiveness, we need to analyze numerous indexes and compare different models using the visualization method before we can select the best model. As an example, assume that we have a multiclass classification task related to handwriting identification. We first obtain two machine learning models (deep learning models are similar) through training: random forest (RF) and SVM. The accuracy of both models is 0.87. How can we determine which one is better? To answer this conundrum, we can use the visualization method. Through a set of histograms and line charts, this method shows how the prediction scores of the two models are distributed for different categories of samples, as shown in Fig. 13.14.

In Fig. 13.14, each histogram represents a category. We can see that the SVM prediction scores are concentrated at 0.9–1.0, whereas the RF prediction scores are distributed within 0.3–0.8. From this, we can determine that SVM classifies samples in each category more effectively, meaning that the SVM model is the optimal choice.

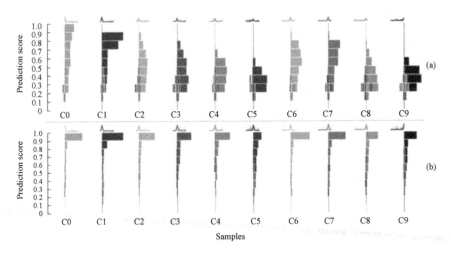

Fig. 13.14 Distribution of the prediction scores of RF (**a**) and SVM (**b**) for samples of different categories[9]

At a star-studded event in Beijing, film makers revealed that they had completed filming of the thriller comedy "Scary Market", co-starring Athena Chu, Feier Li, and Tat-Ming Cheung. The producer expected the film to hit cinemas during this year's Halloween.

Fig. 13.15 Attention to different words in news classification

2.   Case analysis

Taking a text classification task based on the BERT[10] model as an example, this section describes how visualization helps us to gain greater insight into the working mechanism and decision-making process of the model while evaluating its effectiveness.

We can consider BERT as a language model based on extensive text training, and one that relies mainly on the self-attention mechanism to perform computation. In order to train the model for a specific NLP task (e.g., text classification), we can optimize the model based on BERT through transfer learning. In addition, by utilizing BERT's self-attention mechanism, we can visualize attention in order to understand the decisions made by the model. Figure 13.15 shows the distribution of attention when BERT classifies a news message as "entertainment". Highlighted words are those that have attracted the model's attention, where the deeper the highlight, the greater the attention. Because the message contains the names of some celebrities and words such as "thriller comedy", the model classifies the news message as "entertainment". Case analysis in combination with the visualization method can

---

[9] Source: https://ieeexplore.ieee.org/stamp/stamp.jsp?tp=&arnumber=7539404.

[10] See: Devlin J, Chang M W, Lee K, et al. Bert: Pre-training of Deep Bidirectional Transformers for Language Understanding [EB/OL]. (2018–10-11) [2019-10-26] http://arxiv.org/pdf/1810.04805. pdf.

help us intuitively understand the basis of model decision making. Furthermore, in order to quickly identify the cause of a misclassified news message, we can check through case analysis to ascertain whether the model focuses on words that are not related to real labels.

13.2 MindSpore Visualization

The interfaces and processes of MindSpore may constantly change due to iterative development. For all runnable code, see the code in corresponding chapters at https://mindspore.cn/resource. You can scan the QR code on the right to access relevant resources.

Over the past decade, machine learning has developed rapidly in terms of research and application, giving rise to increasingly complex network structures. But as the complexity increases, programmers find it more and more difficult to explain how the involved models work. This hinders the ability of programmers to evaluate model effectiveness, as they need to understand what real-time effects parameter changes have on models and training. The more complex the networks become, the harder it is to perform log-based debugging in terms of both time and cost.

MindSpore visualization is developed to address these issues, offering both model and training visualization. By visualizing images, scalars, and graph structures, it provides the necessary insights for programmers to understand models, structures, and training, enabling them to evaluate models quickly and efficiently based on detailed visualization results. In this section, we describe some of the key concepts involved in MindSpore visualization, including OPS Summary, and explain how to use visualization effectively.

13.2.1 Visualization Process

The MindSpore visualization tool is part of the MindSpore training framework, so we first need to install the framework via pip—Python's package-management system:

```
$ pip install mindspore
```

Once MindSpore is installed, and the visualization tool is installed automatically. We can then use the logs generated by MindSpore after model training (Code 13.2 in Sect. 13.2.3 provides an example of generating such a log).

To start the MindSpore visualization service, we need to run a command on the device that contains the parameters of the directory in which the log is located. Optional parameters can be specified in the command, some of which are as follows:

- datalog: The path to the log required for the model and training visualization module.
- dataset: The path to the dataset required by the dataset visualization module.
- port: Specifies the port, which is 8040 by default.
- host: Specifies the host, which is local host by default.
- help: Displays help information.

After we run this command, the device will display some startup information, including a web address if the server starts successfully. We can access this address to view the visualization information of the modules corresponding to the imported parameters:

```
[2019-08-29 22:46:28 +0000] [85479] [INFO] Listening at:
http//0.0.0.0:8040
```

MindSpore visualization is comprised of four modules, based on the type of content: dataset visualization, model and training visualization, result analysis visualization, and task management visualization.

From Fig. 13.16, which shows the model and training visualization workflow involved in MindSpore visualization, we can see that the content to be visualized depends on the output of MindSpore. Consequently, any data that changes during training needs to be recorded so that we can visualize the training process.

In order to achieve this, we must first use the OPS Summary operator to receive user-specified data during training. OPS Summary is the generic name given to operators such as ScalarSummary and ImageSummary customized by MindSpore for the model and training visualization module. We then need to train the user-defined computational graph to use the SummaryRecord class so that it outputs data contained in the specified OPS Summary operator to the log file containing Summary (described in Sect. 13.2.4). The Summary class refers to the summary data.

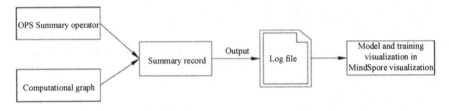

Fig. 13.16 Model and training visualization workflow for MindSpore visualization

Upon startup, the MindSpore visualization service displays summary information of models, training logs, and datasets on the first page, from which we can select individual tasks to view specific modules.

13.2.2 Dataset Visualization

In general, training tasks require three types of raw data: text data, in tasks such as news classification and abstract generation; image data, in tasks such as image classification and object detection; and table data, such as table entries stored in a database, requiring classification or regression prediction. We need to convert this raw data into machine-understandable values before using it as training data, which we obtain by using the word vector method. Prior to this, however, it is beneficial to check what type of data is available, what the characteristics of the data are, and whether the data is balanced.

1. Data overview

The data overview page, as the name suggests, provides an overview of the data involved in classification tasks. It includes a statistical breakdown and histogram of the data, showing the percentage of data per category, as shown in Fig. 13.17. Clicking **View** for a desired entry displays a corresponding page according to the format of the original data.

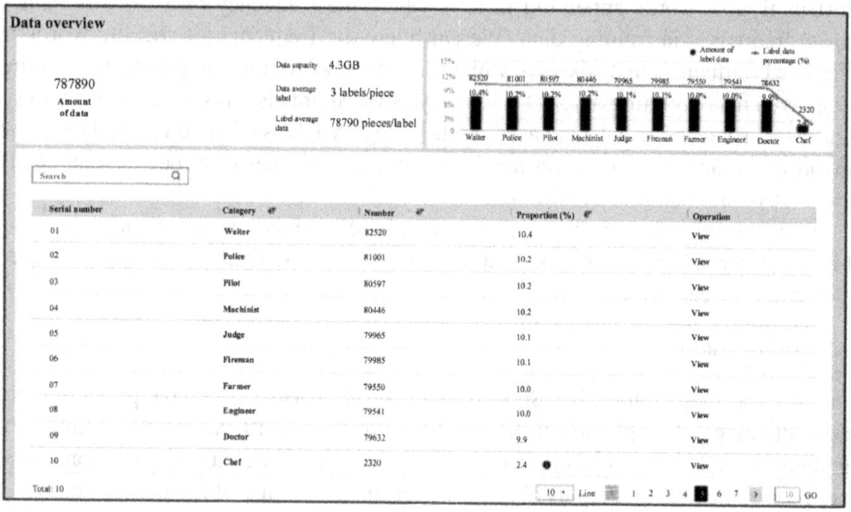

Fig. 13.17 Data overview page for data visualization

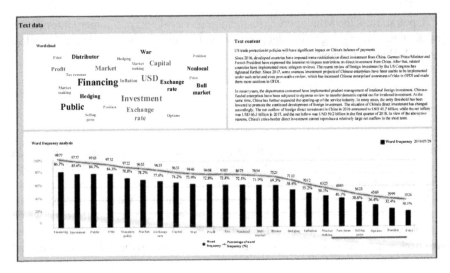

Fig. 13.18 Text data page for dataset visualization

2.   Text data

MindSpore provides a number of visualization schemes for specific tasks. Using text classification tasks as an example, MindSpore provides two visualization methods: word cloud analysis and word frequency analysis, as shown in Fig. 13.18. Word cloud has become a popular method in recent years for displaying the frequency distribution of words appearing in text, where the frequency of a word is related to its frequency in training data. We can view the frequency of specific words in the word frequency analysis area, which shows the word frequency using histograms displayed in descending order of frequency. MindSpore displays word cloud analysis and word frequency analysis based on the category labels of the training datasets to avoid overloading us with too much information on one page, but we can easily switch to other datasets as required.

With the information obtained through text classification visualization, we can broadly infer the word to be focused on when a text classification task model is used to predict the category.

3.   Image data

In terms of image data, MindSpore visualization provides an image preview function for image classification tasks, as shown in Fig. 13.19. Selecting a number of images at random based on different categories, which we can select according to our requirements, can help us obtain a better understanding of the training data.

Fig. 13.19   Image classification page for dataset visualization

4.   Table data

The table data page, as shown in Fig. 13.20, provides key information about table data. We can view attribute information, including a box chart that displays the associated data distribution, as well as statistics of missing and abnormal values, by expanding the collapsible element for each numeric attribute. In addition, we can

Table data

Number of rows: 7000   Number of columns: 4   Number of categories: 3

Serial number	Attribute	Category	Missing number	Missing proportion (%)	Number of anomalies	Proportion of anomalies	Maximum value	Average value	Minimum value	Operation
01	Age	Integer	1400	20%	14	0.2%	100	50	0	Analysis
02	Weight	Floating point number	70	1%	14	0.2%	180	100	20	Analysis
03	Name	Character string	70	1%	.	.	.	.	.	Analysis
04	Height	Floating point number	70	1%	14	0.2%	190	100	140	Analysis

Fig. 13.20   Table data page for dataset visualization

customize the range of normal values and can compare the data distribution of a given attribute between different categories in cases of multi-classification.

13.2.3   Model and Training Visualization

Before we can evaluate and adjust a model based on certain indicators, we often need to wait a long time for model training to finish. By visualizing the model and training, MindSpore provides us with greater insights into how changes of parameters and indexes affect the model and training, enabling us to make necessary model adjustments quickly. With MindSpore, we can also select customized visualization models and analyze their trends in order to make informed decisions for model optimization.

1.   **Scalar**

The OPS.ScalarSummary() operation enables us to view the trends of a specific scalar, such as loss value and accuracy rate of each iteration, throughout the entire training process. The ScalarSummary operator involves two parameters, as shown in Code 13.1.

Code 13.1 ScalarSummary Operator in MindSpore.

```
from mindspore.ops import operations as OPS
scalar_summary = OPS. ScalarSummary (string_in, scalar)
```

In the ScalarSummary operator, the two parameters are defined as follows:
string_in: The name of the scalar displayed in MindSpore visualization, which is of the string type.
scalar: Data that contains the scalar, which is of the tensor type.
Code 13.2 shows an example of writing test scalar data to a log by using the ScalarSummary operator and SummaryRecord module.

Code 13.2 Writing Test Scalar Data to a Log with the ScalarSummary Operator and SummaryRecord Module

```
import random
import numpy as np
from mindspore.trace.Summary.summary_record import SummaryRecord
from mindspore.common.tensor import Tensor
from mindspore.common.api import compile_graph, exec_pip,
import mindspore.nn as nn
from mindspore.ops import operations as OPS


class SummaryDemo(nn.Cell):
    def __init__(self,):
        super(SummaryDemo, self).__init__()
        self.summary = OPS.ScalarSummary()
        self.add = OPS.TensorAdd()

    def construct (self, x, y):
        self.summary ("x1", x)
        z = self.add (x, y)
        self.summary ("z1", z)
        self.summary ("y1", y)
        return z

    def test_scalar_summary_with_ge():
        #Step 0: Create SummaryRecord.
        test_writer = SummaryRecord(SUMMARY_DIR)
        #Step 1: Create a network for writing scalars.
        x = Tensor(np.array ([1.1]).astype(np.float32))
        y = Tensor(np.array ([1.2]).astype(np.float32))
        net = SummaryDemo()
        net.set_train()
        graph, pip = compile_graph (net, x, y, save_graphs=True)
        pip.init_data_graph(graph, net.parameters_dict())

        #Step 2: Create a test training event.
        steps = 100
        for i in range (1, steps):
            #Generate test data.
            x = Tensor (np.array([1.1 + random.uniform (1,
                        10)]).astype(np.float32))
            y = Tensor (np.array(1.2 + random.uniform (1,
                        10))).astype(np.float32))
            output = exec_pip(pip, x, y)
            test_writer.record(i)

        #Step 3: Close SummaryRecord.
        test_writer.close()
```

Code 13.2 draws the changes of scalars ($\times 1$, $y1$, and $z1$ in this example) in the training process by using operations such as ScalarSummary and SummaryRecord, which are used to receive the test data and write it to the log file, respectively. MindSpore visualization reads the log file and displays the results on the web page, and interprets the ScalarSummary operator based on the results.

After MindSpore visualization is started, the Scalar page shows the effect shown in Fig. 13.21 according to the log output generated from Code 13.2, that is, the accuracy written above. MindSpore visualization enables us to view information at any given point on the displayed line graph, including training steps, timestamps, and smoothed values, via an intuitive interface through which we can obtain relevant information. As shown in Fig. 13.22, the control panel on the Scalar page provides numerous options to fine-tune how the information is presented.

2.   Image

The OPS.ImageSummary() operation enables us to view several images on the MindSpore visualization page. For training tasks that involve images, MindSpore visualizes the intermediate results to help us perform model evaluation.

In MindSpore, the ImageSummary operator involves two parameters, as shown in Code 13.3.

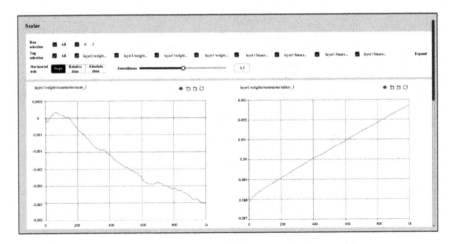

Fig. 13.21 Scalar page for model and training visualization

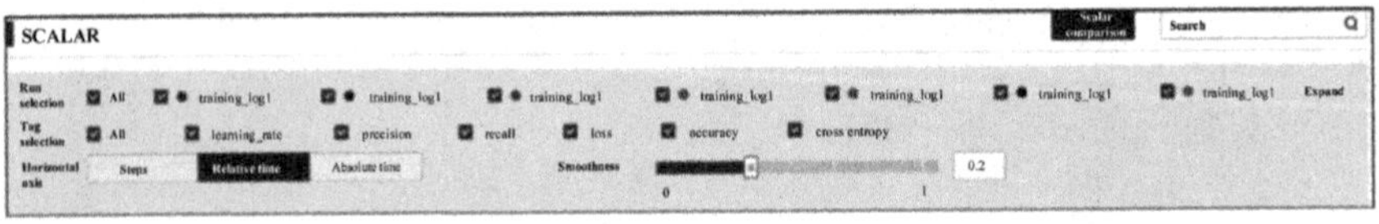

Fig. 13.22 Control panel for the Scalar page

Code 13.3 ImageSummary Operator in MindSpore.

```
from mindspore.ops import operations as OPS
image_summary = OPS.ImageSummary(string_in, image)
```

In the ImageSummary operator, the two parameters are defined as follows:

string_in: The name of the image displayed in MindSpore visualization, which is of the string type.

image: Image data, which is of the tensor type.

After the tensor containing the image data is imported to the OPS.ImageSummary operator, the SummaryRecord module is used to write this image data to the log file. MindSpore visualization reads the log file and displays the results on the web page. However, we first need to define the image information we want to record in the network. Code 13.4 shows an example of defining ImageSummary in the network.

Code 13.4 Code for Defining ImageSummary in the Network.

```
class ResNet(Cell):

    def __init__(self, block, layer_num, num_classes=100):
        super(ResNet, self).__init__()
        self.summary = OPS.ImageSummary()

        #Define the network structure.
        self.conv1 = conv7x7(3, 64, stride=2, padding=3)
        ...

    def construct(self, x):
        self.summary("x_image", x)
        #Define the computation process.
        x = self.conv1(x)
        ...

        return x
```

We need to define SummaryRecord prior to training so that we can subsequently use it as a callback function during training in order to save images in the log file.

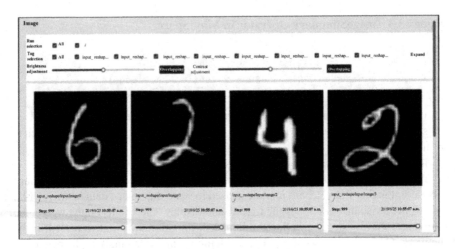

Fig. 13.23 Image page for model and training visualization

Figure 13.23 shows an example of how the sample code is visualized. For each image on the Image page, we can drag the progress bar to view the visualization results of the model and training at different times.

3.   **Computational graph**

The computational graph visualization module is used to display the network structure of the model. We can click a node to view detailed information about it, including its name, attribute, and input/output. Storing the computational graph to the log file does not depend on the OPS Summary operator; instead, we only need to import the defined network when instantiating SummaryRecord. Code 13.5 provides an example of this.

Code 13.5 Using SummaryRecord to Store Information of a Computational Graph into a Log.

```
import os
from mindspore.data import augmentations as augs
import mindspore.nn as nn
from mindspore import Model
from mindspore.trace.summary.summary_record import SummaryRecord
from mindspore.nn.optim import Momentum
CUR_DIR = os.getcwd()
SUMMARY_DIR = CUR_DIR + "/ test_temp_summary_event_file/"


class NET(nn.Cell):
    def __init__(self):
        super(NET, self).__init__()
        self.conv = nn.Conv2d(3, 64, 3, has_bias=False,
        weight_init= 'normal', pad_mode='valid')
        self.bn = nn.BatchNorm2d(64)
        self.relu = nn.ReLU()
        self.flatten = nn.Flatten()
        self.fc = nn.Dense(64*222*222, 3) #padding=0
    def construct(self, x):
        x = self.conv(x)
        x = self.bn(x)
        x = self.relu(x)
        x = self.flatten(x)
        out = self.fc(x)
        return out


def get_dataset():
    data_dir = os.Path.Dirname(
        os.path.realpath(_file_)) + "/../test_data/imagenet_file"
    augmentations = augs.Compose(
        [augs.RandomCropResized(224),
         augs.RandomHorizontalFlip(),
        Augs.ToTensor()])
    dataset = dt.ImageFolder(data_dir, transform=augmentations)
        one_hot_len = len(dataset.class_to_idx)
    def one_hot_fuc(sample):
        lst = [0] * one_hot_len
        data, label = sample
        lst[label] = 1
        data_label = np.array(lst, np.float32)
        return data, data_label
    dataset = dataset.map(one_hot_fuc)
    dataset = dataset.shuffle(buffer_size=3)
    dataset = dataset.batch(batch_size=2, drop_last=False)
```

```
        dataset = dataset.to_tensor()
        return dataset


def test_graph_summary():
    dataset = get_dataset()
    #Step 0: Create SummaryRecord.
    net = NET()
    test_writer = SummaryRecord(SUMMARY_DIR, network=net)
    #Step 1: Create a model.
    loss = nn.SoftmaxCrossEntropyWithLogits()
    optim = Momentum(learning_rate=0.1 momentum=0.9,
    weights=net.trainable_params())
    model = Model(net, loss_fn=loss, optimizer=optim,
    metrics=None)
    model train(2, dataset)
    #Step 2: Store the computational graph.
    test_writer.record(0)
    #Step 3: Close SummaryRecord.
    test_writer.close()
```

Code 13.5 first defines a network structure and then uses the get_dataset() function to read the dataset into memory, following which it uses the test_graph_summary() function to output the log file. The procedure is as follows:

Step 0: Instantiate a SummaryRecord object for outputting a log file, and import the path of the specified output log and the network structure objects of the computational graph.
Step 1: Import the optimizer object and network structure objects into the model, and call the training function for compilation.
Step 2: Call the record function in the SummaryRecord object to output the computational graph to the log file. To simplify this example, real training is not required and no training steps are included, so the imported parameter is 0.
Step 3: Close the SummaryRecord object.

The MindSpore visualization backend then reads and runs the log file to display the computational graph visualization page showing the network structure, where all nodes are collapsed by default, as shown in Fig. 13.24.

In Fig. 13.24, **Parameter** represents the parameter node and contains the network parameters in the computational graph; **Default** represents the default model structure node; and the solid arrows connecting the nodes indicate the flow direction of the tensor data (the associated numbers indicate the pieces of tensor data). In addition:

1. ▭: A rectangular namespace node represents Namescope, which we can expand by double-clicking it to view the subnodes.
2. ⬭: An elliptical operation node represents a specific operator node, which is an atomic node and cannot be expanded.

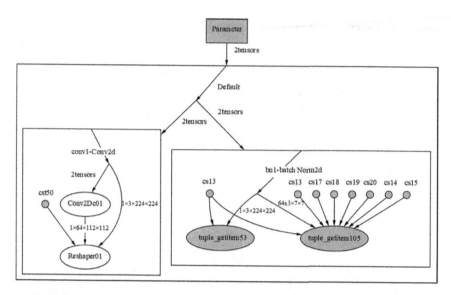

Fig. 13.24 Computational graph for model and training visualization

3. ⬭ : An octagonal aggregation node indicates that some nodes of the same type and at the same layer are displayed as one node, which we can expand by double-clicking it to view specific nodes and their connection relationships.
4. ⬭ A virtual node indicated by a dashed box is a simplified mapping of a node, which we click on to jump to the actual node.
5. A solid arrow indicates a data flow direction edge.
6. A dashed arrow, shown only when the model is large, indicates a control-dependent edge.

Taking the ResNet as an example, after we expand the namespace node by double-clicking it, the main display area shows part of the structure we selected in the computational graph. Expanding the namespace node also reveals its subnodes, where the connection lines between the nodes indicate the directions of data flows and control edges. In addition, the secondary display area (omitted here) shows a higher-level overview of the full computational graph, displaying the location of our selected part of the graph, details of the selected node, and explanations of the legends used.

13.2.4 Format of Summary Data

Summary data contains two embedded classes: Image and Value. Code 13.6 defines Summary in the summary.proto file.

Code 13.6 Excerpt of the summary.proto File.

```
message Summary {
    //Data
    message Image {
      //Image dimension information
      int32 height = 1;
      int32 width = 2;
      //Color space
      //1 - grayscale
      //2 - grayscale + alpha
      //3 - RGB
      //4 - RGBA
      //5 - DIGITAL_YUV
      //6 - BGRA
      required int32 colorspace = 3;
      //Encoded image data
      required bytes encoded_image_string = 4;
    }

    //Numerical information
    message Value {
      //Data tag for managing data
      required string tag = 1;

      //Values corresponding to the tag
      oneof value {
        float scalar_value = 3;
        Image image = 4;
        TensorProto tensor = 8;
      }
    }

    //Set of numerical information contained in summary data
    repeated Value value = 1;
}
```

Event data records basic information about an event, including the timestamp, global steps, and other defined information. This means that for an event instance, we can select event information from only the following fields: file version number, encoded data flow graph, and Summary data. Code 13.7 defines Event selected in the summary.proto file.

Code 13.7 Definition of Event in the summary.proto File.

```
message Event {
   //Event timestamp
   double wall_time = 1;

   //Number of global steps
   int64 step = 2;

   oneof what {
      //Event file version number
      string file_version = 3;
      //Encoded data flow graph
      bytes graph_def = 4;
      //Summary data
      Summary summary = 5
      //Generated logs
   }
}
```

When the timestamp and global steps are provided, Summary can be converted into event data.

References

1. C. Olah, A. Mordvintsev, L. Schubert, Feature visualization. Distill, **2**(11), e7 (2017)
2. D. Cashman, G. Patterson, A. Mosca et al., RNNbow: visualizing learning via backpropagation gradients in RNNs. IEEE Comput Graph Appl **38**(6), 39–50 (2018)

Chapter 14
Data Preparation for Deep Learning

14.1 Overview of Data Format

A data format describes how to organize and save data in files, and can be in the form of numbers, characters, or binary numbers. Storage in a character format typically offers a high level of transparency but consumes more storage space, whereas that in a binary format—a compressed format—offers a low level of transparency but consumes less storage space. While text files can be opened and displayed in readable form using common programs such as Notepad, binary files need to be decoded using specific tools or libraries before they can be displayed in a readable form.

Common data storage formats include TXT, XLS, DOC, PPT, CSV, XML, JSON, JPEG, BMP, and many others.

(1)　TXT mainly stores text information. Such files can be opened and displayed in a readable manner using programs such as Notepad and Notepad + + .

(2)　XLS, DOC, and PPT: formats supported by the Microsoft Office suite. XLS is ideal for processing tables, charts, and data; DOC is suitable if typesetting of text is required; PPT is suitable for product description and charts.

(3)　BMP: a standard format used by Windows to store bitmap digital images. Although the image depth is adjustable, BMP files are not compressed and therefore have a relatively large size.

(4)　JPEG: a lossy compression scheme used to compress images. Due to lossy compression, some repeated or unimportant data may be lost, potentially damaging the image data.

© Tsinghua University Press 2021

L. Chen, *Deep Learning and Practice with MindSpore*, Cognitive Intelligence and Robotics, https://doi.org/10.1007/978-981-16-2233-5_14

```
0000: FF D8 FF E0 00 10 4A 46 49 46 00 01 01 01 00 60
0010: 00 60 00 00 FF DB 00 43 00 08 06 06 07 06 05 08
0020: 07 07 07 09 09 08 0A 0C 14 0D 0C 0B 0B 0C 19 12
0030: 13 0F 14 1D 1A 1F 1E 1D 1A 1C 1C 20 24 2E 27 20
0040: 22 2C 23 1C 1C 28 37 29 2C 30 31 34 34 34 1F 27
0050: 39 30 38 32 3C 2E 33 34 32 FF DB 00 43 01 09 09

                          ...

0220: 89 8A 92 93 94 95 96 97 98 99 9A A2 A3 A4 A5 A6
0230: A7 A8 A9 AA B2 B3 B4 B5 B6 B7 B8 B9 BA C2 C3 C4
0240: C5 C6 C7 C8 C9 CA D2 D3 D4 D5 D6 D7 D8 D9 DA E2
0250: E3 E4 E5 E6 E7 E8 E9 EA F2 F3 F4 F5 F6 F7 F8 F9
0260: FA FF DA 00 0C 03 01 00 02 11 03 11 00 3F 00 E2
0270: E8 A2 8A F9 93 F7 10 A2 8A 28 00 A2 8A 28 00 A2
0280: 8A 28 03 FF D9
```

Fig. 14.1 JPEG image in binary mode

A JPEG image predominantly contains the following data segments: [file header][APP0 segment][DQT segment]…[SOF0 segment][DHT segment]…[SOS segment][image compression data][file trailer].

If we were to draw a 32×24 red square and save it as a JPEG file, its binary representation would be as shown in Fig. 14.1.

14.2 Data Format in Deep Learning

In the field of AI, an extensive range of data is used for training. For example, text, image, audio, and video data can be used as original input, which is then either manually or semiautomatically annotated as training data. Once this input and the annotation information are uploaded to a training platform, the platform uses the annotation information during the training process in order to generate a model.

14.2.1 Original Input

Original input is fed into the training framework and mainly includes text, image, audio, and video data. Each piece of original input has a particular set of features; for example, an image contains attribute information such as type, length, width, and size. This information is referred to as metadata, which the training framework uses in order to better understand the pieces of original input. The following provides some examples of the different types of original input.

(1)   Text: In text classification, labels are used to classify the text, and then the text and label categories are trained to generate a model for text classification detection.

(2)   Image: The most common application is object recognition, in which each training image is labeled as a category. Two lists in a one-to-one mapping—one of the images and one of the categories—are obtained and subsequently used for image classification training.

(3)   Audio: Through training, speech is converted into text, which can then be used as input in an AI application to complete semantic understanding and instructive operations.

(4)   Video: Video data can be labeled efficiently to facilitate operations such as classification and search.

14.2.2   Annotation Information

Annotation information is associated with the type of training the user performs based on the original input. For example, PASCAL VOC, custom CT format, and COCO are different annotation formats. After annotation is performed, annotation files are generated in a variety of formats, some of which are described in this section.

1.   **PASCAL VOC format**
     Mandatory fields are described as follows:
- folder indicates the directory where the data source resides.
- filename indicates the name of the annotated file.
- size indicates pixel information of an image.
- width indicates the width of an image.
- height indicates the height of an image.
- depth indicates the number of channels in an image.
- segmented indicates whether segmentation is performed.
- object indicates object detection information. If multiple objects are annotated, there will be multiple object fields.
- name indicates the category of content.
- pose indicates the shooting angle of content.
- truncated indicates whether content is truncated (0 means no).
- occluded indicates whether content is occluded (0 means no).
- difficult indicates whether it is difficult to identify the target (0 means no).
- bndbox indicates the type of an annotation box. Values are shown in Table 14.1.

Table 14.1 Description of bndbox values

Type	Shape	Annotation information	Remarks
point	Point	Coordinates of the point <x > 100 < x> < y > 100 <y>	–
line	Line	Coordinates of points < x> 100 < x1 > <y1 > 100 <y1> <x2> 200 < x2> <y2 > 200 <y2>	–
bndbox	Rectangular box	Coordinates of the lower left point and the upper right point <xmin> 100 < xmin> <ymin > 100 <ymin> <xmax> 200 < xmax> <ymax> 200 < ymax>	–
polygon	Polygon	Coordinates of points < x1> 100 < x1 > <y1 > 100 <y1> <x2> 200 < x2> < y2> 100 <y2> <x3> 250 < x3 > <y3> 150 <y3> <x4> 200 < x4> <y4 > 200 <y4> < x5> 100 <x5> <y5 > 200 <y5> <x6> 50 < x6> <y6 > 150 <y6>	–
circle	Circle	Center coordinates and radius <cx > 100 <cx> <cy > 100 < cy> <r > 50 <r>	–
rotated_box	Rotated rectangle	–	Reserved, not supported currently
cubic_bezier	Cubic Bezier curve	–	Reserved, not supported currently

An example of PASCAL VOC annotation information is shown in Code 14.1.

Code 14.1 Example of PASCAL VOC annotation information

```
<annotation>
  <folder>test_data</folder>
  <filename>260730932.jpg</filename>
  <size>
    <width>767</width>
    <height>959</height>
    <depth>3</depth >
  </size>
  <segmented>0</segmented>
  <object>
    <name>bag</name>
    <pose>Unspecified</pose>
    <truncated>0</truncated>
    <occluded>0</occluded>
    <difficult>0</difficult>
    <bndbox>
      <xmin>108</xmin>
      <ymin>101</ymin>
      <xmax>251</xmax>
      <ymax>238</ymax>
    </bndbox>
  </object>
  <object>
    <name>circle</name>
    <pose>Unspecified</pose>
    <truncated>0</truncated>
    <occluded>0</occluded>
    <difficult>0</difficult>
    <circle>
      <cx>405</cx>
      <cy>170</cy>
      <r>100</r>
    </circle>
  </object>
</annotation>
```

2. Custom CT format

Custom CT format is a new data annotation format that includes definitions such as template specification used, whether the data is an array, whether a field is required, and field type. As the name suggests, it can be tailored to generate a custom annotation format, based on which it can generate an annotation template, making subsequent annotation easier to perform. The custom CT format is shown in Code 14.2.

Code 14.2 Custom CT format

```
{
  "$schema": "http json-schema org draft-07 schema#",
  "title": "CVAT annotation format schema",
  "description": "...",
  "definitions": {
   "attributes": {
    "type": "array",
    "items": {
     "type": "object",
     "properties": {
      "attr-name": {"type": "string"},
      "data-type": {"type": "string"},
      "attr-value": {}
     }
     "required": ["attr-name", "data-type", "attr-value"]
    }
   }
  },
  "type": "object",
  "properties": {
   "source-ref": {"type": "string"},
   "anno-tool": {"type": "string"},
   "template-name": {"type": "string"},
   "creation-time": {"type": "string"},
   "attributes":{"$ref": "#/definitions/attributes"},
   "entity-instances": {
    "type": "array",
    "items": {
     "type": "object",
     "properties": {
      "entity-name": {"type": "string"},
      "class-id": {"type": "integer"},
      "instance-id": {"type": "integer" , "minimum": 0},
      "attributes": {"$ref": "#/definitions/attributes"}
     },
     "required": ["entity-name", "class-id", "instance-id",
     "attributes"]
    }
   }
  },
  "required": ["source-ref", "anno-tool", "template-name",
  "creation-time"]
}
```

An example of custom CT format annotation information is shown in Code 14.3.

Code 14.3 Example of custom CT format annotation information

```json
{
  "source-ref": "Name of the annotated sample file",
  "anno-tool": "CVAT"
  "template-name": "Human image annotation template",
  "creation-time": "2018-11-13T20:20:39+00:00",

  "attributes": [
    {
      "attr-name": "Image classification",
      "data-type": "image-class",
      "attr-value": [     //attribute value whose multiplicity is*.
        {"value": 1,
         "name": "Human"
        },
        {
          "value": 3,
          "name": "Photography"
        }
      ]
    }
  ],
  "entity-instances": [
    {
      "entity-name": "Human image"
      "class-id": 1
      "instance-id": 1,
      "attributes": [
        {
          "attr-name": "Human scoring",
          "data-type": "body",
          "attr-value": {
            "value": 1,
            "name": "Human is centered and occupies more than 50% of the image"
          }
        },
```

```
{
    "attr-name": "Human face box",
    "data-type": "bounding-box",
    "attr-value": {
    "xmin": 210,
    "yin": 121,
    "xmax": 351,
    "ymax": 435
    }
},
{
    "attr-name": "Multipoint attribute"
    "data-type": "points",
    "attr - value": [
    {"x": 10, "y": 191},
    {"x": 42, "y": 74},
    {"x": 36, "y": 19}
    ]
},
{
    "attr-name": "Face feature",
    "data-type": "face-landmark-5",
    "attr-value": {
        "point0": {"x": 100,"y": 21},
        "point1": {"x": 89,"y": 20},
        "point2": {"x": 13,"y": 21},
        "point3": {"x": 34,"y": 31},
        "point4": {"x": 62,"y": 187}
    }
    }
    ]
    }
    ]
    }
```

14.3   Common Data Formats for Deep Learning

Some of the most common data formats used in deep learning include TFRecord, LMDB, and REC. The TFRecord format corresponds to TensorFlow, LMDB corresponds to Caffe, and REC corresponds to MXNet.

In order to explain why we need deep learning data formats, let us take images and annotation information as an example. Conventionally, training data is stored either locally or on the cloud, and is provided to the training platform in the form of a file list. This approach has a number of drawbacks: It requires many inefficient I/O or network operations, consumes local storage space or network bandwidth, prolongs the training process, and compromises the training efficiency. MindSpore takes a different approach in order to address such issues. The MindSpore data format organizes the image list and annotation information into one or more large files, either locally or on the cloud, reducing the time needed for the training platform to read numerous files and improving training efficiency.

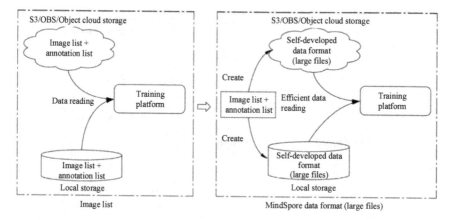

Fig. 14.2 Differences between the conventional approach of reading an image list and the approach MindSpore uses

Fig. 14.3 Time consumption comparison between the conventional approach of reading an image list and the approach MindSpore uses

Figure 14.2 shows the differences between the conventional approach of reading an image list and the approach MindSpore uses.

Figure 14.3 shows a time consumption comparison between the two approaches.

14.3.1 TFRecord Format

TFRecord is a binary storage format in TensorFlow and generates data based on Protobuf. Only the Protobuf format needs to be defined (i.e., what data needs to be written and their types), following which a TensorFlow interface can be invoked to convert the original input and label information to the TFRecord format. TFRecord stores data in a row-based storage mode, enabling efficient reads as well as facilitating transfers and duplication. Of particular note is that it does not require a separate label file. With TFRecord, we can define data types such as bytes_list, float_list, and int64_list, and store both image data and labels in TFRecord files. TFRecord makes it convenient to provide data for TensorFlow, read data from files, and preload data, allowing data to be quickly loaded during training.

The storage format of TFRecord data is shown in Fig. 14.4.

A TFRecord file contains the tf.train.Example protocol buffer. After data is added in the tf.train.Example protocol buffer, the protocol buffer is serialized into a string and written to the TFRecord file through tf.Python_io.TFRecordWriter. An example of a TFRecord write operation is shown in Code 14.4.

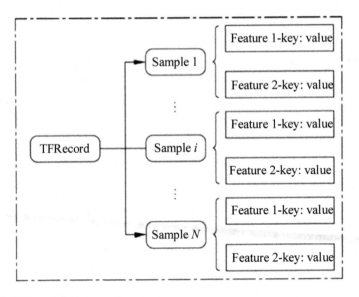

Fig. 14.4 TFRecord data storage format

Code 14.4 Example of a TFRecord write operation

```
classes = {'duck,'cow'}
writer = tf.python_io.TFRecordWriter("train.tfrecord")

for index, name in enumerate(classes):
    class_path = name + '/'
    for img_name in os.listdir(class_path):
        img_path = class_path + img_name

        img = Image.open(img_path)
        img = img.resize((128, 128))
        img_raw = img.tobytes()
        example= tf.train.Example(features = tf.train.Features(
            feature = {
                "label": tf.train.Feature(int64_list =
                tf.train.Int64List(value = [index]))
                "img_raw": tf.train.Feature(bytes_list =
                tf.train.BytesList(value=[img_raw]))
            }
        ))
        writer.write(example.SerializeToString())
writer.close()
```

The tf.parse_single_example parser of tf.TFRecordReader can be used to read data from the TFRecord file. The operation can parse the example protocol buffer to a tensor. An example of a TFRecord read operation is shown in Code 14.5.

Code 14.5 Example of a TFRecord read operation

```
filename_queue = tf.train.string_input_producer([filename])

reader = tf.TFRecordReader()
_, serialized_example = reader.read(filename_queue)
features = tf.parse_single_example(serialized_example,
                       features = {
                           'label': tf.FixedLenFeature([],
                           tf.int64),
                           'img_raw': tf.FixedLenFeature([],
                           tf.string),
                       })

img = tf.decode_raw(features['img_raw'], tf.uint8)
img = tf.reshape(img, [128, 128, 3])
img = tf.cast(img, tf.float32) * (1. / 255) - 0.5
label = tf.cast(features['label'], tf.int32)
return img,label
```

14.3.2 LMDB Storage

Lightning Memory-Mapped Database (LMDB) is a transactional database used in Caffe and based on key-value pairs. Because it uses a memory mapping file, it offers extremely high I/O performance, which is beneficial as numerous read and write operations are performed when Caffe is used. In LMDB, the Datum data structure is used to store original images and annotated labels. Specifically, Datum includes:

(1) Channels indicates channels in an image. A color image has three channels, whereas a grayscale image has only one.
(2) Height indicates the height of the image (i.e., data).
(3) Width indicates the width of the image (i.e., data).
(4) Data indicates the image data (pixel values).
(5) Label indicates the image label.

LMDB is well suited for image dataset scenarios. It saves decoded RGB values of an image, meaning that the saved dataset is larger than the image list.

As mentioned earlier, LMDB uses a memory mapping file, whereby all read operations are to map a to-be-accessed file to virtual memory in a read-only manner through Mmap. Write operations are performed through system calls, mainly to use file system consistency to avoid synchronization on the address being accessed.

LMDB uses a B+ tree structure for storage. Both indexes and values are read from the B + tree page. The B + tree operation mode is provided to the outside: A cursor can be used for performing operations such as create, retrieve, update, and delete (CRUD). The basic architecture of LMDB is shown in Fig. 14.5.

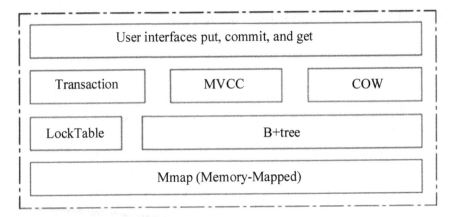

Fig. 14.5 Basic architecture of LMDB

(1) User interfaces put, commit, and get: Interfaces through which users operate LMDB. These interfaces, respectively, correspond to the write, commit, and get operations, allowing users to write data to and obtain data from LMDB.

(2) Transaction: LMDB provides transaction operations to ensure the atomicity, consistency, isolation, and durability (ACID) attributes of data, mainly for data consistency purposes.

(3) MVCC: Multi-version concurrency control (MVCC) addresses issues with write operation time-outs due to multiple long read operations caused by read–write lock. LMDB adds a limit to MVCC, that is, only one write thread is allowed to exist, thereby avoiding read–write conflicts.

(4) COW: Copy-on-write (COW) is an optimization strategy, whereby if more than one caller requests the same resource at the same time (such as data stored in memory or on a disk), the callers will jointly acquire the same pointer that points to the same resource. The system generates a dedicated copy of the resource for a caller only when the caller attempts to modify the resource content, while the resource that other callers see remains unchanged—this process is transparent to all other callers. The main advantage of this approach is that no copies will be generated if the caller does not modify the resource, meaning that multiple callers can share the same resource when they perform only read operations.

(5) LockTable: It is used for read operations in a transaction.

(6) B+ tree: LMDB uses a B + tree structure for storage, and both indexes and values are read from the B+ tree page. The B + tree operation mode is provided to the outside: The pointer can be used to perform CRUD operations.

(7) Mmap: Memory mapping maps physical memory to process address space so that applications can directly use I/O address space. When files are mapped to memory space, applications do not need to perform I/O operations on them. Consequently, no buffer needs to be requested or allocated for the files to be processed, and all file buffering operations are directly managed by the system. Because operations such as uploading the files to memory, writing data from the memory to a file, and releasing memory blocks are omitted, this operation

mode plays an extremely important role in scenarios where large numbers of files need to be processed.

An example of an LMDB write operation is shown in Code 14.6.

Code 14.6 Example of an LMDB write operation

```
def create_db(output_file):
    print(">>>Write database…")
    LMDB_MAP_SIZE = int(1e10)
    env = lmdb.open(output_file, map_size =LMDB_MAP_SIZE)

    checksum = 0
    with env.begin (write = True ) as txn:
    for j in range(0, 128):
        #Custom label, width, and height
        label = j % 10
        width = 64
        height = 32

        img_data = np.random.rand (3, width, height)
        #Randomly generated image data

        #Create TensorProtos
        tensor-protos = caffe2-pb2.TensorProtos()
        img-tensor = tensor-protos.protos add()
        img-tensor.dims.extend(img-data.shape)
        img_tensor.data_type = 1

        flatten-img = img-data.reshape(np.prod(img-data.shape))
        img_tensor.float_data.extend(flatten_img)

        label_tensor = tensor_protos.protos.add()
        label_tensor.data_type = 2
        label_tensor.int32_data.append(label)

        #Write data in "filename: value"mode.
        txn.put('image{}.jpg'.format(j).encode('ascii'),
        tensor_protos.SerializeTbString())

        checksum + = np.sum(img_data) * label
        if j % 16==0:
            print("Inserted {} rows".format(j))

    print("Checksum/write: {}".format(int(checksum)))
    return checksum
```

An example of an LMDB read operation is shown in Code 14.7.

Code 14.7 Example of an LMDB read operation

```
def read_db_with_caffe2(db_file, expected_checksum):
    print(">>> Read database...")
    model = model_helper.ModelHelper(name = "lmdbtest")
    batch_size = 32
    #Obtain data and label object
    _, _ = model.TensorProtosDBInput([], ["data" "label"],
                            batch_size = batch_size,
                            db = db_file,
                            db_type = "lmdb")


    workspace.RunNetOnce(model.param_init_net)
    workspace.CreateNet(model.net)
    checksum = 0
    for _ in range(0, 4):
        workspace.RunNet(model.net.Proto().name)


        img_datas = workspace.FetchBlob("data")
        labels = workspace.FetchBlob("label")
        for j in range(batch_size):
            checksum += np.sum(img_datas[j,:]) * labels[j]

    print("Checksum/read: {}".format(int(checksum)))
    assert np.abs(expected_checksum - checksum < 0.1),
    "Read/write checksums dont match"
```

14.3.3   REC Format

REC is the data format used in MXNet. To generate a file in this format, we need to use the /mxnet/tools/im2rec.py tool to process database images. After we generate a list file, we can then generate a REC file based on this list file.

An example of generating a list is shown in Code 14.8.

Code 14.8 Example of generating a list

```
image_files = os.listdir(data_loc)
random.seed(100)
random.shuffle(image_files)

n_image = len(image-files)
n_train = int(n_image * 0.8)
n_test = n_image - n_train

#Open the list file.
fout = open(os.path.join('./', 'animal_train.lst'), 'w')

duck = 0
cow = 1

for i in range(n_train):
    filename = image_files [i]
    label = duck if 'duck' in filename else cow
    fout.write('%d\t%d\t%s\n'%(i, label, filename))

fout.close()

#View the list file.
fout = open(os.path.join('./', 'animal_test.lst'), 'w')

for i in range(n_test):
    filename = image_files [n_train + i]
    label = duck if 'duck' in filename else cow
    fout.write('%d\t%d\t%s\n'%(i, label, filename))

fout.close()
```

An example of generating the REC format is shown in Code 14.9.

Code 14.9 Example of generating the REC format

```
% python mxnet - /mxnet/tools/im2rec.py -- num tread 4 pass -
through 1 animal datas/train
```

14.3.4   *MindSpore Data Format*

For back-end training, typical data formats such as TFRecord, LMDB, and REC (partial) lack important information and functions, such as schema definition (annotation), statistical information, and retrieval function. Consequently, we are unable to obtain a clear understanding of how data in these formats is defined, how many pieces of data there are, or how labels are distributed, even though such information exists in the dataset management. The MindSpore data format was defined to address these issues and includes schema definition along with statistical, retrieval, raw data, metadata, and annotation information. By enabling us to use and understand the data more effectively when using the local interface and visualization tools, this format ultimately helps us to enhance the overall training effect.

1.   **Features of the MindSpore data format**
(1)   The MindSpore data format is provided as a library and includes a Python interface. This format delivers improved read performance through the library-provided read interface and allows us to easily add schemas, statistics, custom statistical items, index fields, and written data through Python when generating data. Furthermore, index fields speed up the retrieval of specific data, and we can visualize a wealth of statistical information.

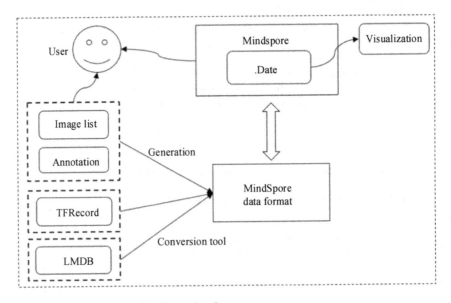

Fig. 14.6 Conversion to the MindSpore data format

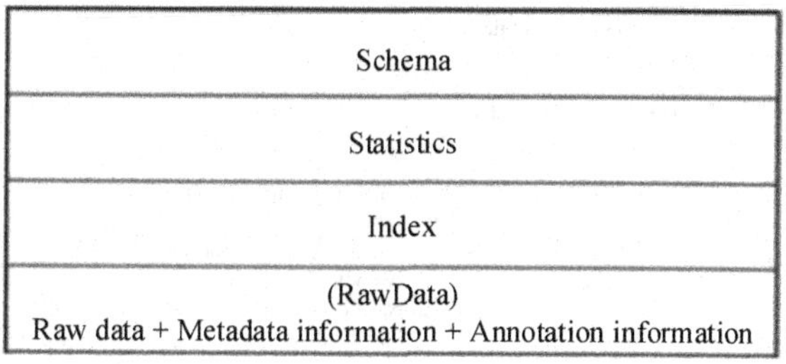

Fig. 14.7 Structure of the MindSpore data format

Schema
Statistics
Index
(RawData) Raw data + Metadata information + Annotation information

(2)   Tools for converting other framework formats (TFRecord, LMDB, and REC) to the MindSpore data format are provided. Figure 14.6 shows the conversion to the MindSpore data format.

2.   Structure of the MindSpore data format

The MindSpore data format consists of four parts that form one or more files on physical storage: Schema, Statistics, Index, and RawData. The structure of this format is shown in Fig. 14.7.

(1)   Schema: Annotation information differs between platforms because they use different tools that employ different annotation formats. Although we could save the annotation information in binary mode, doing so would prevent us from extracting annotation information efficiently because its meaning would be obscured. We therefore need to define metadata (i.e., schema) to describe the format of the annotation information, enabling us to obtain such information more easily. For example, the schema may define multiple pieces of metadata for a raw image, including its length, width, size, and type, each of which needs to be stored in separate field. Code 14.10 shows an example of a schema.

Code 14.10 Schema example

```
//Create a schema.
json schema = {"name": {"type": "string"}, "data": {"type":
"bytes"}, "width": {"type": "int32"}, "height": {"type":
"int32"}, "size": {"type": "int32"}, "label": {"type":
"int64"}};
```

(2)   Statistics describes the distribution and status of data in the MindSpore data format, enabling us to understand the data and determine whether it meets our requirements. Figure 14.8 provides an example of the statistics supported in the MindSpore data format, including the total number of samples, number of samples annotated in the past seven days (daily), month (weekly), and half year (monthly), and hierarchical statistics categorized by entity, attribute, and subattribute.

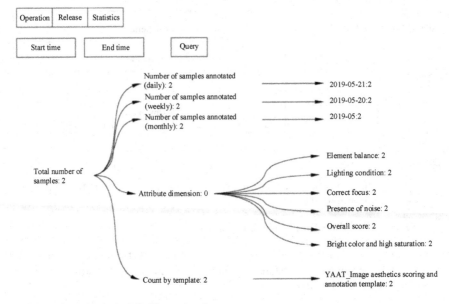

Fig. 14.8 Statistics in the MindSpore data format

Operation	Release	Statistics	Retrieval

Filter criteria

Serial number	Filter parameter	Comparison	Parameter value	Connector
1	Entity name	Equal	Portrait	And
2	Sample name	Not equal	image_00024	And

Result		Query

Serial number	Sample name	Operation
1	Image_0008.jpg	View
2	Image_00012.jpg	View
3	Image_00021.jpg	View

Fig. 14.9 Information retrieval

Fig. 14.10 Image data and
annotation information

{

    "name": "001.jpg",
    "data": "0xFF0xFF0xFF0xFF0xFF0xFF...",
    "width": 1,
    "height": 2,
    "size": 100,
    "label": 76

}

(3) Index provides index fields that enable us to easily retrieve data (or a subset of data) for subsequent processing. Figure 14.9 provides an example showing a list of samples that are related to "portrait" and whose names are not "Image_00024".

(4) RawData combines raw data, metadata information, and annotation information, and must correspond to schema definitions. Figure 14.10 provides an example of image data and annotation information.

14.3.5 MindSpore Dataset

To enhance data reading in the MindSpore computing framework, MindSpore datasets (such as MindDataset, TFRecordDataset, and GeneratorDataset) utilize a new data engine that constructs a pipeline operation for MindSpore input data. This data engine can be customized to satisfy specific requirements in order to provide high-performance data read service.

1. Basic concepts

The following describes some of the key concepts involved in the data engine for data storage.

(1) Data buffer: data storage unit. After data is read from a file, it is stored in a pre-created data buffer. Because the data engine supports different storage formats, it contains different types of data buffers—typically TFBuffer (TFRecord Buffer) is used.

(2) Data batch: batch size during data output. Data batches are built by data buffers.

(3) Data view: description of specific data, including metadata information. It is used to read real data.

(4) Sliding window: stride from one data buffer to the next.

The relationship between these conceptual items is shown in Fig. 14.11.

In terms of data read, one of the key concepts is as follows:

StorageClient: a module that interacts with a data storage layer. Similar to a data buffer, different types of storage clients (such as TFClient, i.e., TFRecord Client) can be created based on different storage formats.

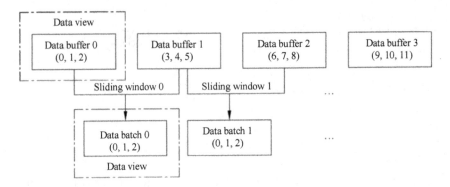

Fig. 14.11 Data storage mode of the data engine

2. **Logical architecture**

The data engine includes the following modules:

(1) **Parallel access module**

This module performs multi-threaded reads in the dataset catalog and concurrently parses data.

(2) **Cache module**

This module improves data read performance during training by caching the training data. The two-layer architecture of the cache module is shown in Fig. 14.12.

Given that the available memory resources are limited, data cached to memory is automatically migrated to the disk cache after a defined threshold is reached according to certain policies. Policies also define when the data cached to disk will be returned to the memory cache.

(3) **Shuffle module**

This module disorders the training data and includes two types of shuffling: shuffling between data buffers and shuffling inside a data buffer.

(4) **Iterator module**

This module constructs data batches, provides external APIs, and implements other functions.

Figure 14.13 shows an overview of the data engine's logical architecture.

Fig. 14.12 Cache module of the data engine

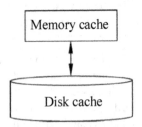

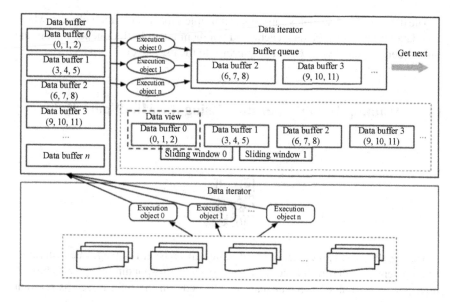

Fig. 14.13 Logical architecture of the data engine

Fig. 14.4 Recommended data operation sequence

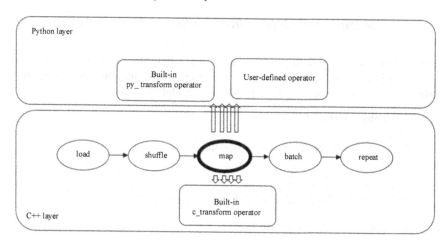

Fig. 14.15 Operation and data pipeline

The data iterator distributes subtasks to multiple subtask execution objects, which read data buffers from the data cache and put them into a buffer queue. Data in the buffer queue is read by the GetNext interface to the user layer.

14.4   Training Data Preparation Using the MindSpore Data Format

The interfaces and processes of MindSpore may constantly change due to iterative development. For all runnable code, see the code in corresponding chapters at https://mindspore.cn/resource. You can scan the QR code on the right to access relevant resources.

This section focuses on how we can generate, read, and retrieve data in the MindSpore data format and provides numerous code examples to facilitate the descriptions.

14.4.1   Generation of Data in the MindSpore Data Format

The Python APIs enable us to easily implement multiple operations, including: creating a schema, creating statistics, creating index information, and writing raw data (picture, annotation, etc.) into the MindSpore data format.

(1)   **Creating a write object**

(1)   Purpose

To create a MindSpore format write object.

(2)   API

```
class FileWriter:
    def __init__(self, file_name, shard_num):
```

(3)   Parameter description (Table 14.2).

(4)   Return value

None.

Table 14.2 Description of parameters for creating a schema

Parameter	Mandatory	Description
file_name	Yes	Path of the file in the MindSpore data format
shard_num	Yes	Number of generated shards

Example

```
FILES_NUM = 4
CV_FILE_NAME = "./imagenet.mindrecord"
writer = FileWriter(CV_FILE_NAME, FILES_NUM)
```

(2) **Adding a schema**

(1) Purpose
   To define a schema.
(2) API
```
def add_schema(self, content, desc=None):
```
(3) Parameter description (Table 14.3).

(4) Return value

   Schema id.

Example

```
cv_schema_json = {"file_name": {"type": "string"}, "label":
{"type": "int32"}, "data": {"type": "bytes"}}
writer.add_schema(cv_schema_json, "img_schema")
```

(3) **Adding an index field**

(1) Purpose
   To add a custom index field.
(2) API
```
def add_index(self, index_fields):
```
(3) Parameter description (Table 14.4).

Table 14.3 Description of parameters for defining a schema

Parameter	Mandatory	Description
content	Yes	Schema defined in the Dict format
desc	No	String, indicating the name of the schema/dataset

Table 14.4 Description of parameters for adding an index field

Parameter	Mandatory	Description
index_fields	Yes	Index field list

(4)   Return value

SUCCESS/FAILED.

Example

```
writer.add_index(["file_name", "label"])
```

(4) **Writing user data**

(1) Purpose
     To write user data to a disk.
(2) API
```
def write_raw_data(self, raw_data, parallel_writer=False):
```
(3) Parameter description (Table 14.5).
(4) Return value

SUCCESS/FAILED.

Example

```
writer.write_raw_data(data)
```

(5) **Closing a local file**

(1) Purpose
     To close a local file.
(2) API
```
def commit(self):
```
(3) Parameter description
     SUCCESS/FAILED.
(4) Return value

Table 14.5 Description of parameters for writing user data

Parameter	Mandatory	Description
raw_data	Yes	User data list, where each element is in the Dict format
parallel_writer	No	Boolean, indicating whether to parallelize data writes

None.

Example

```
writer.commit()
```

Code 14.11 provides a complete example of the code used to generate data in the MindSpore data format.

Code 14.11 Example of Generating Data in the MindSpore Data Format

```
from mindspore.mindrecord import FileWriter, FileReader

FILES_NUM = 1
CV_FILE_NAME = "./imagenet.mindrecord"

"""tutorial for cv dataset writer."""
writer = FileWriter(CV_FILE_NAME, FILES_NUM)

cv_schema_json = {"file_name": {"type": "string"}, "label":
{"type": "int32"}, "data": {"type": "bytes"}}
writer.add_schema(cv_schema_json, "img_schema")
writer.add_index(["file_name", "label"])
data_list = []
data_list.append({"file_name": "001.jpg", "label": 76, "data":
b'xxxxxxx'})
writer.write_raw_data(data_list)
writer.commit()
```

14.4.2 Statistics and Retrieval of Data in the MindSpore Data Format

The MindSpore data format supports data retrieval and statistics based on the index fields we define.

(1) **Enabling the indexing operation**

(1) Purpose
     To enable the indexing of data in the MindSpore data format.
(2) API
```
class MindPage:
    def __init__(self, file_name, num_consumer=4):
```
(3) Parameter description (Table 14.6).

Table 14.6 Description of parameters for enabling the indexing operation

Parameter	Mandatory	Description
file_name	Yes	Path of a local file in the MindSpore data format
num_consumer	No	The number of concurrent read threads (4 by default)

(4)   Return value

None.

Example

```
reader = MindPage(NLP_FILE_NAME + "01")
```

(2)   **Getting an index field**

(1)   Purpose
      To get an index field list.
(2)   API
```
def get_category_fields(self):
```
(3)   Parameter description
      None.
(4)   Return value

fields_list.

Example

```
fields = reader.get_category_fields()
```

(3)   **Setting an index field**

(1)   Purpose
      To set a to-be-retrieved field.
(2)   API
```
def set_category_field(self, category_field):
```
(3)   Parameter description (Table 14.7).

(4)   Return value

Table 14.7 Description of parameters for setting a to-be-retrieved field

Parameter	Mandatory	Description
set_category_field	Yes	Name of the to-be-retrieved field

True/False.

Example

```
ret = reader.set_category_field("rating")
```

(4) **Reading statistics of the current index field**

(1) Purpose

To read the statistics of the current index field.

(2) API

```
def read_category_info(self):
```

(3) Parameter description

None.

(4) Return value

fields_info (String mode, which can be converted to Dict).

Example

```
info = reader.read_category_info()
print("category info: ", info)
```

(5) **Getting data based on statistical ID and schema fields**

(1) Purpose

To get data based on statistical ID and schema fields.

(2) API

```
def read_at_page_by_id(self, category_id, page, num_row):
```

(3) Parameter description (Table 14.8).

(4) Return value

list.

Example

```
data = reader.read_at_page_by_id(0, 0, 1)
```

Table 14.8 Description of parameters for getting data based on statistical ID and schema fields

Parameter	Mandatory	Description
category_id	Yes	The field ID is obtained based on the statistical results
page	Yes	Specifies a page ID
num_row	Yes	Size per page

(6)   **Closing an index file**

(1)   Purpose
      To close an index file.
(2)   API

```
def close(self):
```

(3)   Parameter description
      None.
(4)   Return value

True/False.

Example

```
flag = reader.close ()
```

Code 14.12 provides a complete example of the code used to obtain statistics and retrieve data in the MindSpore data format.

Code 14.12 Example of Obtaining Statistics and Retrieving Data in the MindSpore Data Format

```
from mindspore.mindrecord import MindPage, SUCCESS

CV_FILE_NAME = "./imagenet.mindrecord"

reader = MindPage(CV_FILE_NAME)
fields = reader.get_category_fields()
print("fields: ", fields)

ret = reader.set_category_field("label")
assert ret == SUCCESS, 'failed on setting category field.'

info = reader.read_category_info()
print("category info: ", info)

data = reader.read_at_page_by_id(0, 0, 1)
print(data)
```

14.4.3 Reading MindSpore Training Data

MindSpore provides data loading methods such as MindDataset, TFRecordDataset, ImageFolderDatasetV2, and GeneratorDataset; operations such as repeat, shuffle, and map; and image processing operations such as decode, resize, and rescale.

1. **MindDataset**

(1) Purpose
   To create a dataset based on a directory in the MindSpore data format.
(2) API

```
class MindDataset (Dataset)
```

2. **TFRecordDataset**

(1) Purpose
   To create a dataset based on the dataset directory of a TFRecord file.
(2) API

```
class TFRecordDataset (Dataset)
```

3. **ImageFolderDatasetV2**

(1) Purpose
   To create a dataset based on the dataset directory of a raw image.
(2) API

```
class ImageFolderDatasetV2 (Dataset)
```

4. **GeneratorDataset**

(1) Purpose
   To create custom datasets. We can define a Python dataset parsing function and then create a variety of datasets using the following API.
(2) API

```
class GeneratorDataset (Dataset)
```

5. ***Dataset function description**

   A wide selection of data processing operations is available to us after we load the training data to the dataset. Such operations include shuffle, map, batch, and repeat. Although we can use each one separately, we typically combine them depending on our particular requirements, performing them in the following recommended sequence:

(1) *** repeat**

(1) Purpose
   To copy a dataset.
(2) API

```
def repeat(self, count=None):
```

Example

```
ds = ds.repeat(repeat_count)
```

(2)   **batch**

(1)   Purpose
      To set the batch size of output data.
(2)   API

```
def batch(self, batch_size, drop_remainder=False,
num_parallel_workers=None, per_batch_map=None,
      input_columns=None, pad_info=None):
```

Example

```
ds = ds.batch(2)
```

Before using the API, it is good practice to either preprocess the data or process it using per_batch_map, especially when the image data is read. Alternatively, we can rely on the dataset itself to ensure that the data has the same shape size. This is necessary because an error will be generated if the batch of data does not have the same shape size.

(3)   **shuffle**

(1)   Purpose
      To set data shuffling.
(2)   API

```
def shuffle(self, buffer_size):
```

Example

```
ds = ds.shuffle(10)
```

(4)   **Map**

(1)   Purpose
      To perform the operation described in sub section 5 in Sect. 14.4.3.
(2)   API

```
def map(self, input_columns=None, operations=None,
output_columns=None, columns_order=None,
      num_parallel_workers=None, python_multiprocessing=False):
```

Example

```
resize = transforms.Resize()
#Use the map operation on the dataset
ds = ds.map(input_columns ="image", operation=resize)
```

(5) create_dict_iterator

(1) Purpose

To create an iterator, return a data object of the dictionary type, and obtain the data corresponding to a keyword.

(2) API

```
def create_dict_iterator(self):
```

Example

```
ds1 = de.TFRecordDataset(DATA_DIR, SCHEMA_DIR)
ds1 = ds1.batch(batch_size, drop_remainder=True)
ds1 = ds1.shuffle(buffer_size=buffer_size)

num_iter = 0
for data in ds1.create_dict_iterator():
#Each data entry is a batch.
print(data["image"])
```

6. Operation notes

The mindspore.dataset.transforms module in MindSpore provides a variety of data conversion operations and covers usage scenarios in multiple fields. For example, "vision" provides data augmentation operations commonly used in the field of computer vision and includes two submodules: c_transforms, implemented based on C++ , and py_transforms, implemented based on Python. Furthermore, we can also customize data processing operators in Python. As shown in the figure below, both the built-in operator and the user-defined data transformation operator need to be executed by using the map function of the dataset.

Some of the most common operations are as follows:

(1) Decode

(1) Purpose

To decode an image.

(2) API

```
Decode(rgb=True)
```

Example

```
decode_op = transforms.Decode()
```

(2)   **Resize**

(1)   Purpose
      To resize an image.
(2)   API
```
Resize(size, interpolation=Inter.BILINEAR)
```

Example

```
resize_op = transforms.Resize((resize_height, resize_width))
```

(3)   **Rescale**

(1)   Purpose
      To rescale the pixel value of an image.
(2)   API
```
Rescale(rescale, shift)
```

Example

```
rescale_op = transforms.Rescale(rescale, shift)
```

(4)   **CenterCrop**

(1)   Purpose
      To perform central cropping on an image.
(2)   API
```
CenterCrop(size)
```

Example

```
center_crop_op = transforms.CenterCrop(resize)
```

(5)   **RandomCrop**

(1) Purpose

To perform random cropping on an image.

(2) API

```
RandomCrop(size, padding=None, pad_if_needed=False,
fill_value=0, padding_mode=Border.CONSTANT)
```

Example

```
random_crop_op = transforms.RandomCrop((crop_height,
crop_width))
```

(6) **RandomHorizontalFlip**

(1) Purpose

To perform horizontal flipping on an image (random).

(2) API

```
RandomHorizontalFlip(prob=0.5)
```

Example

```
random_horizontal_flip_op =
transforms.RandomHorizontalFlip(0.3)
```

(7) **RandomVerticalFlip**

(1) Purpose

To perform vertical flipping on an image (random).

(2) API

```
RandomVerticalFlip(prob=0.5)
```

Example

```
random_vertical_flip_op = transforms.RandomVerticalFlip(0.5)
```

(8) **HWC2CHW**

(1) Purpose

To replace a channel of an image.

(2) API

```
HWC2CHW()
```

Example

```
hwc2chw_op = transforms.HWC2CHW()
ds = ds.map(input_columns="image", operation=hwc2chw _op)
```

(9)   **One-Hot**

(1)   Purpose
      To generate a label list and convert data to a one-hot representation.
(2)   API

```
OneHot(num_classes)
```

Example

```
one_hot_encode = transforms.OneHot(num_classes)
ds = ds.map(input_columns="label", operation=one_hot_encode)
```

MindSpore: An All-Scenario Deep Learning Computing Framework

Abstract

MindSpore is a new deep learning computing framework designed to accomplish three goals: easy development, efficient execution, and adaptability to all scenarios. To ease development, MindSpore implements automatic differentiation (AD) using source code transformation (SCT) to express complex compositions with a control flow. The SCT-based AD mechanism transforms functions into intermediate representations (IRs) that construct a computational graph, which can then be parsed and executed on different devices. To improve performance and efficiency in device, edge, and cloud scenarios, a number of software and hardware co-optimization techniques are applied on the computational graph before execution. MindSpore supports dynamic graphs, making it easier to inspect running modes. In addition, mode switching between dynamic and static graphs is extremely simple thanks to the SCT-based AD mechanism. To efficiently train large models on large datasets, MindSpore flexibly supports data parallelism, model parallelism, and hybrid parallelism training by using a high-level manually configured strategy. Furthermore, MindSpore provides the auto-parallel capability, which searches in a comprehensive strategy space to find a fast parallelism strategy (in terms of training time).

In this paper, we describe the MindSpore architecture and several major features that set MindSpore apart from other state-of-the-art training frameworks. We also demonstrate the compelling performance that MindSpore achieves on Huawei Ascend series chips.

© Tsinghua University Press 2021
L. Chen, *Deep Learning and Practice with MindSpore*, Cognitive Intelligence
and Robotics, https://doi.org/10.1007/978-981-16-2233-5

Introduction

Over the past few decades, deep learning research and applications have mushroomed, achieving major success in fields such as image recognition [1], speech recognition and speech synthesis [2], gaming [3], and language modeling and analysis [4]. The increasing development of deep learning frameworks [5–9] facilitates using large amounts of computational resources for training neural network models on large datasets.

At present, there are two types of mainstream deep learning frameworks. One constructs a static graph that defines all operations and network structures before execution and is represented by TensorFlow [5]. This framework offers higher performance during training but does so at the cost of ease of use. The other framework performs immediate execution of dynamic graph computations and is represented by PyTorch [6]. By comparison, dynamic graphs offer greater flexibility and easier debugging but do so at the cost of lower performance. Although the frameworks offer certain advantages, neither of them simultaneously offers easy development and efficient execution.

In this paper, we introduce MindSpore—a new deep learning framework developed to accomplish three goals: easy development, efficient execution, and adaptability to all scenarios. MindSpore consists of several major components, namely MindExpression, MindCompiler, MindRE, MindData, and MindArmour. Table A.1 summarizes the technical contributions that each component makes in helping MindSpore accomplish its intended goals.

1. MindExpression provides a Pythonic programming paradigm for end users, while MindCompiler provides just-in-time (JIT) compilation optimization capabilities based on intermediate expressions. These components have following distinct features:

   - AD: The SCT-based AD mechanism is used, which transforms a piece of Python code into dataflow graph during the training or inference stage. This makes it easy for users to construct complex neural network models by using native control logics in Python.
   - Auto-parallel: Parallelizing DNN training across distributed devices is common practice today due to models and datasets becoming bigger and bigger. However, current frameworks (such as TensorFlow [5], Caffe [10], and MXNet [7]) employ a simple and often suboptimal strategy to parallelize training. In contrast, MindSpore parallelizes training tasks in a transparent and efficient manner. Specifically, in terms of transparency, users can submit one version of Python code to train on multiple devices, with only one line of configuration change. And in terms of efficiency, the parallelizing strategy is selected with the minimum cost, which reduces both computation and communication overheads.

Table A.1 Contributions of different components to goals

Goal	Component								
	MindExpression and MindCompiler				MindRE	MindData			
	SCT-based AD	Dynamic graph	Auto-Parallel	Graph manager	Runtime system	Training dashboard	Profiler	Auto-augment	Auto data acceleration
Easy development	□	□	□	◑	◑	□	◑	□	◑
Efficient execution	□	◑	□	□	◑	◑	□	◑	□
Adaptability to all scenarios	◑	◑	◑	□	□	◑	◑	◑	◑

□ means major contributions; ◑ means minor contributions

- Dynamic graph: MindSpore supports dynamic graphs without introducing additional AD mechanisms (such as the operator overloading AD mechanism). This results in significantly greater compatibility between dynamic and static graphs.

2. MindData is responsible for data processing and providing tools to help developers debug and optimize their models. For data processing, MindData has high-performance pipelines through automatic data acceleration and offers various types of auto-augment policies, eliminating the need for users to find the correct data augmentation strategy. By integrating multiple types of data on one page, the training dashboard makes it easy for users to view the training process. In addition, the profiler makes execution more transparent in that it collects statistics on execution time and memory usage, enabling focused performance optimization.

3. MindArmour is responsible for providing tools to help developers defend against attacks and ensure privacy protection in machine learning. MindArmour can generate adversarial examples, evaluate model performance in specific adversarial settings, and develop models that are more robust. It also supports a wide array of privacy-preserving capabilities, such as differential privacy [11], confidential AI computing [12], and trustworthy collaborative learning [13, 14].

4. MindRE is responsible for AI network execution. To implement this, MindRE extracts and adapts to the operation interfaces in different underlying hardware and supports runtime systems in various device and cloud hardware environments.

The rest of this paper is arranged as follows: Chap. 2 provides an overview of MindSpore, describing its architecture and programming paradigm. Chapter 3 presents the core components of MindSpore—MindExpression and MindCompiler—by illustrating the design details of AD, auto-parallel, and dynamic graphs. In Chaps. 4 and 5, we describe MindData and MindArmour, respectively. Chapter 6 discusses the device–cloud collaborative architecture that MindSpore supports. Chapter 7 uses ResNet-50 as benchmark to evaluate the auto-parallel feature and the performance of training and inference on MindSpore. Finally, we conclude our work and highlight some future research directions in Chap. 8.

MindSpore Overview

MindSpore Architecture

Figure A.1 shows the architecture of MindSpore.

MindExpression provides Python interfaces for defining the user-level application programming interfaces (APIs) that are used to build and train neural networks. Because MindSpore uses the SCT-based AD mechanism, users can program in a

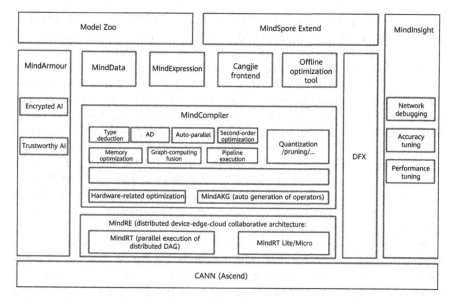

Fig. A.1 MindSpore architecture

Pythonic way. This means that users can build complex models with control flow using typical Python statements such as **if**, **else**, and **while**.

MindCompiler is the core of high-performance execution and AD, which is built on the SCT-based mechanism. If PyNative mode is selected, operators are delivered for execution one by one. If a network model is run in graph mode, MindCompiler uses a "pipeline" to generate a computational graph from the Python code. Specifically, MindCompiler parses the Python code to generate an abstract syntax tree (AST), which is then transformed into A-normal form (ANF) graph [15]. Because the ANF is graphical rather than syntactic, it is much easier to manipulate algorithmically [16]. The pipeline can automatically generate backward computation nodes and add them to the ANF graph if the neural network needs to be trained and applies a number of optimizations (such as memory reuse, operator fusion, and constant elimination) after constructing the complete graph. If a user wants to train the model in distributed environments, the pipeline applies the optimization provided by auto-parallel (see Sect. 3.2). Virtual machines (VMs) in the backend manage the computational graphs by using sessions and call the backend to run the graph and control the lifecycle of graphs.

In terms of data processing, MindData completes data pipelines (including data loading, argumentation, and transfer) during training. It also provides easy-to-use APIs and supports an extensive array of data processing capabilities, covering all scenarios such as computer vision (CV), natural language processing (NLP), and graph neural networks (GNNs). In this process, improving the data processing capabilities to match the computing power of AI chips is key to ensuring the ultimate performance of AI chips. MindInsight, which is within MindData, has four modules: training dashboard, lineage, profiler, and debugger. The profiler makes execution more transparent in that it collects statistics on execution time and memory usage. The debugger is a debugging tool that allows users to view the internal structures of graphs and inputs/outputs of nodes in graph execution mode during training. MindInsight analyzes the summary files generated during the training process and enables developers to easily visualize the training process and compare different trails on the graphical user interface (GUI).

MindArmour helps users develop models that are more robust and protect user privacy in training/inference data. MindArmour's adversarial attack defense has three main modules: attack, defense, and evaluation. The attack module generates adversarial examples in both black-box and white-box attack scenarios. The defense module uses the adversarial examples it receives from the attack module to improve the robustness of models during training. The evaluation module provides multiple evaluation metrics, enabling developers to easily evaluate and visualize the robustness of their models. To achieve privacy-preserving machine learning, MindArmour implements a series of differential privacy-aware optimizers that automatically add noise to the generated gradients during training.

Programming Paradigm

MindSpore provides a Pythonic programming paradigm for users and supports the use of native Python control grammar and advanced APIs such as *tuple*, *list*, and *lambda* thanks to SCT-based AD. In order to maintain simplicity, MindSpore introduces as few interfaces and concepts as possible. For example, users who want to train a simple neural network on a single-node platform need to know only the following five components:

- **Tensor**: A *tensor* is a multi-dimensional matrix that contains elements of a single data type. Different from other training frameworks, MindSpore does not have a *scalar variable* concept. To compute a tensor's gradient, the **requires_grad** attribute of that tensor should be set to **True**. NumPy can then be used to initialize the tensor or transform the value of the tensor into a NumPy object.

- **Dataset**: A *dataset* is a separate asynchronous pipeline that prepares tensors to feed into the rest of the network with no delay in training.
- **Operator**: An *operator* is a basic computation unit of a neural network. In addition to supporting most of the commonly used neural network operators (such as convolution, batch-norm, and activation) and math operators (such as add and multiply), MindSpore also supports custom operators. It allows users to add new operators for specific hardware platforms or combine multiple existing operators into new ones.
- **Cell**: A *cell* is a collection of tensors and operators. It is the base class for all neural network cells. A cell can contain other cells, which are nested in a tree structure. Users express the computation logics of the neural network by defining a *construct* function in a cell. This function then performs the defined computations each time it is called.
- **Model**: A *model* is a high-level API in MindSpore. It encapsulates some low-level APIs to make the inference and training as simple as possible for users. This component can be omitted if users are familiar with the low-level APIs and want to implement fine-grained control on the computation process.

From the user's perspective, writing a program using MindSpore revolves around building a *cell* that corresponds to a neural network. The first step of this process is to input tensors, which should be either constant or parametric. Different operators are then used to further build the cell. The last step involves encapsulating the cell into a model to train the neural network; alternatively, the input data can be passed directly to the cell for inference. In Code 1, we provide an example of a MindSpore program written in Python. This example shows the process of defining a LeNet [17] neural network and training it. The first six lines in the Code import the necessary libraries of MindSpore. Lines 7–25 define the LeNet-5 cell corresponding to the LeNet neural network. The _init_ function instantiates all the operators required by LeNet, and the *construct* function defines LeNet's computation logic. Lines 26 and 27 read data from MNIST datasets and generate an iterator *ds*, which is used as the training input. Line 28 instantiates the LeNet-5 class as a network. The *SoftmaxCrossEntropyWith-Logits* function is used to compute loss (line 29), and *momentum* is used to optimize parameters (lines 30 and 31). *Loss* and *optimizer* are used to create a model. Finally, we call the *train* function of the model by using *epoch* to control the number of epochs and evaluate the model.

Code 1 A MindSpore Implementation of LeNet-5.

```
1   import mindspore.nn as nn
2   from mindspore.ops import operations as P
3   from mindspore.network.optim import Momentum
4   from mindspore.train import Model
5   from mindspore.nn.loss import SoftmaxCrossEntropyWithLogits
6   import mindspore.dataset as de
7   class LeNet5(nn.Cell):
8     def __init__(self):
9       super(LeNet5, self).__init__()
10      self.conv1 = nn.Conv2d(1, 6, 5, pad_mode='valid')
11      self.conv2 = nn.Conv2d(6, 16, 5, pad_mode='valid')
12      self.fc1 = nn.Dense(16 * 5 * 5, 120)
13      self.fc2 = nn.Dense(120, 84)
14      self.fc3 = nn.Dense(84, 10)
15      self.relu = nn.ReLU()
16      self.max_pool2d = nn.MaxPool2d(kernel_size=2)
17      self.flatten = P.Flatten()
18    def construct(self, x):
19      x = self.max_pool2d(self.relu(self.conv1(x)))
20      x = self.max_pool2d(self.relu(self.conv2(x)))
21      x = self.flatten(x)
22      x = self.relu(self.fc1(x))
23      x = self.relu(self.fc2(x))
24      x = self.fc3(x)
25      return x
26  ds = de.MnistDataset(dataset_dir="./MNIST_Data")
27  ds = ds.batch(batch_size=64)
28  network = LeNet5()
29  loss = SoftmaxCrossEntropyWithLogits()
30  optimizer = nn.Momentum(network.trainable_params(),
31  learning_rate=0.1, momentum=0.9)
32  model = Model(network, loss, optimizer)
33  model.train(epoch=10, train_dataset=ds)
```

MindExpression and MindCompiler

SCT-Based AD

Three AD techniques are currently used in mainstream deep learning frameworks:

- Conversion based on static computational graph: This technique converts the network into a static dataflow graph at compile time and then converts the chain rule into a dataflow graph in order to implement AD.

Fig. A.2 SCT-based AD

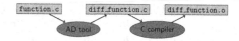

- Conversion based on dynamic computational graph: This technique records the operation trajectory of the network during forward execution with overloaded operators and then applies the chain rule to the dynamically generated dataflow graph in order to implement AD.
- Conversion based on source code: This technique is an evolution of the functional programming framework. It performs AD transformation on the intermediate expression (the expression form of the program during the compilation process) using JIT compilation, supporting complex control flow scenarios, higher-order functions, and closures. SCT-based AD is illustrated in Fig. A.2.

TensorFlow initially adopted static computational graphs, whereas PyTorch used dynamic computational graphs. Although static graphs can utilize static compilation technology to optimize network performance, building or debugging a network is a complicated task. Conversely, while dynamic graphs make operations more convenient, they make it difficult to achieve extreme performance optimization.

MindSpore employs a new mechanism: SCT-based AD. This mechanism supports AD of the control flow, making it easy to build models like PyTorch. In addition, MindSpore can perform static compilation optimization on neural networks to achieve high performance.

The implementation of AD in MindSpore can be understood as the symbolic differentiation of a program itself. Because MindSpore's IRs are functional intermediate expressions, they correspond intuitively with composite functions in basic algebra. The derivation formulas of the composite functions are composed of arbitrary basic functions. Each primitive operation in the IRs corresponds to a basic function in basic algebra, and such basic functions can be used to build flow control with greater complexity.

Auto-parallel

With the advancements of deep learning, training datasets and DNN models are growing larger to support higher accuracy and a wider range of application scenarios. In NLP, for example, the datasets range from 200 MB to 541 TB, while the number of parameters ranges from 340 million in BERT [18] and 800 million in Transformer-xl [19] to 1.5 billion in GTP-2 [19] and over 8 billion in the latest NVIDIA Megatron-LM [20]. In order to train large models on large datasets, deep learning frameworks must therefore support not only data parallelism and model parallelism, but also hybrid parallelism.

Most of today's mainstream frameworks (e.g., TensorFlow [5], Caffe [10], and MXNet [7]) require DNN models to be manually partitioned in order to implement model parallelism. However, manual partitioning is a complex task that relies on expert experience. Implementing hybrid parallelism (data and model parallelism at the same time) adds significant complexity. Recent research works [21–25] have proposed solutions to simplify hybrid parallelism, but they have several limitations. First, they fix the strategy of partitioning tensor dimensions in the entire model. This may result in a suboptimal partitioning strategy because different strategies might be better suited to different parts of the model. Second, [22, 24] cannot apply to many DNNs used for language modeling and person re-identification, as these DNNs tend to be nonlinear networks. Third [21] expresses the partitioning strategy search problem as a mixed integer program and uses an existing solver to find the solution. However, this approach is extremely slow when dealing with large models. Third [21, 24, 25] aim solely to optimize communication or memory cost; however, this approach might not reduce the training time.

MindSpore is designed to allow parallel transition during model training. To this end, tensor redistribution (TR) is introduced into parallel strategy search, enabling the layout of an output tensor among devices to be transformed before being fed into the subsequent operator. This is shown in the red rectangle in Fig. A.3. However, two main challenges exist when TR is considered for parallel strategy search in a complex and large model. First, because TR introduces communication operators (e.g., AllGather) into the dataflow graph, automatically differentiating them from normal operators is required. As such, it is necessary to obtain the backward operator for each corresponding forward operator and use it to update trainable parameters. Current frameworks require experts to manually add SEND and RECV primitives to transmit gradients in the backward phase—this is a challenging task for model developers, especially when the model is complex. Second, because TR significantly expands the strategy space, efficiently finding a suitable strategy for a complex and large model is challenging. In terms of functionality and efficiency, the algorithm should quickly find a strategy for the model that has a nonlinear structure. In terms of performance, the strategy returned by the algorithm should produce a short end-to-end training time. This requires special attention to be paid to running cost modeling, potentially involving a great deal of manual effort.

MindSpore introduces novel solutions to address the preceding two challenges. For the first challenge, MindSpore defines the corresponding backward operator (which is also a communication operator) or a combination of several operators to enable AD of communication operators. For instance, the backward operator of AllGather is ReduceScatter, and the backward operator of SEND is RECV followed by ADD. Defining these backward operators is helpful because doing so enables the Auto-diff procedure to differentiate the entire forward graph in one go without skipping any operator. This is why AD is the subsequent step of auto-parallel. For the second challenge, we build a cost model to select a suitable strategy, paying attention to both computation and communication overheads. We propose two techniques to quickly find such a strategy for complex and large graphs: an algorithm that supports multiple graph operations to transform the original graph into a linear one and a strategy sparsification mechanism that effectively shrinks the search space while guaranteeing good precision of the returned solution. For instance, the time required

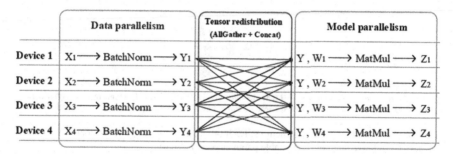

Fig. A.3 Data parallelism transformed into model parallelism

to search for strategies of ResNet-50 in parallel on eight devices is within 1 s, and the returned solution leads to a shorter training time. For a large model containing more than 128 K classes, the returned solution reduces the training time by about 55% compared with the raw data parallelization strategy.

Code 2 Parallelism transition in semi-auto-parallel configuration.

```
1   class Submodel(nn.Cell):
2   def _init_(self, shape):
3     self.bn = BatchNorm(set_strategy={[4, 1]})
4     self.matmul = MatMul(set_strategy={[1, 1], [1, 4]})
5     self.W = Parameter(Tensor(shape), require_grad=True)
6   def construct(self, X):
7     Y = self.bn(X)
8     Z = self.matmul(y, self.W)
9     return Z
```

MindSpore supports user-specified high-level strategy configuration—referred to as *semi-auto-parallel*—making it sufficiently flexible. In Code 2 and Fig. A.3, we provide an example of transforming data parallelism into model parallelism. This submodel, constructed using a BatchNorm operator followed by a MatMul operator, is widely used in classification tasks such as ResNet and ReID. In the BatchNorm operator, X is split into four parts by rows to implement efficient data parallelism. In the MatMul operator, the weight W (a learnable parameter) is split into four parts to implement model parallelism, which is more efficient due to the large number of parameters. Because the output layout of BatchNorm is different from the input layout of MatMul, MindSpore inserts a TR (AllGather and ConCat in this example), which is transparent from users. MindSpore also automatically schedules which device runs which slice of the model, eliminating the need for users to consider such scheduling. However, different model structures have different numbers of parameters in each operator, as shown in Fig. A.4, and they prefer different partitioning strategies. In Fig. A.4 (3), configuring the first operator as model parallelism and the subsequent operators as data parallelism offers better performance and leads to the insertion of a TR.

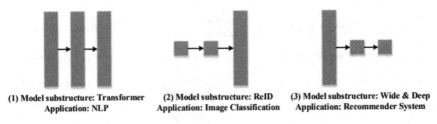

(1) Model substructure: Transformer **(2) Model substructure: ReID** **(3) Model substructure: Wide & Deep**
        Application: NLP   **Application: Image Classification**   **Application: Recommender System**

Fig. A.4 Three widely used substructures. Each box represents a layer (operator), whose height indicates the relative number of learnable parameters at that layer

When a new model is being trained, *set_strategy* is configured many times, leading to greater manual effort. In that case, if *auto-parallel* is configured, the proposed algorithm will find the efficient one, meaning that the *set_strategy* does not need to be specified. For instance, when the number of classifications is greater than 130 K in ResNet, the algorithm returns a strategy that enables one iteration of training to be completed within 50 ms. In contrast, the raw data parallelism enables one iteration of training to be completed in more than 111 ms. For detailed evaluations, see Sect. 8.1.

Dynamic Graph

In most cases, static graph offers better runtime performance because the compiler knows its global information. However, dynamic graph offers greater ease of use, enabling users to construct and modify models more easily. In order to support both static and dynamic graphs at the same time, most state-of-the-art training frameworks need to maintain two kinds of AD mechanisms: tape-based AD and graph-based AD. This requires developers to maintain both mechanisms, increasing the workload. Furthermore, from a user's perspective, switching between static and dynamic modes is complex.

MindSpore supports static and dynamic graphs based on a unified SCT-based AD mechanism, delivering both high efficiency and ease of use. In MindSpore, we call dynamic graph "Pynative mode" because the code is run with the Python interpreter in this mode. As shown in Code 3, only one line of code is needed to switch between static graph mode and Pynative mode. In addition, MindSpore supports a staging mechanism (shown in line 4) to accelerate the Pynative mode's runtime efficiency. Adding the *ms_function* decorator in front of a function (*fc_relu*) leads to the function being compiled and run in static graph mode.

Code 3 A MindSpore implementation of LeNet-5

```
1   from mindspore import context
2   import numpy as np
3   class LeNet5(nn.Cell):
4     @ms_function
5     def fc_relu(self, x):
6       x = self.relu(self.fc2(x))
7       x = self.fc3(x)
8     def construct(self, x):
9       x = self.max_pool2d(self.relu(self.conv1(x)))
10      x = self.max_pool2d(self.relu(self.conv2(x)))
11      x = self.flatten(x)
12      x = self.relu(self.fc1(x))
13      x = fc_relu(x)
14      return x
15    data=np.ones((batch_size,3,224,224),np.float32)*0.01
16    net = LeNet5()
17    # switch to Pynative mode
18    context.set_context(mode=context.PYNATIVE_MODE)
19    pynative_out = net(data)
20    # switch back to static graph mode
21    context.set_context(mode=context.GRAPH_MODE)
22    graph_out = net(data)
```

Figure A.5 shows the design of static graph and dynamic graph. In dynamic graph mode, the framework traverses all operators called for the model, generates a computational graph for each operator, and delivers the graphs to the backend for forward propagation. After the forward propagation is completed, the framework

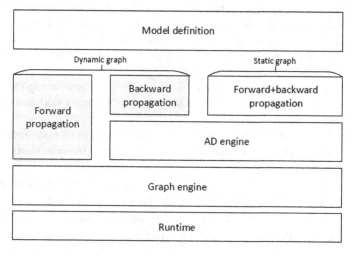

Fig. A.5 Design of static graph and dynamic graph

generates both forward and backward propagation graphs for the model and issues these graphs to the backend. Because MindSpore uses the SCT-based AD mechanism, all code written by users to inspect their models (e.g., *pdb* and *print*) can be omitted when generating backward propagation graphs.

Second-Order Optimization

Deep learning has shown excellent performance in many applications, including image recognition, object detection, and NLP. Driven by the rapid development of deep learning, optimizers—an important part of deep learning—have also attracted extensive research.

Common optimization algorithms are classified as first-order and second-order optimization algorithms. Among first-order optimization algorithms, classical gradient descent (GD) is the most widely used in machine learning. Common first-order optimization algorithms (such as SGD) update parameters according to $\theta = \theta - \eta \nabla_\theta$, where θ is the parameter to be updated, η is the learning rate, and ∇_θ is the gradient of the loss function compared to the parameter.

By introducing strategies like momentum and adaptive learning rate decay, GD brings many variants, such as Momentum, Nesterov, AdaGrad, RMSprop, Adadelta, and Adam. Because these improved optimization algorithms can adaptively update the step size by using historical information about stochastic gradients, they are easier to tune and use. And given that the loss function of neural networks is highly non-convex and surface curvature is unbalanced, engaging more information (such as the second-order matrix) in parameter update helps speed up convergence.

In this regard, second-order optimization algorithms leverage the second-order derivative of the objective function to correct curvature and accelerate first-order descent. Faster convergence enables these algorithms to better approximate to the optimal value and yield a geometric descent path that is more consistent with the optimal real-world descent path. Compared with first-order optimization algorithms, second-order optimization algorithms first multiply ∇_θ and a matrix G^{-1}, giving an update rule of $\theta = \theta - \eta G^{-1} \nabla_\theta$, where G is the second-order matrix. The definition of G is not consistent across different second-order optimization algorithms. For example, it is the Hessian matrix and Fisher matrix in Newton's method and natural gradient method, respectively.

The Hessian matrix is a block matrix consisting of all the second-order partial derivative of a multivariable real-valued function. The Hessian matrix can be expressed as $H_{ij} = \frac{\partial^2 f}{\partial \theta_i \partial \theta_j}$, where f is the loss function, and θ is the parameter to be updated. The Fisher matrix is a covariance matrix derived from the maximum likelihood function. The Fisher matrix can be expressed as $F = E_{(x,y) \sim p(x,y|\theta)}[\frac{\partial \log p(y|x,\theta)}{\partial \theta} \frac{\partial \log p(y|x,\theta)^T}{\partial \theta}]$, where θ is the parameter to be updated. The joint distribution of the model is $p(x, y|\theta) = p(y|x, \theta)q(x)$, where $q(x)$ is the sample distribution of x and is irrelevant to θ, and $\log p(y|x, \theta)$ is the loss function, which is a log-likelihood function.

Although second-order optimization algorithms feature faster convergence, computing the inverse of the second-order matrix involves a time complexity of (n^3). When the parametric meteorology of the model is n_θ, the size of the corresponding second-order matrix is $n_\theta \times n_\theta$. In deep learning models, n_θ often runs into the millions, making it extremely complex—if not impossible—to compute the inverse of the second-order matrix. Therein lies the crux of the matter: how to reduce the computational complexity of second-order matrix inversion.

To address this issue and improve second-order algorithms based on the natural gradient method, MindSpore provides a novel Trace-based Hardware-driven layer-ORiented Natural Gradient Descent Computation algorithm, called THOR. The following discusses the three major improvements.

Matrix Update Frequency

Experiments indicate that the Frobenius norm (or "F norm" for short) of the Fisher matrix changes acutely in the early stage and gradually becomes stable in the later stage. Therefore, it is assumed that $\{F^k\}_{k=1}^n$ is a Markov process and can converge to a steady-state distribution π, where F^k represents the Fisher matrix during the kth iteration. Gradually increasing the update interval of the Fisher matrix is sufficient to shorten the training time without compromising the convergence speed.

Update by Layer

Fisher matrices are decoupled layer by layer, and experiments are performed on each layer. The results of the experiments indicate that some layers of the Fisher matrices reach the steady state faster than others do. This inspired us to finely adjust the update frequency of each layer. Specifically, the Fisher matrix at a layer is updated only when the trace change of the second-order matrix is less than the threshold. Otherwise, the Fisher matrix during the previous iteration is directly used. The update formula is

$$\Delta^k = \frac{\left|\left|tr\left(F_i^k + \lambda I\right)\right| - \left|tr\left(F_i^{k-1} + \lambda I\right)\right|\right|}{\left|tr\left(F_i^k + \lambda I\right)\right|}$$

$$\begin{cases} \text{Update } F_i^k \text{ if } \Delta^k \in (w_1, +\infty) \\ \text{Do not update } F_i^k \text{ but use } F_i^{k-1} \text{ of the previous iteration if } \Delta^k \in [w_2, w_1] \\ \text{Stop updating } F_i^k \text{ and always use } F_i^{k-1} if \Delta^k \in [0, w_2] \end{cases}$$

Hardware-Aware Matrix Splitting

THOR assumes that Fisher matrices are decoupled layer by layer and that the input and output blocks at each network layer are independent of each other. Assuming that the input and output of each network layer are divided into n blocks (n is the balance point between matrix information loss and hardware performance), the n blocks are independent. Based on this assumption, THOR further splits second-order matrices to improve computational efficiency.

First, we determine the matrix splitting dimensions based on the highest-dimension layer. Taking the ResNet-50 as an example in Ascend 910, the range of matrix splitting dimensions is [1, 16, 32, 64, 128, 256, 512, 1024, 2048]. Then, we compute the matrix loss and performance data of each dimension to obtain the following figure. We can see that the intersection point is 106, which is closest to 128. As such, we determine that the matrix splitting dimension is 128 (Fig. A.6).

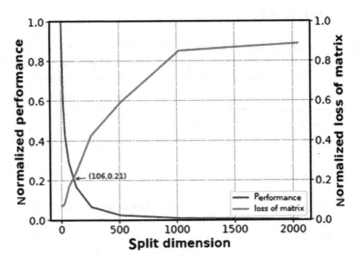

Fig. A.6 Obtaining the matrix splitting dimension

Code 4 Training networks with THOR in MindSpore

```
1   from mindspore.train.train_thor import ConvertModelUtils
2   from mindspore.nn.optim import THOR
3   elif cfg.optimizer == "Thor": #Create a THOR optimizer.
4       from src.utils import get_bert_thor_lr, get_bert_thor_damping
5       lr = get_bert_thor_lr()
6       damping = get_bert_thor_damping()
7       optimizer = THOR(network, lr, damping, cfg.Thor.momentum,
8                        cfg.Thor.weight_decay, cfg.Thor.loss_scale, cfg.batch_size,
9                        decay_filter=lambda x: 'layernorm' not in x.name.lower() and 'bias' not in x.name.lower())
10      context.set_context(max_call_depth=10000)

11  model = Model(net_with_grads)
12  model = ConvertModelUtils().convert_to_thor_model(model, network=net_with_grads, optimizer=optimizer,
    frequency=cfg.Thor.frequency) #Save the second-order information required by THOR.
13  model.train(new_repeat_count, ds, callbacks=callback,
14              dataset_sink_mode=(args_opt.enable_data_sink == "true"), sink_size=args_opt.data_sink_steps)
```

MindData

Data Processing

The data engine MindData is a separate asynchronous pipeline that prepares tensors to feed into the model. Data is organized as a series of rows with different columns. All columns are identified with a name and can be accessed independently. The pipeline always starts with a source dataset operator, which reads data from disks and includes flags to select shuffling and sharding strategies. In order to access the data in the pipeline, an iterator (Python access) or device queue (direct send to accelerator device) is used.

Data processing is intrinsically pipelined and parallelized. The pipelines run asynchronously by default, but they allow users to insert sync points into graphs to support real-time feedback loops for pipeline operators. Default parameters are configured in order to obtain good performance without required manual tuning. In the future, pipelines will be dynamically adjusted to fully utilize all available resources, including hardware accelerators for image processing or available memory for caching.

To enable quick migration for users, data processing supports existing Python user code. Existing Python dataset classes can be passed as an argument to GeneratorDataset, and samplers are supported natively in all random access source datasets. Furthermore, custom Python data transforms can be called from a dataset or map operator, and new workloads can be initially run on MindSpore with minimal porting effort.

Workloads are emerging with new requirements for datasets to support greater flexibility. Data processing supports parameter adjustment (such as batch size) using a user-defined function or schedule. It also supports user-defined custom transforms on an entire batch to support batch-level image size or multi-row operations such as image mix-up. To ensure that augmentations are more diverse, the augmentation of each sample can be randomly chosen from sets of transforms. Transforms candidates can be selected via external search (i.e., fast auto-augment); however, recent research on randomAugment and uniformAugment shows that selecting a wide variety of reasonable transforms will produce comparable results to those obtained without the additional search time for many datasets (i.e., all supported transforms minus those that create unrecognizable images most of the time). In addition, feedback from loss or other metrics collected during training can be passed back into the dataset to perform dynamic adjustments in data processing as demonstrated in adversarial auto-augment.

MindRecord

MindRecord is a dataset format, which stores the users' training data according to different types and pages, establishes a lightweight and efficient index. It also provides a set of interfaces to conveniently convert the training data into the MindRecord format and uses MindDataset to read this data into a dataset. Important metadata (e.g., dataset size or data layout) can quickly be read from the dataset to improve performance or simplify user access. In addition to supporting efficient sequential I/O of small blocks of data, MindRecord also supports efficient random row-access and push-down filtering as per use-case requirements. As new use cases emerge, further optimized functions will be pushed down into this dataset.

MindInsight

MindInsight has four modules: training dashboard, lineage, profiler, and debugger. These modules help developers identify deviations during model training, determine the impact of factors such as hyperparameters and data enhancement, and profile and debug the model. MindInsight enables developers to better observe and understand the training process, leading to greater model optimization efficiency and developer experience. Figure A.7 shows the MindInsight architecture.

MindInsight uses the summary file generated during model training as the input. After file parsing, information extraction, data caching, and chart drawing, MindInsight converts binary training information into charts that are easy to understand and displays them on web pages.

Fig. A.7 MindInsight
architecture

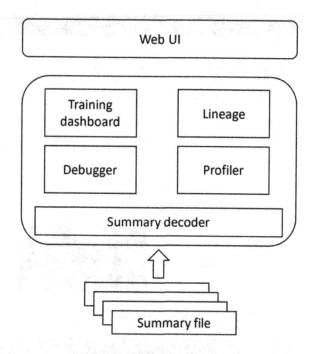

Fig. A.7 MindInsight architecture

Training Dashboard

MindInsight enables users to visualize the training process via training dashboard, which includes modules such as the training scalar information, parameter distribution graph, computational graph, data graph, and data sampling.

MindInsight's training dashboard implements an innovative way to present the training process. By integrating multiple types of data on one page, the training dashboard provides users with an overview of training all on one page. Figure A.8 shows an example of the training dashboard.

Lineage

MindInsight supports lineage visualization, which integrates the lineage information of multiple training runs into tables and charts, enabling users to easily select the optimal data processing pipeline and hyperparameter settings. Lineage visualization includes model and data lineage visualization. Model lineage records key parameter information about model training, such as the loss function, optimizer, number of epochs, and accuracy. Furthermore, MindInsight displays parameters that are trained multiple times, helping users select the optimal hyperparameter. In the future, MindInsight will support aided hyperparameter recommendation to help users optimize hyperparameters quickly. Figure A.9 shows an example of model lineage visualization.

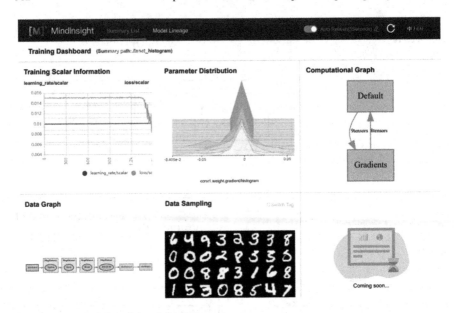

Fig. A.8 MindInsight training dashboard

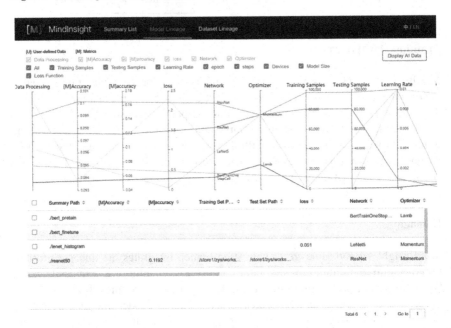

Fig. A.9 MindInsight model lineage

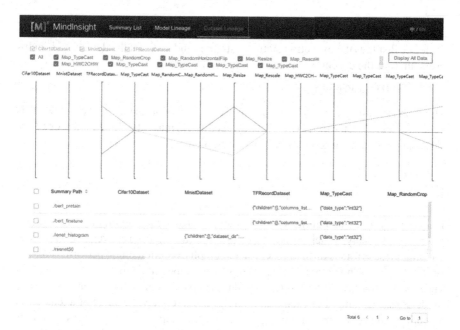

Fig. A.10 MindInsight data lineage

Data lineage visualization records the data processing pipeline used in each model training. MindInsight displays the data processing mode that is trained multiple times, helping users select the optimal data processing pipeline. Figure A.10 shows an example of data lineage visualization.

Profiler

In order to meet requirements for optimizing the neural network performance, we have designed and implemented the profiler, which makes execution more transparent in that it collects statistics such as time and memory usage of each operator. MindInsight then sorts and analyzes the profiling data and displays the results from multiple dimensions and layers, providing valuable information for optimizing neural network performance. The profiler provides the following features:

(1) **Step Trace**

This feature splits neural network execution into multiple stages, including data reading, forward and backward computation, and AllReduce. This facilitates identifying which stage is causing a performance bottleneck.

(2) **Operator Performance**

This feature aggregates and sorts statistics on operator execution time. This enables users to easily identify which operators are consuming the most time.

(3) Timeline

Timeline displays the execution status of streams and tasks on the device. This helps users analyze the execution in a more fine-grained manner.

(4) MindData Profiling

MindData Profiling helps to locate and analyze slowdowns in the input pipeline. This enables users to determine whether they need to increase the thread number of the slow data operators in order to improve performance.

Debugger

During training of neural networks, numerical errors such as infinity often occur. Users want to analyze such errors, which prevent training from converging. However, locating these errors is difficult because the graph execution mode performs computations in a black-box manner. The debugger is a debugging tool that allows users to view the internal structures of graphs and inputs/outputs of nodes in graph execution mode during training. For example, it allows users to view the value of a tensor, set a conditional breakpoint for a group of nodes, and map the node and tensor outputs in a static graph to Python code.

MindArmour

Adversarial Attack Defense

Adversarial attack [26, 27] has become an increasingly prevalent threat to the security of machine learning models. An attacker can compromise machine learning models by adding small perturbations that are not easily perceived by humans to the original sample [28, 29]. To defend against adversarial attacks, MindArmour has three main modules: attack (adversarial example generation), defense (adversarial example detection and adversarial training), and evaluation (model robustness evaluation and visualization).

Taking a model and data as input, the attack module provides easy-to-use APIs to generate corresponding adversarial examples in both black-box and white-box attack scenarios. These examples are then fed into the defense module to improve the generalization of the machine learning model during training. The defense module also implements multiple detection algorithms, which can distinguish between adversarial examples and benign ones based on either malicious content or attacking behaviors. The evaluation module provides multiple evaluation metrics, enabling developers to easily evaluate and visualize the robustness of their models.

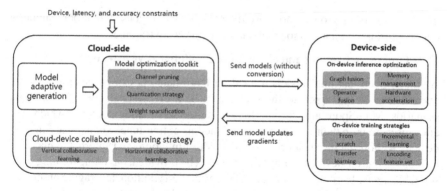

Fig. A.11 Device–cloud collaborative architecture of MindSpore

Privacy-Preserving AI

Privacy preserving is an important topic in AI applications. MindArmour considers several privacy-preserving aspects and provides corresponding features. In order to provide differential privacy guarantee to a trained model, which might leak sensitive information about the training dataset [30, 31], MindArmour implements a series of differential privacy optimizers that automatically add noise to the gradients generated during backpropagation. Specifically, the optimizers adaptively add noise according to the training process, achieving tighter differential privacy budget, faster training, and better utility. Users can use these differential privacy optimizers in the same way as they would use normal ones.

Device–Cloud Collaborative Architecture

MindSpore aims to build an AI framework that covers all scenarios from the device side to the cloud side. MindSpore supports "device–cloud" collaboration capabilities, which include model optimization, on-device inference and training, and device–cloud collaborative learning, as illustrated in Fig. A.11.

(1) Model generation and optimization toolkit

Mobile and edge devices often have limited resources, such as limited power and memory resources. To help users deploy models within these constraints, MindSpore supports a collection of optimization techniques (shown on the left side of Fig. A.11). Model adaptive generation based on neural architecture search (NAS) [32] supports latency estimation of different hardware and different searching strategies. Once the user specifies constraints related to the device, latency, and accuracy, a MindSpore model can be generated adaptively. Quantization strategies reduce the model size and inference latency by reducing the precision of the models. As such, it is necessary for the inference engine to support these reduced precision types. MindSpore supports both post-training quantization and quantization-aware training.

(2)   On-device training and cloud–device collaborative learning

Although deep learning models trained on large datasets can be generic to some extent, they do not apply to the user's own data or personalized tasks in some scenarios. MindSpore aims to provide the on-device training solution, which will allow users to train their own personalized models or fine-tune existing ones on their devices without facing data privacy, bandwidth limitation, and Internet connection issues. Various on-device training strategies will be provided, including training from scratch, transfer learning, and incremental learning. In addition, leveraging on-device training capabilities, MindSpore supports "cloud–device" collaborative learning to share different data by sending model updates/gradients to the cloud side, as shown in Fig. A.11. With collaborative learning strategies, models can learn a greater volume of general knowledge.

(3)   Deployment on mobile and edge devices

MindSpore provides a lightweight computation engine for executing models efficiently on devices. Typically, model conversion is necessary before pre-trained models can be deployed to the user side, potentially leading to unexplainable performance and accuracy loss. In MindSpore, the on-device inference schema is compatible with on-cloud training, eliminating the need for such conversion and avoiding the potential performance deterioration. Furthermore, MindSpore has a variety of built-in automatic optimizations for devices, such as graph/operator fusion, sophisticated memory management, and hardware acceleration, as shown on the right side of Fig. A.11.

MindSpore Serving

Introduction

MindSpore Serving is a lightweight high-performance inference module designed to help MindSpore users efficiently deploy their online inference services in production environments. After training a model on MindSpore, users can export the model and then create an inference service for it using MindSpore Serving.

Functions

MindSpore Serving provides the following functions:

- Loading model files to generate an inference engine and provide the inference function.
- Predicting the message exchanges between a request and its result. (The gRPC and RESTful requests are supported.)
- Predicting interface invocation and returning the prediction results.
- Managing the lifecycle of models.
- Managing the lifecycle of services.
- Managing multiple models and versions.

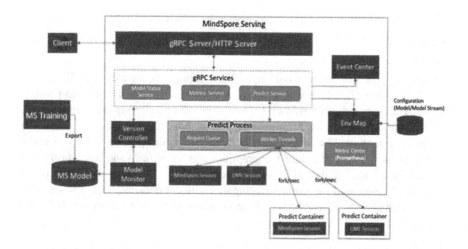

The following describes the functions of the key components in the MindSpore Serving architecture:

- gRPC Server: handles gRPC requests in synchronous or asynchronous mode.
- HTTP Server: handles HTTP requests in synchronous or asynchronous mode.
- gRPC Services: serves as the basic execution unit for services (such as prediction and model version query) provided by MindSpore Serving. The services' interfaces can be defined using gRPC.
- Predict Process: handles inference requests in the cache queue and worker thread pool. The number of worker threads is the same as the number of cards. Each worker thread corresponds to an inference session, which can be managed by Predict Container (isolated at the process level) or directly managed by MindSpore Serving (isolated at the thread level).
- Version Controller: loads MindSpore models and manages versions. Version policies are configurable.
- Model Monitor: detects MindSpore models through periodic polling.

Evaluation

In this section, we evaluate the performance of MindSpore on auto-parallel. We also run experiments on Huawei Ascend chip clusters and compare the performance with mainstream frameworks. The results obtained from the experiments show that our system has the following features: (i) high throughput and (ii) stable speedup as the clusters increase. Furthermore, we provide inference performance on several models and achieve higher performance than that of mainstream frameworks.

Auto-parallel

We conduct experiments on an Ascend cluster comprised of eight devices. We use the standard ResNet-50, which is trained under raw data parallelism and auto-parallel. Figure A.12 shows the comparison between raw data parallelism and auto-parallel, in which the number of classes ranges from 1 K to about 1024 K. When the number of classes is fewer than 32 K, we observe that the two modes produce nearly identical iteration times. This is because the proposed algorithm finds the data parallelism strategy. When the number of classes exceeds 64 K, the auto-parallel mode offers significantly increased performance compared with the data parallelism mode. This is because the strategy returned by the proposed algorithm in such cases is hybrid

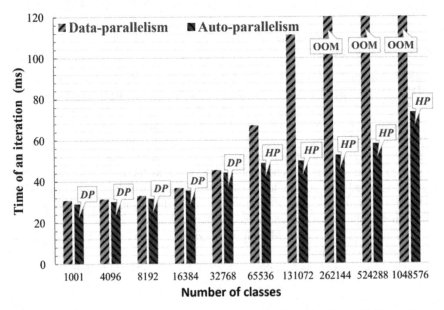

Fig. A.12 Performance comparison of training ResNet-50 using naive data parallelism and auto-parallel

Table A.2 Comparison of inference performance on Huawei Mate 30 smartphones using MindSpore and TensorFlow lite

Model	Threads	MindSpore (ms)	TensorFlow lite (ms)
Inception v4	1	657.921	787.012
	2	345.307	431.289
	4	231.397	312.81
MobileNet v1 1.0 224 frozen	1	33.028	37.471
	2	17.156	20.4
	4	11.761	13.871
MobileNet v1 1.0 224 quant frozen	1	17.216	56.246
	2	9.614	39.333
	4	6.508	31.902
NASNet-Mobile	1	59.885	70.212
	2	39.121	47.017
	4	32.559	33.539
SqueezeNet	1	40.308	53.488
	2	21.776	30.313
	4	16.049	21.298

in Table A.2. We execute the experiments on the CPU and compare the inference latency with TensorFlow. The results demonstrate that MindSpore has significantly lower inference time than TensorFlow does.

Conclusion and Future Work

In this paper, we introduce MindSpore—our new deep learning framework— and highlight its key components (MindExpression, MindCompiler, MindData, and MindArmour) and features (auto-parallel, AD, and device–cloud collaborative training). These components and features enable MindSpore to accomplish its three goals: easy deployment, efficient execution, and adaptability to all scenarios. Furthermore, MindSpore offers visualization and defense tools to make the training process visible and robust to various adversarial attacks. Huawei released the first version of MindSpore on March 28, 2020. Currently, MindSpore has been successfully paired with chip A series processors and applied in company H's products, ranging from smart phones to clouds. In the future, we hope to improve several aspects of the Mind-Spore system. For MindExpression, we want to consider topology-aware scheduling in order to meet different communication requirements in a multi-node cluster. For MindData, we will focus on providing tools that offer greater flexibility for AI engineers to process and argument different types of data. And for MindArmour, we will develop our defense against various adversarial attacks in the CV and NLP domains.

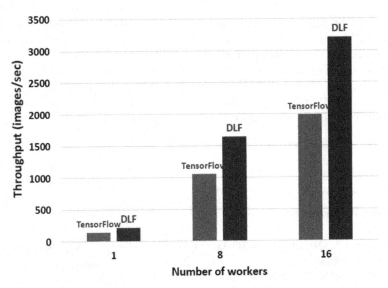

Fig. A.14 Comparison of training throughput on BERT-large using MindSpore and TensorFlow

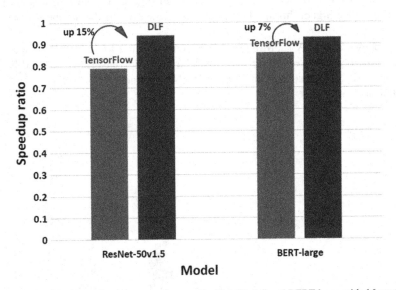

Fig. A.15 Comparison of training speedups on ResNet-50v1.5 and BERT-large with 16 workers using MindSpore and TensorFlow

Inference Performance

We also run experiments for mobile inference using different lightweight models on Huawei Mate 30 smartphones. The results of these experiments are provided parallelism. Specifically, operators in the head of the model are in data parallelism, while the MatMul operator is in model parallelism. This minimizes communication overheads because model parallelism avoids the huge AllReduce incurred by synchronizing learnable parameters in the MatMul operator. When the number of classes exceeds 256 K, the data parallelism mode fails to run because an "out of memory" (OOM) event occurs, whereas the auto-parallel mode achieves successful training of ResNet-50 with only a minor increase in the iteration time.

Benchmark

Training Performance

We focus on ResNet-50 and BERT-large models and configure MindSpore across a cluster of company H chip A. For these experiments, we compare the performance of training ResNet-50 and BERT-large on MindSpore and TensorFlow (TensorFlow uses NVIDIA DGX-2, integrating 16 NVIDIA V100 32G GPUs) and vary the number of workers using different clusters. As shown in Figs. A.13 and A.14, MindSpore achieves much higher throughput than TensorFlow even as the number of workers increases.

As shown in Fig. A.15, MindSpore with chip A can achieve over 93% speedups on training both ResNet-50v1.5 and BERT-large, while TensorFlow with GPUs can achieve only 79% speedups on training ResNet-50 and 86% speedups on training BERT-large.

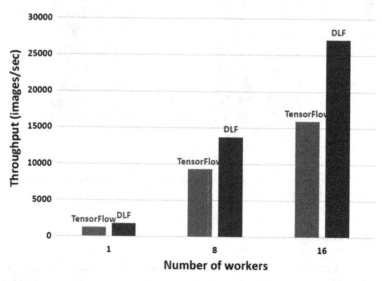

Fig. A.13 Comparison of training throughput on ResNet-50v1.5 using MindSpore and TensorFlow

References

1. A. Krizhevsky, I. Sutskever, G.E. Hinton, ImageNet classification with deep convolutional neural networks, in *Advances in Neural Information Processing Systems* (2012), pp. 1097–1105
2. G. Hinton, L. Deng, D. Yu, G. Dahl, A. Mohamed, N. Jaitly, A. Senior, V. Vanhoucke, P. Nguyen, B. Kingsbury et al., Deep neural networks for acoustic modeling in speech recognition. IEEE Sig. Proc. magaz. **29** (2012)
3. M. Volodymyr, K. Koray, S. David, A.R. Andrei, V. Joel, Human-level control through deep reinforcement learning. Nature, **518**(7540), 529–533 (2015)
4. Y. Bengio, R. Ducharme, P. Vincent, C. Jauvin, A neural probabilistic language model. J. Mach. Lear. Res. 3(Feb), 1137–1155 (2003)
5. M. Abadi, A. Agarwal, P. Barham, E. Brevdo, Z. Chen, C. Citro, G.S. Corrado, A. Davis, J. Dean, M. Devin, et al., TensorFlow: large-scale machine learning on heterogeneous distributed systems. arXiv preprint arXiv:1603.04467 (2016)
6. A. Paszke, S. Gross, S. Chintala, G. Chanan, E. Yang, Z. DeVito, Z. Lin, A. Desmaison, L. Antiga, A. Lerer, Automatic differentiation in PyTorch (2017)
7. T. Chen, M. Li, Y. Li, M. Lin, N. Wang, M. Wang, T. Xiao, B. Xu, C. Zhang, Z. Zhang, MXNet: a flexible and efficient machine learning library for heterogeneous distributed systems. arXiv preprint arXiv:1512.01274 (2015)
8. G. Neubig, C. Dyer, Y. Goldberg, A. Matthews, W. Ammar, A. Anastasopoulos, M. Ballesteros, D. Chiang, D. Clothiaux, T. Cohn et al., Dynet: the dynamic neural network toolkit. arXiv preprint arXiv:1701.03980 (2017)
9. S. Tokui, K. Oono, S. Hido, J. Clayton, Chainer: a next-generation open source framework for deep learning, in Proceedings of Workshop on Machine Learning Systems (LearningSys) in the Twenty-Ninth Annual Conference on Neural Information Processing Systems (NIPS), vol. 5 (2015), pp. 1–6
10. Y. Jia, E. Shelhamer, J. Donahue, S. Karayev, J. Long, R. Girshick, S. Guadarrama, T. Darrell, Caffe: convolutional architecture for fast feature embedding, in *Proceedings of the 22nd ACM International Conference on Multimedia* (ACM, 2014), pp. 675–678
11. C. Dwork, J. Lei, Differential privacy and robust statistics, in *Proceedings of the Forty-First Annual ACM Symposium on Theory of Computing*, pp. 371–380 (2009)
12. R. Gilad-Bachrach, N. Dowlin, K. Laine, K. Lauter, M. Naehrig, J. Wernsing, Cryptonets: applying neural networks to encrypted data with high throughput and accuracy, in *International Conference on Machine Learning* (2016), pp. 201–210
13. L. Melis, C. Song, E. De Cristofaro, V. Shmatikov, Exploiting unintended feature leakage in collaborative learning, in *2019 IEEE Symposium on Security and Privacy (SP)*. (IEEE, 2019), pp. 691–706
14. L. Zhao, Q. Wang, Q. Zou, Y. Zhang, Y. Chen, Privacy-preserving collaborative deep learning with unreliable participants. IEEE Trans. Inf. Forensics Secur. **15**, 1486–1500 (2019)

© Tsinghua University Press 2021
L. Chen, *Deep Learning and Practice with MindSpore*, Cognitive Intelligence and Robotics, https://doi.org/10.1007/978-981-16-2233-5

15. C. Flanagan, A. Sabry, B.F. Duba, M. Felleisen, The essence of compiling with continuations, in *Proceedings of the ACM SIGPLAN 1993 conference on Programming Language Design and Implementation* (1993), pp. 237–247

16. B. van Merrienboer, O. Breuleux, A. Bergeron, P. Lamblin, Automatic differentiation in ml: Where we are and where we should be going, in *Advances in Neural Information Processing Systems* (2018), pp. 8757–8767

17. Y. LeCun et al., LeNet-5, convolutional neural networks. http://yann.lecun.com/exdb/lenet, **20**(5) (2015)

18. J. Devlin, M.-W. Chang, K. Lee, K. Toutanova, Bert: Pre-training of deep bidirectional transformers for language understanding. arXiv preprint arXiv:1810.04805 (2018)

19. A. Radford, J. Wu, R. Child, D. Luan, D. Amodei, I. Sutskever, Language models are unsupervised multitask learners. OpenAI Blog **1**(8) (2019)

20. M. Shoeybi, M. Patwary, R. Puri, P. LeGresley, J. Casper, B. Catanzaro, Megatron-LM: training multi-billion parameter language models using GPU model parallelism. arXiv preprint arXiv: 1909.08053 (2019)

21. N. Shazeer, Y. Cheng, N. Parmar, D. Tran, A. Vaswani, P. Koanantakool, P. Hawkins, H. Lee, M. Hong, C. Young, R. Sepassi, B. Hechtman, Meshtensorflow: deep learning for supercomputers, in *Advances in Neural Information Processing Systems (NeurIPS)*, (Curran Associates, Inc., 2018), pp. 10414–10423

22. Z. Jia, S. Lin, C.R. Qi, A. Aiken, Exploring hidden dimensions in accelerating convolutional neural networks, in *Proceedings of the 35th International Conference on Machine Learning (ICML)* (PMLR, 2018), pp. 2274–2283

23. Z. Jia, M. Zaharia, A. Aiken, Beyond data and model parallelism for deep neural networks, in *Proceedings of the 2nd Conference on Machine Learning and Systems (MLSys)* (ACM, 2019)

24. M. Wang, C. Huang, J. Li, Supporting very large models using automatic dataflow graph partitioning, in *Proceedings of the Fourteenth EuroSys Conference (EuroSys)*. (ACM, 2019)

25. L. Song, J. Mao, Y. Zhuo, X. Qian, H. Li, Y. Chen, Hypar: towards hybrid parallelism for deep learning accelerator array, in *2019 IEEE International Symposium on High Performance Computer Architecture (HPCA)*. (IEEE, 2019), pp. 56–68

26. I.J. Goodfellow, J. Shlens, C. Szegedy, Explaining and harnessing adversarial examples. arXiv preprint arXiv:1412.6572 (2014)

27. N. Akhtar, A. Mian, Threat of adversarial attacks on deep learning in computer vision: a survey. IEEE Access **6**, 14410–14430 (2018)

28. A. Kurakin, I. Goodfellow, S. Bengio, Adversarial examples in the physical world. arXiv preprint arXiv:1607.02533 (2016)

29. N. Carlini D. Wagner, Towards evaluating the robustness of neural networks, in *2017* IEEE *Symposium on Security and Privacy (SP)* (IEEE, 2017), pp. 39–57

30. M. Fredrikson, S. Jha, T. Ristenpart, Model inversion attacks that exploit confidence information and basic countermeasures, in *Proceedings of the 22nd ACM SIGSAC Conference on Computer and Communications Security*, (2015), pp. 1322–1333

31. R. Shokri, M. Stronati, C. Song, V. Shmatikov, Membership inference attacks against machine learning models, in *2017 IEEE Symposium on Security and Privacy (SP)*, (IEEE, 2017), pp. 3–18

32. T. Elsken, J.H. Metzen, F. Hutter, Neural architecture search: a survey. arXiv preprint arXiv: 1808.05377 (2018)

Printed in the United States
by Baker & Taylor Publisher Services